Finding, Freezing and Attaching Assets

Finding, Freezing and Attaching Assets

A Multi-jurisdictional Handbook

Edited by

Jacob C. Jørgensen

Wolters Kluwer

Published by:
Kluwer Law International B.V.
PO Box 316
2400 AH Alphen aan den Rijn
The Netherlands
Website: www.wklawbusiness.com

Sold and distributed in North, Central and South America by:
Wolters Kluwer Legal & Regulatory U.S.
7201 McKinney Circle
Frederick, MD 21704
United States of America
Email: customer.service@wolterskluwer.com

Sold and distributed in all other countries by:
Turpin Distribution Services Ltd
Stratton Business Park
Pegasus Drive, Biggleswade
Bedfordshire SG18 8TQ
United Kingdom
Email: kluwerlaw@turpin-distribution.com

Printed on acid-free paper.

ISBN 978-90-411-6741-5

Printed in the United Kingdom.

Editor

Jacob C. Jørgensen is the editor and co-author of this book. He is a qualified Danish attorney and holds an LLM in international commercial law from the University of Cambridge (Jesus College), as well as a BA and an MA in Law from the University of Copenhagen. He is a Fellow of the Chartered Institute of Arbitrators (FCIArb) and a registered Trust and Estate Practitioner (TEP). He specializes in cross-border litigation, international arbitration and construction law and has authored several articles in these fields of law. The editor can be contacted by e-mail at: jcjorgensen@cantab.net.

Contributors

Dr Yonathan Arbel is a Private Law Post-Doctoral Fellow at Harvard Law School and a partner at Lexidale International Policy Consulting. He holds an SJD degree from Harvard Law School, a JSM degree from Stanford Law School, and an LLB from the Hebrew University of Jerusalem (summa cum laude). He is an expert on the law and economics of enforcement of private obligations and has advised governments and policymakers on issues of collection and enforcement. The author can be contacted by e-mail at: arbel@lexidale.com.

Sidney J.H.M. Berendsen is a Dutch attorney at law and a partner in the Litigation & Risk Management practice group of Loyens & Loeff in Amsterdam. He specializes in corporate law disputes, such as disputes involving transactions, disputes between shareholders, proceedings with the Enterprise Chamber of the Court of Appeals, directors' and officers' liability and (international) arbitration. He also specializes in corporate fraud cases and is a member of the Corporate Investigations Team. Sidney lectures and publishes regularly on corporate law-related issues. He is a member of the International Bar Association, the Association Internationale des Jeunes Avocats (AIJA) and the Dutch Corporate Litigation Association. The author can be contacted by e-mail at: sidney.berendsen@loyensloeff.com.

Michele Bonomini is a member of the Milan Bar with extensive experience in commercial law as well as domestic and cross-border commercial litigation. He graduated in law from the University of Brescia in 2002, and was an exchange student at Ghent University. He obtained an LLM in International and European Law from the Catholic University of Louvain in 2003 and an MA in International Trade and Finance from the State University of Milan in 2004. The author can be contacted by e-mail at: mbonomini@studiopadovan.com.

Ruth Byrne is a partner and solicitor-advocate based in the London office of King & Spalding. She is a member of the firm's International Arbitration Group. She is also Co-chair of the Young International Arbitration Group (YIAG). Ruth has represented clients from a wide range of different industry sectors in dispute resolution. She has been involved as counsel in numerous arbitrations under the rules of the leading international arbitral institutions, as well as sitting regularly as arbitrator. She has extensive experience advising on and appearing in proceedings in support of arbitration in the English Commercial Court. She also regularly acts in commercial disputes before the English High Court and advises on questions of public and private international law. The author can be contacted by e-mail at: RByrne@KSLAW.com.

James Cairney is an associate at Meredith Connell, Auckland, New Zealand. He holds an LLB (Hons) from The University of Auckland. James is a commercial litigator with experience in financial markets law, commercial and contract law, misrepresentation, professional negligence and complex fraud. He has acted on high-profile finance cases related to the fallout from the global financial crisis, in litigation resulting from high-profile corporate failures, and for insurers on professional indemnity and public liability claims. The author can be contacted by e-mail at: james.cairney@mc.co.nz.

Colin Cohen is a partner of Boase Cohen & Collins in Hong Kong. He was qualified as a solicitor in England and Wales and in Hong Kong in 1981. He holds an LLM from the University of Cambridge (1978). He was appointed a Notary Public in November 1991. Colin has extensive experience in corporate litigation arbitration and dispute resolution matters. He has been in Hong Kong since 1981. Between 1983 and 1988, he was a Lecturer at Law at The University of Hong Kong where he was appointed as an Honorary Lecturer. The author can be contacted by e-mail at: Colin@boase cohencollins.com.

Utku Coşar is a partner at Coşar Avukatlık Bürosu, and has particular expertise in dispute resolution. In addition to acting as counsel in commercial and investment treaty arbitrations, where she has represented both state and private parties, Ms Coşar also sits as an arbitrator and, is a leading litigator, having represented both foreign and Turkish clients before the Turkish courts. A graduate of Marmara University Law School, she received two LLM degrees from Georgetown University Law Center, and is admitted to practise law in New York and Turkey. The author can be contacted by e-mail: utku.cosar@cosar.av.tr.

Renato Costagliola is the chief litigator at Studio Legale Padovan. He graduated in law at the State University of Milan in 1983 and was admitted to the Milan Bar in 1986. Before joining Studio Legale Padovan, he worked as a litigator at two major law firms in Milan mainly involved in commercial, bankruptcy and competition law. With three decades of court room experience, Renato is a seasoned litigator in all areas of civil law, either before ordinary or arbitration tribunals. The author can be contacted by e-mail at: rcostagliola@studiopadovan.com.

John Daerr is currently a sole practitioner specialized in international contractual relations, dispute resolution proceedings and in particular mediation proceedings. He began his legal career in Indianapolis, Indiana with the law firm of Locke Reynolds Boyd and Weisell in 1989 where he practised law for twenty years in the firm's Litigation Department. While practicing in the United States John received an AV rating from Martindale-Hubbell (its highest rating) and represented clients in hundreds of cases in all court levels. He was a longstanding member of both the American and Indiana bar associations. After moving to Sweden, John joined one of Sweden's largest international law firms and worked in one of Sweden's largest privately owned companies. There he assisted clients with complex contractual relationships, cross-border litigation, arbitration and the resolution of disputes via mediation. John is a CEDR Accredited Mediator. The author can be contacted by e-mail at: jdaerr046@gmail.com.

Maria Dolotova is an associate in the dispute resolution practice of Herbert Smith Freehills. She specializes in domestic litigation and international arbitration, and represents clients in commercial, construction, corporate, bankruptcy disputes and restructuring proceedings. Maria also advises on labour law issues and enforcement procedures. Maria graduated from the Moscow State Academy of Law in 2006. Before joining Herbert Smith Freehills in 2013, Maria worked in several other international law firms. The author can be contacted by e-mail at: maria.dolotova@hsf.com.

Bart-Jaap van Emmerik is a Dutch attorney at law and a member of the Litigation & Risk Management practice group of Loyens & Loeff in Amsterdam. He specializes in corporate law disputes, such as disputes involving transactions, disputes between shareholders, proceedings with the Enterprise Chamber of the Court of Appeals and directors' liability. He also specializes in disputes concerning banking and securities law. The author can be contacted by e-mail at: bart-jaap.van.emmerik@loyens loeff.com.

Henry Farris is a senior associate in King & Spalding's disputes team in London. He specializes in international arbitration and litigation. Henry's practice includes fraud and corruption cases, asset tracing and contractual disputes. He also has significant experience dealing with interim relief, principally freezing and search orders. Most of his cases have an international dimension, including Russia, Libya, the Middle-East and mainland Europe. The author can be contacted by e-mail at: HFarris@KS LAW.com.

Mauro Pedroso Goncalves is an attorney of the law firm Trench, Rossi e Watanabe Advogados (in cooperation with Baker & McKenzie International) and the head of the Dispute Resolution practice group in Brasilia. He specializes in litigation before the High Courts, and is an author of law books and articles. He holds a JD and a graduate degree (specialization in Civil Procedural Law) from the University Center of Brasilia. He was a member of the Committees on Constitutional Affairs and on Institutional Affairs of the Brazilian Bar Association (OAB/DF). He also served as law clerk to the Brazilian Superior Court of Justice (STJ) and as a legal adviser to the Legislative Chamber of the Federal District (CLDF). The author can be contacted by e-mail at: mauro.goncalves@trenchrossi.com.

Norla Gu is a former associate of Advokatfirman Vinge KB's Shanghai Office. She holds an LLB from Fudan University and specializes in commercial and general corporate law. The author can be contacted by e-mail at: norla_joy@hotmail.com.

Mac Imrie is a partner at Maples and Calder, and is qualified to practise BVI and Cayman Islands law. He has broad experience in multi-jurisdictional commercial litigation, arbitration and regulatory matters. Mac regularly works on mutual fund and hedge fund disputes and in crisis situations. He has represented clients in several high-profile fund collapses and resultant litigation and arbitration. Many of his cases involve obtaining interim protection for creditors and shareholders. Mac has significant advocacy experience having appeared as counsel before numerous courts and tribunals around the world. The author can be contacted by e-mail at: mac.imrie@maplesandcalder.com.

Arabella di Iorio is a partner in Maples and Calder's British Virgin Islands office, where she is head of the BVI litigation and trusts practice groups. Arabella previously served as the Managing Partner of the BVI office for six years. She specializes in complex international commercial litigation, including insolvency, distressed funds, shareholder issues, asset tracing, trust disputes, insurance and reinsurance, professional negligence and contractual claims. She has considerable arbitration and mediation experience and is a solicitor-advocate. Arabella also advises on non-contentious trusts matters. The author can be contacted by e-mail at: arabella.diiorio@maplesandcalder.com.

Alexander Jolles is a partner in Schellenberg Wittmer's Dispute Resolution Group in Zurich. His focus is on international arbitration and litigation, including enforcement, interim measures and appeals. In addition, he has extensive experience in inheritance matters, trust and estate law, and in art law, including art-related litigation. Alexander graduated from the University of Bern and gained admission to the bar in Switzerland in 1988. He is a lecturer on international arbitration at the University of Zurich's LLM programme in international business law and at the Swiss Arbitration Academy. The author can be contacted by e-mail at: Alexander.Jolles@swlegal.ch.

Aleksandar Jovanovic is a commercial litigation lawyer at Torkin Manes LLP. He has a broad range of experience litigating commercial and business related disputes. Aleksandar has represented clients on a variety of matters including the defence of oppression actions and the enforcement of various debt instruments and contractual provisions at private arbitrations and in Court. The author can be contacted by e-mail at: AJovanovic@torkinmanes.com.

Michalis Kyriakides is a partner at Harris Kyriakides LLC and heads the Corporate Department of the firm. His practice covers the full range of company and commercial litigation, arbitration and advisory work. He has particular expertise in cases involving international litigation, injunctions, equity investments, cross-border mergers/acquisitions, corporate restructuring and large asset finance transactions in Europe. He is often instructed by leading international firms, and he regularly represents local and international clients before Cyprus Courts, national authorities and arbitration tribunals. He is a member of the Cyprus Bar Association and he holds an LLB from the University of Athens, an LLM from University College London, and an MSt from the

University of Oxford. The author can be contacted by e-mail: m.kyriakides@harris kyriakides.com.

Nicolas Kyriakides is a civil litigation lawyer at Harris Kyriakides LLC and a researcher in the area of provisional and protective measures. He is a member of the Cyprus Bar Association, and he holds an LLB from the University of Athens, an LLM from UCL, an LLM from NYU and an MSt from the University of Oxford. The author can be contacted by e-mail: n.kyriakides@harriskyriakides.com.

Dr Stefan Leimgruber is a partner in Schellenberg Wittmer's Dispute Resolution Group in Zurich. His main areas of practice are domestic and international commercial litigation and arbitration with a focus on post-M&A and banking disputes, interim measures and debt enforcement. Stefan graduated from the University of Zurich in 2002. Before joining Schellenberg Wittmer in 2007, he worked as a law clerk and as a substitute judge at the Zurich District Court. He obtained a doctorate in law from the University of Lucerne in 2013 for his thesis on declaratory relief in international arbitration. The author can be contacted by e-mail at: stefan.leimgruber@swlegal.ch.

Larry Lian is a former associate of Advokatfirman Vinge KB's Shanghai Office. He holds an LLM from Xiamen University and specializes in commercial and general corporate law. The author can be contacted by e-mail at: lianyuxiong@hotmail.com.

Finn Madsen is a partner at Vinge Law Firm in Malmö. He is the author of several articles on Swedish and international arbitration and procedural law, as well as the book '*Commercial Arbitration in Sweden*', which has been published in Swedish, English and Mandarin. Finn Madsen has been awarded an honorary doctoral degree, juris doctor h.c., by the law faculty of Lund University on account of his contribution to international arbitration law. The author can be contacted by e-mail at: Finn.Mad sen@vinge.se.

Gledson Marques de Campos is a partner of the law firm Trench, Rossi e Watanabe Advogados (in cooperation with Baker & McKenzie International). He specializes in dispute resolution and commercial litigation. He holds a JD, an LLM in procedure law, an LLM in civil law and a Ph.D. in procedure law from the Pontifical Catholic University of São Paulo. He also holds an LLM from the London School of Economics and Political Science. The author can be contacted by e-mail at: gledson.campos@trenchrossi.com.

Kathleen Morrison is an associate at Meredith Connell, Auckland, New Zealand. She holds an LLB and a BSc from Victoria University of Wellington. Kathleen has particular expertise in all aspects of insolvency, in both the personal and corporate insolvency spheres. She has acted for a variety of private commercial and public-sector clients in relation to commercial and civil litigation, including the Official Assignee, private liquidators and receivers, and creditors, both in and out of court. She regularly advises clients in regard to a wide spectrum of civil claims, and on a range of regulatory matters relating to personal and corporate insolvency. The author can be contacted by e-mail at: kathleen.morrison@mc.co.nz.

Jan Heiner Nedden, MM is the managing partner of Hanefeld Rechtsanwälte in Hamburg. He acts as arbitrator and counsel in institutional as well as ad hoc arbitration proceedings and is frequently appointed as German law expert witness in proceedings before foreign courts. Before joining Hanefeld Rechtsanwälte, Heiner served as Counsel at the ICC International Court of Arbitration for several years. He is co-editor of the German language standard article-by-article Practice Commentary on the ICC and DIS Rules. Heiner is an appointed member of the ICC Commission on Arbitration and ADR, and appointed member of the International Dispute Resolution Committee of the Danish Institute of Arbitration. He is a trained mediator and teaches domestic and international arbitration law at the University of Hamburg, the Summer Academy on International Dispute Resolution at the University of Heidelberg and the Swiss Arbitration Academy in Zurich/Geneva. Heiner studied at the universities of Heidelberg and Freiburg in Germany and at Ottawa Law School in Canada. Heiner speaks German, English and French. The author can be contacted by e-mail at: nedden@hanefeld-legal.com.

Gemma Newell is an associate in the Cayman Islands office of Maples and Calder. She has a broad range of experience in commercial litigation and insolvency proceedings. Gemma regularly advises company directors, stakeholders, trustees, liquidators and other fiduciaries on both contentious and non-contentious matters. Her areas of practice also include security enforcement and restructuring. The author can be contacted by e-mail at: gemma.newell@maplesandcalder.com.

Katarina Nilsson is Vice President Legal Asia for the Sapa group, and the Chairman of the Swedish Chamber of Commerce in China. She is based in Hong Kong and holds a BA (Hons) degree in Chinese studies from SOAS, London University, and an LLM from the University of Lund. She specializes in corporate and commercial law as well as Mergers & Acquisitions. The author can be contacted by e-mail at: Katarina.Nilsson @sapagroup.com.

Marco Padovan is the founding member of Studio Legale Padovan. He graduated in law at the University of Rome 'La Sapienza' in 1981 and was admitted to the Italian Bar in 1983. He obtained an MA in International and Comparative Business Law at the London Guildhall University in 1995. He then joined the Legal Department of the European Investment Bank (EIB) in Luxembourg, and from 1993 until 1995 he represented EIB on the Board of Directors of the European Bank for Reconstruction and Development (EBRD) in London. Although he focuses mainly on project financing, financial and securities matters, construction law, private equity, energy and oil law, international trade and finance law, he deals with litigation matters on a regular basis as well. The author can be contacted by e-mail at: mpadovan@studiopadovan.com.

Alexei Panich is a partner in the dispute resolution practice of Herbert Smith Freehills in Moscow and a specialist in litigation and arbitration. For more than eighteen years, he has been representing clients in commercial, construction, banking, regulatory, customs and tax cases as well as in bankruptcy proceedings. Alexei has extensive experience in advising on complex Russian and international litigation matters affecting the activities of both foreign investors and national Russian companies. For the period from 2007 to 2014, Alexei won over 200 litigations, including 6 in the High Arbitration Court. Alexei graduated from the Moscow State Academy of Law in 1999 and has been a member of the Moscow Bar since 2002. He joined Herbert Smith Freehills from Salans (now Dentons), where he was the head of the Moscow dispute resolution practice. The author can be contacted by e-mail at: alexei.panich@hsf.com.

Adv. Dr Elad Peled is an associate at Nir Cohen, Leshem & Co. in Tel Aviv, Israel. He obtained his LLB from the Hebrew University of Jerusalem, his LLM from New York University, and his Ph.D. from the University of Haifa, and is a former Visiting Fellow at the Max Planck Institute for Comparative and International Private Law in Hamburg. His legal experience includes, inter alia, serving as a law clerk and a senior law clerk at the Israeli Supreme Court, heading the Research Division at Lexidale International Policy Consulting, and teaching legal courses. The author can be contacted by e-mail at: peledelad@nyu.edu.

Daniel Prawitz is a senior associate at Vinge Law Firm in Malmö. He focuses exclusively on Swedish and international arbitration and litigation matters. The author can be contacted by e-mail at: Daniel.prawitz@vinge.se.

Dr Friedrich Rosenfeld is an attorney with Hanefeld Rechtsanwälte in Hamburg. He acts as counsel in arbitration and state court proceedings, as expert witness, and as arbitrator. The focus of his practice is international arbitration and public international law. Before joining Hanefeld Rechtsanwälte, Friedrich worked as a consultant for the United Nations Assistance to the Khmer Rouge Trials in Cambodia. Friedrich is also Global Adjunct Professor of Law at NYU School of Law in Paris, Visiting Professor at the International Hellenic University in Thessaloniki and Lecturer at the Bucerius Law School in Hamburg. In 2014, he was appointed Global Hauser Fellow from Practice & Government at NYU School of Law. Friedrich studied at Bucerius Law School in Hamburg and at Columbia Law School in New York. He earned his doctoral degree summa cum laude and speaks German, English, French and Spanish. The author can be contacted by e-mail at: rosenfeld@hanefeld-legal.com.

James A. Round practises all forms of commercial and business related litigation as a partner at Torkin Manes LLP located in Toronto, Ontario. James has litigated complex commercial disputes before all levels of Court in Ontario, including Toronto's specialized Commercial Court, as well as private arbitrations. James has considerable experience in obtaining interlocutory and interim relief, and in particular, with the types of proceedings and forms of relief referred to in this book. The author can be contacted by e-mail at: jround@torkinmanes.com.

Dr Suat Sarı is an associate professor at Istanbul University, Faculty of Law. As a leading scholar of Turkish law, he has published numerous works. Dr Sarı received his LLB, LLM and PhD from Istanbul University and is admitted to practise law in Turkey. The author can be contacted by e-mail: suatsari@istanbul.edu.tr.

Signe A. Vest is an assistant attorney of the law firm Kromann Reumert in Copenhagen, Denmark. She holds a BA and an MA in law from the University of Aarhus and specializes in banking and finance law as well as insolvency law. The author can be contacted by e-mail at: sav@kromannreumert.com.

Summary of Contents

Table of Contents

Foreword

Win the battle and lose the war. You may have a wonderful court room victory, which will greatly impress your client, but when the celebrations end and the judgment is uncollectible, your client will not only be disappointed - if you are paid on an hourly basis, he is likely to consider bringing a legal action against you. Even worse, if you are paid on a contingency basis, your victory will be a loss for both you and your client.

As litigators we will often, instinctively commence our work on any given dispute that lands on our desk by analysing the merits – identifying the optimal litigation strategy, exploring the relevant procedural issues, handling the evidentiary challenges ahead, quantifying the damages, finding suitable experts, etc. – in other words, our first and paramount focus is nearly always on *winning* the case because that is what makes litigation so interesting.

We rarely start by examining the more fundamental question of whether our client is likely to actually get any money out of the case if we manage to win it. The answer to this question of course largely depends on whether the party we are about to sue will have sufficient assets that are likely to be available for enforcement if we manage to eventually secure a successful outcome of the dispute.

The present book is about how to find out – before you go to trial – whether the defendant has any assets, and if so how to freeze such assets with the aim of eventually enforcing a judgment or award. These topics have attracted increasing interest and focus among international litigators over the past decades due to the rise in cross-border disputes and due to how easily assets can be moved around the world with the help of online banking and fiduciary service providers.

Jacob C. Jørgensen and his co-authors have managed to cover an impressive amount of jurisdictions – nineteen in total – including several of the offshore havens that are frequently used to hide assets in. The authors provide the reader with practical guidance into the complex area of cross-border asset tracing and do so in a very down-to-earth way, without the academic hyperbole that generally burdens modern legal textbooks. As such, I believe that this book will quickly become an indispensable tool for international litigators and arbitration lawyers as well as lawyers involved in cross-border insolvency and debt recovery proceedings.

Robert Shapiro
California, November 2015
Partner at Glaser Weil Fink Howard Avchen & Shapiro LLP

Acknowledgments

I would like to thank all of my co-authors for making this publication possible by contributing with chapters of an exceptionally high level of quality and detail. It has been a pleasure working with so many brilliant legal experts from all over the world, and it has been a privilege editing this book. I am particularly grateful to my Danish co-author, Ms Signe A. Vest, for her assistance and support. Finally, a great debt of gratitude is owed to Ms Eleanor Taylor of Kluwer Law International for her patience, support and kind help throughout the project.

Jacob C. Jørgensen (Editor)
Copenhagen, November 2015

CHAPTER 1

Introduction

Jacob C. Jørgensen

Commercial dispute resolution proceedings are typically initiated in order for the plaintiff to gain some sort of financial advantage, which runs counter to the interests of the defendant. Sometimes litigants are driven into legal proceedings by motives that are not purely financial, such as a desire to gain more time in a certain context or inflict nuisance or duress on the counterparty, but usually lawsuits and arbitrations are initiated in order for a party to achieve an economic advantage.

The globalization of trade and commercial relations in general has resulted in an increase in cross-border disputes over the past decades, and since clients are increasingly finding themselves suing or being sued outside their home jurisdictions, the need for information concerning how to conduct oneself in the context of dispute resolution proceedings taking place in foreign countries is on the rise, as reflected in the ever growing pool of publications about various kinds of procedural issues that might arise in the context of international litigation or arbitration proceedings.

In the seemingly endless flow of legal articles, PhDs, books, blogs, newsletters and periodicals about procedural issues, it is surprising to find that relatively few writers have shown interest in perhaps the most fundamental of all questions, which any experienced lawyer should at least try to answer before going to trial or initiating insolvency proceedings, namely: Will my client eventually get any money out of this? The ambition behind this book is to provide international litigators with a tool to answer this basic question.

The book is written by international lawyers with decades of hands-on experience in helping their clients find, freeze and attach assets belonging to defendants in their home jurisdictions and abroad. The book first and foremost seeks to provide practical guidance to legal professionals representing parties in cross-border commercial lawsuits, international arbitration proceedings, simple debt collection matters, enforcement proceedings, divorce proceedings, inheritance matters and other legal matters where the assets in dispute are thought to be located abroad. However, academics and scholars involved in legal research projects or law reform programmes may also find inspiration in this book as it seeks to describe not just what the law says, but how the law actually works in the nineteen jurisdictions, which we have covered.

Most of the chapters are structured in the same way, and are all kept relatively short and to the point as the idea was to provide the reader with an overview rather than an in-depth analysis of the pre-trial asset tracing techniques and rules regulating freezing orders and enforcement methods of each jurisdiction.

Importantly, it should be noted that the authors have not (or only superficially) addressed the insolvency rules of their respective jurisdictions since the focal point of this book is to shed light on how to find and freeze assets belonging to an opposing party *without* first having to initiate costly litigation, arbitration or insolvency proceedings, which will almost inevitably involve the risk of giving the opposing party a chance to hide his assets.

As the book's title indicates, the authors have first of all addressed the practical issue of pre-trial asset tracing techniques, or in plain English: How to find out whether a future defendant or respondent has any assets before suing or initiating arbitration or insolvency proceedings.

As will be seen, nearly all of the jurisdictions allow a party to trace assets through public registers, many of which are available on the Internet. The reader should therefore get a fairly broad, yet detailed, picture of how anyone with an Internet connection (and the right language skills) can go about investigating whether a potential counterparty owns for example vessels, aircrafts, motor vehicles, real estate, intellectual property rights, etc. in any of the nineteen jurisdictions covered in this book.

Interestingly, when it comes to *court-assisted* pre-trial asset discovery, the laws of the civil law jurisdictions offer surprisingly little help, whereas the common law systems appear more flexible and pragmatic – at least this is the case when court assistance is requested along with a request for interim relief in the form of a freezing order.

Once available assets have been identified and the decision of initiating a lawsuit or arbitration has been made, a new and far more risky issue arises, namely the issue of whether any steps should or could be taken to freeze such assets to ensure that they are available in the context of enforcement proceedings after the lawsuit or arbitration has ended. This issue has been addressed separately in each of the chapters, which offer useful overviews of the rules regulating injunctive relief sought prior to or during both arbitration proceedings and civil proceedings. As will be seen, several authors have also commented on the relatively new EU Regulation No. 655/2014 that establishes the so-called European Account Preservation Order procedure, which most of the EU countries have implemented.

Furthermore, each of the chapters gives practically useful insight into how the different legal systems tackle the complex issue of how to enforce a foreign judgment or arbitral award. This issue has recently attracted new attention with the Hague Convention on Choice of Court Agreements coming into force on 1 October 2015. This convention provides for the mutual recognition and enforcement of judgments rendered in civil and commercial matters in all of the convention member states, in cases where the judgment is rendered by a court exclusively chosen by agreement of the parties. At present, the only contracting parties are Mexico and the EU Member States (excluding Denmark), whereas Singapore and the US have signed the convention, but are yet to ratify it.

During the course of lawsuits or arbitrations, defendants/respondents sometimes take steps to remove valuable assets from their sphere to thereby shield them against enforcement proceedings. Asset shielding manoeuvres can take many different forms - from the straightforward transfer of assets to a family member or a corporate entity, to sophisticated schemes involving offshore trusts, sham investments designed to generate a (fictitious) loss of assets, securitization schemes designed to reduce or eliminate the equity value of assets, etc.

In the final sections of each chapter, the authors have provided an overview of the remedies that are available to a party facing these types of asset shielding manoeuvres. The rules regulating D&O liability and debtor fraud etc. of each jurisdiction are addressed in this regard.

CHAPTER 2
Brazil

Gledson Marques de Campos & Mauro Pedroso Gonçalves

§2.01 INTRODUCTION

Brazil is a civil law country. Its body of law was developed from Roman and German concepts of codified law. Consequently, Brazilian law relies primarily on legislation, but there are also other sources of law, such as case law, legal doctrine, customs and trade usages.

The Federal Republic of Brazil became an independent country in 1822. It is a federation of twenty-six states, each of which has their own State Constitution, based on the Federal Constitution. The Federal Union has exclusive authority to legislate in broader areas of law such as those related to contracts, tort, property, family, civil and criminal procedure, etc.

Accordingly, Brazil's principal source of law is the Federal Constitution and the various statutes that systematically regulate individual legal areas. Given that only the Federal Union can legislate on *procedural* law, the Civil Procedural Code (Act No. 5869 of January 11, 1973)[1] establishes all of the judicial practices and procedural steps that are to be applied by the courts in relation to, for example, proceedings for the freezing and attaching of assets.

It is worth mentioning that the Brazilian judicial system comprises the federal and the regular courts, both of which have two levels. Decisions of the lower courts emanate from a single judge. At the second level, the federal or state courts are comprised by a panel of judges. At the higher court level, the judges may review and rule only on issues of law, but not on evidentiary issues.

As in other countries, the arbitral institutions in Brazil are independent of the court system. Arbitral proceedings are governed by the Brazilian Arbitration Act (BAA)

1. A Portuguese version of "Civil Procedural Code" is available here: http://www.planalto.gov.br/ccivil_03/leis/l5869.htm.

(Law No. 9307 of September 23, 1996).[2] Brazil has ratified the 1958 New York Convention on the Recognition and Enforcement of Foreign Arbitral Awards.

In general, it is not easy to identify and freeze assets in Brazil. As is the case in most other jurisdictions that have been described in this book, Brazilian procedural law does *not* provide any leverage to pre-trial asset investigations through the court system. As set out in further detail below under section §2.02, the most efficient way to find assets located in Brazil is to resort to online databases, which in some cases can provide useful information about a defendant's assets. The most useful databases, however, are only available to Brazilian judges during the enforcement proceedings.

In relation to the possibility of freezing and attaching assets in the context of arbitral or civil proceedings, we have described the relevant rules under section §2.03.

The enforcement of judicial decisions and arbitral awards is dealt with at the lower court levels whose interlocutory decisions may be appealed to the higher courts. In section §2.04 below, we provide an overview of how foreign decisions and arbitral awards may be enforced in Brazil.

Finally, under section §2.05, we have addressed the remedies offered by Brazilian law to plaintiffs facing illicit asset shielding maneuvers.

§2.02 IDENTIFYING ASSETS IN BRAZIL

In the pre-trial phase, a plaintiff may search for assets belonging to the defendant in a limited number of public registers, such as those administrated by public notaries and the Department of Motor Vehicles (DETRAN). In general, however, the probability of success is low due to Brazilian bank and tax secrecy rules and due to the absence of public registers in Brazil concerning real estate, vehicles, vessels, aircraft, tangible assets, etc. Even when a company is initiating a bankruptcy proceeding or any other type of insolvency proceeding, a party, involved in enforcement proceedings against the same company, cannot obtain information about its assets.

However, in cases involving a risk of fraud the plaintiff may file an injunction suit to freeze assets belonging to the defendant. In these types of cases, the plaintiff can request a court order to be published in the Official Gazette and in a main local newspaper in order for third parties and the public in general to formally acknowledge that any transfer of assets by the defendant may be challenged in the future and eventually declared null and void because of the injunction. Furthermore, the plaintiff can request public agencies to register the freezing order in regard to any assets owned by the defendant to thereby ensure compliance with the injunction.

It is also possible for the plaintiff, when commencing enforcement proceedings, to request that the existence of the proceedings be registered by public agencies in order to thereby inform third parties that any dispositions involving the transfer of assets from the defendant could be challenged in the future.

2. A Portuguese version of "Brazilian Arbitration Act" is available here: http://www.planalto.gov.br/ccivil_03/leis/l9307.htm.

Once a judicial decision or an arbitral award becomes final and non-appealable (or, at least, when enforcement is possible), the plaintiff can obtain a wider range of information about the assets belonging to the defendant through three main databases that are used by judges handling enforcement proceedings. The databases which contain information about different types of assets held by corporations and individuals are: (i) BACENJUD; (ii) RENAJUD; and (iii) INFOJUD.

[A] Attachments

Through the BACENJUD system, plaintiffs can apply for an online attachment of securities and cash deposited in bank accounts by a defendant. It is a very effective and swift way for a creditor to secure a claim, but it requires the court ordering the Brazilian Central Bank to provide information and freezing the defendant's bank accounts. Once an amount equal to the debt has been frozen, the amount is transferred to a court-held bank account.

[B] Motor Vehicles

In relation to motor vehicles, the RENAJUD database should be mentioned. This database connects the courts to the National Traffic Agency (DENATRAN), allowing the judges to levy an online attachment of motor vehicles belonging to a defendant in Brazil.

[C] Assets Declared for Tax Purposes

Finally, the INFOJUD system enables an online connection between the courts and the Brazilian Federal Revenue, allowing creditors to find known assets of the debtor protected by bank and tax secrecy. Thus, INFOJUD allows access to information about assets declared on the debtor's tax return, such as real estate, vessels, aircrafts, tangible assets, financial reports, etc.

If the court finds that an online attachment would be too burdensome or if the online attachment is futile, other assets that are known to the creditor can be attached. In some cases, the judge may find that certain assets cannot be attached because the debtor depends on them to carry out his business. This rule could, for example, apply to the basic tools belonging to a carpenter.

§2.03 INTERIM MEASURES

Under Brazilian law, interim measures are classified as: (i) "cautelares," which are designed to preserve the "status quo," facilitating the later enforcement of a judgment or an award; and (ii) "antecipação dos efeitos da tutela," which are granted in anticipation of the outcome of a lawsuit or arbitration (without prejudice of course to the outcome of the proceedings).

Despite the differences, both measures can be obtained urgently where there is an imminent risk of irreparable harm to the claimant, if interim relief is not granted, and where the claimant can show that he will most likely prevail in the dispute.

Interim measures are thus used to mitigate the creditor's risk of not being paid despite a successful outcome of the dispute. The effectiveness of an interim measure largely relies on a proper sanctioning of the debtor if he disposes of assets that have been included under a freezing order; and by informing third parties of the freezing of the assets.

An interim measure may be requested prior to the filling of or during a lawsuit or arbitration. If the interim measure is requested prior to the filing of a lawsuit or arbitration and aims to preserve the "status quo" ("*cautelar*"), the plaintiff must file his request with the court, which has jurisdiction over the dispute. If the parties have entered into an arbitration agreement the plaintiff must file the request for an interim measure with the judge that would have been competent if there had not been an arbitration agreement.

As indicated, the judge can levy a penalty if the order places an obligation on the defendant to do or refrain from doing certain things and if the order is not complied with. Such a penalty will apply once the interim measure has been granted and has become effective. The judge or arbitrator(s) has discretion to establish a penalty in an amount which would be high enough to motivate the debtor to comply with the freezing order. However, several scholars and court decisions support the contention that the amount of the penalty cannot exceed the amount of the obligation based on which the order has been granted. It should be noted that the proceeds of the penalty belongs to the party and not to the court.

Finally, if an interim measure is granted and the final decision revokes it, the party that requested the interim measure may be obliged to pay compensation for any loss or damages suffered by the defendant as a result of having had to comply with the freezing order.

§2.04 ENFORCEMENT ISSUES

[A] Enforcement Based on a Judgment or Arbitral Award Obtained in Brazil

In Brazil, enforcement proceedings may be conducted on the basis of either a judgment or an arbitral award obtained in Brazil; or on the basis of certain "extrajudicial instruments," such as bills of exchange, promissory notes, trade bills, checks, etc. In the following, we will provide a brief overview of how Brazilian judgments and arbitral awards are enforced. Below under section §2.04[B], we will take a closer look at how foreign judgments and arbitral awards may be enforced against assets in Brazil.

The rules of enforcement of judicial decisions apply equally to arbitral awards, provided that the arbitral award, defined in Article 31 of the BAA,[3] has been approved by a Brazilian court for enforcement purposes.[4]

If a party does not comply with a judicial decision or an arbitral award, the counterparty may initiate enforcement proceedings against the defaulting party.[5]

According to Article 475-J of the Civil Procedural Code, at the beginning of the enforcement proceedings, the defendant will be requested to comply with the judgment or award within fifteen calendar days. If the defendant remains inert, a fine of 10% of the total amount owed according to the judgment or award will be levied, and the debtor's assets will be subject to attachment.

If the debtor fails to pay the fine, the creditor can request the court to order the debtor to disclose his assets within five calendar days after having been notified of the order, compare Article 600 of the Civil Procedural Code. If the defendant still refuses to comply with the disclosure order, the judge can levy an additional fine of up to 20% or the amount owed according to the judgment or award, compare Article 601 of the Civil Procedural Code.

After the debtor's assets have been identified and attached, they will be appraised by a court appraiser. The creditor will then have the following options:

(i) The creditor may offer to claim title to the asset by setting off his claim. If the value of the claim is higher than the value of the assets, the enforcement proceedings will continue with the aim of attaching other assets belonging to the debtor. If the value of the claim is lower than the attached assets, the creditor must deposit an amount equal to the difference with the court.

(ii) If the creditor is not interested in obtaining ownership to the asset, he can alternatively request that a private broker, duly approved by the court, sell the asset. The court will set the conditions for the sale, including, the minimum price, guarantees, broker's commission, etc. The proceeds from the sale will be used to pay the creditor. If the proceeds do not suffice, the enforcement proceedings will continue for the purpose of attaching other assets belonging to the debtor.

(iii) The creditor can also request the sale of the debtor's assets on a public auction. The auction is carried out judicially over the course of two days: On the first day, bidders will be allowed to place bids. On the second day, the asset will be sold at the highest bid price.

3. According to Article 31 of the Brazilian Arbitration Act – "*the arbitral award shall have the same effect on the parties and their successors as a judgment issued by a State Court, and if it includes an obligation for payment, it shall constitute an enforceable instrument therefore.*"
4. The Brazilian Arbitration Act considers the arbitration award a sentence, similar to as occurs in France and Switzerland. However, we cannot disregard that arbitration is a private form to solve conflicts in which the parties waive the submission of the conflict to a court of law. The possibility that the parties have to solve their conflicts without the intervention of a court of law has always existed, as far back as the world's very existence. Negotiation, conciliation and mediation support the foregoing statement.
5. José Eduardo Carreira Alvim. *Direito Arbitral*. Rio de Janeiro: Forense, 2004. p. 359.

(iv) Finally, the creditor can request the usufruct of the asset. This option is rarely used except for assets that can easily be leased.

Within fifteen calendar days from the date of the attachment of the assets, the debtor may file an objection to the enforcement. Only a limited number of defenses can be raised in support of an objection, such as: (i) a lack of service of process, (in case a summary judgment has been rendered); (ii) the claim is not enforceable; (iii) an undue attachment of the assets in question has been levied, or the assets have been incorrectly appraised; (iv) the creditor or the debtor has no standing to sue or be sued; (v) the value of the attached assets exceeds the value of the claim; (vi) any cause that may impair the right to collect the debt, such as payment, set off or time bar, provided that such cause arose *after* the judgment or award was rendered.

In principle, an objection does not stay the enforcement; however, the judge may decide to grant a stay if the defenses are deemed well-founded, and there is an imminent risk of irreparable harm to the debtor if the enforcement proceedings are allowed to carry on.

If the judge stays the proceedings, the case will continue only up to and including the attachment and appraisal of the assets. The creditor will not be able to exercise any of the four options described above until the court has ruled on the objection.

The judge may order an expert appraisal or schedule a hearing for witness depositions before ruling on an objection by the debtor to proceed with the enforcement. Once a decision has been rendered by a lower court, the parties can appeal to the State Court of Appeals and later to the Superior Court of Justice and/or to the Supreme Court.

[B] Enforcement Based on a Foreign Judgment or Arbitral Award

[1] Foreign Arbitral Awards

The "BAA" distinguishes between *national* arbitral awards and international arbitral awards.[6] According to Article 34 of the BAA "*a foreign award is an award that has been rendered outside of the national territory.*" Accordingly, an arbitral award will be considered national if it is rendered by a tribunal sitting in Brazil and international if rendered by a tribunal which has its seat outside Brazil.

On September 5, 2002, Brazil ratified the 1958 New York Convention on the Recognition and Enforcement of Foreign Arbitral Awards. Under the BAA, it is relevant to distinguish a national award from an international award as the former may be enforced directly before a federal court whereas the latter, (like a foreign judicial decision) is required to be *homologated* by the Superior Court of Justice (STJ), as described in further detail below.

6. Article 31 provides that "*the arbitral award shall have the same effect on the parties and their successors as a judgment issued by a State Court, and if it includes an obligation for payment, it shall constitute an enforceable instrument there for.*" On the other hand, Article 35 states that "*in order to be recognized or enforced in Brazil a foreign arbitral award is subject only to homologation by the Federal Supreme Court.*"

[2] Foreign Judgments

In relation to the recognition and enforcement of foreign judicial decisions and foreign arbitral awards,[7] the Federal Constitution and the BAA require homologation of the judgment or award.

The scope of the homologation procedure which is administrated by the Superior Court (STJ) is limited and does not involve a review of the merits of the judgment or award and will therefore not give rise to any modification of the decision in any way whatsoever.[8]

Before a federal court grants the enforcement of an international judgment or award, it is necessary to appoint an "enforcement judge" from the Superior Court of Justice (STJ), who will analyze whether the decision or award meets the requirements of enforceability established by Brazilian law.

As in most other countries any judgment or award considered offensive to national sovereignty, public policy or costumes will not be recognized and can therefore not be enforced Brazil.

In addition, in order to be homologated, the judgment or award must have been issued by a court that has jurisdiction over the defendant and the dispute. Furthermore, the judgment or award must be preceded by due service of process on the Defendant, and have become final.[9]

There are other formal requirements that must be met in order for a foreign judgment or award to be homologated. The claimant is for instance required to attach a certified copy of the judgment or award that is sought to be recognized along with a duly translated Portuguese language version, prepared by a sworn translator.

The claimant is not obliged to request the recognition of the *entire* judgment or award. He can, for instance, request recognition only of the part related to compensation for damages.

If the homologation petition meets all of the requirements, the President of the Superior Court will order the defendant's service of process.

The defendant will be given the opportunity to present his/her defense against the homologation, which – according to the Internal Rules of the Superior Court – must be limited to: (i) lack of authenticity of the documents; or (ii) non-fulfillment of the requirements established in the Superior Court's internal regulations. As already underlined, it is not possible to revisit the merits of an award or judgment in the homologation proceedings.

7. Article 34 of the Brazilian Arbitration Act: "*a foreign arbitral award is an award issued outside of the national territory.*"
8. Although Article 35 of the Brazilian Arbitration Act (Law No. 9307 of September 23, 1996) provides for a homologation procedure before the Federal Supreme Court (STF), Constitutional Amendment No. 45 of 2004 to the Federal Constitution changed its authority in Article 105, I, "i." Initially the Supreme Court (STF) held such authority and later it was attributed to the Superior Court of Justice (STJ), which is the Higher Court for non-constitutional matters.
9. Only the final decision is subject to homologation. Interlocutory decisions rendered by foreign courts during the course of litigation and procedural awards rendered by arbitral tribunals cannot be homologated.

If a declaration of enforceability ("exequatur") is issued by the Superior Court the foreign decision may be enforced by one of the federal courts that has jurisdiction over the defendant's domicile.

§2.05 D&O LIABILITY IN RELATION TO ASSET PROTECTION SCHEMES

[A] Civil Law

Brazilian law offers several remedies to plaintiffs facing illicit asset shielding maneuvers by a defendant. The rules especially relate to the liability of directors and officers of Brazilian companies and are found both in criminal law and in tort.

Generally, Brazilian law prohibits the dissipation of assets designed to frustrate legitimate debt collection attempts by creditors. If a given transaction is considered to be a "fraud against enforcement," the legal effect under Brazilian law is simply to render the transaction null and void and allow the disgruntled creditors to claw back dissipated assets.

This principle is for example reflected in the Article 593 of the Civil Procedural Code, which provides that the sale of assets belonging to a debtor during the course of a trial may be rendered ineffective if the sale did not take place on arm's length terms.

Consequently, if a debtor commits any act that is aimed at harming the legitimate financial interest of the creditors, such as a transfer of commercially sound agreements to other companies, or a transfer assets without suitable consideration, such acts may be rendered null and void upon request by disgruntled creditors.

With respect to piercing the corporate veil, Article 50 of the Brazilian Civil Code provides as follows:

> *in case of abuse of the legal entity, characterized by misuse of purpose or by patrimonial confusion, the judge may decide, at the request of a party, or at the request of the Public Prosecutor Office when it is entitled to intervene in the lawsuit, that the effects of certain and determined obligations be extended to the private assets of the managers or partners of the corporate entity.*

The piercing of the corporate veil doctrine applies, in general, to situations where a party engages in a fraudulent operation and/or abuses its rights acting through a legal entity, to its own benefit and sometimes even to the benefit of third parties, resulting in damages to the company, to third parties or to the public.

A piercing of the corporate veil requires the court to review: (i) the specific facts of the matter to determine whether the respective conduct may be considered fraudulent and/or abusive; (ii) which shareholder participated in the conduct that caused the piercing of the corporate veil; and (iii) the true need to pierce the corporate.

With regard to fraud Articles 158–163 of the Civil Code (Law No. 10406 of January 10, 2002)[10] provides a creditor with the possibility of challenging a fraudulent transaction when: (i) the debtor transfers assets free of charge to another person (e.g.,

10. A Portuguese version of "Brazilian Civil Code" is available here: http://www.planalto.gov.br/ccivil_03/leis/2002/l10406.htm.

a gift or any other act under which the debtor voluntarily transfers title of an asset without any consideration) or forgives debts and, as a consequence, the debtor becomes insolvent; (ii) the debtor sells/transfers/assigns assets/rights and, as a consequence, becomes insolvent and the acquirer is aware of such circumstance.

In case the judge recognizes the transaction as being fraudulent, the transaction may be rendered null and void and the transferred assets or forgiven debt is returned to the debtor. This may apply to a debtor company's managers, shareholders and – depending on the situation – even affiliated companies or subsidiaries of the same company group as the defendant company.

Moreover, under Brazilian law even third parties may be held responsible for inflicting damages on creditors by helping a debtor hide its assets.

[B] Criminal Liability

Finally, a few comments should be made with respect to how the Brazilian Penal Code may be used to counter illicit assets shielding schemes.

Article 179 of the Brazilian Penal Code[11] concerns the crime of "fraud against enforcement." This provision may apply in cases where a party sells or diverts assets or generates sham debts to avoid enforcement. Under Article 179, these types of actions may be sanctioned with a fine or with incarceration of between six months to two years.

11. A Portuguese version of "Brazilian Civil Code" is available here: http://www.planalto.gov.br/ccivil_03/decreto-lei/del2848.htm.

CHAPTER 3
British Virgin Islands

Arabella di Iorio

§3.01 INTRODUCTION

The British Virgin Islands (BVI) is one of fourteen Overseas Territories which by settlement, conquest or annexation belong to the British Crown. Lying on the northeast edge of the Caribbean Sea, the BVI is an archipelago of some sixty islands in the Leeward Islands of the Lesser Antilles of the West Indies. The most populated island is Tortola, on which is situated Road Town, the capital of the BVI. Tortola was annexed for the Crown by the Governor of the Leeward Islands in 1672, and other islands were annexed in later years.

The power to provide for the government of the BVI by Order in Council is set out in the West Indies Act 1962. The current constitution was adopted in 2007 (the Virgin Islands Constitution Order 2007), and the country is led by the Premier, who is elected in a General Election, appointed by the Governor and who nominates a cabinet. The Monarch (through the Governor) is responsible for foreign affairs, internal security, defence and the administration of the courts. There is, however, a large degree of internal self-government.

The legislature consists of the Monarch and the House of Assembly. The legislature has power, subject to the Constitution, to make laws for the peace, order and good government of the BVI.

The BVI is one of the nine members of the Eastern Caribbean Supreme Court (ECSC) (the others are Anguilla, Antigua and Barbuda, Dominica, Grenada, Montserrat, Saint Kitts and Nevis, Saint Lucia, and Saint Vincent and the Grenadines). The High Court and the Court of Appeal of the ECSC have jurisdiction in the BVI. The ECSC is headquartered in Castries, Saint Lucia, although each territory has its own registry and judiciary. The BVI High Court has three resident judges, one of whom (Barry Leon J) is assigned to the Commercial Division. The Court of Appeal sits in the BVI usually three times a year, although additional special sittings can be arranged as necessary.

Final appeal in both civil and criminal cases is to the Judicial Committee of the Privy Council in London. There is a Magistrates Court, which has both criminal and civil jurisdiction, with final appeal to the Court of Appeal.

By the Common Law (Declaration of Application) Act 1705, the common law of England was declared to be in force. The majority of the law currently in force is enacted by the local legislature, as supplemented by some UK statutes and orders in Council which have been specifically extended to the BVI. The ECSC (Virgin Islands) Act 1969 provides that in cases where common law and equity conflict, equity shall prevail.

Although only Privy Council decisions are technically binding in the BVI, decisions of the English Court of Appeal and Supreme Court are highly persuasive and will, save in exceptional circumstances, generally be followed. Authorities from other Commonwealth jurisdictions are also often cited.

The BVI is a very popular jurisdiction for the incorporation of companies, investment funds, and limited partnerships. Its bespoke company legislation, the BVI Business Companies Act, 2004, provides very significant flexibility, and it is a creditor friendly jurisdiction also with bespoke insolvency legislation: the Insolvency Act 2003. With the enactment of the Arbitration Act 2013, it is also committed to playing an increasing role on the international arbitration stage.

§3.02 IDENTIFYING ASSETS IN THE BVI

The vast majority of BVI registered companies will not have assets within the jurisdiction. Although BVI companies are obliged to file certain information win the Registry of Corporate Affairs, that information is limited and does not include share registers, registers of directors or financial statements. Information that is disclosable by way of court order, including prior to the commencement of proceedings, is considered in section §3.03 below.

The following sets out details of the registration of assets.

[A] Land

The BVI has the Torrens system of land registration. Details are kept at the BVI Land Registry and are publicly searchable. The documents of title will record any encumbrances currently registered against the property (e.g., charges, restrictive covenants and cautions) as set out in the Registered Land Act 1970.

[B] Vessels

Road Harbour in the BVI is a British Port of Registry, part of the UK's Red Ensign Group of Registries.

The BVI has a modern registration system, which also allows for the registration and discharge of mortgages, changes of ownership, and other services. As of 2007, the Registry also offers Category 1 registrations, including large cargo vessels of unlimited tonnage and mega-yachts grossing below 3,000 tonnes. The BVI register is independent from the UK register, and manually searchable by members of the public, on payment of the relevant fee, or transcripts can be requested. The name of the relevant vessel is a key to the process.

[C] Aircraft

Aircraft may be registered in the BVI, and a Register of Aircraft is maintained pursuant to the Air Navigation (Overseas Territories) Order 2013. It is also possible to register an aircraft mortgage or an aircraft engine mortgage pursuant to the Mortgaging of Aircraft and Aircraft Engines Act 2011.

[D] Bad Debtors

A company search will reveal whether a company is in receivership or liquidation. Applications for, and notices of, appointment of liquidators and bankruptcy trustees are also advertised in the Gazette and the BVI Beacon, both of which offer online search facilities.

There is no system for registering or identifying bad debtors.

[E] Intellectual Property Rights

The BVI has its own patents and trademarks registry. The Register is publicly searchable; searches incur a modest fee.

The BVI legislation dealing with trademark applications is well established. Original applications are made under the Trade Marks Act 1887 and the Trade Marks Rules 1937 (both as revised). The registration of existing UK trademarks is governed by the United Kingdom Trade Marks Act 1946 and the Registration of the United Kingdom Trade Marks Rules 1947 (both as revised). Recently the BVI Trade Marks Act, 2013 was enacted by the Legislature of the Virgin Islands, though is not yet in force. The 2013 Act will revoke the current legislation and provides a broader scope for applications including well-known trademarks and those entitled to protection under the Paris convention.

The BVI legislation dealing with patent applications is similarly well established. Original applications are made under the Patents Act 1906 and the Patents Regulations 1906 (both as revised). The registration of existing UK patents is governed by the Registration of United Kingdom Patents Act 1925 and the Registration of the United Kingdom Patents Rules 1927 (both as revised).

[F] Other Pre-action Relief

The BVI court has jurisdiction to grant search orders (formerly known as Anton Piller Orders) and Norwich Pharmacal Orders prior to the commencement of legal proceedings. Each of these is considered below. The court may also be prepared (in very urgent cases) to grant a Freezing Order (formerly known as a Mareva Injunction) or a disclosure or preservation order before proceedings are commenced, but will require an undertaking from the claimant that proceedings will be commenced in short order. Freezing, disclosure and preservation orders are considered in section §3.04.

[G] Search Orders

These are available under Part 17 of the Civil Procedure Rules 2000 (as amended), and are usually made so as to safeguard vital evidence, although they are also frequently used to preserve property which might otherwise be destroyed or dissipated. Applications for search orders are usually made ex parte, and as with all such applications, the applicant must comply with its duty of full and frank disclosure. The applicant will also be required to give undertakings to the court as to the manner in which the order is to be executed, and breach will be a contempt of court.

Search orders are rarely made in the BVI and require an applicant to satisfy the court that:

(a) there is an extremely strong prima facie case;
(b) the actual or potential damage to the applicant is very serious;
(c) there is clear evidence that the respondents have in their possession incriminating material;
(d) there is a real possibility that the material will be destroyed before an *inter partes* application can be made; and
(e) the harm likely to be caused by the execution of the search order to the respondent and his business affairs will not be excessive or out of proportion to the legitimate object of the order.

[H] Norwich Pharmacal Orders

The basic principle is well known, and is that if a person through no fault of his own, gets mixed up in the wrongful acts of others so as to facilitate that wrongdoing, he comes under an obligation to assist the person who has been wronged by giving him full information (including information about what the wrongdoer has done with its assets) and disclosing the identity of the wrongdoer.

The ‘mere witness’ rule operates so as to exclude ordering discovery against someone who would in due course be compellable to give that information as a witness at trial or pursuant to a witness summons. The jurisdiction cannot, therefore, be used to obtain a pre-trial deposition from a potential witness.

Much of the jurisprudence in the BVI has turned on the question whether Norwich Pharmacal relief is available against the registered agent of a BVI incorporated company. At first instance, the court was reluctant to 'harass' registered agents with disclosure orders on the basis that they were mere onlookers, except in circumstances where the registered agent was involved in *and* had knowledge of the wrongdoing. This severely restricted the availability of the relief, since the vast majority of registered agents have absolutely no knowledge of the commercial activities of the companies they administer. However, the Court of Appeal held the reverse in *JCC BTA Bank v. Fidelity Corporation Services* (HCVAP2010/35). The Court of Appeal was unequivocal that: '.... *by virtue of their very role in providing registered agent services to companies, a role which is voluntary, [the agents] cannot on any view be considered as mere onlookers*'.

The Court of Appeal's decision is very important. All BVI companies must have a registered agent and maintain a registered office in the BVI. Certain documents must be kept at the registered office, and the registered agent must obtain extensive due diligence information and satisfy itself as to the ultimate beneficial ownership of the company. The Court of Appeal has in essence held that facilitating the wrongdoing, however innocently, renders the registered agent liable to a Norwich Pharmacal Order in appropriate circumstances.

Norwich Pharmacal Orders can be obtained in support of both domestic and foreign proceedings, but the applicant is not obliged to commence proceedings after the information has been disclosed. A BVI order may expressly restrict the applicant from making use of the information disclosed without further sanction of the court.

[I] Gagging Orders

Any Norwich Pharmacal disclosure would likely be rendered ineffective if the registered agent were to notify its client of the application. The BVI court will accordingly frequently 'gag' the registered agent, preventing it from revealing the existence of the application until a certain number of days after the order has been complied with have passed.

[J] Appointment of a Receiver

The BVI court has jurisdiction to appoint a receiver, pursuant to section 24 of the ECSC (Virgin Islands) Act 1969, which provides as follows:

> *24(1) A mandamus or an injunction may be granted or a receiver appointed by an Interlocutory Order of the High Court or of a Judge thereof in all cases in which it appears to the Court or Judge to be just and convenient that the Order should be made and any such Order may be made either unconditionally or upon such terms and conditions as the Court or Judge thinks just.*

The jurisdiction is therefore discretionary, and is simply based on the court's assessment of it being 'just and convenient' for the relief to be granted, hence the lack of a rigid framework of rules (other than procedural rules governing the manner in which an application is to be made, which is contained in Part 51 of the Civil Procedure Rules 2000).

Prior to the development of the other well-known interim jurisdiction – the granting of freezing (or 'Mareva') relief – the statutory jurisdiction to appoint a receiver was rarely employed, but it is now a frequently used tool in the BVI court's armoury, very often deployed together with freezing orders and disclosure orders, particularly in situations where other interlocutory relief alone is not considered sufficient to protect the assets in question.

In order to obtain such interlocutory relief, an applicant will have to overcome certain hurdles, including demonstrating to the court that its substantive case is a good arguable one, with a realistic prospect of success.

The BVI court is familiar (indeed possibly more so than its English counterpart) with the jurisdiction to appoint a receiver, and (both at first instance and in the Court of Appeal) have approved the rationale for the appointment of receivers as expressed in *Kerr on the Law and Practice as to Receivers and* Administrators, 17th edition. This text is now in its 18th edition and known as *Kerr and Hunter on Receivers and Administrators*, but the principles expressed remain the same. The learned authors state, at paragraphs 1–6:

> *A receiver can only be properly appointed in a claim for the purpose of getting in and holding or securing funds or other property, which the court at the trial, or in the course of the claim, will have the power, and the means, to distribute amongst, or make over to the persons or person entitled thereto.... The object sought by such appointment is therefore the safeguarding of property for the benefit of those entitled to it. There are two main classes of cases in which the appointment is made: (1) to enable person who possess rights over property to obtain the benefit of those rights and to preserve the property pending realisation, where ordinary legal remedies are defective; and (2) to preserve property from some danger which threatens it.*

In appropriate cases, the initial application for the appointment of a receiver is made ex parte by the claimant (usually in cases of urgency and so as not to 'tip off' the defendant, thus enabling him to place assets beyond the jurisdiction of the court). If the claimant is successful in obtaining relief, the court will order the matter to be re-listed for a further hearing, once the defendant has been served with the court documents and the order, so that the defendant has an opportunity at that further hearing to make submissions to the court that the order should not be continued. If the court remains satisfied, after that further hearing, that an order is appropriate, it will continue it, usually by way of a further order.

Given the absence of set rules, the specific powers and duties of a receiver appointed by the BVI court will be those set out in the order appointing him or her, as supplemented, unless the order provides otherwise, by the powers set out in the Insolvency Act 2003. This is expressly confirmed in the 2003 Act itself, which provides as follows at section 127:

> *127(1) A receiver has the powers expressly or impliedly conferred on him:*

> *(a) in the case of a receiver appointed out of court, by the charge or other instrument by which he was appointed; or*
> *(b) in the case of a receiver appointed by the Court, by the Court order under which he was appointed.*
>
> *Unless the charge or other instrument under which, or Court order by which, he was appointed expressly provides otherwise, a receiver may*
>
> *(a) demand and recover, by action or otherwise, income of the assets in respect of which he was appointed;*
> *(b) issue receipts for income recovered;*
> *(c) manage, insure, repair and maintain the assets in respect of which he was appointed; and*
> *(d) exercise, on behalf of the company, a right to inspect books or documents that relate to the assets in respect of which he was appointed in the possession or under the control of a person other than the company.*

This has been confirmed by the court, for example in *Danone Asia PTE Limited & Ors v. Golden Dynasty Enterprise Limited & Ors* (BVIHCV 2007/0262) where Charles J stated: 'The powers of the Receivers are derived from the Order'. In the 2007 edition of their work *The Law of Administrators and Receivers of Companies*, Messrs Lightman and Moss state: 'In general, the powers of a receiver appointed by the court are governed by the terms of the order appointing him.'

Providing that the receiver acts within the terms of the Order appointing him, there is no requirement for him to revert to the court.

Under section 118 of the Insolvency Act 2003, a receiver must, forthwith upon being appointed, send a notice of his appointment to the company, and file a notice of the appointment with the Registrar of Corporate Affairs. If the company is a regulated entity, notice must also be filed with the Financial Services Commission.

In addition, under section 119(2)(c) of the Insolvency Act (page 64 of the bundle), where a receiver has been appointed over specific assets of a company, every public document issued by or on behalf of the company relating to those assets must contain a statement that a receiver has been appointed.

§3.03 THE EFFECT OF THE RECEIVERSHIP ORDER

The effect of the Receivership Order is that, from the date of the receiver's appointment, the powers of the owner to deal with the specific assets are paralysed. As a legal entity, the owner of course continues to exist, and indeed is able to continue to deal with any of its assets other than the specific assets, but its powers, and – in the case of a company – those of its board of directors, are suspended in relation to the specific assets. Those powers are exercisable by the receiver, subject to the terms of the Receivership Order and under the direction of the court.

In *Moss Steamship Company v. Whinney* [1912] AC 254, Lord Atkinson put matters this way:

> This appointment of a receiver and manager over the assets and business of a company does not dissolve or annihilate the company, any more than the taking

possession by the mortgagee of the fee of land let to tenants annihilates the mortgagor. Both continue to exist; but it entirely supersedes the company in the conduct of its business, deprives it of all power to enter into contracts in relation to that business, or to sell, pledge, or otherwise dispose of the property put into the possession, or under the control of the receiver and manager. Its powers in these respects are entirely in abeyance.

§3.04 INTERIM MEASURES

[A] Bankers Trust Orders

These are very similar to Norwich Pharmacal Orders, with two exceptions. First, there is no requirement to prove any involvement in the wrongdoing by the discovery defendant; and second, the remedy is only available where the claimant has a proprietary interest. It is not, therefore, available in connection with a freezing order where the claimant is not seeking to take assets.

These orders are available ex parte (subject to the usual duties and safeguards) upon or after the proceedings have been issued.

[B] Interim Measures in Support of Arbitration

On 1 October 2014, the BVI brought the Arbitration Act 2013 into force, following the BVI's accession to the New York Convention.

An arbitral tribunal is given wide discretion to award interim measures, unless otherwise agreed by the parties. Article 17A of the Model Law sets out the relevant conditions to be satisfied by a party applying for such relief, namely that it must satisfy the tribunal that:

(a) harm (which cannot be compensated by an award of damages) is likely to result if the interim order is not made and such harm substantially outweighs the harm that is likely to result to the party against whom the order is made; and
(b) there is a reasonable possibility that the applicant will succeed on the merits of the claim. Any such determination is expressly stated not to affect the discretion of the tribunal in making any subsequent determination.

The conditions shall only apply to the extent that the tribunal considers appropriate where the interim relief sought is an order for the preservation of evidence.

Article 17 of the Model Law sets out the types of relief available, unless otherwise agreed by the parties:

(a) An order for the maintenance or restoration of the status quo pending determination of the dispute.

(b) An order that a party take action that would prevent, or refrain from taking action that is likely to cause, current or imminent harm or prejudice to the arbitration process itself.
(c) An order that a party provides a means of preserving assets out of which a subsequent award may be satisfied.
(d) An order for the preservation of evidence that may be relevant and material to the resolution of the dispute.

It is expressly provided that whilst an interim measure may include an injunction, it will not include an order made under section 54, which deals with the general powers exercisable by the tribunal in relation to matters such as ordering security for costs, directing disclosure, or the inspection and preservation of property and similar orders.

[C] Injunctions and Disclosure Orders

These are again slightly different to the more traditional freezing orders in that they are available to preserve property and to oblige a defendant to disclose information about the location of that property, in circumstances where the property is the subject of a claim. Applications can therefore be made to preserve assets which are the subject of a tracing claim and to obtain information about them.

As with freezing orders, these can be granted ex parte at the same time as the issuing of the claim, and if an undertaking is provided to file the claim as soon as practicable, shortly before the claim is filed.

[D] Freezing Orders

Freezing orders are a critical weapon for claimants restraining a defendant from disposing of, dealing with, or diminishing the value of its assets, whether those assets are situated within the BVI or outside its jurisdiction.

They can be granted before and after judgment, and in aid of domestic and foreign proceedings, including arbitrations, and in aid of enforcement of a judgment or arbitration award. In contradistinction to the other forms of interim relief discussed above, they operate in personam against a defendant and the principles on which they are available closely follow English law.

The development of the freezing order jurisdiction in the BVI owes much to its first Commercial Court Judge, Edward Bannister QC. Before his decision in *Black Swan Investment ISA v. Harvest View Ltd & Anor* (BVIHCV 2009/399), the position in the BVI was that interim relief was only available if substantive proceedings had been issued in the BVI. While claimants often tried to circumvent this by issuing proceedings and then seeking or agreeing a stay, Bannister J held in Black Swan that the lack of statutory jurisdiction to grant relief in aid of foreign litigation was not a bar. His views have been affirmed by the Court of Appeal in *Yukos CIS Investments Limited & Ors v. Yukos Hydrocarbons Investments Limited & Ors* (BVIHCAP 2010/028).

As set out above, the point of a freezing order is to preserve assets against which the claimant may ask to execute judgment. Accordingly, if the claimant claims the assets themselves, a freezing order is not the appropriate relief, although another form of interim order may well be available.

The initial application for a freezing order is almost invariably made ex parte. Under the BVI Civil Procedure Rules 2000, an interim order made without notice to the defendant cannot be granted for a period longer than twenty-eight days.

The requirements for the grant of freezing relief are:

(a) A good arguable case.
(b) A real risk that the judgment or award will go unsatisfied.

[E] Good Arguable Case

This is a lower hurdle than having to show that the claimant will win, but a higher hurdle than that applicable to other injunction applications, which is that there is a serious issue to be tried.

[F] Risk of Dissipation

The claimant's evidence must demonstrate that there is a real, or serious, risk that unless the Order is granted, the assets will be dissipated such that they will no longer be available when the judgment or award is made. It is no longer the case that evidence that a defendant holds its assets through offshore structure will, by itself, be sufficient to raise the inference that it will remove or dissipate those assets.

[G] Duty of Full and Frank Disclosure

This is a duty which applies to all ex parte applications and is particularly important in a case where the court is being asked to deploy one of its 'unclear weapons'. It is also one of the first things a defendant will scrutinise when considering its position on the *inter partes* return date or on an application to discharge the injunction.

The obligation is to place before the court all matters which are relevant to the court's assessment of the application. Because the court is essentially performing a 'weighing up' function, in deciding whether justice and convenience favours the grant of the Order, the applicant's duty extends to disclosing matters which are or may be adverse to the applicant, and to disclosing matters which would have been known to it had it made relevant enquiries before issuing the application. Neither is the applicant able to excuse itself by including the relevant material in an exhibit: the court's attention must be drawn to it. It goes without saying that potential defences to the substantive claim should also be highlighted. The requirement for a cross-undertaking in damages is discussed below, but it will be a breach of the duty of full and frank disclosure for an applicant not to bring to the court's attention matters relevant to that cross-undertaking, for example solvency issues which may affect the applicant's ability to comply with the undertaking.

[H] Cross-Undertaking in Damages

The practice of the BVI court is to require the applicant for freezing relief to undertake to compensate the defendant, should the defendant suffer loss as a result of the grant of the Order. The undertaking is given to the court, by counsel for the applicant.

If the applicant does not have the financial means to meet a cross-undertaking, the court may nevertheless – in rare cases – grant the relief, particularly in circumstances where alleged acts of the defendants are responsible for, or have contributed to, that impecuniosity.

[I] Fortification of the Undertaking

The BVI court has, on relatively few occasions, required fortification of the cross-undertaking by a payment into court or the provision of some other form of security.

[J] Ancillary Disclosure Order

The BVI court will frequently grant relief which is ancillary to a freezing order, in order to ensure that the Order is effective. The most common of these is an order requiring the defendant to give disclosure (on oath) as to the whereabouts of and information about its worldwide assets. This will enable notice of the freezing order to be given to relevant third parties, or enable freezing orders to be sought from courts in other jurisdictions. In return for orders such as these, the court will usually require some form of undertaking from the applicant about the use of the information obtained from the defendant, and will usually require an undertaking not to use the information other than for the purposes of the pending claim, without the leave of the court.

§3.05 ENFORCEMENT OF JUDGMENTS IN THE BVI

[A] Enforcement of Domestic Judgments

Execution of domestic judgments can be obtained by any of the following methods: writs of execution; charging orders; 'garnishee' orders (i.e., attachment of debts including bank deposits); receiverships (to collect receivables or even run a business); statutory demand; or the appointment of a liquidator.

[B] Enforcement of Foreign Judgments

Foreign judgments may be enforced by action at common law or by registration under the Reciprocal Enforcement of Judgments Act 1922 (the '*Act*') and the Foreign Judgments (Reciprocal Enforcement) Ordinance 1964 (the '*Ordinance*').

Not every foreign judgment is capable of enforcement in the BVI. Some may only be recognised by the court.[1] As a general rule, only foreign money judgments may be enforced.

A foreign judgment creditor may be able to achieve its objectives by other legal means, without enforcement. For example, if judgment is entered against a BVI company overseas and the company does not satisfy the judgment debt, the foreign judgment creditor can petition the BVI court for an order to wind up the company on the basis that it is unable to pay its debts.

The Act and the Ordinance codify the common law rules relating to enforcement. The Act applies to judgments of the Courts of England, Northern Ireland and Scotland. The Ordinance applies to judgments of the Courts of Australia and its states and territories, the Bahamas, Barbados, Belize, Bermuda, Nigeria, Guyana, Jamaica, St Lucia, St Vincent, and Trinidad and Tobago.

§3.06 REQUIREMENTS FOR ENFORCEMENT BY ACTION AT COMMON LAW

[A] General Principles

The enforcement of foreign money judgments is based upon the principle that the judgment of a foreign court of competent jurisdiction imposes upon the judgment debtor (i.e., the unsuccessful litigant) an obligation to pay the sum for which judgment has been given.

A number of important consequences flow from this principle. Specifically, the BVI court will:

(a) enforce a foreign judgment even though the relevant foreign court would not enforce a BVI judgment in similar circumstances;
(b) not enquire into the merits of the original action;
(c) not conduct an enquiry aimed at establishing that the legal system of the foreign country meets basic standards of justice;
(d) not review the measure of damages or compensation and seek to substitute its own judgment for that of the foreign court.

The defences available to a judgment debtor are therefore limited.

1. For example, a judgment dismissing a claim (although an adverse costs order may be enforced); a declaratory judgment; and orders relating to the bankruptcy of individuals or the liquidation of companies. The BVI court may also recognise a foreign judgment as a defence to an action or recognise it as constituting an assignment of property.

A foreign judgment may be enforced by action at common law, provided that it meets certain criteria:

(a) It must be made by a court of competent jurisdiction.
(b) It must be for a debt or definite sum of money.
(c) It must not be a sum payable in respect of taxes or other charges of a like nature or in respect of a fine or other penalty.
(d) It must be final and conclusive.

[B] The Foreign Judgment Must Have Been Given by a Court of Competent Jurisdiction

The BVI court will regard the foreign court as competent only in the following circumstances:

(a) Where the judgment debtor was present in the foreign jurisdiction at the time the proceedings were commenced.
    For a company incorporated under the law of one country to be treated as being present within the territorial jurisdiction of the courts of another, it must have either:
    (i) established and maintained a fixed place of business in the other country and for more than a minimal period of time carried on its own business from such premises; or
    (ii) had a representative carry on its business in the other country for more than a minimal period of time.
(b) Where the judgment debtor was the claimant, or counterclaimed, in the foreign proceedings.
(c) Where the judgment debtor voluntarily appeared in the foreign proceedings.
    If the judgment debtor has appeared in the foreign proceedings and contested the action on its merits without raising jurisdictional objections, it will be unable to challenge the foreign court's jurisdiction when defending an enforcement action. Difficulties may arise where a defendant participates only to the extent of contesting the jurisdiction of the foreign court and, having lost, takes no further part in the foreign proceedings.
(d) Where the judgment debtor expressly agrees to submit to the jurisdiction of the foreign court.

An agreement to submit to the jurisdiction of a foreign court must be express. A provision in a contract that its terms will be governed by and construed in accordance with the law of a particular country does not amount to an agreement to submit to the jurisdiction of that country's courts, but an agreement to accept service at a particular place in a particular country will be treated as an agreement to submit to jurisdiction.

[C] The Foreign Judgment Must Be 'Final and Conclusive'

The foreign judgment must constitute a final adjudication of all the issues raised in the action, and must not be liable to be varied by the foreign court.

[D] The Foreign Judgment Must Be for a Definite Sum of Money

The foreign judgment need not specify the actual sum payable by the judgment debtor, provided it contains all figures necessary for the court to ascertain the sum payable by means of simple arithmetical calculation. The court can only enforce an order for costs (i.e., legal fees) if the foreign court has determined the amount payable.

[E] Foreign Judgments in Respect of Taxes or Penalties Will Not Be Enforced

The court will not enforce a foreign judgment for payment of taxes or other charges of a like nature or in respect of a fine or other penalty. Punitive damages awarded to private individuals or penalties payable under the terms of contracts made between private individuals, are unlikely to fall within this category but may, nevertheless, be unenforceable for public policy reasons.

In certain civil jurisdictions, a victim of a crime may intervene in criminal proceedings, and obtain compensatory damages. The BVI court will treat those damages as severable from the penal order and will allow enforcement.

[F] Judgments Impeachable on Grounds of Fraud

A foreign judgment will not be enforced if it is impeachable for fraud on the part of the party in whose favour it was given or on the part of the court itself.

[G] Judgments Offending Natural Justice

Foreign judgments will not be enforced if the proceedings in the foreign court offend against BVI views of substantial justice. In practice, such a defence will be difficult to maintain because the court will not generally entertain any suggestion that a foreign country's procedural rules offend against natural justice.

[H] Judgments Contrary to Public Policy: Generally

A foreign judgment will not be enforced if its enforcement would be contrary to public policy in the BVI. In practice, it is extremely unlikely that circumstances could arise where the BVI court would refuse to enforce a foreign judgment on this ground.

[I] Punitive Damages and Multiple Damages

The circumstances in which an award of punitive damages (usually referred to in this jurisdiction as 'exemplary damages') may theoretically be available under BVI law are extremely limited, and we are not aware of any case in which an award has actually been made. A claimant seeking to enforce a foreign judgment for punitive damages in circumstances in which exemplary damages could not have been awarded had the original cause of action arisen in the BVI, must expect to be faced with the argument that enforcement would be contrary to public policy.

§3.07 PROCEDURE FOR ENFORCEMENT

[A] General

A common law enforcement action is commenced by the issue of a claim form with a statement of claim setting out:

(a) the basic facts relating to the nature of the original cause of action;
(b) the basis upon which the foreign court had jurisdiction over the debtor;
(c) particulars of the judgment; and
(d) the fact that the judgment remains unsatisfied in whole or in part.

The judgment creditor has available to him all the usual interlocutory remedies and rights of appeal available to any claimant including pre-trial freezing injunctions.

[B] Default and Summary Judgments

Given the limited range of defences available to the judgment debtor, a claimant may be able to obtain a default or summary judgment relatively easily and expeditiously. There is of course nothing to prevent a judgment debtor raising a counterclaim which is properly justiciable in the BVI. If successful on the counterclaim, the amount of the judgment in favour of the creditor will be reduced or extinguished.

[C] Interest

The award of interest is discretionary, and the court is likely to exercise that discretion so as to avoid awarding a penal rate of interest. The judgment will carry post-judgment interest under BVI law at the prescribed rate.[2]

2. In most cases, pre-judgment interest will have been awarded under the foreign jurisdiction and will therefore already be included in the judgment to be registered in the BVI. In the case of a foreign jurisdiction which did not award post-judgment interest, leading to a 'gap' between the date of the foreign judgment and the date of registration, it is possible that the BVI court would

[D] Execution

Having obtained judgment, the claimant will have available a wide range of enforcement procedures. These include: writs of execution; charging orders; 'garnishee' orders (i.e., attachment of debts including bank deposits); or receiverships (to collect receivables or even run a business).

[E] Execution of Judgments Denominated in Foreign Currencies

The BVI court has jurisdiction to give judgments expressed in foreign currencies and routinely does so. When commencing enforcement proceedings, the judgment creditor must file a certificate stating the exchange rate between the foreign currency and the US Dollar (the latter being the currency of the BVI) as at the close of business on the previous day.

[F] Limitation

In an enforcement action, the BVI court is usually only concerned with its own limitation rules. The limitation period is six years from the date upon which the sum specified in the judgment becomes payable.[3] That date is determined in accordance with the foreign law of the judgment, and may be considerably later than the actual date of the foreign judgment if, for example, there was a stay of execution pending an appeal.

The fact that enforcement of the foreign judgment may have become statute barred in the country in which it was made is generally irrelevant, unless the effect of the foreign limitation law was not simply to bar the action but also to extinguish the obligation.

§3.08 ENFORCEMENT OF JUDGMENTS UNDER STATUTE

The Act and the Ordinance provide a scheme for registering and enforcing relevant foreign judgments. A judgment creditor may apply to the court for registration at any time within six years after the date of judgment. The court will register the judgment, provided the judgment has not been wholly satisfied and is enforceable by execution in the foreign country. The circumstances in which registration may or must be set aside coincide with the position at common law.

Application for registration is made without notice, supported by affidavit evidence exhibiting a copy of the foreign judgment, verifying the amount due, and

award pre-judgment interest for that period. It should be emphasised that the BVI court's jurisdiction to award pre-judgment interest has not been tested, although in our view the jurisdiction exists.

3. Section 4 of the Limitation Ordinance 1961.

setting out other details required by the Civil Procedure Rules. The order for registration will provide that the debtor may apply to set the order aside within a specified time limit. If no application is made, the creditor can proceed to execution. Registered judgments have the same force and effect as judgments originally given by the BVI court.

§3.09 LIABILITY OF DIRECTORS AND OFFICERS

Broadly speaking, the duties owed by a director to a company fall into two categories. First, fiduciary duties and second, duties of skill and care.

[A] Fiduciary Duties

The BVI Business Companies Act 2004 provides that in exercising his powers and performing his duties, a director shall act honestly and in good faith and in what the director believes to be the best interests of the company. In a departure from previous legislation, and subject to there being express permission in the company's constitutional documents, a director is permitted to act in the best interests of the holding company or – in a joint venture context – in the best interests of the shareholder who appointed him. The 'best interests' test is subjective, and the court will only interfere if it concludes that no reasonable director would have acted as the director in question.

A director must not exercise his powers for a collateral purpose and must not improperly fetter the exercise of a future discretion. Neither should he put himself in a position where there is a conflict between his duty to the company and his personal interests.

[B] Duties of Care and Sill

The 2004 Act provides that when exercising powers or performing duties, a director shall exercise the care, diligence and skill that a reasonable director would exercise in the same circumstances, taking into account, but without limitation, the nature of the company, the nature of his decision, his position and the nature of his responsibilities. Provision is also made for the circumstances in which a director may rely on information and advice.

[C] To Whom the Duties Are Owed

A director's duties are owed to the company, and not to fellow directors, affiliated companies, or shareholders. Once, however, a company is insolvent or of doubtful solvency, and the principal economic interest in the company belongs to its body of general creditors, the directors must consider the creditors' interests as part of their duty to act in the best interests of the company itself.

[D] Other Liabilities

In addition to what is set out above, there are of course other statutory provisions which impact on the conduct of directors, for example regulatory provisions, and other conduct – for example the commission of a criminal act – which will result in liability.

Of perhaps more relevance in the context of this chapter, are the liabilities which may be incurred under the Insolvency Act 2003. In particular, a court may make an order requiring a director to pay compensation or to make a contribution to an insolvent company's assets in circumstances where the company has continued to trade despite being insolvent, or where at any time before the commencement of its liquidation any business of the company has been conducted with the intent to defraud its creditors, to defraud the creditors of any other person, or for any fraudulent purpose. Unless a director can demonstrate that he had no intention of defrauding creditors a director who has made or caused to be made any transfer of the company's assets during the twelve months prior to liquidation, may be found guilty of fraudulent conduct.

The court also has the power to disqualify a director, where there has been misfeasance, fraud or any breach of duty, and where the court is of the view that the director's conduct makes him unfit to be concerned in the management of a company.

[E] Claims by Shareholders

Although, as stated above, directors owe their duties principally to the company, a shareholder may be able to claim against a director either in respect of a personal right, or, more commonly, where the company has a claim against it directors, but is not taking action. A derivative claim of this nature, where the shareholder either brings proceedings in the name of the company, or intervenes in existing proceedings, may only be brought with the leave of the BVI court, even if the actual substantive proceedings will be taking place outside the BVI. The BVI Business Companies Act 2004 sets out a list of factors which the court must take into account in deciding whether to grant leave. These include whether the shareholder is acting in good faith, whether the proceedings are likely to succeed and how costly they will be, and whether an alternative remedy is available to the shareholder. In particular, the court must be satisfied, that it is the interests of the company that the conduct of the claim should not be left to the directors of the determination of the shareholders as a whole.

[F] Director Indemnities

A company's memorandum and articles of association will more often than not provide for the directors to be indemnified by the company against judgments, legal fees and other expenses. If, however, the directors did not act honestly and in good faith and in what they believed to be the best interests of the company, or if, in the context of criminal proceedings, they had reasonable to cause to believe that their conduct was unlawful, any purported indemnification by the company will be void.

CHAPTER 4

Canada

James A. Round & Aleksandar Jovanovic[*]

§4.01 INTRODUCTION

[A] History

Canada is composed of ten provinces and three territories, each of which maintains an autonomous judicial system. The contemporary Canadian legal system was established during the time of British and French colonization of North America. The colonial process that created the Dominion of Canada was completed by virtue of the *Constitution Act, 1867* (the '*Constitution Act*'), originally known as the *British North America Act*, enacted by Parliament of the United Kingdom. The *Constitution Act* provided for the union of the provinces and territories into a federal state with a parliamentary system modelled after that of the United Kingdom.[1]

Section 91 of the *Constitution Act* provides the federal government jurisdiction over areas of law that pertain to the nation as a whole. The *Constitution Act* established that banking, criminal law, international trade, immigration, income tax and admiralty law were to be within the purview of the federal government. Section 92 of the *Constitution Act* gives the provinces the capacity to legislate in the areas of personal and property rights, including contracts, real estate and business.[2] There is naturally some degree of overlap between provincial and federal legislation that has been and continues to be reconciled by the Courts. The majority of Canada's common law

* The authors of this chapter thank students-at-law Rebecca Ying and Lauren Crosby for their valuable assistance in preparing this work.

1. Department of Justice Canada, 'Where Our Legal System Comes From,' (7 May 2015) online: < http://www.justice.gc.ca/eng/csj-sjc/just/03.html >, [DOJ].
2. WH Mcconnell, 'Constitution Act 1867,' The Canadian Encyclopedia, (30 January 2015) online: < http://www.thecanadianencyclopedia.ca/en/article/constitution-act-1867 >.

principles concerning the identification, tracing and freezing of assets and the declaratory relief discussed within this chapter derive mainly from British common law, and are substantially similar to many other Commonwealth jurisdictions discussed in this book.

[B] Common and Civil Law Jurisdiction

Each Canadian province receives its governmental authority directly from the *Constitution Act*, whereas the powers of the territories were delegated by the Canadian federal government. All provinces and territories (except for Québec) follow the common law tradition of Great Britain. Québec retained the civil law traditions of France from the time of colonization, making Canada a uniquely 'bijural' jurisdiction, where the common and civil law systems co-exist simultaneously within one nation.

The Civil Code of Quebec applies to all private law matters in Québec. As in the other provinces and territories of Canada, the common law is applied in Quebec for matters of public law.[3] All legislation enacted in Canada is drafted in both English and French, and federal legislation must take into account both the common law and civil law traditions.[4] The federal Courts of Canada must take into account the bijural nature of Canadian law when rendering decisions.

[C] Choosing the Correct Jurisdiction

As a result of Canada's legal system, litigants must take care of commence proceedings in the appropriate jurisdiction that pertains to the subject matter of the claim. All proceedings relating to matters exclusively under the purview of the federal government, as provided for in the *Constitution Act*, must be commenced in the Federal Court of Canada.[5]

Commercial matters generally fall under provincial jurisdiction and, subject to *forum conveniens* considerations, are usually commenced in the province in which the debtor's assets are located. Each province and territory (except for Nunavut) has its own three-tiered court system.[6] The Supreme Court of Canada is the final and ultimate Court of Appeal for all proceedings. The various provinces and territories have slightly different Court structures that take into account the needs of various regions and communities, such as the Commercial List in the Toronto region that deals exclusively with complex commercial litigation.[7]

3. DOJ, *supra* note 1.
4. Department of Justice Canada, 'About Bijuralism,' (7 January 2015) online: <http://www.justice.gc.ca/eng/csj-sjc/harmonization/bijurilex/aboutb-aproposb.html>.
5. The Federal Courts consist of: (1) the Federal Court of Canada; (2) the Federal Court of Appeal; and (3) specialized Federal Courts such as the Tax Court of Canada and Military court.
6. The provincial Courts consist of: (1) Provincial/Territorial Courts; (2) Provincial/Territorial Superior Courts; and (3) Provincial/Territorial Appellate Court.
7. Department of Justice Canada, 'Dispute Resolution Reference Guide,' (19 January 2015) online: <http://www.justice.gc.ca/eng/rp-pr/csj-sjc/dprs-sprd/res/drrg-mrrc/06.html>.

The jurisdiction of a particular Court is also defined by the source of its power. Courts that derive their power from the common law tradition, which stems from the Magna Carta, are considered to be Courts of 'inherent jurisdiction' while Courts that derive their power from statute are limited to adjudicating matters that fall within the scope of that particular statute.[8]

Injunctive relief can only be granted by Courts of 'inherent jurisdiction' unless the injunctive relief is being sought against the Federal Government in which case the litigation must be commenced in Federal Court (which is a statutory Court). The titles of the Courts of 'inherent jurisdiction' vary from province to province. For example, in Ontario, the Court of 'inherent jurisdiction' is the Superior Court of Justice, while in Manitoba it is the Court of Queen's Bench.

§4.02 IDENTIFYING ASSETS IN CANADA

[A] Overview

As is the case with other nations whose legal systems are described in this book, in Canada, there are essentially two methods to identify a Canadian company's or private individual's assets: (a) public searches and investigations, and (b) by Court ordered disclosure.

[B] Public Searches and Investigations

[1] Real Estate

In the majority of Canadian provinces and territories, real estate holdings can be identified by conducting investigations through governmentally controlled databases of real estate holdings. Through these records, interested parties can determine whether a corporation or private individual owns real estate in specific jurisdictions. However, these searches and investigations are subject to inherent frailties. Real estate that is held through a holding company, or some other intermediary, may not be readily identifiable. Moreover, it may be difficult to identify real estate holdings owned by a private individual, depending on variations in name spelling. Nevertheless, real estate searches ought to be part of any preliminary investigation to identify assets of any corporation or individual, and can usually be completed quickly and for a modest fee. The majority of provinces[9] maintain an online database of real estate holdings that can be accessed either directly through the provincial government's website or through an intermediary.

It is notable that these real estate searches will not reveal the estimated value of the real estate holdings, nor will they reveal the amount of equity that the owner of the

8. For example, in Ontario, the *Courts of Justice Act*, RSO 1990, c C.43 defines the jurisdiction of the Small Claims Court which adjudicates matters with a monetary value of up to CAD 25,000.00.
9. Prince Edward Island, the Northwest Territories, Yukon and Nunavut do not have online real estate databases.

property holds. But such real estate searches will usually list the amount for which the property was most recently transferred, and the amount of charges/mortgages or other encumbrances on the property. This information can often provide valuable insight into a corporation or individual's financial status.

[2] Motor Vehicles

There is no publicly available database in Canada to identify motor vehicles by a corporation or individual's ownership. However, authorized persons can carry out investigations to identify driver licence numbers for individuals. The driver's licence numbers can then be used to identify licence plates associated with the driver. The licence plate searches will reveal the vehicles. As indicated, these searches can only be carried out by appropriately authorized individuals for authorized purposes, and usually require private investigators or paralegals be retained for a modest fee.

[3] Marine Vessels

The registration and licensing of vessels are different for pleasure crafts[10] versus non-pleasure vessels.[11] Although both types of vessels can be registered, there are more stringent regulations that require non-pleasure vessels to be registered. Registration will be mandated if the vessel is not a pleasure craft, is wholly owned by qualified persons[12] and has not been registered, listed or recorded in a foreign state.[13] Non-pleasure vessels powered by an engine of 10hp (7.5kw) or more, and all commercial river rafts, must be registered with Transport Canada's Canadian Register of Vessels or Small Vessel Register.[14] All commercial vessels must be registered, regardless of size.[15]

---

10. A 'pleasure craft' is a vessel used for recreation that does not carry passengers. It is of a prescribed class under the *Canada Shipping Act, infra* note 12. Within the meaning of pleasure craft, a 'passenger' is a person who has paid a fee to be transported in a commercial vessel. A 'guest' does not need to pay a fee.
11. A vessel used for anything other than pleasure, recreation or daily living is a non-pleasure vessel.
12. Part 2 of the *Canada Shipping Act*, SC 2001, c 26 states that to qualify as a registered owner(s), one must be:

    - A Canadian citizen or a permanent resident;
    - A corporation incorporated under the laws of Canada or a Canadian province;
    - A corporation incorporated under the laws of a foreign state if a subsidiary of that corporation is incorporated under the laws of Canada or a Canadian province and that subsidiary acts with respect to all matters relating to the vessel;
    - an employee or a director in Canada of a branch office of the corporation that is carrying on business in Canada, or
    - a ship management company incorporated under the laws of Canada or a province.

13. *Canada Shipping Act*, *supra* note 12, s. 46(1).
14. Transport Canada, 'Small Vessel Register (Commercial),' (27 May 2015), online: <http://www.tc.gc.ca/eng/marinesafety/oep-vesselreg-smallcomm-menu-542.htm#general>, [Small Vessel Register].
15. Transport Canada, 'Pleasure Craft Licenses,' (27 May 2015), online: <http://www.tc.gc.ca/eng/marinesafety/debs-obs-paperwork-paperwork_boat_licence-3211.htm#g3>.

The Canadian Register of Vessels can be understood as 'a title system for the ownership of vessels,' similar to a land registry.[16] When a vessel is registered, both the ownership and mortgage details of the vessel are publicly available on the Vessel Registration Query System (VRQS).[17] In terms of the ownership information, both the owner's name and address are identified.[18] Although the number of encumbrances on the vessel are listed in the registry, the estimated market value or the purchase price of the vessel is not disclosed.

The availability of ownership and mortgage information of pleasure craft depends on whether the craft is licensed or registered. All pleasure craft equipped with motors of 10 hp or greater must be licensed or registered. The owner can opt to register their pleasure craft in certain situations, as opposed to simply licensing it. The ownership and mortgage information of registered pleasure craft is publicly available on the VRQS. However, there is no publicly available database for vessels that have been merely licensed.[19]

[4] Corporate Searches

Whether incorporated pursuant to provincial, territorial or federal law, Canadian corporations must provide certain minimum corporate information to the respective provincial or federal Ministry. This information usually requires the identification of the corporation's directors and officers, including their contact information. Corporate searches can be performed online through an authorized service provider and can provide information concerning a corporate debtor's principals and a general sense of the corporation's scope. However, the information set out in the corporate searches is subject to the diligence of the corporation's reporting and is often out of date. Corporate searches will not reveal a corporation's annual financial statements as private corporations[20] are not required to disclose their annual financial statements to the public.

[5] Personal Property Security Searches

In most Canadian jurisdictions, a person can investigate whether a corporation or individual has provided a security interest in personal property, such as motor vehicles, industrial equipment or other chattels. Most provinces have legislation in place that dictates the manner in which a person may provide a security interest in personal property, including the registration of those security interests.

---

16. Small Vessel Register, *supra* note 14.
17. The link to the VRQS can be found at: http://wwwapps.tc.gc.ca/Saf-Sec-Sur/4/vrqs-srib/eng/vessel-registrations.
18. Section 76 of the *Canada Shipping Act, supra* note 12, provides access to the Canadian Register of Vessels as a public register, and a person may examine or obtain copies of any entries in the Register with respect to a vessel.
19. Pleasure Craft Licenses, *supra* note 15.
20. As opposed to publicly traded corporations that are required to adhere to strict disclosure regulations.

Most jurisdictions maintain publicly accessible databases that monitor security interests in personal property to allow creditors to determine whether a particular chattel is encumbered. As is the case with real estate searches, personal property security searches can be completed for a modest fee and can be conducted online through an authorized service provider.

[C] Court Intervention to Identify Assets

An interested person could also obtain information regarding a Canadian corporation or an individual's assets through the judicial process. This is usually achieved in one of three ways. The interested person could seek to have an 'inspector' appointed by a court to carry out investigations pursuant to provincial or federal legislation. The interested person could apply to have a Court issue a *Norwich* Order, requiring the disclosure of a debtor's assets by persons and entities (such as banks) other than the debtor itself. Finally, the interested person could apply to a Court for an *Anton Piller* order, otherwise known as a 'civil search warrant'. Obtaining this type of order places a more onerous burden on the interested party, as will be discussed below.

[1] Appointing an Inspector

An inspector can be appointed to undertake an investigation under either provincial or federal corporate legislation, depending on the statute of incorporation.[21] Many provincial corporate statutes are similar to the federal corporate statute, the *Canada Business Corporations Act* (CBCA).[22] For ease of reference, the CBCA will be discussed in this section; however, it should be noted that the provincial corporate statutes may differ from the CBCA.

Under the CBCA, a security holder[23] may apply to the court that has jurisdiction to obtain an order for an investigation of a corporation and any of its affiliated corporations.[24] Where a corporation is incorporated under provincial statute, that statute must be consulted to determine the process and scope of the investigation order. The primary purpose of appointing an inspector is to gather information not otherwise available to security holders. Information yielded from an investigation will often reveal what legal rights a security holder may have, and what remedies may be available to them.

21. Edmond FB Lamek and Andrew Derksen, Student-at-law, 'OBA Remedies Fast Forward – OBCA (and CBCA) Inspectors' Fasken Martineau Publication 1. [Lamek].
22. Canada Business Corporations Act, RSC 1985, c C-44, online: <http://laws-lois.justice.gc.ca/eng/acts/C-44/index.html>, [CBCA].
23. Lamek and Derksen conclude at pages 5–6 that based on the combined definitions of 'security' and 'debt obligation' under the CBCA, both shareholders and bondholders can make an application for investigation, and thus are considered 'security holders.' Furthermore, they assert that under both the CBCA and OBCA 'security holders' include both registered holders and beneficial owners of securities.
24. Lamek, *supra* note 21 at 5.

The CBCA outlines conduct that will justify an order for investigation, including: (i) whether the corporation or any of its affiliates have acted with the intention to defraud; (ii) whether the business has been carried on in an oppressive or unfairly prejudicial manner, or in a way that unfairly disregards the interests of a security holder or creditor; (iii) whether the corporation was formed or is being dissolved to serve a fraudulent or unlawful purpose; or (iv) whether any persons participating in the formation, business or affairs of the corporation or its affiliates have acted in a fraudulent manner.[25] Canadian courts are given broad discretion to alter the scope of the inspector's powers and mandate based on the specific situation.[26]

The information contained in the inspector's report will often be strictly controlled. The report carries a limited evidentiary function, and serves primarily to provide a factual basis upon which the applicant can learn the case they must establish. Usage of the report in proceedings may be limited.[27]

[2] Before Commencing an Action: Norwich Order

As indicated above, a *Norwich*[28] order compels the disclosure of a corporation or individual's assets by an entity other than said corporation or individual. A *Norwich* order can be used to locate and preserve assets, identify defendants and determine whether a cause of action exists.[29] *Norwich* orders grant litigants 'the right to pre-action discovery of non-parties'.[30] As the purpose of the order is to prevent evidence from being destroyed or concealed, it is often sought on an ex parte basis.[31] Because of the intrusive nature of these orders, Courts must carefully weigh the costs and benefits, including potential prejudice to the target of the *Norwich* order and/or non-parties.[32] A *Norwich* order would typically be sought where information must be obtained from a bank or service provider, for example.[33]

In Canada, the Court will consider the following factors to determine whether to grant a *Norwich* order in the specific circumstances of each case:

(1) Whether the application provided sufficient evidence to raise a valid claim.
(2) Whether the application has shown that the third party was somehow involved in the wrong.

25. *Ibid* at 2-3.
26. *Ibid* at 3.
27. *Ibid* at 13.
28. Norwich orders are named from the case: *Norwich Pharmacal Co v. Customs and Excise Commissioners* [1973] 2 All ER 943.
29. *Alberta Treasury Branches v. Leahy* 2000 ABQB 515 aff'd (2002) 202 AR 63 (CA), leave to appeal to SCC refused (2002) 303 NR 392, [*Leahy*].
30. Todd J Burke, Jahmiah Ferdinand-Hodkin, 'Interim Relief in Complex Litigation,' (2011) presented at conference: Complex, Mega and Advanced Litigation at 2.
31. *Leahy, supra* note 29 at paragraph 106.
32. *Ibid* at 3.
33. Caroline Abela, Krista Chaytor, Marie-Andree Vermette of Weirfoulds LLP, 'Litigation and Dispute Resolution, Canada' Global Legal Group, 2nd Ed at 41. [Litigation and Dispute Resolution].

(3) Whether the third party is the only practicable source of information.
(4) Whether the third party could be indemnified should any harm come of the order, if granted.
(5) Whether the interests of justice favour the disclosure.[34]

The recent Ontario Court of Appeal decision in *GEA Group AG v. Ventra Group Co and Timothy Graham*[35] suggests that this list is not exhaustive. In this case, the requirement that the plaintiff demonstrate necessity in certain cases was added to the *Leahy* list of factors.[36] Generally speaking, parties seeking a *Norwich* order should be guided (but not strictly constrained) by the underlying principles of the implied/deemed undertaking to not use any information acquired for any collateral purpose.[37]

[3] Anton Piller Order

The *Anton Piller* order is often described as a civil search warrant, without the ability to authorize forcible entry.[38] The order is obtained ex parte. When an *Anton Piller* order has been granted by the Court, the person under investigation pursuant to the order can face contempt proceedings for denying entry or otherwise frustrating the process.[39] Since the originating case, *Anton Piller KB v. Manufacturing Processes Ltd*[40] was decided in 1976, this remedy has rarely been employed due to its invasive nature. In the digital age, however, it has become increasingly common for courts to issue this type of relief to prevent the concealment of documents.[41]

Presently, the leading Canadian decision regarding *Anton Piller* orders is the 2006 Supreme Court of Canada decision in *Celanese Canada Ltd. v. Murray Demolition*. In this case, the Supreme Court clarified the appropriate scope for an *Anton Piller* order, including how the orders should be obtained and executed. Provisions were also set out to protect the rights of the parties involved. Specifically, the Court affirmed that it should be 'truly exceptional' for a Court to authorize this type of intrusion.[42]

The Supreme Court affirmed a four-part test that must be met by a plaintiff or applicant to obtain an *Anton Piller* order: (i) the plaintiff must demonstrate a strong prima facie case; (ii) the effect of the defendant's misconduct must result in serious harm to the plaintiff; and the plaintiff must demonstrate that there is clear and convincing evidence that (iii) the defendant is in possession of incriminating documents or materials and (iv) is likely to destroy or conceal the evidence if informed of

34. *Ibid* at paragraph 106.
35. 2009 ONCA 619 [*Ventra*].
36. *Ibid* at paragraph 91.
37. *Leahy, supra* note 29 at paragraph 257.
38. 2006 SCC 36 at paragraph 28, [*Celanese*].
39. *Ibid*.
40. [1975] EWCA Civ 12, [*Anton Piller*].
41. LE Trent Horne, 'Anton Piller Orders,' (5 February 2007) Ontario Bar Association, [Horne].
42. *Celanese, supra* note 38 at paragraph 30.

the proceedings.[43] More generally, the Supreme Court acknowledged the need for the Court to have faith that the plaintiff has provided the Court with complete and candid disclosure, and that the lawyers overseeing the exaction of the order demonstrate professional responsibility.[44]

The Supreme Court also reiterated protections and safeguards for targets of *Anton Piller* relief, including: the need for the supervision of the process by an independent Court-appointed solicitor, the need for the plaintiff to provide an undertaking and/or security to pay damages if the order is later revealed to be unjustified or unlawfully executed, and a limited scope to be applied to the order to ensure that items not covered are not be removed from the premises.[45]

§4.03 INTERIM MEASURES

[A] Tracing or Following Assets

'Following' an asset is the process of tracking assets as they move from one party to another. Assuming that a person has legal title to the assets in question, following could help a client obtain an asset based on the *nemo dat* principle.[46] However, if that asset is ultimately found in the possession of an owner with good legal title to the asset, the follower will not be able to recover ownership of the asset.[47]

Tracing assets (sometimes referred to as 'claiming' assets) can result in a legal or equitable claim on the assets in question. There are several different methods by which these claims can be obtained judicially, including *Mareva* injunctions, claims for 'oppression' by a corporation and in the context of a bankruptcy.

[B] Using *Mareva* Injunctions to Freeze Assets

A *Mareva* injunction can be sought to prevent a party from 'removing, spending or dissipating his or her assets in the course of litigation'.[48] Canadian Courts have issued domestic as well as extraterritorial *Mareva* injunctions.[49] *Mareva* injunctions will have the effect of freezing the assets of a debtor before further liquidations occur.[50]

The legal test to obtain a *Mareva* injunction requires the moving party to establish:

43. *Ibid* at paragraph 34.
44. *Ibid* at paragraph 36.
45. *Ibid* at paragraph 40.
46. The *nemo dat* principle means that one cannot sell (or encumber) what one does not own. Litigation and Dispute Resolution, *supra* note 33 at 39.
47. Litigation and Dispute Resolution, *supra* note 33 at 39.
48. Litigation and Dispute Resolution, *supra* note 33 at 39.
49. Extraterritorial orders can be issued where a Canadian court has in personam jurisdiction over the defendant, *Ibid.*
50. Paul G Macdonald, Jeffrey Levine, 'Creditors' Use of the Oppression Remedy and the Mareva Injunction to Protect Corporate Assets, (25 May 2009), at 1, [Levine].

(1) a prima facie case;
(2) that the defendant is either:
  (a) removing, or there is a real risk that he is about to remove, his assets from the jurisdiction to avoid the possibility of judgment; or
  (b) that the defendant is otherwise dissipating his assets in a manner which would render the possibility of future tracing of the assets remote, if not impossible.
(3) that the balance of convenience is in favour of freezing the assets.[51]

Significantly, a plaintiff must go further than simply demonstrating that there is a possibility that judgment will be frustrated in order to obtain a *Mareva* injunction. The plaintiff must instead demonstrate that the very purpose of the removal or dissipation of assets is an attempt by the defendant to frustrate potential judgments.[52] As is the case with *Anton Piller* orders, the person seeking a *Mareva* order must make full and frank disclosure to the Court and undertake to pay any damages that the target of the *Mareva* order might incur.

§4.04 ENFORCEMENT ISSUES

[A] Guiding Principle

Canadian law has responded to the realities of global commerce and multi-jurisdictional litigation by developing a comprehensive statutory and common law regime to aid the recognition and enforcement of foreign judgments and arbitral awards.[53] The guiding principle of this regime is comity; a concept which has been described by the Supreme Court of Canada as the Courts of one jurisdiction giving effect to the laws and judicial decisions of another jurisdiction, not as a matter of obligation but out of mutual deference and respect.[54]

[1] The Enforcement of Monetary Judgments Intra-provincially

As mentioned in the introductory portion of this chapter, Canada is a federal state that is composed of provincial and territorial jurisdictions. Since commercial matters fall within the purview of provincial Courts,[55] a monetary judgment obtained in one province cannot automatically be enforced in another. Indeed, a judgment obtained in British Columbia would be considered a 'foreign' judgment in Ontario. As such, to

51. *Popack v. Lipszyc*, [2008], OJ No 3380 at paragraph 36. (SCJ)(QL) [*Popack*].
52. *DiMenza v. Richardson Greenshields of Canada Ltd*, (1989) 74 OR (2d) 172 (Div Ct) at 174, [*DiMenza*].
53. While a foreign judgment must first be recognized by a domestic Court before it can be enforced, for ease of reference, this section will refer to both concepts as the 'enforcement' of foreign judgments.
54. *Zingre v. The Queen et al*, [1981] 2 SCR 392. [*Zingre*].
55. *Constitution Act, 1867*, 30 & 31 Victoria, c. 3 (UK), s. 92(13); Commercial matters fall within the provincial jurisdiction as they are considered 'property and civil rights'.

enforce a judgment intra-provincially, a judgment creditor can either rely on existing reciprocal enforcement legislation to register the judgment or they can sue on the judgment.

Canadian provinces[56] have enacted reciprocal enforcement legislation to provide litigants with a streamlined process to enforce judgments obtained in other provinces.[57] While the scope of the legislation differs between provinces, the process of registering a judgment is similar.

A judgment creditor must commence an application to register the judgment in the jurisdiction in which they want enforcement within six years[58] of the original judgment date. In order for the Court to register the judgment, the judgment creditor must demonstrate that the Court of First Instance had jurisdiction to adjudicate the matter, that the judgment is final,[59] that the defendant was provided with sufficient notice of the proceedings and that certain specific defences (set out in the legislation) do not apply.

Alternatively, a judgment creditor can sue to enforce a monetary judgment if it can satisfy the following criteria:

(1) the judgment must be issued by a Court properly exercising jurisdiction;
(2) the judgment must be final and conclusive; and
(3) the defendant is unable to raise 'impeachment' defences.[60]

The most difficult hurdle that the judgment creditor must overcome is demonstrating that the issuing Court validly exercised jurisdiction in adjudicating the matter. The issuing Court will have prima facie validly exercised jurisdiction if the judgment debtor defended the first action[61] or if the contract between the parties contains a forum selection clause favouring that jurisdiction.[62] Otherwise, the judgment creditor must

56. The commentary contained herein excludes any representations with respect to the laws in the Province of Quebec, Northwest Territories, Yukon or Nunavut. Further, the following analysis does not generally apply to orders relating to the enforcement of support or maintenance in family law proceedings.
57. British Columbia: *Enforcement of Canadian Judgments and Decrees Act, SBC 2003 c 29,* Alberta: *Reciprocal Enforcement of Judgments Act, RSA 2000, c R. 6*; Saskatchewan: *Reciprocal Enforcement of Judgments*, RSS 1996, c R-3.1 and *Enforcement of Canadian Judgments Act, SS 2002, c. E-9.1001*; Manitoba: *The Enforcement of Canadian Judgments Act, CCSM. 2005, c E116*; Ontario: *Reciprocal Enforcement of Judgments Act, RSO 1990, c. R. 5*; New Brunswick: *Canadian Judgments Act, SNB 2000, c C-0.1*; Nova Scotia: *Enforcement of Canadian* Judgments *and Decrees Act, SNS 2001, c. 30*; Prince Edward Island: *Reciprocal Enforcement of Judgments Act, RSPEI 1988, c. R-6*; Newfoundland: *Reciprocal Enforcement of Judgments Act, RSNL 1990, c. R-4, as amended 2001, c. N-3.1, s. 2.*
58. The prescribed period varies from province to province but is generally six years.
59. The Court will refuse to register a judgment that is the subject of an appeal or where the defendant is entitled to appeal and intends to exercise that right.
60. *Beals v. Saldanha*, 2003 SCC 72 [*Beals*].
61. If the defendant takes steps in the action, other than defending solely on jurisdictional grounds, the Court deems the defendant to have attorned to the jurisdiction of the Court.
62. *ZI Pompey Industrie v. ECU-Line NV* 2003 SCC 27; the Court will defer to the forum selection clause agreed to by the parties in all but exceptional cases.

establish that there is a 'real and substantial' connection between the Court of First Instance and the conduct giving rise to the action and/or the defendant.

[2] The Enforcement of International Foreign Judgments

A number of Canadian provinces have passed reciprocal enforcement legislation that allows judgment creditors to register international foreign judgments using the same process described above. However, the foreign jurisdictions for which the registration process is available varies widely among the provinces. The most permissive jurisdiction is Saskatchewan[63] which allows any foreign judgment to be registered. British Columbia,[64] Alberta,[65] Prince Edward Island,[66] Manitoba,[67] Newfoundland[68] allow certain jurisdictions in the United States, Australia and Europe to register foreign judgments. Except for Alberta, all of the provinces allow judgments from the United Kingdom to be registered. Ontario, Nova Scotia and New Brunswick only allow judgments from the United Kingdom to be registered.

If the registration process is unavailable, a judgment creditor must commence a proceeding to sue to enforce the international foreign judgment. The same criteria apply to enforcing international judgments as intra-provincial judgments. Again, the most arduous task faced by a judgment creditor is demonstrating that the foreign Court properly assumed jurisdiction through the 'real and substantial' connection test.

Courts will only enforce judgments that are final; meaning that the judgment is res judicata and that the foreign Court no longer has the authority to rescind or vary it. Courts will not refuse to enforce a judgment that is the subject of an appeal in the foreign jurisdiction.[69] However, the judgment debtor may be granted a stay of the proceedings pending the outcome of the appeal.

In *Beals,* the Supreme Court of Canada established that, under Canadian law, three defences are available to a domestic defendant contesting the recognition of a foreign judgment: (i) fraud; (ii) lack of natural justice; and (iii) public policy.[70] The judgment debtor may not raise merit-based defences that were already adjudicated by the foreign Court. A foreign judgment can be challenged for fraud based on new allegations that were not the subject of prior adjudication. To successfully defend on the basis of a lack of natural justice, a defendant must prove that the foreign Court did not apply minimum standards of fairness. The defence of public policy may be used to challenge the enforcement of a foreign judgment by condemning the foreign law on

63. *The Enforcement of Foreign Judgments Act,* SS 2005, Chapter E-9.121.
64. *Court Order Enforcement Act*, RSBC 1996, c. 78: WA, AL, CA, OR, CO, ID, Australia, Germany, Austria.
65. *Reciprocal Enforcement of Judgments Act*, RSA 2000, c. R. 6: WA, ID, MO, Australia.
66. *Reciprocal Enforcement of Judgments Act*, RSPEI 1988, c. R-6: WA.
67. *The Reciprocal Enforcement of Judgments Act*, CCSM c. J20, WA, ID, Australia; *The Enforcement of Judgments Conventions Act*, CCSM 2000, c. E117: France.
68. *Reciprocal Enforcement of Judgments Act*, RSNL 1990, c. R-4, as amended 2001, c. N-3.1, s. 2: Australia.
69. *Four Embarcadero Center Venture v. Mr. Greenjeans Corp.*, [1988] OJ No 210.
70. *Beals, supra* note 60.

which the judgment is based as contrary to the Canadian concept of justice and basic morality.[71]

In Canada, interim injunctions *cannot* be simply registered.[72] As such, a litigant who has obtained a foreign interim order, such as a *Mareva* order, must commence a fresh proceeding in Canada and then obtain the same interim order in the Canadian proceeding. In *Brotherhood,* the Supreme Court of Canada affirmed that Canadian Courts have inherent jurisdiction to grant injunctive relief, even though the final relief may be granted in another forum.[73] Although *Brotherhood* concerned a labour dispute, the case has been interpreted by lower Courts as authority for the granting of *Mareva* injunctions where the foreign proceeding is still yet to be determined.

As with the enforcement of foreign monetary judgments, the onus is on the person seeking to have the foreign order enforced to demonstrate that the Court can properly assume jurisdiction over the dispute. The real and substantial connection must be established between the defendant (against whom the injunction is being sought) and the injunctive relief.

The party seeking to have the relief enforced is not required to establish a real and substantial connection between the underlying claim in the foreign jurisdiction and the defendant.[74] In *Obégi,* the Court enforced a foreign *Mareva* injection and found that a real and substantial connection existed where the defendants had a bank account in Ontario that had significant sums of money flow through it.[75]

[3] Arbitral Awards

The Canadian federal government ratified the Convention on the Recognition and Enforcement of Foreign Arbitral Awards (the 'New York Convention') in 1986, and more recently ratified the Convention on the Settlement of Investment Disputes between States and Nationals of Other States (the 'ICSID Convention'). Every province has enacted laws implementing the New York Convention in some fashion.

Each province has separate legislation for domestic arbitration and international commercial arbitration. For example, Ontario has enacted the *Arbitration Act*[76] for domestic arbitration and the *International Commercial Arbitration Act*[77] for international commercial arbitration. Further, each provincial statute is based on and incorporates to some extent the Model Law on International Commercial Arbitration adopted by the United Nations Commission on International Trade Law on 21 June 1985. Much like foreign judgments, arbitral awards are enforced by applying to the Court in the jurisdiction in which the debtor or the debtor's assets are located.

71. *Yaiguaje v. Chevron Corp* [2013] OJ No 1955, aff'd (CA), citing *Beals supra* note 60.
72. The registration process is reserved for judgments that are for a sum of money.
73. *Brotherhood of Maintenance of Way Employees Canadian Pacific System Federation v. Canadian Pacific Ltd.,* [1996] 2 SCR 495.
74. *Obégi v. Kilani,* 2011 ONSC 1636.
75. *Ibid.*
76. SO 1991, c 17.
77. RSO 1990, c I.9.

Canada also has federal arbitral legislation, the *Commercial Arbitration Act*,[78] for arbitrations in which Her Majesty the Queen in Right of Canada, a departmental corporation or a federal Crown corporation is a party or if the dispute relates to maritime or admiralty matters.[79]

[4] Limitation Periods

A major issue affecting the enforcement of foreign judgments and arbitral awards in Canada is the applicability of provincial limitation periods. Litigants need to be mindful that while intra-provincial judgments can be enforced for six years from the date of the judgment, arbitral awards and international judgments are subject to provincial limitation statutes. Canadian law considers arbitral awards and international judgments to be simple contractual debts between the parties. Accordingly, provincial limitation periods apply to their enforcement.[80]

Canadian Courts rigidly apply limitation period legislation and as such, judgment creditors should be careful to commence a proceeding to enforce the foreign judgment or arbitral award within two years.[81] Indeed, the Supreme Court of Canada held that a foreign arbitral award could not be enforced in Alberta since two years had passed from the date that the judgment creditor first learned that the defendant would not honour the award.[82]

[5] Letters Rogatory/ Letter of Request

Discovery evidence for use in a foreign proceeding can be obtained in Canada through a letter of request (also known as 'letter rogatory') process. The foreign Court, of competent jurisdiction, must duly authorize the letter of request for judicial assistance to the appropriate Canadian Court and identify that the witness is located within the jurisdiction in which the request is being made.[83] The evidence being sought must be in relation to a pending civil, commercial or criminal matter before the requesting Court.[84] Once these preconditions are met, the Court will consider the following six criteria in deciding whether to exercise its authority to enforce the letter of request:

(1) whether the evidence sought is relevant;
(2) whether the evidence sought is necessary for trial and will be adduced at trial, if admissible;

78. RSC 1985, c 17 (2nd Supp).
79. *Ibid*, s. 5(2).
80. *Commission de la Construction du Québec v. Access Rigging Services Inc.*, 2010 ONSC 5897.
81. The applicable limitation period varies from province to province and can be either two years or six years depending on the jurisdiction. The majority of jurisdictions have a two-year limitation period.
82. *Yugraneft Corp. v. Rexx Management Corp.*, [2010] 1 SCR 649.
83. *Canada Evidence Act*, RSC 1985, c C-5, s. 46. [*Canada Evidence Act*]; *Evidence Act* (Ontario), RSO c E. 23., 60(1). [*Ontario Evidence Act*].
84. *King v. KPMG*, (2003), 37 C.P.C. (5th) 333.

(3) the evidence is not otherwise obtainable;
(4) whether the order sought is consistent with public policy;
(5) whether the documents sought are identified with reasonable specificity; and
(6) whether the order sought is unduly burdensome.[85]

The decision that established these factors emanated from Ontario; however, the underlying rationale has been adopted by Courts throughout Canada.

§4.05 DIRECTORS' AND OFFICERS' LIABILITY

In Canada, a corporation is a separate legal personality, distinct from its employees, management and shareholders.[86] Generally, these affiliates do not bear responsibility for the debts of the corporation. As a result, incorporation can facilitate the shielding of assets and protect management from exposure to personal liability. In certain circumstances, however, assets can be recovered from a corporation or from its directors and officers.

Directors' and officers' powers and responsibilities are primarily regulated through corporate statute, as supplemented by the common law. Directors and officers owe a fiduciary duty to the corporation to 'act honestly and in good faith with a view to the best interests of the corporation'.[87] The scope of directors' and officers' duty requires that they 'exercise the care, diligence and skill that a reasonably prudent person would exercise in comparable circumstances'.[88] A breach of this duty can result in the directors or officers themselves being held liable for their acts or omissions. The scope of the duty owed may vary somewhat between jurisdictions.[89]

In the seminal case *Peoples Department Stores Inc. (Trustee of) v. Wise,*[90] the Supreme Court of Canada held that directors and officers owe a duty of care not only to the corporation, but also to other stakeholders,[91] including creditors.[92] Importantly, *Peoples* clarified that Courts must exercise restraint in interfering with the decisions of management. Where management makes a decision that falls within a range of reasonable choices, Courts ought to defer to their expertise.[93] *Peoples* also clarified that creditors can assert claims based on a breach of the statutory duty of care, as well as in oppression.

85. *re Friction Division Products, Inc v. E.I. DuPont de Nemours & Co et al (No. 2)*, (1986), 56 OR (2d) 722.
86. *Salomon v. A Salomon & Co Ltd* [1897] AC 22.
87. CBCA, *supra* note 22 s. 122(1)(a).
88. *Ibid* at s. 122(1)(b).
89. For example, s. 134(1) of the Ontario Business Corporations Act expressly provides that the duties owed by officers and directors are owed to the corporation. In contrast, s. 122(1) of the CBCA omits the phrase 'to the corporation,' suggesting that directors and officers may owe a duty of care to other stakeholders.
90. *Peoples Department Stores Inc. (Trustee of) v. Wise* (2004), 2004 SCC 68.[*Peoples*].
91. *Peoples* was concerning a federally incorporated company.
92. *Peoples supra note 90* at paragraph 57.
93. The 'business judgment rule' provides that as long as directors and officers make decisions that fall within 'a range of reasonableness' a court ought not to substitute its own opinion for that of the board's, see *Peoples, supra* note 90 at paragraph 65.

Corporate legislation in Canada prevents directors and officers from contracting out of their fiduciary duties or duty of care. Directors are permitted to designate offices and delegate duties and powers to officers to manage the business and affairs of the corporation.[94] Accordingly, where a director has relied in good faith upon the representations of a qualified and credible professional,[95] they may rely upon the defences of good faith and reasonable diligence[96] to avoid liability for a breach of fiduciary duty or duty of care, respectively.

[A] Piercing the Corporate Veil

Where a company has been incorporated for an 'illegal, fraudulent or improper purpose'[97] courts may disregard the separate legal personality principle and thereby 'pierce the corporate veil'. Veil piercing has commonly been used where small, privately held companies do not have a clear separation of ownership and control. In the recent Ontario Court of Appeal decision, *Shoppers Drug Mart Inc. v. 6470360 Canada Inc*,[98] the Court held that directors and officers can be exposed to personal liability where they have expressly ordered that a 'wrongful thing' be done.

[B] Relief for Oppression

Oppression is an equitable remedy that is meant to allow courts to enforce 'not just what is legal, but what is fair'.[99] The leading case on oppression is the 2008 Supreme Court of Canada case, *BCE Inc v. 1976 Debentureholders*. Prior to *BCE*, the 'reasonable expectations' of the parties were examined to determine if the conduct in question justified an oppression remedy.[100] *BCE* established that a court must also consider whether the defendant's conduct[101] constitutes oppression, unfair prejudice or unfair disregard of the interests of corporate stakeholders.[102] The oppressive conduct is not limited to acts of the corporation as an entity, however. Section 241(2)(c) of the CBCA states that a court may grant a remedy in oppression where the oppressive conduct has been carried out by the directors of the corporation or any of its affiliates.

Typically, oppression actions are used to protect the interests of minority shareholders of a corporation, oppression relief can be sought by any security holder,

94. CBCA, *supra* note 22 at s. 121(a).
95. For example, where a director has relied in good faith upon financial statements provided by an auditor, they may be exempt from liability.
96. CBCA, *supra* note 22 at s. 122(4).
97. *642947 Ontario Ltd v. Fleischer* (2001), 56 OR (3d) 417 (CA). [*Fleischer*].
98. 2014 ONCA, [*Shoppers*].
99. *BCE Inc. v. 1976 Debentureholders*, 2008 SCC 69, at paragraph 58. [*BCE*].
100. *Ebrahimi v. Westbourne Galleries Ltd*, [1973] AC 360 (HL).
101. Conduct that can be oppressive includes any act or omission, the manner in which the business or affairs are conducted, and the exercise of power of directors of either a corporation or its affiliates, see CBCA, *supra* note 22 at s. 241.
102. Levine, *supra* note 50 at 12. See also CBCA, *supra* note 22 at s. 241(2).

creditor, director or officer of the corporation as of right[103] as well as 'any other person who, in the discretion of the court, is a proper person to make an application'.[104]

In some cases, directors have been found to be personally liable for oppression. This is most commonly the case where the director has personally benefited or furthered their control of the corporation through misconduct.[105] Another rationale for holding a director liable for oppression would be in the case of a closely held corporation where the director exercises a great deal of control.[106] For example, in a recent Ontario case,[107] the director of a closely held corporation was found liable in oppression for the unpaid wages and related expenses of his employees.[108]

[C] Remedies for Oppression

Significantly, oppression actions allow courts considerable latitude to determine an appropriate remedy that is context specific.[109] Under the CBCA and the Ontario Business Corporations Act, (OBCA) a court is entitled to make 'any interim or final order it thinks fit'.[110] The broad and discretionary nature of the oppression remedy could be a useful tool to aid a victim in tracing, freezing and recovering assets; however, it must be noted that the relief granted ought to be that which is necessary to 'rectify' the matters complained of.

103. *BCE, supra* note 99 at paragraph 52. 'Creditor' defined in these terms in CBCA, *supra* note 22 at s. 238, *Ontario Business Corporations* Act, RSO 1990, c B 16 at s. 245, [OBCA].
104. CBCA, *supra* note 22 at s. 238, OBCA *supra* note 103 at s. 245.
105. *Budd v. Gentra Inc.* [1998] OJ No 3109 (CA) at paragraph 52, [*Budd*].
106. *Ibid.*
107. *El Ashiri v. Pembroke Residence Ltd.*, 2015 ONSC 1172, [*El Ashiri*].
108. In this case, the corporation was OBCA incorporated.
109. Levine, *supra* note 50 at 13.
110. OBCA, *supra* note 103 at s. 248(3).

CHAPTER 5

Cayman Islands

Mac Imrie & Gemma Newell

§5.01 INTRODUCTION TO THE JURISDICTION

The Cayman Islands consists of three islands in the western Caribbean Sea around 460 miles south of Miami, Florida and 170 miles northwest of Jamaica. The country has a democratic government based upon the British Westminster model.[1] Judicial independence in the Cayman Islands is protected by the Constitution and is a cornerstone of the system of government.

All civil litigation takes place in George Town on Grand Cayman, the largest of the three islands. Litigation is conducted on the adversarial system, based generally on English principles of civil procedure. Due to the Islands' status as a leading offshore financial centre, the Cayman Islands courts are accustomed to dealing with complex commercial disputes involving, for example, mutual funds, SPVs, insolvencies, disputes between shareholders of private companies, asset finance, corporate fraud, insurance and trusts, often with significant cross-border aspects.

The Grand Court of the Cayman Islands (the '*Grand Court*') is the superior court of record of first instance for the Cayman Islands. The caseload of the Grand Court is divided amongst five divisions: Financial Services, Civil, Family, Admiralty and Criminal.

Commercially significant civil litigation cases classified as 'financial services proceedings' are tried in the Financial Services Division. Financial services proceedings include:

(a) Proceedings relating to investment funds.

1. The Westminster system is a democratic parliamentary system of government. Essentially, Westminster is the system of parliamentary democracy used in the United Kingdom, Canada, Australia, New Zealand and other common law countries.

(b) Insurance actions where the amount claimed exceeds KYD 1 million.
(c) Applications made pursuant to any Cayman Islands regulatory law.
(d) Actions or applications relating to trusts (except where the net asset value of the trust or the estate is less than KYD 1 million).
(e) Applications under the Companies Law.
(f) Actions for breach of contract or breach of duty by or against professional service providers (except for non-payment or over-payment of fees where the amount claimed is less than KYD 250,000).

Every proceeding in the Financial Services Division is assigned to a Commercial Judge, that is, one of a number of experienced commercial judges including the Chief Justice. Commercial Judges sit alone, without a jury. Where the assigned judge is unavailable, urgent applications may be heard or determined by another Commercial Judge. Visiting Judges and senior lawyers from, in particular, England, Jamaica and Canada sometimes sit as acting Judges. Enforcement proceedings and freezing injunctions are almost always dealt with in the Grand Court; usually in the Financial Services Division or Civil Division.

Appeals from the Grand Court are to the Cayman Islands Court of Appeal (which usually sits three times each year, although expedited appeals can be arranged by way of special sitting). The ultimate appellate court is the Privy Council in England. The Cayman Islands legal system is a common law system based on the English model. It comprises statute law and binding case precedents. Cayman Islands law has generally developed in line with English law, although some statutes, including the Companies Law and the Grand Court Rules, differ materially from English law. English (and other British Commonwealth) case authorities are generally persuasive, subject to relevant differences in the underlying legislation and local considerations.

The Grand Court Rules are modelled on the former English Rules of the Supreme Court (i.e., the 1999 White Book). The specific terms of the Grand Court Rules are interpreted by reference to an 'overriding objective' to deal with matters in a just, expeditious and economical way.

The issues in litigation are defined by pleadings exchanged by the parties, usually including a statement of claim, a defence and (if necessary) a reply (although certain types of claims are commenced by originating summons or petition). The pleadings set out the parties' various factual allegations, and in the case of the plaintiff, the relief sought. All such allegations must be pleaded with a reasonable degree of particularity, to a level which is generally higher than what would be typical in the United States. At trial, the parties are limited to those matters set out in their pleadings.

Parties' discovery obligations are broad, and extend to all documents which are relevant to matters in issue on the pleadings, or which may reasonably lead to a train of enquiry. Certain classes of privilege apply, including most significantly, legal professional privilege.

Depositions do not form part of the usual civil procedure. There is a mechanism known as 'discovery by oral examination' which is in some ways similar to a deposition; however, only the parties may be examined, not the witnesses. Discovery by oral examination will only be ordered in exceptional or unusual circumstances.

Evidence at trial is usually by way of live oral evidence, although, at the Judge's discretion, video link is available. Interlocutory matters are usually decided on affidavit evidence.

The court has wide-ranging powers at an interim stage to trace and preserve assets, to require the provision of information, to preserve documents, to appoint interim receivers, etc.

There is no requirement that the plaintiff be located in or have any connection with the Cayman Islands. It is possible to commence proceedings in the Cayman Islands against a defendant located outside the Cayman Islands, although the permission of the court is required. Obtaining permission involves an ex parte application, at which the plaintiff must show, among other things, that the claim raises a serious issue to be tried, and that the claim has a relevant connection to the jurisdiction. However, a defendant may seek a stay of the Cayman Islands proceedings, if it can demonstrate that the Cayman Islands is not the most appropriate forum for the litigation.

Although the court controls the pace of litigation, it does so with regard to practicalities and the particular dispute, and a reasonable timetable framework is set out within the court's overriding objective. Court hearing times in the Cayman Islands compare very favourably with those in other jurisdictions. Complex interlocutory hearings can be heard within weeks and urgent applications sooner. Hearing dates depend on the size and complexity of the litigation, court availability and at times the availability of counsel. Straightforward trials can usually take place within twelve months of the commencement of proceedings and sometimes less. The fees for commencing proceedings vary, but there is a fixed fee of about USD 6,000 to issue proceedings in the Financial Services Division, and variable (usually lower) fees for filings in the Civil Division.

Punitive or exemplary damages are almost never available. Damages are almost invariably designed to compensate the wronged party for their loss, not to punish the 'wrongdoer'. One exception to the compensation principle is in cases of fraud or breach of fiduciary duty, where the court may, in appropriate circumstances, order that the wrongdoer render an account for any profits made from the wrongdoing.

The court will normally order that the unsuccessful party pay the successful party's costs of the litigation. The costs which are recoverable on a typical costs order are assessed on a 'standard' basis by reference to a set of prescribed rates. The prescribed rates are invariably lower than the actual cost of litigation, and indicatively, a party could expect to recover between around 50% and 70% of their actual costs. However, if the court takes the view that losing party's conduct of the litigation has been unreasonable, improper or negligent, it may order that party to pay costs on an 'indemnity' basis. In that case, recovery is not limited to the prescribed rates and the taxation officer will only disallow costs where he/she is satisfied that they were unreasonably incurred.

Only the costs of attorneys admitted to practise in the Cayman Islands are recoverable if costs are assessed on the 'standard' basis. However, the costs of foreign attorneys who have not been admitted to practise in the Cayman Islands may also, in principle, be recoverable on the 'indemnity' basis.

The Cayman Islands' courts are very experienced in dealing with complex and high value commercial disputes. Its legal system is generally considered to be 'creditor friendly' for the purposes of tracing and recovering assets.

As explained in more detail below, generally, foreign judgments will be enforced in the Grand Court without difficulty if, among other things, the judgment for a sum of money is final and has been made by a court of competent jurisdiction. The defences available to a judgment debtor are limited.

Similarly, applications to freeze assets can be straightforward where certain requirements are met and can be made to assist foreign legal proceedings in the absence of substantive local proceedings. Although certain confidentiality laws apply in the Cayman Islands, there are numerous gateways through which information can be obtained.

§5.02 IDENTIFYING ASSETS IN THE CAYMAN ISLANDS

Most legal work involving asset tracing and recovery in the Cayman Islands is concerned with financial assets. Prior to proceedings being commenced, there are limited means by which financial assets can be covertly investigated as statute law restricts the disclosure of confidential information held by professional service providers such as banks, trustees, corporate service providers and administrators without client consent or a court order.

However, some publicly available information is available about certain types of assets, which may be of assistance in asset tracing exercises involving specific types of assets (mainly non-financial assets).

[A] Public Registers

[1] Land

The Cayman Islands has the Torrens system[2] of land registration, and details are kept at the Cayman Islands Land Registry, and are publicly searchable. The documents of title will record the name of the legal owner, any encumbrances currently registered against the property (e.g., charges, restrictive covenants, and cautions).[3]

[2] Vessels

The Cayman Islands has a modern ship registration system, which also allows for the registration and discharge of mortgages, changes of ownership and other services. The

2. Torrens title is a system of land title in which a register of holders of land which is maintained by the state which guarantees an indefeasible title to those included in the register. Land ownership is transferred through registration of title as opposed to using deeds.
3. See http://www.caymanlandinfo.ky/ for online access.

Cayman Islands shipping register is searchable by the public, on payment of a fee, or transcripts can be requested. The name of the relevant vessel is a key to the process.

[3] Aircrafts

Aircrafts may be registered in the Cayman Islands, and a Register of Aircrafts is maintained pursuant to the Air Navigation (Overseas Territories) Order. It is also possible to register an aircraft mortgage and aircraft engine mortgage.[4]

[4] Bad Debtors

There is no public system for registering or identifying bad debtors. However, a company search will reveal whether a company is in receivership or liquidation. Applications for, and notices of, appointment of liquidators and bankruptcy trustees are also advertised in the Cayman Islands Gazette.[5] There are also a number of companies which provide local investigation and debt collection services, and it is usually possible for them to locate personal assets such as cars and pleasure craft. In relation to motor vehicles, in practice because the Cayman Islands are so small, it is usually not difficult to locate motor vehicles (i.e., through a private investigator or otherwise).

[5] Intellectual Property Rights

The Cayman Islands has a patents and trademarks register which is publicly searchable.[6]

[6] Court Searches

It is possible to conduct a physical (i.e., copy of hard file) search of proceedings filed in the Grand Court registry (or have an agent do so) although public access is limited to the originating document used to commence the action. Pleadings, affidavits, witness statements and documentary evidence cannot be inspected by member of the public unless they are a party to the proceedings, or a Judge grants access to these. An online register of reported and unreported judgments is also available.[7]

4. See http://www.caacayman.com/portal/page?_pageid = 3321,6647377&_dad = portal&_schema = PORTAL for online access.
5. See http://www.gazettes.gov.ky/portal/page?_pageid = 5281,1&_dad = portal&_schema = PORTAL for online access to the Gazette.
6. See http://www.ciregistry.gov.ky/portal/page?_pageid = 3521,6697052&_dad = portal&_schema = PORTAL for online access.
7. See https://www.judicial.ky for online access.

[7] *Company Information*

The level of company information available to members of the public depends on whether it is an 'exempted company' or a 'resident company'. An exempted company is a company incorporated in the Cayman Islands which does not trade or do business in the Islands. Most Cayman Islands companies are therefore exempted companies. Other than an exempted company's: (i) date of incorporation; (ii) registered address; and (iii) status, no other company information is generally available to members of the public.

In relation to resident companies (i.e., those which trade in the Cayman Islands), in addition to that company's date of incorporation, registered address and status; a register of members[8] must be kept at the registered office of the company and shall be open to inspection and copying by any member of that company free of charge and any member of public on payment of KYD 10 or such less sum as the company may specify for each inspection. Information on the identity of a company's directors or its assets (whether held in trust or otherwise) is not publicly available.

Every limited company must keep a register of all mortgages and charges specifically affecting property of the company at its registered office. A short description of the property mortgaged or charged, the amount charged and the names of the mortgagees or persons entitled to such charge is detailed on this register. Any creditor or member of the company can inspect this register.

CORIS is an online system which is available to certain service providers (i.e., registered office services) licensed by the Cayman Islands Monetary Authority which gives certain information on annual returns generally limited to a company's registered office address and information as to whether the company is still listed as active, or is subject to a liquidation process or a pending or actual strike-off.

[8] *Confidentiality and Bank Secrecy*

Cayman Islands confidentiality law is governed by both common law[9] and statute.

The Confidential Relationships (Preservation) Law (CRPL) makes it a criminal offence to divulge, attempt, offer or threaten to divulge confidential information or to wilfully obtain or attempt to obtain it. The CRPL essentially codifies the English common law duty of confidentiality owed by a bank to its customer and applies to other professional relationships. It covers all confidential information with respect to business of a professional nature which arises in or is brought into the Cayman Islands and to all persons coming into possession of such information at any time thereafter whether they are within the jurisdiction or not. The definition of 'confidential

8. Commencing from the date of the registration of the company.
9. The common law of confidence arises where confidential information comes within the knowledge of a person in circumstances where that person has notice or is deemed to have agreed that the information in question is confidential, and that it would be just in all the circumstances that he should be prohibited from disclosing it. A duty of confidence does not arise where any such disclosure is required by law.

information' in the CPRL includes information concerning any property which the recipient is not, otherwise than in the normal course of business authorised by the principal to divulge. Confidential information under the CRPL must be '*with respect to business of a professional nature*' which includes the relationship between a professional person and a principal however the latter may be described.

The CPRL has no application to the seeking, divulging or obtaining of confidential information by or to any 'professional persons' acting in the normal course of business or with the consent, express or implied of the relevant principal. Furthermore the CPRL will not apply where the Grand Court directs that information be provided. Section 4 of the CRPL expressly refers to the holder of the information's obligation to apply for directions where they intend or are required to give in evidence in, or in connection with, any proceeding being tried, inquired into or determined by any court, tribunal or other authority (whether within or outside of the Cayman Islands) any confidential information within the meaning of the CRPL.

Unless assistance from the court is sought, the level of information publicly available in relation to trustees and assets held in trust is very limited.

[B] Pre-action Asset Tracing by Court Order

The Grand Court has jurisdiction to grant search orders, disclosure orders and freezing orders prior to the commencement of legal proceedings.

[1] Search/Preservation Orders

Search/Preservation Orders are usually made so as to safeguard evidence, although they are also frequently used to preserve property which might otherwise be destroyed or dissipated. Applications for search orders are usually made ex parte, and the applicant must comply with its duty of full and frank disclosure and will also be required to give undertakings to the court as to the manner in which the order is to be executed.

Search orders are rarely made in the Cayman Islands and require an applicant to satisfy the court:

(a) that there is an extremely strong prima facie case;
(b) that the actual or potential damage to the applicant is very serious;
(c) that there is clear evidence that the respondents have in their possession incriminating material;
(d) that there is a real possibility that the material will be destroyed before an *inter partes* application can be made; and
(e) that the harm likely to be caused by the execution of the search order to the respondent and his/her/its business affairs will not be excessive or out of proportion to the legitimate object of the order.

Search and preservation orders are sometimes issued in conjunction with freezing orders and disclosure orders of the type referred to below. For example, the Grand Court has, in aid of a freezing injunction, ordered discovery going beyond the usual process of disclosure of assets by affidavit; namely by the inspection and copying of the defendant's financial documents, where access to the documents was threatened by the risk of their removal overseas and their destruction by the defendant.[10]

[2] Disclosure Orders/Norwich Pharmacal Orders

As most other common law jurisdictions, the Cayman Grand Court is prepared to make disclosure orders by way of Norwich Pharmacal orders applying the usual equitable principles to such applications. A Norwich Pharmacal Order requires the disclosure of certain documents or information to the applicant. Orders are commonly used to identify the proper defendant to an action or to obtain information to plead a claim. If a person through no fault of their own becomes mixed up in the wrongful acts of others so as to facilitate that wrongdoing, he/she/it comes under an obligation to assist the person who has been wronged by disclosing the identity of the wrongdoer and providing information (including information about what the wrongdoer has done with assets).

Norwich Pharmacal relief an equitable remedy, and will be granted only where 'necessary' in the interests of justice. It is not generally available against a respondent who is likely to be a party to the potential proceedings. It must be shown that the respondent is a person who was mixed up in, or facilitated the wrongdoing (even innocently). There are no specific Cayman Islands civil procedure rules dealing with Norwich Pharmacal relief. As with other equitable remedies, the Court has discretion as to whether it is right that an order should be made in all the circumstances. In this respect, the Court may balance any interest in disclosure against any other public and private interest in order to decide whether, in all the circumstances, it is appropriate to order disclosure.

The 'mere witness' rule[11] operates so as to exclude ordering discovery against someone who would in due course be compellable to give that information as a witness at trial or pursuant to a witness summons.

Norwich Pharmacal orders can be obtained in support of both domestic and foreign proceedings, but the applicant is not obliged to commence proceedings after the information has been disclosed. The order may expressly restrict the applicant from making use of the information disclosed without further sanction of the court.

As the purpose of obtaining any Norwich Pharmacal disclosure could be rendered ineffective if the recipient were to notify the alleged wrongdoer of the application, the court may prevent the disclosing party from revealing the existence of the application until a certain number of days have passed after the order has been complied with.

---

10. *Laager v. Kruger* (Unreported, Grand Court, 3 May 1996).
11. The 'mere witness' rule prevents the applicant from obtaining information against a person who will in due course be compellable to give that information either by oral testimony as a witness at trial or on a witness summons for the production of documents.

The Grand Court also has jurisdiction to issue Bankers Trust relief, requiring the disclosure of documents and information to enable a Plaintiff to trace property of which it has been defrauded.[12]

In *Braga v. Equity Trust Company (Cayman) Limited,*[13] the Plaintiff sought orders for disclosure in aid of foreign proceedings regarding and alleged fraud in Brazil. The Grand Court had ordered that certain corporate services companies disclose information about the ultimate beneficial owners (i.e., Norwich Pharmacal orders) and disclosure orders (i.e., Bankers Trust relief) about the financial affairs of certain persons. Restrictions were placed on the use of the documents without leave of the Court. A dispute arose as to whether the Plaintiffs had breached the terms of the Court's order, and those affected by the disclosure applied to set aside the Norwich Pharmacal orders and reduce the scope of the Bankers Trust relief. This gave the Court an opportunity to review the approach to such applications in detail.

The Court confirmed that to make a Norwich Pharmacal order, the party from which disclosure was sought must have been 'involved' – innocently or otherwise – in the wrongdoing. This was true of the defendants. As fiduciary service providers to shareholders allegedly involved in fraudulent activity, the defendants were more than 'mere witnesses'. The Court held that the jurisdiction to make Norwich Pharmacal orders was broad, flexible and developing and one in which a common sense, non-technical approach would be taken. The Court also held that there was no absolute requirement to show that a Norwich Pharmacal order was necessary to enable an action to be brought, and such orders were not limited to cases where the wrongdoer's identity needed to be ascertained. They could be granted in circumstances in which the wrongdoer's identity was known but information was needed to prove the wrongdoing.

However, the Court concluded that the Bankers Trust disclosure orders had been drawn too widely and should be limited in scope to what is required to locate and preserve assets which had been fraudulently diverted.

[3] Freezing Injunctions

Freezing injunctions are not uncommon in the Cayman Islands. The Grand Court Rules set out the procedural steps required, and there is a standard form of order which is usually made (also found in the Grand Court Rules).

Freezing orders (i.e., Mareva injunctions) restrain assets and prevent a defendant from disposing of, dealing or diminishing the value of the assets (subject to reasonable expenses being paid). The requirements for the grant of a freezing order are:

(a) A good arguable case.
(b) A real risk of disruption of assets such that the judgment or award will go unsatisfied if the order is not granted.

12. *Bankers Trust Co v. Shapira* [1980] 1 WLR 1274.
13. 2011(1) CILR.

(c) That the balance of convenience between the parties favours the grant of the order.

The applicant for a freezing order has a duty of full and frank disclosure and must place before the court all matters which are relevant to the court's assessment of the application. The applicant's duty extends to disclosing matters which are or may be adverse to the applicant, and to disclosing matters which would have been known to it had it made relevant enquiries before issuing the application.

The applicant for freezing relief will be required to undertake to compensate the defendant, should the defendant suffer loss as a result of the grant of the order. The undertaking is given to the court, by counsel for the applicant. The court may require fortification of the cross-undertaking by a payment into court.

If the applicant does not have the financial means to meet a cross-undertaking, the court may nevertheless grant the relief, particularly in circumstances where alleged acts of the defendants are responsible for, or have contributed to, that impecuniosity.

The court will frequently grant relief which is ancillary to a freezing order, in order to ensure that the order is effective. The most common of these is an order requiring the defendant to give disclosure (on oath) as to the whereabouts of and information about worldwide assets. This will enable notice of the freezing order to be given to third parties, or to enable freezing orders to be sought from courts in other jurisdictions. The court will usually require some form of undertaking from the applicant about the use of the information obtained from the defendant, and will usually require an undertaking not to use the information other than for the purposes of the pending claim, without the leave of the court.

[4] Interim Relief to Support Foreign Proceedings

The Grand Court is able to grant interim relief in the Cayman Islands (including by way of freezing order) in support of substantive proceedings in other jurisdictions – i.e., free-standing interim relief.[14]

In 2013, the Cayman Islands Court of Appeal confirmed the availability of 'free-standing' freezing injunctions in support of foreign legal proceedings, against Cayman Islands entities against which no wrongdoing is alleged[15] (i.e., non-cause of action defendants located within the Cayman Islands).

However, in an earlier decision, the Court of Appeal had concluded that there was no jurisdiction to serve a defendant out of the jurisdiction where the only relief sought was an interim freezing injunction in support of foreign proceedings. This meant that a plaintiff could seek a freezing injunction in the Cayman Islands in support of foreign proceedings, but only if the party against whom the injunction was sought

14. The Grand Court may grant an order for security for costs against a foreign plaintiff with no assets in the jurisdiction. In the case of individuals (as opposed to companies), the amount awarded is likely to be limited to the additional expenses of enforcing a costs order in the relevant jurisdiction. *Gong v. CDH China Management Co Ltd* 2011(1) CILR 57.
15. *VTB Capital PLC v. Universal Telecom Management* [2013] 2 CILR 94.

was present in the Cayman Islands. If the defendant was not present in the Cayman Islands, but merely had assets located here, the court could not assist. To remedy the situation, in 2014 an amendment to the law was made specifically allowing for the service out of the jurisdiction of any action, with leave of the Court, where the claim is brought in relation to proceedings which have been or are to be commenced in a court outside of the Cayman Islands and are capable of giving rise to a judgment which may be enforced within the Cayman Islands.[16]

§5.03 ENFORCEMENT ISSUES

Other than the Foreign Judgments Reciprocal Enforcement Law (1996 Revision) (discussed below), there are no other applicable statutes (domestic or international) dealing with the recognition or enforcement of domestic or foreign proceedings.

Order 72, rule 1(l) of the Grand Court Rules provides that the enforcement of foreign judgments, whether at common law or pursuant to the Foreign Judgments Reciprocal Enforcement Law (1996 Revision), are proceedings which fall under the Financial Services Division of the Grand Court.

[A] Domestic Judgments

Execution of domestic judgments can be a wide range of enforcement proceedings, including writs for seizure and sale of goods; charging orders in respect of land and securities, which may then be sold; 'garnishee' orders (i.e., attachment of debts including bank deposits); or receiverships (to collect receivables or even run a business). If Cayman Islands companies do not pay judgment debt, they may be wound up by liquidators and dissolved. It is also possible to engage in wide-ranging post-judgment discovery either in advance of, or concurrently with, execution proceedings.

[B] Foreign Judgments

Foreign judgments may be enforced by action at common law or, in the case of certain Australian judgments, by registration under the Foreign Judgments Reciprocal Enforcement Law (1996 Revision).

Not every foreign judgment is capable of enforcement in the Cayman Islands. Some may only be recognised by Cayman Islands courts. Special considerations may arise in relation to the enforcement of money judgments given in foreign insolvency proceedings.

A foreign judgment creditor may be able to achieve its objectives without enforcing a foreign judgment in the Cayman Islands. For example, if a judgment is entered against a Cayman Islands company overseas and the company does not satisfy

16. See Grand Court Rule Order 11 rule 1(n).

the judgment debt, the foreign judgment creditor can petition the Cayman Islands court for an order to wind up the company on the basis that it is unable to pay its debts.

The enforcement of foreign money judgments is based upon the principle that the judgment of a foreign court of competent jurisdiction imposes upon the judgment debtor (i.e., the unsuccessful litigant) an obligation to pay the sum for which judgment has been given.

A number of important consequences flow from this principle. Specifically, the Cayman Islands court:

(a) will enforce a foreign judgment even though the relevant foreign court would not enforce a Cayman Islands judgment in similar circumstances;
(b) will not enquire into the merits of the original action;
(c) will not conduct an enquiry aimed at establishing that the legal system of the foreign country meets basic standards of justice; and
(d) will not review the measure of damages or compensation and seek to substitute its own judgment for that of the foreign court.

The defences available to a judgment debtor are therefore limited.

A foreign money judgment may be enforced by action at common law, provided that it meets certain criteria:

(a) It must be made by a court of competent jurisdiction.
(b) It must be for a debt or definite sum of money.
(c) It must not be a sum payable in respect of taxes or other charges of a like nature or in respect of a fine or other penalty.
(d) It must be final and conclusive.
(e) It must not be impeachable on the grounds of fraud.
(f) It must not offend natural justice.
(g) It must not be contrary to public policy.

A common law enforcement action is commenced by the issue of a writ endorsed with a statement of claim setting out:

(a) the basic facts relating to the nature of the original cause of action;
(b) the basis upon which the foreign court had jurisdiction over the debtor;
(c) particulars of the judgment; and
(d) the fact that the judgment remains unsatisfied in whole or in part.

The Cayman Islands courts will also permit the direct enforcement of foreign non-money judgments, although the court retains a discretion in such applications. The court will have regard to general considerations of fairness and ensure that domestic law is not extended to suit foreign litigants. Recognition and enforcement of foreign judgments for specific performance and enforcement is therefore possible.[17]

Having obtained judgment, the plaintiff will have available, in theory at least, the wide range of enforcement procedures available in respect of domestic judgments.

[C] Arbitral Awards

Under the Arbitration Law 2012, an arbitral award rendered in the Cayman Islands may be enforced in the same manner as a judgment or order of the court to the same effect, and where permission is given, judgment may be entered by the court in the same terms as the award.[18]

There are two types of foreign arbitral awards under Cayman law:

(a) '*Convention Awards*', i.e., awards made in pursuance of an arbitration agreement in the territory of a state, other than the Cayman Islands, that is a party to the New York Convention on the Recognition and Enforcement of Foreign Arbitral Awards, 1958 (the '*New York Convention*').
(b) Other awards by foreign arbitrators ('*non-Convention awards*').

The New York Convention has been adopted by the Cayman Islands.

The Foreign Arbitral Awards Enforcement Law (1997 Revision) (the '*Law*') provides for the enforcement of Convention Awards in the Cayman Islands and specifies the required procedure. The Arbitration Law 2012 applies the same principles of enforcement to non-Convention awards.[19] The substantive ingredients of the cause of the action and/or conditions for enforcement and the defences available are, however, those laid down by the New York Convention.

A foreign award will be enforced in the Cayman Islands unless the party against whom enforcement or recognition is being sought (the 'respondent') establishes certain specific defences:[20]

(c) That he/she/it was (under the applicable law) under some incapacity when he/she/it entered into the arbitration agreement.
(d) That the arbitration agreement was not valid under the law to which the parties subjected it (the proper law of the arbitration agreement[21]) or, failing any indication thereon, under the law of the country where the award was made (the law of the arbitration[22]).

---

17. *Bandone SDN. BHD. and Brunei Investment Agency v. Sol Properties Incorporated* [2008] CILR 301.
18. See section 72(1) and (2) of the Arbitration Law, 2012.
19. *GlobeOp Financial Services LLC v. Titan* 2014(1) CILR 412.
20. Section 7(2) of the Law. Note that such defences do not include set-off (*Re Swiss Oil Corporation* [1988–1989] CILR 277).
21. That is the substantive law by which the validity and effect of the arbitration agreement is governed.
22. That is the law of the country in which the arbitration proceeding took place.

(e) That he/she/it was not given proper notice of the appointment of the arbitrator or of the arbitration proceedings or was otherwise unable to present his/her/its case.
(f) That the award deals with a difference not contemplated by, or not falling within, the terms of the submission to arbitration or contains decisions on matters beyond the scope of the submission to arbitration.
(g) That the composition of the arbitral authority or the arbitral procedure was not in accordance with the agreement of the parties or, failing such agreement, with the law of the country in which the arbitration took place.
(h) That the award has not yet become binding on the parties, or has been set aside or suspended by a competent authority of the country in which, or under the law of which, it was made. The Cayman Islands court has held that the words 'suspended by a competent authority' mean suspended by a decision of a court, tribunal or other body having jurisdiction to make such decisions in the country where the arbitration took place.[23]

An application for enforcement is made ex parte for 'leave to enforce the award in the same manner as a judgment or order to the same effect'. The application must be supported by an affidavit which exhibits: (i) the duly authenticated original award or a duly certified copy of it; (ii) the original arbitration agreement or a duly certified copy of it; and (iii) where the award or agreement is in a foreign language, a translation of it certified by an official or sworn translator or by a diplomatic or consular agent. Unless the respondent makes an application to set aside any order made within a specific period, the applicant is permitted to enforce it.

When making an application to enforce a foreign award, the applicant has available to him all the usual pre-trial remedies available on an action for the enforcement of a foreign judgment, such as interim freezing injunctions, discovery in aid of execution and receiverships.

Generally speaking, 'enforcement' of foreign awards means the process of enabling the award to have the same force and effect as a judgment of the court. Once the application to enforce an award has been granted, the court will consider enforcement procedures, sometimes known as 'execution'.

Having obtained judgment on the award, the applicant will have available a wide range of enforcement or execution procedures. These include seizure and sale of goods; charging orders in respect of land and securities, which may then be sold; attachment of debts including bank deposits; and the appointment of a receiver (who might collect receivables or even run a business). In general terms, an enforced award involving an obligation to pay a definite sum of money or to take, or refrain from taking, a particular course of action will be enforceable through one or more of these processes of execution.

23. The Cayman Islands court has held that a French award was not to be treated as having been suspended for these purposes merely because the French law imposed an automatic stay pending an appeal (*Republic of Gabon v. Swiss Oil Corp.* [1988-89] CILR N-1).

A party seeking to rely upon an enforced foreign award not to execute it and recover money or property, but rather to resist a claim or an allegation by another party or to have the terms of a declaratory award adopted and recognised as if they were the terms of a court order, is said to seek 'recognition' of an award.

A foreign award entitled to recognition may give rise to: (a) cause of action estoppel, or (b) issue estoppel. A cause of action estoppel prevents a party to proceedings from asserting or denying, as against the other party, the existence of a cause of action, the non-existence of which has been determined by a foreign award. An issue estoppel prevents a matter of fact of law which has necessarily been decided by a foreign award from being re-litigated in the Cayman Islands.

Awards of a declaratory nature should be capable of recognition, provided they are sufficiently certain and clear.[24] In all cases, consideration must been given to what process of the Cayman court is required to give effect to the terms of the enforced foreign award (i.e., whether by way of execution or recognition).

§5.04 DIRECTOR AND OFFICER LIABILITY IN RELATION TO ASSET PROTECTION SCHEMES

The duties of a director (loyalty, honesty, good faith, care and skill) are owed to the company. The directors must act in what they consider to be in the best interests of the company. In the ordinary course, the best interests of the company will be equated with the best interests of the company's shareholders. However, when a company encounters financial difficulties and is insolvent or is of doubtful solvency, the directors must consider the creditors' interests as part of their duty to act in the interests of the company itself. Upon insolvency or doubtful solvency, it is the general body of the company's creditors that has the principal economic interest in the company and therefore in considering what is in the company's best interests in those circumstances, the directors must have regard to what is in the best interests of the general body of creditors.

This does not mean that creditors will have a direct right of action against the directors or the company for not considering their interests, but it does mean that the company itself (usually through a liquidator appointed following the company's insolvency) can bring an action against a director for breach of duty.

The circumstances in which a company shall be deemed to be 'unable to pay its debts' (i.e., insolvent) under Cayman Islands law emphasise a company's cash flow position. However for the directors of a company, the question of whether the fair value of the company's assets exceeds the value of its liabilities (taking into account its

24. See *IPOC International Growth Fund Limited v. LV Finance Group Limited*, Civil Appeal No. 30 of 2006, unreported, in which the Court of Appeal of the British Virgin Islands concluded that purely declaratory Convention Awards were capable of enforcement and recognition if sufficiently certain and precise, and clarified suggestions to the contrary arising from the English Court of Appeal cases *Margulies Brothers Ltd v. Dafnis Thomaides & Co (UK) Ltd* [1958] 1 Lloyds Rep 205 and *Tongyuan International Trading Group v. Uni-Clan* (unrep, 19 January 2001) in which it was held that purely declaratory awards were not enforceable. Note, however, that Convention Awards may be treated differently from non-Convention Awards for these purposes.

prospective and contingent liabilities) (the 'balance sheet' test) is a test which will also be likely to be relevant in considering whether a company is insolvent or of doubtful solvency, even if the company is cash flow solvent at the time.

As a general rule, directors must not prefer the interests of one creditor (or group of creditors) over the general body of the company's creditors unless there is a legitimate commercial reason for doing so. For example, if a director causes the company to repay a sum owed to a creditor connected to that director in circumstances where the company's other creditors are unlikely to recover their debts in full, that director risks personal liability, and the amounts paid to that creditor could in certain specific circumstances be recovered by a liquidator with the company in due course.

The law is not intended to discourage directors from taking legitimate business risks, but it is intended to ensure that directors act properly and responsibly. The steps listed above are intended to enable the directors' conduct, as far as possible, to withstand scrutiny at a later date.

If the directors suspect that the company is (or may become) insolvent, for example because in their view the company fails the 'balance sheet test' or it simply cannot meet its obligations on an ongoing basis, the basic principles of director's duties remain the same: the directors must act in the best interests of the company. As indicated above, in those circumstances, the best interests of the company will be equated to the best interests of the company's creditors.

The directors will therefore need to consider whether it is appropriate for the company to continue to trade. A decision to continue to trade may be justifiable if the directors can reasonably form the view that the company has a good prospect of trading out of its difficulties, for example by reaching a compromise or negotiating amended terms with its principal creditors. The directors' position will be assisted if they have the benefit of appropriate professional advice, such as revised business plans, cash flow projections and the like prepared by accountants.

If the directors form the view that there is no reasonable prospect of the company trading out of its current difficulties, the most appropriate course of action will invariably be for the directors to take advice (if they have not already done so) from an expert in reconstruction and insolvency on the formal procedures which exist to protect the interests of creditors, and to reorganise a company's affairs.

Any formal steps against the directors on the basis that they did not act in the best interests of the company will almost invariably have to be taken by the company itself. If the company is in liquidation, such action will be taken by a liquidator who may, as agent of the company, seek damages from the directors for breach of their common law duties. Typically, a liquidator will be encouraged by the company's creditors to investigate the role played by the directors in the company's collapse and if appropriate to pursue the relevant directors personally.

In the most serious cases, directors may be prosecuted, either by the Attorney General or by the liquidator (on the order of the court, by its own motion or on the application of any person with an interest in the liquidation) if it appears that a director has been guilty of a criminal offence in relation to the company. The Companies Law (2013 Revision) (the 'Law') makes directors criminally liable in the circumstances listed below. These sections of the Law apply in both insolvent and solvent liquidations:

(a) Fraud in anticipation of winding up – section 134 of the Law
Directors will be accountable for certain prescribed actions taken in the twelve months prior to the liquidation with the intent to defraud the company's creditors or contributories. Such actions include fraudulently concealing or removing company property to the value of KYD 10,000 or more; falsifying or destroying company documents; and disposing of company property obtained on credit. These actions are an offence and liable on conviction to a fine or imprisonment for five years or both.
(b) Transactions in fraud of creditors – section 135 of the Law
It is an offence for a director to have transferred, gifted or charged any company property or concealed or removed company property with the intent to defraud creditors or contributories. It is also an offence for a director to have caused the levying of any execution against the company's property. Such actions are liable on conviction to a fine or imprisonment for five years or both.
(c) Misconduct in the course of winding up – section 136 of the Law
This section makes it an offence to conceal relevant information or property of the company from the liquidator with the intent to defraud creditors or contributories. Such actions are liable on conviction to a fine or imprisonment for five years or both.
(d) Material omissions from statement relating to the company's affairs – section 137 of the Law
Where a company is being wound up, this section makes it an offence for a director to make any material omission in any statement relating to the company's affairs with an intent to defraud creditors or contributories. Such statements are liable on conviction to a fine or imprisonment for five years or both.

Directors may also be made personally liable to contribute to the assets of the company where a director is knowingly party to the carrying on of a business with an intent to defraud creditors of the company or of any other person or for any fraudulent purpose.

In some jurisdictions, a formal procedure exists whereby the conduct of directors of insolvent companies is formally reviewed, and if appropriate proceedings are brought against that director by the government with the aim of disqualifying that director from acting as a director of any company for a specified time in the future. The length of any disqualification is likely to depend on the director's culpability in the company's collapse. In the Cayman Islands, a formal general disqualification mechanism of that nature does not exist, and indeed there are no general statutory provisions identifying the duties of a director when a company encounters financial difficulties.

However, the importance of specific regulation of certain types of company incorporated in the Cayman Islands must be borne in mind in this context. For example, under the Banks and Trusts Companies Law (2013 Revision), the Cayman Islands Monetary Authority must give its written approval to the appointment of a director or other senior officer by a licensee. The Monetary Authority is obliged to refuse to grant such approval if it is of the opinion that the director or other senior officer to whom the application relates is not a fit and proper person to hold such office. Any such approval may be revoked by the Monetary Authority with the approval of the governor (and will lapse if the individual concerned becomes bankrupt or is convicted of an offence involving dishonesty).

CHAPTER 6
People's Republic of China

Katarina Nilsson, Larry Lian & Norla Gu

§6.01 INTRODUCTION

The People's Republic of China (the "PRC" or "China") is the successor to an imperial system of government first unified under Emperor Qin Shi Huang in 220 B.C. Shortly after its founding in 1949, the PRC government dismantled the former legal system and created a socialist legal system. Since China's economic reforms began in 1979, the Chinese legal system has gradually developed into a civil law system, with similarities to the German and French systems. China's legal system is mainly based on codified law, whereas case law only plays a limited role. China lacks a formal system of judicial precedent. Instead the Supreme People's Court and the Supreme People's Procuratorate are authorized to make binding interpretations of laws.

China's legislative system is organized on a hierarchical basis, with the Constitution being the principal law, which all other laws must be aligned with. The National People's Congress (the "NPC") and its permanent body, the Standing Committee of the NPC (the "Standing Committee"), are vested with a supreme, legislative authority in China. The enactments promulgated by the NPC and its Standing Committee may be broadly categorized as laws. The Standing Committee is also empowered to interpret statutes. China's cabinet, the State Council and its subordinate ministries and administrative departments are authorized to issue more detailed regulations and measures as well as to adopt regulations required for the implementation of laws passed by the NPC and its Standing Committee. The People's Governments at local levels have the power to enact local regulations based on local political, economic and cultural conditions. Local regulations must first be reviewed by the Legal Work Commission of the Standing Committee to ensure that they do not conflict with the Constitution. Any conflict between different levels of statutes will usually be resolved by the NPC and the State Council.

Although the modern legal system of China has developed significantly over the last thirty years, its development appears to have happened on an ad hoc basis in many aspects. For instance, experimental regulations are often issued pending the issuance of "final" regulations. Sometimes so-called neibu or internal regulations are circulated without being directly disclosed to external parties but serving as prescriptive guidelines for Chinese officials, departments and units. Foreign investors often learn of these regulations through a summary supplied by their business partners, or through their Chinese lawyer.

China is signatory to a large number of international treaties, such as the United Nations Convention on Contracts for the International Sale of Goods and the 1958 New York Convention on the Recognition and Enforcement of Foreign Arbitral Awards (the "NYC").[1] Such treaties have the force of law in China, except for those provisions to which the Chinese government has made explicit reservations when ratifying the relevant treaty.

The Chinese courts are generally divided into courts of general jurisdiction and courts of special jurisdiction. The trial work of these courts is supervised by the Supreme People's Court. The courts of special jurisdiction include the military courts, the railway transport courts and the maritime courts. The courts of general jurisdiction include the Supreme People's Court at the national level and the basic-level People's Courts, the intermediate People's Courts and the higher People's Courts at local and provincial levels. The Chinese courts are collectively referred to as the "People's Courts" in the following.

PRC law does not require debtors to disclose information about their assets, unless insolvency proceedings are first initiated or the debtors fail to perform their obligations in accordance with an enforceable judgment. As described in further detail below under section §6.02, there are only a limited number of national and local public databases in China with detailed information about different types of assets. Accordingly, successful pre-trial asset investigations are generally very difficult to conduct in the PRC.

Upon satisfaction of certain legal requirements, the People's Court may order the adoption of preservation measures such as attaching, sealing, seizing or freezing of property prior to or during a trial. We have described the relevant PRC laws and regulations on asset preservation measures below in section §6.03.

Below under section §6.04, we have provided an overview of the rules concerning the enforcement of foreign judgments and awards in the PRC.

Finally, under section §6.05, we have addressed the remedies, which PRC law offers plaintiffs with respect to countering illicit asset shielding maneuvers.

§6.02 IDENTIFYING ASSETS IN CHINA

It is a challenge to identify a debtor's assets in China.

1. http://www.uncitral.org/pdf/english/texts/arbitration/NY-conv/XXII_1_e.pdf.

Under PRC law, there is no compulsory legal requirement for a debtor to reveal his assets, unless: (a) a bankruptcy proceeding has been initiated against the debtor before a People's Court, or (b) a final and enforceable judgment has been rendered, which the debtor refuses to fulfill.

However, there are some publicly available registers and databases in the PRC with information concerning different types of assets, which we will describe in the following.

[A] Real Estate

There is no uniform nationwide database or register of real estate in the PRC. The local land resources bureaus at the county level are responsible for administrating a register of land ownership and land use rights.[2] Further, the local housing bureau, at the county level, is responsible for the administration of a register of properties erected on plots of land within that county. In some areas, there is one single local bureau in charge of both land resources and housing, which is responsible for the preparation of a uniform register of both land and properties.

According to the Property Law, legal right holders and interested parties[3] may examine and copy the information recorded in the real estate registers. Different local authorities may adopt different practices in relation to handling requests for public search. For example, some authorities may not accept the request for a public search if the applicant does not have a search warrant issued by the People's Court.

[B] Motor Vehicles

According to the Law on Road Traffic Safety of the PRC, a motor vehicle cannot be driven on public roads unless and until it has been registered with the traffic control authority. There is no uniform, nationwide database or register of all motor vehicles in China. The register of motor vehicles is administrated by the local vehicle registration authority at the city level and contains information concerning the ownership, transfer and pledging of the motor vehicles.

In the pre-trial phase, it is possible to conduct a title search with the local vehicle registration authority of the city where vehicles belonging to the debtor are thought to be registered.[4]

---

2. Land in China is divided into state-owned land and collectively owned land. The ownership of state-owned land belongs to the nation and corporations and individuals may obtain land use right to state-owned land through certain legal procedures. The ownership of collectively owned land belongs to peasant collectives (such as a village or a township). Land use right holders or land owners may build properties on the land and obtain building ownership to the properties they have built through certain legal procedures.
3. There is no clear definition of "an interested party" under PRC law. The definition of the term is subject to the interpretation of the local authorities.
4. The registration city of a motor vehicle could be indicated from the license plate number of the vehicle.

[C] Vessels

There is no uniform, nationwide database or register of all vessels in China. A vessel owner in China is required to register its ownership to the vessel with the local vessel registration authority at the port where the vessel is registered. Information concerning mortgages and charter agreements is also required to be registered with the same authority.

According to Chinese law, right holders and interested parties are allowed to check the information recorded on the vessel register.

[D] Aircrafts

All aircrafts for civil use in China are required to be registered with the registration department under the PRC Civil Aviation Administration. The nationwide, uniform aircraft register contains information about aircrafts for civil use, including information about the aircraft owner, the estimated value of the aircraft and any third-party rights to the aircraft.

According to Chinese law, the information recorded on the aircraft register is publicly available.

[E] IP Rights

Intellectual property rights represent a significant part of the asset portfolios of Chinese companies. In the pre-trial phase, it is therefore advisable to conduct a thorough search for different types of registered intellectual property rights in the PRC.

Information regarding trademarks registered in China is available for public search on the official website of the Trademark Office of the State Administration for Industry and Commerce (http://sbj.saic.gov.cn/sbcx/). On this website, creditors may search for information about all registered trademarks and trademark applications under the name of a debtor.

Information regarding patents (including inventions, utility models and design patents) registered in the PRC is available for public search through the official website of the State Intellectual Property Office (http://www.sipo.gov.cn/zljsfl/). On this website, creditors may search the information about all registered patents and patent applications under the name of a debtor.

There is no compulsory requirement under PRC law for a copyright owner to register his copyrights. Hence there is no uniform register or database of copyrights in China. However, most software copyright owners tend to register their copyrights to software, and such information is recorded in the nationwide uniform register maintained by China Copyright Protection Centre, which is publicly accessible.

Furthermore, Internet domain names can sometimes represent significant economic value. Owners of domain Chinese domain names can be found on public websites such as: www.net.cn and www.xinnet.com.

[F] Financial Reports

Any pre-trial asset search involving companies incorporated in China should include the latest annual financial reports of such companies.

Publicly listed companies in the PRC are required to publicize their financial reports periodically, and such reports are available on the websites of the stock exchange where the companies are listed, see www.sse.com.cn and www.szse.cn.

In case the debtor is a non-listed company, it is advisable to conduct a company search for the most recent annual report with the local Administration for Industry and Commerce (AIC) where the company is registered. However, it is uncertain whether any useful information concerning the company's assets can be found in the annual report, because financial information (such as balance sheets and income statements) of a non-listed company is classified as confidential information. Such information is made publicly available at the company's own discretion.

[G] Tangible Assets

Any collateralization of tangible assets (such as equipment, raw material and products) owned by a company incorporated in China must be registered with the local AIC where the company is registered.

[H] *Database of the Supreme* People's Court

Last but not least, there is an online database of the Supreme People's Court, which publicizes information relating to enforcement orders issued against PRC corporations and natural persons. The database is established to facilitate public access to information about PRC corporations and natural persons who are subject to but have failed to perform an enforcement order issued by one of the People's Courts. However, this database is neither complete nor up to date. It therefore does not cover all of the People's Courts throughout China, nor does the database contain any information about ongoing court proceedings or outstanding court judgments. The database is available at: www.shixin.court.gov.cn.

§6.03 ASSET PRESERVATION MEASURES

The rules on asset preservation measures are mainly provided in the Code of Civil Procedure of the PRC, and in the corresponding judicial interpretations issued by the Supreme People's Court from time to time.[5]

Although the legal system of the PRC allows for asset preservation measures, creditors are likely to run into obstacles in pursuit of such measures. Sometimes the

5. On January 1, 2013, a "common law type" of interim measure became available under Article 100 of the revised Chinese Civil Procedure Law allowing the People's Courts to grant certain types of preservation orders.

obstacles are procedural because creditors are usually required to produce detailed and often unavailable information about the target assets as well as security. However, in most cases, especially where the debtors are Chinese enterprises that have contributed significantly to local tax revenue, "local protectionism" is the main obstacle because judges in the People's Courts are under pressure from the local governments, which fund the courts and decide on personnel matters relating to the courts.

[A] Rules in Relation to Court Action

In the following two scenarios, a People's Court may issue an order to grant asset preservation measures (such as seal-up, seizure, freezing and other methods as prescribed by law) against a debtor:

(i) *before* a lawsuit is initiated and upon the request of an interested party whose legitimate rights and interest would, due to urgent circumstances, suffer irreparable damage in the absence of immediate asset preservation measures; or

(ii) *after* a lawsuit or an arbitration is initiated but before the judgment or the award is rendered, in cases where the enforcement of a judgment or an award may become impossible or difficult. The People's Court will normally grant such an order upon request from a party. However, in certain circumstances (e.g., where the disputed asset in the lawsuit is at risk of being damaged or lost, or where evidence shows that the debtor is likely to conceal, transfer or sell his assets), the People's Court may also issue such an order on its own initiative.

In the scenario described under (i) above, the party must first submit an application for the asset preservation measures to the People's Court in the region where the assets are located, or at the domicile of the debtor against whom the application is made, or with the competent People's Court having jurisdiction over the case. With the application, the applicant must provide security in an amount equal to the estimated value of the assets against which the asset preservation measures are sought. In addition, most People's Courts will require the applicant to provide very specific and detailed information in relation to the target assets, because the People's Courts rarely take the initiative to investigate the debtor's assets due to their limited resources. Moreover, the applicant must initiate the lawsuit against the debtor within thirty days after the issuance of the court order; otherwise, the People's Court must revoke such order.

In the scenario described under (ii) above, the People's Court may require the applicant to provide security. In most cases, a security will be required to ensure that the debtor receives compensation for any loss suffered as a result of the asset preservation order in case the measure subsequently proves to be unjustified. If the provision of security is required by the People's Court and the applicant fails to comply, the asset preservation measures will not be granted. As in the first scenario, most

People's Courts will also require the applicant to provide very specific and detailed information in relation to the target assets.

If an asset preservation order is granted, the execution of the order will begin immediately. The scope of the preservation measures is restricted to the assets in dispute or to the assets belonging to the debtor. No asset preservation measures can be adopted with regard to assets originally belonging to a third party or with regard to disputed assets, which have been received from the debtor by a third party in good faith. Furthermore, in case the debtor provides other types of assets as adequate security for the claim, the People's Court must revoke any asset preservation measures granted by it.

[B] Rules in Relation to Arbitration

According to the PRC Arbitration Act, a tribunal established under the rules of an arbitration institution in China, such as the China International Economic and Trade Arbitration Commission, is not empowered to order an asset preservation measure against any party. Therefore, in case the parties have agreed to resolve their dispute through arbitration in China, the claimant wishing to pursue an asset preservation measure has to apply to the competent People's Court under the above described procedure.

Under the following two scenarios, the People's Courts may grant an asset preservation order *prior to or during* the course of arbitration:

(i) *before* arbitration procedures are initiated and upon the request of an interested party whose legitimate rights and interests would, due to urgent circumstances, suffer irreparable damage in the absence of an asset preservation measure; or
(ii) *after* arbitration procedures are initiated but before the award is rendered, in cases where enforcement of the award may otherwise become impossible or difficult.

The legal requirements for obtaining an asset preservation order in the scenario described under section (i) above are generally the same as those described under section §6.03[A](i). The interested party must first submit an application to the People's Court in the region where the assets are located, or at the domicile of the respondent, or to the competent People's Court, which would have had jurisdiction in the absence of a valid arbitration agreement. With the application, the claimant must provide security. Moreover, the claimant must initiate the arbitration proceedings within thirty days after the asset preservation order has been rendered.

With respect to an application made after arbitration proceedings have been initiated, the claimant must submit the application for an asset preservation order to the relevant arbitral institution, which will then forward the application to the competent People's Court.

This "two-step" application approach is not ideal. In most cases when creditors apply for asset preservation measures, the situation is usually urgent and requires swift action. The current "two-step" application process inevitably takes more time than a direct application to the People's Court. The risk is that the debtors use the time lapse as an opportunity to hide, transfer or dissipate the assets concerned, before a court order is obtained.

§6.04 ENFORCEMENT ISSUES

If the dispute resolution proceedings take place in another country but the defendant holds assets that are located in China, the issue arises whether it is possible to enforce the foreign judgment or arbitral award in China.

It can be very difficult to enforce foreign judgments in China. In general, the People's Courts seldom enforce foreign judgments, (although the plaintiff may apply for recognition and enforcement in China according to Article 265 of the PRC Law of Civil Procedure). Theoretically speaking, foreign judgments can be enforced in China where there is either: (i) a recognition treaty between the two nations; or (ii) reciprocity in enforcement of judgments between the two nations.

China has entered into bilateral treaties on reciprocal judgment recognition and enforcement with several countries, including Macau, Hong Kong, Argentina, Australia, France, Italy, Russia, Spain and Turkey.[6] If China and the country where the forum for dispute resolution is located are parties to such bilateral treaties, the court that granted the foreign judgment may make a judgment recognition and enforcement request to the competent People's Court in accordance with the relevant treaties.

In a limited number of cases, the People's Courts may also recognize and enforce foreign judgments under multi-lateral treaties acceded to by China, e.g., the International Convention on Civil Liability for Oil Pollution Damage of 1969.

On April 22, 1987, China ratified the 1958 "NYC," which has been ratified by over 135 countries. When foreign arbitral awards are enforced in China, it is usually pursuant to the NYC. An arbitral award made abroad in another contracting state will in principle be recognized and enforced in China. In this regard, it may be noted that Hong Kong and Macau are no longer considered "foreign" to China. However, due to the "one country-two systems" policy, the laws in Hong Kong and Macau shall be maintained. In this context, several special arrangements[7] have been implemented so that the judgments and arbitral awards made in Hong Kong and Macau will be enforced in China similarly to foreign awards pursuant to the NYC.

---

6. Other countries include but not limited to Cuba, DPRK, Peru, Romania, Hungary, Morocco, Ukraine, Greek, Cyprus, Egypt, Lithuania, United Arab Emirates, Kuwait, Tunisia, Poland, Laos, Vietnam, Mongolia, Uzbekistan, Kyrgyzstan, White Russia, Kazakhstan, Bulgaria and Tajikistan.
7. The Arrangement on Recognition and Enforcement of Judgments in Civil and Commercial Matters by the Courts of the Mainland and of the Hong Kong Special Administrative Region, the Arrangement between the Mainland and Macao Special Administrative Region on the Mutual Recognition and Enforcement of Civil and Commercial Judgments, the Memorandum of Understanding Concerning the Mutual Enforcement of Arbitral Awards between the Mainland and Hong Kong Special Administrative Region and the Memorandum of Understanding Concerning the Mutual Enforcement of Arbitral Awards between the Mainland and Macao Special Administrative Region.

In the below section §6.04[A], we will further describe the conditions and practical situations concerning the enforcement of foreign judgments in China. Under section §6.04[B], we will provide a brief overview as to how international arbitral awards can be enforced in China.

[A] Enforcement of Foreign Judgments

As mentioned, it is very difficult to have a judgment of a foreign court recognized and enforced in China, since foreign judgments must satisfy a number of requirements set forth in Chinese laws and in bilateral treaties between China and the forum state.

If a bilateral treaty does not exist between China and the forum state, the People's Courts may recognize and enforce a foreign judgment on the basis of reciprocity, which is interpreted as willingness by the foreign court of the forum state to enforce a judgment rendered by a People's Court. This may be extremely difficult to establish.

In 2009, a federal district court in the United States recognized and enforced a judgment granted by a People's Court.[8] It remains to be seen whether this decision alone will establish *general* reciprocity between the US and China for the purpose of recognizing and enforcing each other's judgments. In our view, this is doubtful in that an applicant must prove that a judgment *identical* to the one that is sought to be recognized and enforced in China would be recognized and enforced in the forum state, had it been rendered under the same circumstances by a People's Court.

PRC law does not specify the conditions under which a People's Court may refuse to recognize and enforce a foreign court's judgment. Generally, if a bilateral treaty is available, that treaty would regulate the issues to be considered by the People's Court in reviewing judgments granted by the foreign court for the purpose of enforcement in China. The request for enforcement may be refused for various reasons. For instance, the People's Court may find that the relevant foreign judgment was made by a court lacking jurisdiction. The People's Court may also take the view that the relevant foreign judgment has no effect under the laws of the forum state, the same cause of action may have already proceeded to trial in China (litis pendens), or the recognition and enforcement of the relevant foreign judgment would damage Chinese sovereignty, security or public order.[9]

If neither a treaty nor reciprocity is available to a foreign judgment holder, the last resort is to bring action (again) before the competent People's Court. However, if the parties have agreed to the exclusive jurisdiction of a foreign court and such an agreement is valid according to PRC law, the People's Courts are very likely to refuse jurisdiction. To avoid this situation in contractual relationships involving Chinese parties who for some reason refuse to agree on arbitration, it should be considered including a forum clause in the contract, which allows the courts of for example Hong Kong or Macau to exercise non-exclusive jurisdiction.

8. *Hubei Gezhouba Sanlian Industrial Co., Ltd. et. al. v. Robinson Helicopter Co., Inc.*, 06-01798 (C.D. Cal 2009).
9. *See* Ming Dong "Recognition and enforcement of Foreign Judgment in China", posted at http://ming-chineselawyer.blogspot.hk/2011/06/recognition-and-enforcement-of-foreign.html.

[B] Enforcement of International Arbitral Awards

The PRC has made a "commercial relationship" reservation under the NYC, according to which the PRC will apply the NYC only to disputes arising out of legal relationships, whether contractual or not, which are considered as "commercial" under Chinese law. The term "commercial legal relationship" refers to "economic rights and obligations arising from contracts, torts or in accordance with statutory provisions," e.g., technology transfers. The law does not provide a more specific definition of what is considered "commercial" and what is not, and this is therefore left to the interpretation of the People's Courts.

The competent People's Court for enforcement of a foreign arbitral award is the intermediate People's Court at the domicile of the party against whom enforcement is requested or at the place where the asset, which is subject to enforcement, is located.

Foreign arbitral awards must be submitted to a People's Court for enforcement within two years from the last day of the period specified in the award for its performance.

When filing an application for enforcement of a foreign arbitral award, the applicant should submit the following documents: (i) an application for enforcement; (ii) documents identifying the applicant, e.g., an individual's passport or an entity's certificate of incorporation etc.; (iii) an original or a notarized and certified copy of the arbitral award; (iv) an original or a notarized and certified copy of the arbitration agreement or the contract containing the arbitration clause; and (v) a certified Chinese translation of the award and the arbitration agreement.

There are no formal means of appeal against the People's Courts' decision granting enforcement. Instead, China has implemented a pre-reporting system to encourage the People's Courts to enforce foreign arbitral awards. If the Intermediate People's Court considers that enforcement should be refused, it is required to report this to the competent High People's Court in the local province. If the High People's Court also agrees that recognition and enforcement should be refused after review of the Intermediate People's Court's decision, it is required to report that decision to the Supreme People's Court for a final review.

Enforcement of foreign arbitral awards in China usually involves many obstacles, which are often very frustrating to the applicants. For instance, documents such as the company registration file have to be translated into Chinese by a translation agent designated or recognized by the People's Court. Since the People's Courts at different locations may have differing standards for document and translation requirements and since the People's Court may come up with unforeseen and illogical requirements when reviewing the documents submitted, the enforcement procedures may be delayed due to document preparation. Such delays are more the rule than the exception and sometimes the delays are lengthy. As already mentioned, local protectionism is another possible problem. If the debtor is a big enterprise that provides tax revenue to the region where it is located, the local People's Court may hesitate to grant an enforcement order.

§6.05 D&O LIABILITY IN RELATION TO ASSET PROTECTION SCHEMES

Debtors might, prior to, during or after a court trial in various ways, attempt to foil enforcement efforts by hiding or removing assets, transferring assets without any consideration, trading at an unreasonably low price, paying off debts that are not due, fabricating debts or acknowledging fictitious debts.

Such acts are usually carried out by the directors and officers of the companies. It thus becomes interesting to look into whether the directors and officers can be held liable for engaging in what one could call (illicit) asset protection schemes.

In the following, we will provide a brief overview of the relevant rules under PRC law concerning liability for directors and officers.

[A] Civil Liability

According to the PRC Company Act, where any director or senior management personnel of a company violates laws, regulations or the company's articles of association, in the performance of their duties, he/she shall be liable to pay compensation if any loss is suffered by the company. The same applies where the damages are suffered by shareholders. However, the PRC Company Act does not extend the director's liability to cases where the damages are inflicted on a third party, e.g., the company's creditors.

Pursuant to the PRC Insolvency Act, asset shielding maneuvers made within a certain period prior to the initiation of or during the course of insolvency proceedings may be declared invalid by the competent People's Court. In case of asset shielding maneuvers, which undermine the interests of an insolvent company's creditors, the legal representative[10] and the person directly in charge of the day-to-day operations of the company are liable for any loss suffered by creditors of the company.

Under the PRC Company Act, the legal representative of a company is the chairman of the board of directors, or the managing director, or the general manager. The term "persons-in-charge," as the concept is used under PRC law, may include the directors. Though the chairman of the board is regularly considered the person who is ultimately in charge of the company, it is still likely that the directors will first attract civil liability in case of illicit asset shielding maneuvers under PRC Insolvency Law.

It should be mentioned that D&O insurance is not yet common in China. Insurance for directors and officers was only introduced in China in 1996 and the first

10. Under PRC law, the legal representative of a company is the person who acts in the name of the company and represents the company in the exercise of its rights and obligations. The legal representative is a fundamental part of a company's corporate governance structure. The person who is appointed as "legal representative" is authorized to conduct many of the company's affairs.

policy, written in Chinese, was sold in 2002 to a locally listed company. At present, less than 10% of listed companies in China have D&O insurances in place.[11]

[B] Administrative Liability

Pursuant to provisions in the PRC General Principles of Civil Law and other related laws and regulations, a company's legal representative may also be subject to administrative sanctions, administered by the relevant authorities, such as fines if there is misconduct within the company. Punishable misconduct includes, for example, a secret withdrawing of funds or hiding of assets to evade repayment of debts. A legal representative may avoid being penalized if he can prove that he was not aware of such acts and was not, subjectively, at fault or delinquent in his duties.

As stated above, the legal representative may be a director of the company. Thus it is possible for a director to assume also *administrative* liability if he acts as the legal representative and the company removes or hides valuable assets prior to or in the course of dispute resolution proceedings.

[C] Criminal Liability

If a company illegally disposes of assets, which are subject to an existing asset preservation order, and the disposal is considered "serious," the company is in violation of Article 314 of the PRC Penal Code, according to which, anyone who seriously conceals, transfers, sells or intentionally destroys or damages assets that are sealed, seized or frozen by a judicial body shall be subject to criminal liability. In addition, the refusal to execute a judgment or an order made by a People's Court by way of concealing, transferring, intentionally destroying or damaging the assets etc. may constitute a violation of Article 313 of the PRC Penal Code.

According to a judicial interpretation of the Supreme People's Court, any person in charge of a company who hides assets on behalf of the company in order to interfere with the execution of a judgment by a court attracts criminal liability under Article 313 of the PRC Penal Code. It is still unclear and debated in practice whether persons-in-charge may also be penalized in case of a violation of Article 314 of the PRC Penal Code. Again, as mentioned above, persons-in-charge may include the company's directors.

11. *See* "China: D&O liability insurance expected to take off", available at http://prolink-consulting.com/china-do-liability-insurance-expected-to-take-off/. *See also* p. 152 ff. of this guide: http://view.pagetiger.com/directors-and-officers-guide for a more detailed overview of D&O liability rules in China.

CHAPTER 7

Cyprus

Michalis Kyriakides & Nicolas Kyriakides

§7.01 INTRODUCTION

As a result of the British rule in Cyprus from 1878 until 1960, the country's legal system has been strongly influenced by the English common law tradition.[1] Cypriot private law and criminal law is mostly based on English common law. Procedural law is also based on common law, whereas, public law derives from the continental tradition.[2]

Article 188 of the Constitution of Cyprus provides that the laws that applied in Cyprus in 1960 shall remain in force, to the extent that they do not contravene the Constitution, until they are replaced by new laws. Some branches of Cypriot law were codified in 1959, e.g., the Civil Wrongs Law (Cap. 148), the Contracts Law (Cap. 149), the Criminal Code (Cap. 154), etc.[3] To avoid gaps in the Cypriot legal system, Law no. 14 of 1960 stipulates, *inter alia* that when not otherwise provided by applicable statutes, the courts of Cyprus would continue to apply English common law and the principles of equity. This provision constitutes the formal gateway of common law into the legal system of Cyprus.

More than half a century after the independence of Cyprus, Cypriot law has developed autonomously, and in recent years under the heavy influence of the EU, which Cyprus became a member of in 2004.[4]

1. Symeon C. Symeonides, *The Mixed Legal System of the Republic of Cyprus*, 78 Tulane Law Review 441, 441 (2003).
2. Nikitas E. Hatzimichael, *Cyprus as a Mixed Legal System*, 6 Journal of Civil Law Studies 38, 38 (2013).
3. Andreas Neocleous & Co, *Introduction to Cyprus Law*, 12 (Dennis Campbell, Yorkhill Law Publishing 2000).
4. Nikitas E. Hatzimichael, *Cyprus as a Mixed Legal System*, 6 Journal of Civil Law Studies 38, 71 (2013).

Cyprus presently maintains a two-tier judicial system. The primary trial court, i.e., the court of general jurisdiction, is the District Court whose jurisdiction extends over most civil and criminal matters. At the apex of the administration of the country's justice system sits the Supreme Court of Cyprus, which serves *inter alia* as an appellate court in civil and criminal matters, as an administrative Court of First Instance, and as a constitutional court.[5]

In a number of cases, judges of the Cyprus District Courts have – simultaneously with the granting of freezing orders – imposed a requirement on respondents to disclose the value and location of their assets. This issue is described in further detail below under section §7.02.

The freezing of assets in civil proceedings can be based on a variety of provisions of Cypriot law, depending on the circumstances of each case. We will take a closer look at this issue under section §7.03 below where we will also examine the European Account Preservation Order Regulation, which will enter into force in 2017 in Cyprus.

In relation to the enforcement of foreign judgments and arbitral awards, the Brussels Regulation (recast) and the New York Convention both apply in Cyprus. We will address the issue of enforcement in section §7.04 of this chapter.

Finally, under section §7.05, we will describe under which circumstances the board of directors, company officers, and/or owners of a company incorporated in Cyprus may be held liable if they attempt to hide company assets prior to or pending a lawsuit or arbitration proceedings to which the company is a party.

§7.02 IDENTIFYING ASSETS IN CYPRUS

On the basis of a long line of English case law, Cypriot courts may order a defendant to disclose, under oath, information about the value and location of its assets, provided that this is done in the context of proceedings for the granting of a freezing order.[6] For example, in a case before the Limassol District Court,[7] the court made reference to the decision in *Ashianti v. Kashi*[8] where the English court said:

> *In the present case we are concerned not only with a Mareva injunction but also with an order for discovery which was made ancillary to the injunction. [...]. It seems to me that in the present state of the law the only basis for such an order is that it is made in aid of and ancillary to an injunction in the Mareva form. The power to order discovery exists, but it is a power which exists to make the injunction effective.*

However, since an order to disclose information about assets will usually be a significant burden on the respondent, Cypriot courts have been reluctant to grant this

5. Nikitas E. Hatzimichael, *Cyprus as a Mixed Legal System*, 6 Journal of Civil Law Studies 38, 61 (2013).
6. Costas Stamatiou and Panayiotis Neocleous, *Cyprus: Freezing Orders, Ship Arrest Warrants, Anti-suit Injunctions, Disclosure Orders and Norwich Pharmacal Relief in Aid of Court or Arbitration Proceedings in Cyprus and Overseas*, 21(2) International Company and Commercial Law Review 54, 56 (2010).
7. *Divino Distribution LLP v. CP Media (Cyprus) Ltd*, 4250/2013 (Limassol District Court).
8. *Ashianti v. Kashi* [1987] QB 888 (CA).

type of relief. Courts have referred *inter alia* to the English case *Bekhor & Company Ltd v. Bilton* where it was said that 'the power to order discovery in support of a Mareva injunction should be sparingly exercised and if too readily resorted to could easily become a most oppressive procedure'.[9]

An alternative way of obtaining information about a defendant's assets is through public registers and databases, which contain information about different types of assets belonging to corporations and private individuals. In the following, we will provide a brief overview of some of the main public asset registers in Cyprus.

[A] Real Property

Real property in Cyprus is registered with the Department of Lands and Surveys of Cyprus. According to the law, the land registry must be up to date at all times. A plaintiff may apply to the Department of Land and Surveys enquiring whether a defendant has any real estate in Cyprus registered on his name.[10] Moreover, the website: http://parcel.dls.moi.gov.cy gives access to a public database in English and in Greek, which contains information about real estate located in Cyprus. Users are able to search for a specific property using a street address or a digital map. The database contains among other things a valuation of the property.

[B] Vessels and Aircrafts

The Register of Cypriot Ships and the Cypriot Aircraft Register contain information about owners of Cypriot vessels and aircrafts respectively.

The Register of Cyprus Ships is not available online. Information about the Department of Merchant Shipping, which administers the register may be found at http://www.mcw.gov.cy/mcw/dms/dms.nsf/registerships_en/registerships_en?Open Document.

The Cypriot Aircraft Register can be found here: http://www.mcw.gov.cy/mcw /dca/dca.nsf/DMLregister_en/DMLregister_en?OpenDocument.

[C] Intellectual Property Rights

In relation to disputes against corporations with ties to Cyprus, a pre-trial asset search should in most cases include an investigation into the corporation's trademarks, patents, copyrights, domain names and other intellectual rights.

The Office of the Registrar of Industrial Designs (which is a division of the Cyprus Registrar of Companies' Office and Official Receiver) administers the Cypriot trade-marks, patents, copyrights and industrial rights.[11]

9. *Bekhor & Company Ltd v. Bilton* [1981] QB 923 (CA).
10. The website of the Department of Land and Surveys is www.moi.gov.cy/dls.
11. The relevant register is not available online.

The University of Cyprus is the Official Registrar for the '.cy' top level domain and handles such domain name applications.[12]

[D] Company Information

Another useful source of information related to a defendant's financial situation is the Department of Registrar of Companies and Official Receiver, which can provide information regarding the ownership of a legal entity.[13]

[E] 'Bad Debtors'

Finally, there are two registers in Cyprus with details about 'bad debtors'.

One is the Central Information Register (CIR) for the Issuers of Dishonoured Cheques (CIR), where all issues of cheques that have not been honoured are registered. Interested parties, wishing to examine the possibility to establish economic relations with other parties can subscribe for access to the data of the CIR via the First Cyprus Credit Bureau Ltd (FCCB), which will forward the application to the CIR Managing Committee for approval.[14]

The second register is called 'Artemis', which has been created and is administered by banks in Cyprus. This register is not accessible by the public, only by financial institutions.[15]

§7.03 INTERIM MEASURES

As already indicated above, Cypriot law offers litigants the possibility of obtaining a freezing order under different circumstances, which we will take a closer look at in the following section of this chapter.

First, it should be mentioned that the Cyprus District Courts have *general* jurisdiction to grant in personam freezing orders (also called 'Mareva injunctions') in the context of proceedings, which are pending before Cyprus courts; or in relation to an arbitration,[16] which takes place in Cyprus. According to well established case law, such freezing orders are not restricted to assets in Cyprus but may also embrace assets located *outside* the jurisdiction.

12. The database to look up.cy domains may be accessed at http://www.nic.cy/nslookup/online_database.htm.
13. One may search online for a registered organisation at https://efiling.drcor.mcit.gov.cy/DrcorPublic/SearchForm.aspx?sc = 0&lang = EN.
14. More details about the CIR can be found at http://www.centralbank.gov.cy/nqcontent.cfm?a_id = 11371&lang = en.
15. More details about Artemis can be found at https://www.artemis.com.cy/company_en.aspx.
16. This includes both a domestic arbitration conducted under Cap. 4 and an international commercial arbitration conducted pursuant to Law 101/1987.

Second, provisional and protective measures can also be issued pursuant to Regulation (EU) 1215/2012 ('Brussels Regulation (recast)') in aid of *foreign* proceedings pending before the courts of another EU Member State; or in aid of *international* arbitration proceedings taking place in another EU Member State.

Third and finally, provisional and protective measures can be issued by a court in Cyprus pursuant to bilateral or multilateral conventions in aid of foreign proceedings pending before the courts of another country, or in aid of international arbitration proceedings taking place in another country.

[A] Freezing Orders in the Context of Judicial or Arbitration Proceedings Pending in Cyprus

The Supreme Court of Cyprus has recognised that the Cyprus District Courts have power to grant Mareva injunctions, identical to those granted in England on the basis of the principles laid down in the famous judgment in *Mareva Compania Naviera SA v. International Bulkcarriers SA*[17] in 1975. As is the case under English law, a Cypriot Mareva injunction allows for the freezing of a respondent's assets that may be at risk of dissipation pending the final determination of judicial proceedings.

The first decision, which established the power of the Cypriot courts to grant interim relief in the form of a Mareva Injunction was *Nemitsas Industries Ltd v. S & S Maritime Lines Ltd.*[18] In this case, the court stated that the legal basis for granting a freezing order of this type is section 32 of the Courts of Justice Law (Law 14/1960), which empowers the court to grant an injunction 'in all cases in which it appears to the court just or convenient so to do'. According to the same provision, there are three key conditions that must be met before the court can grant interim relief:

(1) there must be a serious matter to be heard;
(2) there must be a probability that the applicant is entitled to relief; and
(3) it will be difficult or impossible to do complete justice at a later stage without granting the order.

A Mareva Injunction, however, is not granted automatically where the above three conditions are met. The issue of whether or not to grant the injunction is left entirely to the discretion of the court. The court will assess whether it is just and convenient to grant the order in light of all the facts and circumstances of the matter.[19]

It should be noted that a party pursuing a freezing order must not necessarily demonstrate that the respondent is likely to dispose of the assets. It is enough to show that if the assets are removed or dissipated, a later court decision will most likely not

17. *Mareva Compania Naviera SA v. International Bulkcarriers SA* [1980] 1 All ER 213 (CA).
18. *Nemitsas Industries Ltd v. S & S Maritime Lines Ltd* [1976] 1 CLR 302.
19. *Odysseos v. Pieris* [1982] 1 CLR 557.

be fulfilled.[20] Accordingly, where the respondent proves that he is able to fulfil a judgment, a freezing order will usually not be issued.[21]

Cypriot courts enjoy a wide degree of discretion with respect to the type of assets that can be frozen. However, an applicant may find it easier to establish the risk that he will be deprived of future relief where the asset that might be disposed of by the respondent is in a bank account rather than in the form of for example real estate.[22]

Finally, it must be stressed that the affidavit to support an application for a freezing order must be filed after filling proceedings on the merits.[23]

Another legal basis for obtaining a freezing order under Cypriot law is found in section 5[24] of the Cypriot Code of Civil Procedure (Cap. 6), relating to the freezing of immovable assets. By virtue of this provision, the court may issue an interim order, in a case where the recovery of a debt or damages are claimed, restraining the dissipation of immovable property registered in the name of the defendant.

An order pursuant to section 5 may be granted, provided that the plaintiff shows a good cause of action, and demonstrates that it is probable that the plaintiff will be prevented from enforcing a judgment in his favour in the case of a sale or a transfer of the defendant's property.

It is possible to apply to the court for a freezing order on an ex parte basis pursuant to section 9 of the Cypriot Code of Civil Procedure (Cap. 6). The courts will allow an ex parte application only if there is an element of extreme urgency.

In most cases, an ex parte *order* will be conditional upon the applicant providing an undertaking for any damages, which the respondent can show to have suffered as a result of the freezing order, if the freezing order later turns out to be unwarranted.

Moreover, there is a duty of full and frank disclosure in ex parte applications.[25] When the order is issued ex parte, a return date is given on which the respondent will be given the chance to appear before the court and oppose the order. The case law shows that a reasonable amount of time must be given for the order to be served.[26]

Upon the granting of injunctive relief any party for which the injunction is intended is (obviously) under a legal obligation to comply with the order, compare Article 42 of the Courts of Justice Law 14/1960. Any violation of the order constitutes contempt of court, which is punishable by imprisonment, a fine or a sequestration of assets. Any person inciting or facilitating a violation of the injunction may also be held in contempt of court.

Cypriot courts also have power to grant so-called Chabra orders designed to block assets in the hands of a co-defendant as ancillary and incidental to a claim raised

20. See e.g., *Potlava Petroleum Company v. Mexana Oil Limited* [2001] 1 CLR 1301.
21. *Marketrends v. Georgiou* [2002] 1 CLR 1759.
22. *Potlava Petroleum Company v. Mexana Oil Limited* [2001] 1 CLR 1301.
23. See *Re Stavros Hotel Apartments* [1994] 1 CLR 836.
24. In the case *Lakatamitis v. Theodorou*, the Court said that it is possible pursuant to section 32 of the Courts of Justice Law (Law 14/1960) to make an order as envisaged by section 5 of Cap. 6, but, in making such an order under section 32, the specific criteria laid down in section 5 should also be taken into account insofar as they do not coincide with the criteria set out in the said section 32.
25. *Zachariades v. Liveras* [1989] 1 CLR 437.
26. Re *Henry Chalhoub* [1999] 1 CLR 1333.

against the principal defendant. Such an order does not require any direct cause of action against the co-defendant.[27] Based on the English decision in *T.S.B Private Bank International S.A. v. Chabra*,[28] these orders are available where there are reasons to believe that a co-defendant is in possession or control of assets to which the principal defendant is beneficially entitled.

As already mentioned, Cypriot courts have extended the reach of Mareva-type injunctions to include assets that are located outside Cyprus, following the example of the English courts, which have a long tradition of granting Worldwide Freezing Orders. In the case of *Seamark Consultancy Services Ltd v. Joseph Lasala*,[29] the Supreme Court said that taking into account the modern changes to the way commercial transactions are conducted, the Court of First Instance had the power to grant the orders in question pursuant to which the assets of the respondents outside the jurisdiction were frozen.

Cypriot courts may also issue freezing orders in aid of arbitration proceedings pending in Cyprus, which are not 'international' and 'commercial'.[30] Such orders may be based on section 26 and Schedule B of the Arbitration Law (Cap. 4), which relate to the granting of security for costs, the disclosure of documents and interrogatories, the taking and preservation of evidence, the issuance of provisional or protective relief, etc. In practice, however, the courts of Cyprus are generally reluctant to intervene in local arbitral proceedings, and there is therefore no recorded Supreme Court case law showing how the mentioned rules are applied in practice.

[B] Freezing Orders in Aid of Judicial or Arbitration Proceedings Pending in EU Member States

The Brussels Regulation (recast), which is directly applicable in Cyprus, provides in Article 35 that a party may apply to the courts of a Member State for such provisional measures as may be available under the law of that Member State, even if the courts of another Member State have jurisdiction as to the substance of the matter.

The Court of Justice of the EU (the 'CJEU') decided in *Van Uden Maritime BV t/a Van Uden Africa Line v. Kommanditgesellschaft in Firma Deco-Line*[31] that provisional measures can be ordered on the basis of Article 31 of Regulation (EC) 44/2001 ('Brussels I Regulation'), which is identical to Article 35 of the Brussels Regulation (recast)), irrespective of whether the main proceedings in the other Member State are in the form of arbitration or a court action.

Moreover, in *Van Uden*,[32] the CJEU also stated that there must be a real connecting link between the subject-matter of the measures sought under Article 31 of

27. *Re Hellington Commodities Ltd* [2009] 1 CLR 926.
28. *T.S.B Private Bank International S.A. v. Chabra* [1992] 1 WLR 231 (Ch).
29. *Seamark Consultancy Services Ltd v. Joseph Lasala* [2007] 1 CLR 162.
30. When arbitration proceedings pending in Cyprus are 'international' and 'commercial', Law no. 101/1987 applies. See below.
31. Case C-391/95 *Van Uden Maritime BV t/a Van Uden Africa Line v. Kommanditgesellschaft in Firma Deco-Line* [1998] ECR I-7091, paragraphs 33–34.
32. Case C-391/95 *Van Uden Maritime BV t/a Van Uden Africa Line v. Kommanditgesellschaft in Firma Deco-Line* [1998] ECR I-7091, paragraph 40.

the Brussels Convention and the territorial jurisdiction of the state of the court before which those measures are sought. In other words, there must be a reason that a litigant is applying in another Member State instead of the Member State where the proceedings are taking place. In this respect, the litigant may, for example, point to the fact that the assets are located in the other Member State or that the respondent resides there.

As stated in Article 73 of the Brussels Regulation (recast), the Regulation does not affect the 2007 Lugano Convention,[33] which has an identical provision in Article 31.

[C] European Account Preservation Orders

Regulation (EU) No 655/2014 has established a new regime of rules regarding the so-called European Account Preservation Order (EAPO). The rules will apply in Cyprus from 18 January 2017. The EAPO rules allow a plaintiff to obtain an order preserving a defendant's bank account if there is proof that the defendant is likely to thwart the enforcement of a future judgment. Banks throughout the EU are thus under an obligation to enforce orders issued pursuant to the EAPO rules.

An EAPO is only available in the context of pecuniary claims in civil and commercial matters and only in cross-border cases. Article 3 of the regulation defines a cross-border case as one in which the bank account to be preserved is maintained either: (i) in a Member State other than the Member State of the court where the plaintiff has commenced proceedings, or (ii) in the Member State in which the plaintiff is domiciled.

The Regulation's recitals state that an EAPO is available only to applicants who are domiciled in a Member State, bound by the Regulation, and that orders issued under the regulation should relate only to the preservation of accounts, which are held by banks in such a Member State. All EU Member States, apart from the United Kingdom and Denmark, have adopted the EAPO regulation. Consequently, litigants will be able to obtain an EAPO from a court in Cyprus, freezing bank accounts in other Member States, while bank accounts held in *Cyprus* may be preserved by virtue of an EAPO granted by a court in another Member State *or* on the basis of the above-described Cypriot rules on freezing orders.

[D] Freezing Orders in Aid of Judicial or Arbitration Proceedings Pending in Non-EU Member States

There is no specific legal basis similar to Article 35 of the Brussels Regulation (recast) upon which provisional and protective measures in aid of court actions in countries outside the Brussels or Lugano area may be requested. As a consequence, the ability of courts in Cyprus to issue freezing orders in aid of such judicial proceedings is questionable. However, in our opinion this should not necessarily be interpreted as meaning that they will not devise a way to exercise their discretionary powers to issue

33. Non-EU contracting states to the Lugano Convention are Switzerland, Iceland and Norway.

such orders when justice requires. Nevertheless, this has not been affirmed so far by the Supreme Court of Cyprus.[34]

As regards arbitration proceedings, section 9 of the Cypriot International Commercial Arbitration Law (Law no. 101/1987) provides the legal basis upon which Cypriot courts may grant provisional and protective measures in aid of international commercial arbitration. The Law applies exclusively to international, commercial arbitrations and contains a very wide definition of what is deemed to be 'commercial'. Specifically, it provides that commercial is the arbitration which refers to matters that arise out of relations of a commercial nature, contractual or otherwise. Moreover, the requirement that the arbitration must be 'international' is satisfied when the parties are located in different countries. An arbitration may also be considered as international if a substantial part of the obligation that constitutes the subject-matter of the dispute was to be performed in a different country, or if the parties have expressly agreed that the arbitration will take place overseas, or if the subject-matter of their dispute is related to more than one country. Finally, the arbitration must derive from a *written* arbitration agreement or clause in order to fall under the scope of the statute.

Section 9 of the Cypriot International Commercial Arbitration Law provides that Cypriot courts have the power to order protective measures before or during arbitral proceedings. The text of this provision is almost identical to Article 9 of the UNCITRAL Model Law on International Commercial Arbitration of 1985 amended in 2006, which states that it is not incompatible with an arbitration agreement for a party to seek and obtain, before or during arbitral proceedings, an interim measure of protection from a court.

§7.04 ENFORCEMENT ISSUES

[A] Enforcement of Foreign Judgments

Under the Brussels I Regulation, a judgment creditor, seeking to enforce a judgment from one Member State before the courts in another Member State, was required to file an application for a declaration of enforceability (*exequatur*). The Brussels Regulation (recast) (the 'Recast Regulation') has abolished the exequatur and has introduced a simplified mechanism for the mutual recognition and enforcement of Member State judgments.

Now, a judgment creditor simply has to present a copy of the judgment and a standard form certificate (found in Annex I to the Recast Regulation), and can then begin the enforcement process (cf. Article 39 of the Recast Regulation). The judgment and the certificate, issued by the court of origin must be served on the judgment debtor before enforcement (cf. Article 43 of the Recast Regulation).

34. Costas Stamatiou and Panayiotis Neocleous, *Cyprus: Freezing Orders, Ship Arrest Warrants, Anti-suit Injunctions, Disclosure Orders and Norwich Pharmacal Relief in Aid of Court or Arbitration Proceedings in Cyprus and Overseas*, 21(2) International Company and Commercial Law Review 54, 59 (2010).

However, orders granted ex parte in one Member State may not be recognised and enforced in another Member State. This was decided in the case *Denilauler v. Couchet Frères*[35] where the CJEU ruled that an order, which is made without the defendant having been summoned to appear and is intended to be enforced without prior service on him is not enforceable in other Member States. The principles established by this decision are now reflected in Article 42 of the Recast Regulation.

In relation to judgments granted in jurisdictions governed by the Lugano Convention, formalities for the recognition and declaration of enforceability of a judgment are still necessary. A party seeking enforcement under the Lugano rules must thus file an application by summons at the court where enforcement is sought and produce a copy of the judgment together with a certification that the judgment is enforceable in the Member State of issue. The court of the Member State where the judgment was given will then issue, at the request of any interested party, a certificate using the standard form in Annex V to the Convention. The applicant must also give an address for service of process on the respondent within the area of jurisdiction of the court applied to.

Regarding countries outside the Brussels and Lugano area, Cyprus is party to a number of bilateral treaties in relation to the recognition and enforcement of foreign judgments. Specifically, it has signed and ratified such treaties with Syria (Rat. Law 160/86, 13/97), Russia (Rat. Law 172/86), Ukraine (Rat. Law 172/86 and 8/2005), Georgia (Rat. Law 172/86), Serbia (Rat. Law 179/86), China (Rat. Law 19/95, and others.

Cyprus is also a signatory to a number of multilateral conventions relating to the recognition and enforcement of foreign judgments including the Hague Convention on Foreign Judgments in Civil and Commercial Matters. With regards to the Hague Convention, it is important to note that even though Cyprus has signed the Convention, the Convention has no practical effect on its own because according to Article 21 decisions rendered in a contracting state shall not be recognised or enforced in another contracting state unless the two states, being parties to the Convention, have signed a *supplementary* agreement to this effect.

In order to simplify procedures for the enforcement and execution of foreign judgments in Cyprus, the Foreign Judgments Law (Law no. 121(I)/2000) has been introduced. As the title indicates, the procedures laid down in this Law apply to foreign judgments (but obviously not to judgments rendered by courts in Brussels or Lugano Member States).

According to Article 5 of the Law, an application for enforcement may be filed together with an affidavit with the District Court in accordance with the applicable Rules of Civil Procedure.

The application, which must be served on the respondent, is subject to an oral hearing. The respondent is given the opportunity to contest the application by filing a written objection accompanied by an affidavit at least two days before the date of the hearing.

35. Case C-125/79 *Denilauler v. Couchet Frères* [1980] ECR 1553.

[B] Enforcement of Foreign Arbitral Awards

The Recast Regulation applies to court judgments or orders but not to arbitral awards (cf. Article 1(2)(d) of the Recast Regulation).

Foreign arbitral awards can, however, be enforced in Cyprus by virtue of the provisions set out in the Cyprus International Commercial Arbitration Law (Law no. 101/1987) and the New York Convention on the Recognition and Enforcement of Foreign Arbitral Awards of 1958, which was ratified by Law no. 84/1979 in Cyprus.

A party seeking enforcement of a foreign award must file an application by summons accompanied by an affidavit according to the Foreign Judgments Law mentioned above. Such application must be served on the other party, and pursuant to Article 35 of Law no. 101/1987 and Article IV of the New York Convention the application must also be accompanied by the duly authenticated original award or a duly certified copy hereof and by the original arbitration agreement or a duly certified copy hereof.

If the award is not drafted in Greek, the party applying for recognition must also produce an official translation of the aforementioned documents in Greek. Again, according to the Foreign Judgments Act, once the application is served upon the other party, he is given the opportunity to appear before the court and oppose the registration of the award. The application will be fixed for a hearing within four weeks from the filing of the application, and the respondent will be given the opportunity to contest the application by filing a written objection.

Recognition and enforcement of an arbitral award may be refused for the reasons stated in Article 36 and Article V of the New York Convention.

§7.05 D&O LIABILITY IN RELATION TO ASSET PROTECTION SCHEMES

[A] Provisions That May Apply in Cases Where an Interim Injunction Is in Place

Freezing injunctions serve the purpose of prohibiting asset dissipation pending proceedings in order to protect a creditor against the phenomenon of 'emptying' a company in order to avoid enforcement of a potential judgment or award.

Once an injunction has been issued and has been served on the officials or employees of a company, any dissipation in breach of the injunction would constitute contempt of court, and consequently lead to a sanctioning of the officers and/or directors of the company.

In addition, a Cypriot court may, pursuant to a complaint of an aggrieved party, punish any person who acts as an aider and abettor in violating the injunction. This offence requires some form of active participation in the breach.

[B] Provisions That Can Be Applied in the Absence of a Freezing Injunction

In the absence of a freezing order, it is easier for companies, especially during the course of dispute resolution proceedings, to attempt to remove valuable assets from the corporate entity involved in the dispute.

Asset shielding tactics can take many different forms: from the straightforward transfer of assets and business activities to an affiliated entity to sophisticated schemes involving offshore entities, sham creditors, the creation of fictitious losses, etc.

The ability to pierce the corporate veil is theoretically existent but it is rarely successful in practical life, since Cypriot courts are very reluctant to undermine the principle that a company is a separate legal entity whose owners' liability is limited to value of their shares.

Importantly, under Cypriot law, board members are not personally liable to any third party, and creditors do not have a direct right to claim damages from a director. Nevertheless, there are some mechanisms which can be used by aggrieved parties, compare right below.

[1] Provisions Establishing Civil and Criminal Liability under the Cyprus Companies Act (Cap. 113)

The Cyprus Companies Act (Cap. 113) includes certain provisions that guard creditors against fraudulent or preferential transfers to third parties prior to a company being wound up.[36]

Any conveyance, charge, mortgage or other act relating to an asset belonging to a company, within six months before the commencement of its winding up,[37] may be deemed invalid if considered fraudulent or preferential. Similarly, any conveyance or assignment by a company of *all* of its property to a trustee may also be voidable if considered fraudulent or preferential.

It is worth noting that any third party who benefits from the preferential payment may become directly liable towards the disgruntled creditors of the debtor.

In addition, criminal provisions may be applied to penalise company officials who have taken actions for the purpose of defrauding the creditors of a company.

Finally, if in the course of a winding up of a company it appears that the directors continued to allow the company to incur debts when they already knew or ought to have known that the company had no reasonable prospect of repaying the debt, then they may become *personally* liable for that debt under sections 307 and 312 of the Companies Act. Such liability may be avoided if the said directors can show that they

36. See sections 301–303 of the Cyprus Companies Act.
37. For the purposes of this provision, the commencement of the winding up is deemed to occur on the date of filing of the petition, not on the date when the order is eventually made by the court. See section 218(2) of the Cyprus Companies Act. Even under this interpretation, the timeframe covered by this section is rather small.

have taken 'every step with a view to minimising the potential loss to the company's creditors as they ought to have taken'.

[2] Provisions under Other Laws or Principles

As noted, Cypriot law generally does not consider directors or board members to be *personally* liable towards any third party (other than the company itself), and creditors do generally not have a direct right to claim damages from a director or a board member.

Nevertheless, the officials of a Cypriot company may become liable personally as a result of transactions made against the best interests of the company, if such transactions amount to a violation of their fiduciary duties.[38] The fiduciary duty of a Cypriot company official involves an obligation towards the company to act in good faith and in the best interests of the company at all times. It is a breach of this duty if assets of the company are sold at sub-value or channelised away from the company via transactions, which are not concluded or performed on arm's length terms.

There are also provisions in individual legislative instruments, which could be invoked for the purpose of clawing back assets wrongfully removed from a Cypriot company in an effort to defraud creditors. Cap. 62 on fraudulent transfers thus provides for the ability to claw back movable or immovable assets transferred with the purpose of defrauding creditors.

Further, civil and criminal liability may also be attracted by Cypriot company directors or officials on the basis of Law no. 60(I)/2008 on defrauding judgment creditors, although the major drawback of this law is that it only applies to acts or omissions, which have taken place after the date when the judgment was rendered.

Finally, it should be mentioned that the wrongful dissipation of assets could give rise to a trust being created, whereby the company could eventually seek the recovery of the asset.[39]

38. Such a claim can be brought only by the company and not directly by an affected creditor. Given that usually the company is controlled by the persons who have made or authorised this transfer, this avenue presupposes that the company enters into liquidation, so that the relevant decision is taken by the liquidator.
39. This usually would apply when the company enters into liquidation, all powers of control are vested in the liquidator and the liquidator, acting in the best interests of the creditors and in an effort to maximise the liquidation dividend, initiates proceedings against third parties which benefited from wrongful transactions prior to the company been placed in liquidation.

CHAPTER 8
Denmark

Jacob C. Jørgensen & Signe A. Vest

§8.01 INTRODUCTION

The Danish legal system is probably unknown to most lawyers outside Denmark. In spite of Denmark's historically powerful position in Northern Europe and our colonies in the Caribbean, Africa, India, etc. that were established and held throughout the seventeenth, eighteenth and nineteenth centuries, Danish law never really made an impact in the formation of foreign legal systems, like for example Swiss, French, German and English law. There are several reasons for this:

Danish is not a particularly easy language to understand, let alone speak, and very little literature on Danish law is available in languages other than Danish. Our legal system has therefore never been able to attract the academic interest and international popularity of, for example, French, English or German law, which have been widely studied by foreign scholars and used as a basis for law reform work in several jurisdictions throughout the world (with or without colonial ties).

Danish law is relatively difficult to access because of the legal system itself. In spite of very early law reform initiatives in the seventeenth century, which resulted in King Christian V's '*Danske Lov*' of 1683 – a codification, which unified Denmark's legal system for the first time under the absolute monarchy[1] – Denmark never adopted a modern civil code like most other countries on the Continent. Instead the Danish legal system was developed on the basis of a number of *leges speciales*.

1. Until 1683, Denmark had been divided into three main jurisdictions: Jutland, Zealand and Scania. Each of these jurisdictions had a 'provincial code' (the so-called Landskabslove), the most well known being the 'Jutlandic Law' ('*Jydske Lov*') from 1241.

Still, large and important areas of Danish law, notably tort law, property law in regard to movables and various areas of contract law, have never been systematically regulated in individual statutes. As a result, these areas are, even today, mainly governed by legal principles codified in *Danske Lov*[2] and ancient principles of Roman law that have developed by the Danish courts throughout centuries. With respect to these areas, Danish law can be said to resemble common law more than its civil law neighbours although decisions rendered by Danish judges are usually brief, to the point and very rarely contain useful obiter dictae.

Accordingly, foreign practitioners looking for a clear set of rules under Danish law concerning a specific problem, which would usually be regulated in a civil code, will sometimes be surprised to find that Danish law does not offer any clear rules.

Danish procedural law does not provide any leverage with regard to conducting pre-trial asset investigations through the courts, unless insolvency proceedings are first initiated against the defendant. However, as described in further detail below under section §8.02, there are several online databases in Denmark with detailed information about different types of assets, which are available to the public.

In relation to the possibility of freezing assets, Danish law appears to be less well developed compared to other European jurisdictions. For example, the new EU rules on Account Preservation Orders have not been implemented into Danish law, and the Danish Arbitration Act (DAA) from 2005 has not been updated with the 2006 UNCITRAL Model Act rules on interim measures. We have examined the Danish rules on freezing orders below under section §8.03.

With regard to the judiciary system, the Danish courts are composed of: The Supreme Court ('*Højesteret*'), two High Court Divisions ('*Landsretten*'), the Copenhagen Maritime and Commercial Court ('*Sø- og Handelsretten i København*') and twenty-four city courts ('*Byretten*'). The two main Danish arbitral institutions should also be mentioned here, namely the Danish Institute of Arbitration ('*Voldgiftsinstituttet*') and the Danish Arbitration Board for Building and Construction ('*Voldgiftsnævnet for bygge- og anlægsvirksomhed*').

The enforcement of judgments and arbitral awards is administrated by the enforcement division of the city courts – 'fogedretten' – whose decisions can be appealed to the High Court. Denmark has ratified the 1958 New York Convention on the Recognition and Enforcement of Foreign Arbitral Awards as well as the Lugano and Brussels Conventions. Below under section §8.04, we have provided an overview of how foreign judgments and awards can be enforced in Denmark.

Finally, under section §8.05, we have addressed the remedies, which Danish law offers plaintiffs in regard to countering asset shielding manoeuvres.

2. A Danish version of '*Danske Lov*' is available in PDF here: http://bjoerna.dk/DL-1683-internet.pdf.

§8.02 IDENTIFYING ASSETS IN DENMARK

Under Danish law, it is not possible to obtain a court order compelling a party to reveal its assets, unless insolvency proceedings are first initiated.

There are, however, a number of public registers and databases in Denmark containing information about different types of assets belonging to corporations and private individuals. In the pre-trial phase, these registers and databases are the most relevant asset research sources.

[A] Real Estate

It is estimated that more than two-thirds of Danish privately owned wealth is placed in real estate located in Denmark. Any pre-trial asset search involving a Danish defendant should therefore include a search for Danish real estate.

The website www.ois.dk gives access to a public database containing information about real estate located in Denmark. The website makes it possible to search for a specific property using a street address or a digital map. The OIS database contains information about among other things the fiscal property appraisals, which indicate the market value of properties in Denmark.

If the property has been sold in recent years, a more accurate indication of its current market value can be found on the website www.boligejer.dk, which contains information about the recently obtained purchase prices for all properties located in Denmark.

In order to estimate the equity value of a Danish property, it is necessary to also conduct a research in the Danish Land Registry (*'Tingbogen'*) to establish among other things whether, and if so to which degree, the property has been mortgaged and/or whether other creditors might have already levied attachments on the property or initiated foreclosure proceedings.

The Danish Land Registry is available here: www.tinglysning.dk.

[B] Motor Vehicles

In the Danish car registry (*'Bilbogen'*) creditor rights, such as retention of title, mortgages and attachments are registered as well as bankruptcy or other types of insolvency proceedings affecting motor vehicles belonging to the debtor.

In the pre-trial phase, the car registry should be checked to see if the debtor owns any motor vehicles that could be attached after the judgment or award is rendered or targeted by a freezing order prior to or during trial.

The car registry is also available at www.tinglysning.dk.

[C] Vessels

The Danish International Ship Register ('DIS' or 'Skibsregistret') contains information about ownership to Danish vessels. DIS also contains registrations of third-party rights over the vessels, including mortgages, attachments, usufructs, etc.

The DIS is available here: www.skibsregister.dma.dk.

[D] Aircrafts

The Danish Transportation Authority ('*Trafikstyrelsen*') administrates the Danish Aircraft Register ('*Luftfartøjsregistret*'), which contains information about civilian aircrafts registered in Denmark, including information about who owns the aircrafts.

The Danish Aircraft Register can be accessed here: www.dcaa.trafikstyrelsen.dk.

[E] IP Rights

A very significant part of corporate wealth is invested in intellectual property rights. In particular in relation to disputes against large corporations with ties to Denmark, any pre-trial asset search should involve a thorough investigation into the corporation's trademarks, patents, models, Internet domain names and designs.

The Danish Patent and Trademark Office ('*Patent- og Varemærkestyrelsen*') administrates the Danish patent, model, design and trademark registers, which are available here: www.dkpto.dk.[3]

Furthermore, Internet domain names – like trademarks – can often represent significant economic value. Owners of Danish domain names can be found here: www.dkhostmaster.dk.

[F] Financial Reports

Any pre-trial asset search involving a counterpart with incorporated entities in Denmark should include copies of the latest annual financial reports filed by such entities.

Financial reports must be filed by Danish public limited liability companies ('Aktieselskaber') and – unless they have been exempted from the duty to file – also by Danish private limited liability companies ('Anpartsselskaber'). The financial reports are available at the website of the Danish Company Register ('*CVR-registret*'): www.cvr.dk.

[G] Tangible Assets

Third-party rights over tangible assets, such as machinery, raw materials, goods, etc. belonging to corporate entities are registered in '*Personbogen*'. A search in

3. Access to the EU and International databases for patents, trademarks and designs (EPOline, Espacenet, TMview, Designview and WIPO) is also available through this link.

'Personbogen' using the company's registration number will thus show whether the company has issued a letter of indemnity (often in combination with a floating charge) or whether the entity has mortgaged any of its major tangible assets in favour of other creditors.

The 'Personbogen' can be accessed here: www.tinglysning.dk.

[H] RKI Register

Lastly, the so-called RKI Register, which is Denmark's largest register containing details of more than 750,000 'bad debtors', both private individuals and companies domiciled in Denmark, should be mentioned here. Against payment of a fee, the RKI Register can be researched online via this website: www.experian.dk/rki/.

§8.03 INTERIM MEASURES

The rules on interim measures, including freezing orders, are found in sections 627–640 of the Danish Administration of Justice Act[4] (the 'DAJA') and – with regard to interim measures issued in the context of arbitration proceedings – in section 17 of the DAA.[5]

Denmark has not adopted the new EU rules on European Account Preservation Orders, which allow creditors to preserve funds in bank accounts under the same conditions in all EU Member States (except the UK and Denmark).[6] Accordingly, the above-mentioned national rules are currently the only legal basis for freezing assets in Denmark.

[A] Freezing Orders Issued by the Danish Courts

As mentioned in the introduction to this chapter, the Danish city courts each have a special division ('*Fogedret*'), which handles enforcement issues.

A request for a freezing order must be filed with the enforcement division of the city court, either (i) where the debtor is domiciled, (ii) where the debtor is working, (iii) where there is security for the claim, or (iv) where the assets are located.[7]

The request has to be in writing and must contain the plaintiff's arguments for freezing the defendant's assets. Any relevant documents, on which the plaintiff relies, must be enclosed with the request.[8]

4. Act No. 1139 dated 24 September 2013. The rules in the DAJA on interim measures were amended with effect as of 1 July 2013, however, the rules on freezing orders in sections 627–640 were not amended.
5. See Jacob C. Jørgensen et al., 'The New Danish Arbitration Act', International Arbitration Law Review, 2005.
6. The European Account Preservation Order rules have been described elsewhere in this book.
7. DAJA section 487. The court fee amounts to DKK 300 + ½% of the amount of the claim exceeding DKK 3,000. The court fee has to be paid with the request for freezing order. If the court fee is not paid, the request will be denied.
8. DAJA section 631.

The request must be followed by an action (a so-called *justifikationssag*) brought before the city court to confirm the freezing of the asset(s). Such an action must be initiated within one week, from the date of the freezing order, in accordance with section 634, subsection 1 of the DAJA.[9] If the plaintiff loses the '*justifikationssag*', the domestic courts will in accordance with section 639 in the DAJA decide on the plaintiff's liability for any damage, which the freezing order may have caused.[10]

The following basic conditions have to be fulfilled before the freezing of assets can be allowed under the rules of the DAJA:[11]

- The claim has to be pecuniary and existing. In other words, the plaintiff has to demonstrate the existence of a financial obligation owed by the defendant.[12]
- It is impossible to seize the defendant's goods directly. (If this possibility exists, the court will not issue a freezing order but instead refer the plaintiff to seize the defendant's assets).
- The possibility of securing payment would deteriorate if the defendant's assets were not frozen, (e.g., because the defendant is rapidly moving assets out of the country or giving assets away).[13]

Furthermore, as mentioned above, the plaintiff will normally have to provide security as a condition for the freezing of the defendant's assets. This is done in order to provide security for any damages that the plaintiff may inflict upon the defendant as a result of the freezing of his assets. Security can be provided in the form of a bank guarantee or a cash deposit.

If assets, which are registered in public records, such as real estate, vessels, aircrafts, motor vehicles, etc. are frozen, the plaintiff must undertake the relevant act of perfection to secure his right to the assets against bona fide third parties. In case the defendant goes bankrupt, the freezing order will become void.[14]

A freezing order can be levied with respect to as many of the defendant's assets as needed to provide adequate security for the claim and any expenses related to the freezing.[15] The freezing of assets will deprive the defendant of the right to dispose over the assets in any manner, which is not in line with the terms of the freezing order.[16] This does not exclude the defendant's common use of the assets.[17] Accordingly, if a bank account is frozen, the defendant may still pay bills and usual expenses while the freezing order is in place. Should the defendant dispose of the assets to the detriment of the plaintiff, the defendant may be held liable according to the Danish Penal Code

9. Jakob Juul and Peter F. Thommesen, 'Voldgift' (2003), p. 129 and Bernt Hjejle, 'Voldgift' (1987), p. 69.
10. Jakob Juul and Peter F.Thommesen, 'Voldgift' (2003), p. 130.
11. DAJA sections 627–629.
12. Bernhard Gomard, 'Fogedret' (1997), p. 223.
13. See for example UfR 1996.1688 H where the debtor had already moved abroad and was receiving an amount from a settlement in a different case. However, according to UfR 2001.667 V the fact that the debtor is living abroad is in itself not enough to grant a freezing order.
14. Bernhard Gomard, ' Fogedret' (1997), p. 236.
15. DAJA section 632, subsection 1 and UfR 1976.998.
16. DAJA section 632, subsection 2.
17. Bernhard Gomard, 'Fogedret' (1997), p. 233.

and attract liability in tort, see below under section §8.05, where this issue is addressed in greater detail.[18]

Pursuant to DAJA section 630, the defendant can prevent the freezing order by providing adequate security for the claim including any possible interest on the claim. The enforcement court will decide whether the security is sufficient. The parties can appeal the enforcement court's decision within a four-week deadline.[19]

[B] Freezing Orders Issued by Arbitral Tribunals

Regardless of whether a party needs to obtain a freezing order in the context of court proceedings or arbitration proceedings, it would usually be preferable to seek the order through the courts, which – as opposed to arbitral tribunals – are empowered to issue *enforceable* interim measures. Section 9 of the DAA allows the parties to seek interim measures through the domestic courts regardless of the fact that their dispute falls within the scope of an arbitration clause.

If a party involved in Danish arbitration proceedings for some reason prefers that the freezing order is issued by the arbitral tribunal rather than the courts, section 17 of the DAA provides the legal basis for taking this step. The DAA does not, however, specify the conditions for issuing a freezing order. Section 17, subsection 2 merely provides that the tribunal may require the requesting party to provide 'adequate security'.

The DAA, which is based on the 1985 UNCITRAL Model Law, came into force on 1 July 2005. Accordingly the act did not implement the detailed additional provisions on interim measures, which were added in Chapter IV A of the Model Law in 2006. The detailed rules on interim measure in the Model Law are yet to be implemented in the DAA. Meanwhile, it is thought that Danish arbitrators would tend to apply the above-mentioned rules of the DAJA by analogy when determining whether or not to grant an interim measure.

§8.04 ENFORCEMENT ISSUES

If the defendant holds assets that are located in Denmark, but the dispute resolution proceedings take place in another country, the question arises whether it is possible to enforce the foreign judgment or arbitral award against the Danish assets.

With regard to foreign judgments it is first of all worth noting that the Regulation (EU) No. 1215/2012 dated 12 December 2012 of the European Parliament and of the Council on jurisdiction and the recognition and enforcement of judgments in civil and commercial matters (recast) ('Brussels I Recast'), came into force on 10 January 2015, replacing Council Regulation (EC) No. 44/2001 of 22 December 2000[20] on jurisdiction

18. Penal Code sections 283, subsection 1, 292 and 293, subsection 2.
19. DAJA sections 640 and 586, subsection 1.
20. See http://eur-lex.europa.eu/legal-content/EN/TXT/PDF/?uri=CELEX:32001R0044&from=DA.

and the recognition and enforcement of judgments in civil and commercial matters (the 'Brussels I Regulation').[21]

However, the Brussel I Recast only applies to court proceedings commenced on or after 10 January 2015, thus, proceedings commenced before that date remain subject to the Brussels I Regulation.

The Brussels I Recast makes it possible to initiate enforcement proceedings in Denmark on the basis of a judgment rendered by a court in a Brussels I Recast Member State.

The same applies to judgments rendered in a state,[22] which is a member to the Lugano Convention on Jurisdiction and the Enforcement of Judgments in Civil and Commercial matters (the 'Lugano Convention') in that Denmark ratified the Lugano Convention on 24 September 2009.

With respect to foreign arbitral awards, Denmark ratified the 1958 New York Convention on the Recognition and Enforcement of Foreign Arbitral Awards (the 'NYC')[23] on 22 December 1972.

Accordingly, foreign arbitral awards and judgments from most European countries can be enforced in Denmark. However, judgments rendered by courts of countries that have not ratified the Brussels or Lugano Conventions will not be recognized or enforced by the Danish enforcement courts.[24]

Thus, a plaintiff, who has obtained a judgment from for instance a US court against a defendant holding assets located in Denmark, will have to initiate a new lawsuit against the defendant before the courts - if possible - in Denmark[25] or in

21. Due to Denmark's non-participation in EU legislation relating to civil matters, the Council Regulation (EC) No. 44/2001 of 22 December 2000 on jurisdiction and the recognition and enforcement of judgments on civil and commercial matters (the Brussels I Regulation) did not enter into force in Denmark until 1 July 2007 where Denmark ratified a Parallel Agreement, the Agreement of 19 October 2005 between the European Community and the Kingdom of Denmark on jurisdiction and the recognition and enforcement of judgments in civil and commercial matters. Under the Parallel Agreement, Denmark is obligated to adopt future amendments of the Brussels I Regulation and to take adequate account of the decisions of the European Court of Justice. Thus, the Brussels I Recast will apply uniformly in all Member States, however in Denmark via an international treaty and the principles of international public law and not via Community law. Cf. Lookofsky, J. & Hertz, K., pp. 34–35. Recital 34 of the Brussel I Regulations provides that continuity between the 1968 Brussels Convention, the Brussels I Regulation and the Brussels I Recast should be ensured and that the same need for continuity applies as regards the interpretation by the Court of Justice of the European Union of the 1968 Brussels Convention and of the Regulations replacing it. Thus, the Brussel I Recast resembles the Brussel I Regulation in large parts.
22. The European Community, Denmark, Iceland, Norway and Switzerland.
23. http://www.uncitral.org/pdf/english/texts/arbitration/NY-conv/XXII_1_e.pdf.
24. The DAJA section 223a and section 479 authorize the Minister of Justice to implement regulations regarding granting recognition and enforceability. However, this authorization has never been exercised.
25. In regard to obtaining jurisdiction over the dispute before the Danish courts, the rules set out in sections 235–248 of the Danish Administration of Justice Act (DAJA) should briefly be mentioned here: In particular, section 246 of the DAJA provides for jurisdiction over a defendant who owns assets that are present in Denmark - such assets may include real estate, financial assets, tangible assets, etc.

another Brussels I Regulation or Lugano Convention Member State in order to obtain a new judgment, which can be enforced in Denmark.[26]

In the following, we will provide a brief overview as to how foreign judgments rendered by a court in a Lugano Convention or Brussels I Recast Member State can be enforced in Denmark, see section §8.04[A] right below. Under section §8.04[B], we will address how international arbitral awards can be enforced in Denmark.

[A] Enforcement of Foreign Judgments

A judgment rendered by a court in a Member State of the European Union is as a main rule enforceable in Denmark without any declaration of enforceability being required, see Article 39 of the Brussels I Recast.[27] The applicant only needs to provide the competent enforcement authority with: (a) a copy of the judgment which satisfies the conditions necessary to establish its authenticity; and (b) a certificate issued by the court of origin pursuant to Article 53 of the Brussels I Recast, certifying that the judgment is enforceable and containing an extract of the judgment as well as, where appropriate, relevant information on the recoverable costs of the proceedings and the calculation of interest.[28]

Under the Brussels I Regulation, a judgment rendered in an EU Member State, which is enforceable there, can only be enforced in another Member State after being declared enforceable there, (the so-called *exequatur*), on application by anyone who has an interest in the matter.[29]

Accordingly, with respect to enforcement proceedings commenced before 10 January 2015, an application must be made to the court that has territorial jurisdiction on the basis of the domicile of the defendant or on the basis of the place of enforcement.

The declaration of enforceability, the '*exequatur*', is issued after certain formalities have been completed and must be served on the other party, who may challenge it only in the courts. The plaintiff must present a certified copy of the judgment as well as proof that the judgment is enforceable in its state of origin.

There are no provisions on enforcement as such. Therefore, once a judgment from another Member State has been declared enforceable in Denmark, the judgment can be enforced in the same way as judgments rendered by a Danish court.

The Lugano Convention extends the sphere of mutual recognition and enforcement of civil judgments beyond the borders of the European Union, encompassing also Iceland, Norway and Switzerland.

26. Such a new lawsuit brought before the Danish courts will as a rule involve a *révision au fond*, i.e., a complete retrial of all the evidence and legal issues of the dispute, cf. Allan Philip, 'Dansk International Privat- og Procesret', 3rd edition, p. 118 ff.
27. For the purposes of the Brussels I Recast and the Brussel I Regulation, 'judgment' means any judgment given by a court or tribunal of a Member State, whatever the judgment may be called, including a decree, order, decision or writ of execution, as well as the determination of costs or expenses by an officer of the court, cf. Article 2(a) of the Recast and Article 32 of the Brussel I Regulation.
28. Cf. Article 42(1) of the Brussels I Recast.
29. The Brussel I Regulation, Article 38.

As is the case with the Brussels I Recast and Brussel I Regulation, the Lugano Convention solely regulates the recognition and enforcement of civil judgments, and the Lugano Convention is, in substance, largely similar to the Brussels I Regulation.[30] Therefore, only the rules of the Brussels I Recast and, where relevant, the Brussel I Regulation will be discussed in the following.

The Danish courts can only refuse to recognize a judgment rendered in another Member State for the following reasons specified in Articles 46, cf. Article 45 of the Brussels I Recast, if:[31]

- such recognition is manifestly contrary to public policy (ordre public) in Denmark; or
- the judgment was given in default of appearance, if the defendant was not served with the document which instituted the proceedings or with an equivalent document in sufficient time and in such a way as to enable him to arrange for his defence, unless the defendant failed to commence proceedings to challenge the judgment when it was possible for him to do so; or
- it is irreconcilable with a judgment given between the same parties in Denmark; or
- it is irreconcilable with an earlier judgment given in another EU or non-EU country involving the same cause of action and the same parties, provided that the earlier judgment fulfils the conditions necessary for its recognition.

[B] Enforcement of International Arbitral Awards

With respect to foreign arbitral awards it is worth noticing that the 'DAA',[32] which implements the NYC, provides for a *wider* recognition than the NYC itself, in that the DAA allows for enforcement of all foreign arbitral awards, regardless of their country of origin.

Usually, the enforcement will concern the payment of a sum of money; however, awards granting non-monetary relief can also be enforced by the intervention of the Danish courts.[33]

When it comes to the commencement of legal proceedings for the enforcement of foreign awards, it should be noted that section 5 of the Danish Act on the limitation of monetary claims[34] provides that when it comes to monetary claims, which have been

30. The Lugano Convention was formed as a modified version of the 1968 Brussels Convention, and its main purpose was to join the EFTA and the European Union Member States together under one jurisdictional and enforcement system.
31. The grounds for refusing to recognize a judgment is largely similar under the Brussels I Regulation, cf. the Brussels I regulation, Article 45, cf. Articles 34 and 35.
32. Act No. 553/2005, which can be accessed here in English: http://www.voldgiftsinstituttet.dk/en/Materiale/Files/Danish+Arbitration+Act+2005.
33. The enforcement of non-monetary is carried out on the basis of DAJA sections 528–536.
34. Act No. 522/2007.

established by a 'binding decision' a ten-year period of limitation applies. The term 'binding decision' includes arbitral awards.[35]

Further, DAJA section 480(1), which also applies to arbitral awards, cf. section 38 of the DAA, establishes that legal proceedings before the enforcement court can only be initiated after a period of two weeks from the date on which the award was rendered.[36] If the award provides for a different timeframe for enforcement, the two-week period will be replaced by the period stated in the award.

An action for the enforcement of a foreign arbitral award should be brought before the enforcement division of the city court at the place where the respondent is domiciled or has its place of business, or at the place where the respondent keeps his assets, cf. DAJA sections 235–247.

A court fee of DKK 300 (about EUR 40) plus 0.5% of the amount sought to be enforced excluding the first DKK 3,000 (about EUR 400) must be paid when the proceedings are initiated before the enforcement court.[37]

In order to have an arbitral award recognized and enforced in Denmark, the plaintiff must provide the original award in its entirety or a certified copy thereof and a duly certified copy of the relevant parts of the document containing the arbitration clause.[38]

Documents in a language other than Danish must be filed with a translation into Danish unless both parties to the proceedings agree not to have a translation filed and the court is comfortable with the foreign language in question, cf. DAJA section 149. Citizens from other Nordic countries may file documents in their own language, which will be translated into Danish on the court's initiative if required by the other party or if the court considers it necessary. An authorized translator must certify the translation.

The first decision granting enforcement can be appealed to the High Court. In practice, appeal to the Danish Supreme Court will not be granted unless the case presents legal questions of principal importance.

A Danish court can stay the proceeding for enforcement pending the outcome of an application for setting aside or suspending the award, cf. DAJA section 345 and DAA section 39, subsection 3.[39]

---

35. The 2007 Act on the limitation of monetary claims came into force on 1 January 2008 and will therefore apply to arbitral awards rendered on or after this date. Before 1 January 2008, a twenty-year limitation period applied pursuant to the 1908 Act on the limitation of monetary Claims, L 1908-12-22 No. 274.
36. See DAJA section 480. Execution against assets before the execution court is carried out as mentioned above in section V.
37. Court Fees Act, LBKG 2014-11-27 No. 1252, section 16.
38. There are no requirements for other documents in the file to be submitted in original or certified copies.
39. Under DAA section 39(3), granting of the stay of the legal proceedings are only conditional of the provision of security, when the party seeking recognition and enforcement of the award has asked the court to order the other party to provide appropriate security.

§8.05 D&O LIABILITY IN RELATION TO ASSET PROTECTION SCHEMES

It is sometimes seen that companies, during the course of protracted dispute resolution proceedings involving substantial claims, take steps in an attempt to remove valuable assets from the corporate entity involved in the dispute.

Asset shielding manoeuvres can take many different forms – from the straightforward transfer of assets and business activities to a parent or sister entity, to sophisticated schemes involving, for example, the transfer of assets to offshore trusts or foundations, sham investments designed to generate a (fictitious) loss of assets, securitizations designed to reduce or eliminate the equity value of assets without removing them, the abuse of insolvency proceedings, etc.

Danish law will as a rule not allow for a piercing of the corporate veil, and accordingly it will rarely be possible for the plaintiff to drag the entity receiving the assets into the proceedings. The initiation of insolvency proceedings is expensive and as a rule never an expeditious solution, although filing for bankruptcy is sometimes necessary in order to trigger the application of claw-back provisions.

An oftentimes efficient counter move when faced with an asset shielding manoeuvre can be to raise or threaten to raise a claim for damages directly against the directors and officers of the entity attempting to shield its assets – to most people the imminent threat of litigation is a strong motivating factor.

In the following, we will provide a brief overview of the relevant rules under Danish law concerning D&O liability.

[A] The Danish Companies Act

Section 361, subsection 1 of the Danish Companies Act provides as follows with regard to the liability of board members:

> (1) Founders and members of management who, in the performance of their duties, have intentionally or negligently caused damage to the limited liability company are liable to pay damages. The same applies where the damage is caused to shareholders or any third party.[40]

The provision is merely a reflection of the general principle of Danish tort law that the plaintiff must show that the defendant has acted negligently and that a foreseeable loss has been suffered as a result of the negligence.[41]

Under Danish law, board members are jointly liable and their liability is personal and unlimited.[42] Often, professional board members, such as lawyers, will take out insurance against liability, but the insurance policy will not cover a liability arising out

40. An English version of the Danish Companies Act is available at: https://danishbusinessauthority.dk/sites/default/files/danish_companies_act.pdf.
41. See Dr Bernhard Gomard 'Aktieselskaber og Anpartsselskaber' 2006, p. 470 ff. An excellent and very comprehensive analysis of the issue of D&O liability under Danish law is found in Dr Thorbjørn Sofsrud 'Bestyrelsens beslutning og ansvar'.
42. See Paul Krüger Andersen 'Aktie- og anpartsselskabsret' 2008, p. 448 ff. See also Dr Jan Schans Christensen 'Kapitalseskaber' 2009, p. 689 ff.

of gross negligence or wilful misconduct. If a board member has accepted that the company engages in active asset shielding activities in relation to an upcoming or pending dispute, this would in our view most likely amount to wilful misconduct. Accordingly, a board member must - in order to avoid liability - clearly voice his objections to any activities by the company aimed at or involving the risk of removing or depleting assets in order to undermine subsequent enforcement proceedings.[43]

A liability can arise even though the activities are not in violation of the articles of association of the company or the provisions of the Companies Act if it is considered that the board member has acted in a dishonest or disloyal manner in an attempt to safeguard the interests of the company.

Pursuant to section 363 of the Companies Act, the liability of a board member can be reduced if this is considered fair and reasonable considering the degree of negligence, the magnitude of the loss inflicted and the circumstances of the matter in general.[44] If certain board members are covered by a professional liability insurance and others are not, this provision is often invoked on behalf of the board members who do not have insurance cover. However, as already mentioned it is doubtful whether a Danish insurance policy would cover the liability of board members who are faced with lawsuits after having actively engaged in asset shielding manoeuvres.

[B] The Danish Criminal Code

In addition to the above rules and principles arising out of the Danish Companies Act in relation to D&O liability, two provisions in the Danish Criminal Code deserve mentioning here:

The removal of assets from a company involved in litigation or arbitration proceedings, can amount to a violation of section 283, subsection 1 no. 3 of the Danish Criminal Code concerning debtor fraud, which *inter alia* provides that a person shall be punished for debtor fraud if he - with the intention of gaining an unlawful enrichment on his own behalf or on behalf of others - removes his belongings or receivables so that they may not be used to satisfy any debts owed to his creditors.[45]

An asset protection exercise may involve an infringement of section 280 of the Danish Criminal Code concerning breach of trust. In particular, section 280, subsection 1, no. 1 is of relevance with regard to board members in that this provision concerns the abuse of a legal right to act on behalf of someone else. If the board members resolve to remove the assets from a company in order to evade enforcement, this may amount to a breach of trust vis-à-vis thecompany, which is punishable under section 280, cf. the ruling of the Danish Supreme Court in UfR 1985.940H where the director and major shareholder of a Danish company was held to have violated section 280 by having abused his position to inflict a substantial financial loss on the company and thereby on its creditors.

43. On the issue of insurance, see Klaus Stubkjær Andersen 'Ledelsesansvar og ledelsesansvarsforsikring', 2011.
44. See Dr Bernhard Gomard in UfR 1971B.117, 'Aktieselskabsledelsens erstatningsansvar'.
45. See 'Kommenteret straffelov. Speciel del, 9. edition', p. 538 ff.

CHAPTER 9
England and Wales

Ruth Byrne & Henry Farris

§9.01 INTRODUCTION

The legal system in England and Wales is a Common Law system in which sources of legal power are derived from statutes and from case law. The principal sources of English law[1] can be summarised in three ways. The first is statute, which derives from legislation from the UK Parliament and devolved parliaments. Next is the Common Law, made through principles established in case law over the centuries during the standardisation of law throughout England and Wales. Judicial precedent forms the basis of the Common Law, with the decision of each Court binding that Court and those below it. Finally, the law of the European Union is binding upon the Courts in England and Wales.

There is no written constitution and so, in addition to statute and case law, other aspects of the legal system are embedded within non-binding and often unwritten conventions, parliamentary rules and royal prerogative. In terms of enforcement of judgments and arbitration awards, this means that there are different sources of authority depending on the original jurisdiction and the type of remedy sought.

The Court of England and Wales has several different divisions and layers, depending on the type of claim and the value and the stage of proceedings (e.g., first instance or appeal). This chapter will focus on enforcement in England and Wales in a civil law commercial context. The civil Courts of First Instance are the County Court and the High Court. Generally the High Court deals with claims in excess of GBP

1. It is important to note that there is not a single, unified legal system in the United Kingdom. The legal system that operates in England and Wales is separate from those of Scotland and Northern Ireland: they are considered as separate jurisdictions whose legal systems are beyond the scope of this chapter. Throughout this Chapter, the term 'English law' will be used as a short-hand term to denote the law of England and Wales.

100,000 and is the focus of this chapter. The High Court is also sub-divided into areas of specialism, with the three main divisions being the Chancery, the Queen's Bench and the Family divisions.

The Chancery division deals with company matters such as insolvency and tax, as well as disputes relating to trusts and wills. The Queen's Bench Division is much broader and deals with general commercial disputes. It also has further sub-divided specialist courts: the Commercial Court and the Technology and Construction Court. The former deals with complex commercial cases (particularly banking and financial disputes).

The first appellate court from the High Court is the Court of Appeal. An appeal in this court is usually heard by three Lord or Lady Justices. If an appeal raises an issue of public interest, permission may be granted to appeal to the Supreme Court, where appeals are usually heard by five Lord or Lady Justices (or occasionally seven). Finally, if a case raises a matter of EU law, it may be referred to the European Court of Justice in Strasbourg for guidance.

The Civil Procedure Rules (the 'CPR'), set out in the 'White Book', provide an important framework detailing the Court's powers and how to obtain appropriate relief. The CPR are applicable to the Court of Appeal, High Court and County Courts in England and Wales. The Supreme Court has its own procedural rules. The CPR are referred to extensively throughout this chapter.

There are three distinct steps to enforcing a judgment or arbitration award, some or all of which may be required in each case. First, it may be necessary for the party who wishes to enforce a foreign judgment in England and Wales to identify the assets of the judgment debtor. Second, interim measures may be needed to preserve those assets. Third, specified steps must be taken actually to enforce the judgment or award.

§9.02 IDENTIFYING ASSETS IN ENGLAND AND WALES

A party seeking to enforce in England and Wales should, if it does not already have the necessary information, seek to identify whether there are any or sufficient assets in this jurisdiction to satisfy the judgment or award debt. The enforcing party can apply to the Court to obtain information from the defendant or third parties. Alternatively, there are a variety of searches that can be undertaken of public information.

[A] Public Searches

[1] Search for Real Property through Land Registry

Evidence of ownership of land and property in England and Wales is documented under the Land Register. This can be searched in order to identify the owner of any interest of a property in England and Wales. Searches can only be conducted on properties, rather than on owners. Therefore a search can be performed on a particular property to see who owns it, but a search to identify what particular properties are owned by a particular person or entity is not possible by this means.

[2] Companies House Search

A search can be undertaken of all companies registered in the UK. Companies are required to file annual accounts and registers of shareholders, amongst other things. A Companies House search is therefore a valuable tool for ascertaining whether a company or corporate body has assets in this jurisdiction. Further, the shareholders of a company and the number of shares they own can usually be identified by means of such a search.

An individual can also be searched for to see if he/she has any current or past directorships of registered companies. Directors often have shares in the company as well.

[3] Vessels

A party may search for vessels under the UK Ship Register for merchant ship and bareboat charter. The register provides a database for ships operating under the UK flag.

[4] IP Rights

The Intellectual Property Office (IPO) in the UK possesses registers relating to copyright, patents, designs and trademarks. UK trademarks can be searched for by trademark number, by owner, or by phrases or images using the IPO's website. The website also gives the same information in relation to EU intellectual property.

[5] Motor Vehicles

A party may also search for vehicle registrations at the Driver and Vehicle Licensing Agency (DVLA). The DVLA provides a list of registered vehicles for personal use and motor trade.

[6] Aircraft

Aircrafts are registered at the UK Register of Civil Aircrafts, and a party may search the G-INFO database which holds details of registered aircrafts in the UK. Details can be obtained by inserting information in relation to serial numbers, aircraft type/name fields, registration owner and ICAO 24 bit aircraft address fields.

[B] Appointing an Enquiry Agent

A common tactic when identifying the assets of a judgment debtor is the use of enquiry agents to perform thorough searches of public records and produce a report on the assets of the company or individual in question. Such reports should be produced in a way that can be relied upon by the enforcing party in Court – either as a stand-alone affidavit or as an exhibit to the affidavit of the enforcing party's solicitor.

[C] Using the Court's Assistance

[1] Pre-recognition/Enforcement

[a] Pre-action Disclosure against a Potential Defendant

The Court has the power to order a potential party to subsequent proceedings to disclose documents on the application of another potential party to those proceedings under CPR rule 31.16.

The documents sought by such an application must be documents that the respondent would be required to disclose by way of standard disclosure. In other words, they must be documents as to which there would likely be a disclosure order once proceedings have been commenced because they either support or adversely affect one or other of the parties' respective cases. In addition, pre-action disclosure must be necessary to dispose fairly of the anticipated proceedings, to assist the dispute to be resolved without proceedings, or to save costs.

[b] Non-party Disclosure Order (Assumed Not to Be Defendants)

Similar powers are available against non-parties, although the applicable threshold is higher. At the pre-action stage, a party may obtain documents and information from a third party who may have been involved in any potential wrongdoing against that party (whether knowingly or not) under what is known as *Norwich Pharmacal*[2] jurisdiction. This procedure is usually invoked to assist in identifying an actual wrongdoer, a cause of action or the location of assets. This procedure can be used at any stage of proceedings, but it is unclear whether the Court would make such an order in support of enforcement proceedings. Once proceedings have commenced, a non-party can be ordered to produce documents under CPR rule 31.17. Again, it is unclear whether this would be an effective tool in enforcement proceedings.

Separately, a *Bankers Trust* order is a type of disclosure order which requires a bank to provide details ordinarily protected by the bank's duties of confidentiality. In *Bankers Trust Co v. Shapira* [1980] 1 WLR 1274 CA, the order sought was disclosure of all relevant documents relating to the accounts of two fraudsters, including the balance of the accounts, cheques, debit vouchers and transfer applications. The order was granted on the basis that it gave effect to the claimant party's right to trace assets which, without such disclosure, would have been impossible. It did not matter that the bank itself had not incurred any liability for the fraud.

2. *Norwich Pharmacal Company & Ors v. Customs And Excise* [1973] UKHL 6, [1974] AC 133 (26 June 1973).

This is similar to a *Norwich Pharmacal* order, although it is focussed on the location of missing assets (usually money), rather than the commission of the underlying cause of action.

[2] Post-recognition/Enforcement

Once judgment has been obtained, an order can be obtained pursuant to CPR rule 71 requiring a judgment debtor to attend Court to provide information about its means or any other information needed for the purpose of enabling a judgment creditor to enforce a judgment. Where the judgment debtor is an individual, the order will be made against him directly and in the case of a defendant company or corporate body, the order can be made against an officer thereof. An order under rule 71 also contains a penal notice, warning that failure to comply with the order may be contempt of court, leading to imprisonment, a fine or seizure of assets.[3]

The scope of the documents and information that the judgment debtor must provide is relatively wide and CPR rule 71.2(6) states that:

A person served with an order issued under this rule must-

(a) attend court at the time and place specified in the order;
(b) when he does so, produce at court document in his control which are described in the order; and
(c) answer on oath such questions as the court may require.

There are important points to note about the territorial scope of such an order. Whilst a judgment debtor is required to answer questions about assets outside of the jurisdiction,[4] an order of this kind cannot be made against a judgment debtor (or officer thereof) who is outside of the jurisdiction.[5] The protection afforded to individuals outside of the jurisdiction is particularly important when considering that companies and corporate bodies have separate legal personalities to their officers.

In respect of a foreign judgment, this procedure would become available once the judgment has been registered (as to which, see below).

§9.03 INTERIM MEASURES

The English Court has significant powers to assist an enforcing party to identify and protect the assets of a judgment debtor at the interim stage. These powers can be invoked at any stage of proceedings, including post-judgment. Further, pursuant to section 44 of the Arbitration Act 1996, the Court's powers may be invoked in support of Arbitration proceedings.

3. CPR 71.2(7).
4. *Interpool Ltd v. Galani* [1988] QB 738.
5. *Masri v. Consolidated Contractors International Co SAL and another* [2009] UKHL 43.

[A] Section 44 of the Arbitration Act 1996

Section 44 of the Arbitration Act 1996 grants the courts general powers which can be exercised in support of arbitral proceedings including making orders in relation to the taking of evidence from witnesses and to the preserving evidence (which is likely to be used if there is a suspicion that documents may be destroyed). The courts may also make orders allowing a party to inspect, preserve or detain property and/or allowing a party to enter property for the purposes of carrying out investigations. This relief may also be extended to third parties such as expert witnesses. For instance, if a third party needs access to premises urgently to examine a biodegradable product, then the Court may give an order permitting such an examination by an expert. The court can also take a step further and order the product to be sold before it perishes in order to mitigate losses.

Finally, the court may also grant an interim injunction such as a freezing injunction (discussed below) in support of arbitral proceedings. This may be particularly helpful if suspicions arise that one party is seeking to move its assets out of the reach of the other party, whether before, during or after an arbitration.

[B] Freezing Orders (Injunction)

One of the most well-known interim measures is a freezing order, previously known as a *Mareva* Injunction. The purpose of a freezing order is to prevent a defendant from dissipating or dealing with its assets up to the value specified in the order outside the ordinary course of business, with the effect that assets up to a certain value should be preserved until a judgment or award can be enforced. Importantly, it does not give security over the defendant's assets. meaning that other claims may in any event still be made against the defendant in respect of its assets by third parties, including in insolvency proceedings, and in the event of any such proceedings, a freezing injunction will not necessarily confer priority on the beneficiary.

The Court's jurisdiction to grant a freezing order comes from several different sources. First was the case from which it takes its name: *Mareva Compania Naviera SA v. International Bulk Carriers SA* [1975] 2 Lloyds Rep 509. Second (chronologically speaking), section 37(1) of the Senior Courts Act 1981 gives statutory authority for granting a freezing order. Third, CPR Rule 25.1(1)(f)[6] lists a 'freezing injunction' amongst the interim remedies that the English Court may make.

The jurisdiction of the English Courts to make a freezing order is very wide. It is most often used in respect of English proceedings and, by virtue of section 25 of the Civil Jurisdiction and Judgments Act 1982 as extended by the Civil Jurisdiction and Judgments Act 1982 (Interim Relief) Order 1997, a freezing order may be made by the English Court in support of foreign substantive proceedings.[7] Foreign substantive

6. 2015 Rules.
7. The 1982 Act had previously stated that a Freezing Order may be made in support of foreign substantive proceedings in a contracting state under the Brussels or Lugano Conventions, and this limitation has now been removed.

proceedings include the enforcement of overseas judgments and awards. There is also no requirement that the defendant to an application for a freezing order should be based in England. In fact, in *Mareva Compania Naviera SA v. International Bulk Carriers*, the Defendant was based overseas and it was another four years before a Freezing Order was made against an English defendant.[8] Finally, pursuant to section 37(1) of the Senior Courts Act 1981, the Court may make a Freezing Order against assets in England and those located overseas. The different iterations of freezing orders, and how to obtain them, are explained in greater detail below.

A freezing order binds any third party who has notice of it. In particular, this means that banks which hold accounts belonging to a defendant must ensure that the terms of a freezing order are complied with. This is an important feature of a freezing order because it means that a defendant is unable to dissipate its assets even if it was minded to.

Finally, a significant additional feature of a freezing order is that it contains a clause requiring the defendant to disclose its assets within a certain period. The precedent freezing order attached to the Annex of Practice Direction 25A of the CPR contains a clause (clause 9) entitled 'Provision of Information', which sets out the standard terms on which a defendant will be ordered to make this disclosure. This is the precedent upon which both domestic and Worldwide Freezing Orders (WFOs) are based and, as such, this disclosure is required as a matter of course when a freezing order is made.

A defendant must give the 'value, location and details' of all its assets above a certain specified value to the applicant's solicitors by a certain date. The requirement to give this information is often as valuable as the freezing of assets itself and ensures that the freezing order can be policed effectively. It is particularly important in WFOs because the defendant's assets may have been 'hidden' in other jurisdictions.

[C] Domestic Freezing Order: English Proceedings and Assets

In addition to demonstrating the risk of dissipation of assets and that there are assets in the jurisdiction against which an award or judgment could be enforced, an applicant for a freezing order must also show that it has a cause of action to bring substantive proceedings in England and Wales and a good arguable case on the merits. This is important to remember as it reflects the fact that a freezing order is relief granted in support of extant (or anticipated) proceedings, rather than being stand-alone relief.

An applicant for a freezing order must act promptly and the Court will consider whether there has been any delay when exercising its discretion whether to make an order. An unjustified delay may indicate to the Court that a freezing order is not urgently required because of the lack of the risk of dissipation. Conversely, a delay may have allowed the defendant to have dissipated its assets already, such that a freezing order would be ineffective. For similar reasons, the Court may refuse to grant a freezing order if the defendant has been forewarned or notified of a freezing order.

8. *Third Chandris Shipping Corp v. Unimarine SA* [1980] 1WLR 107.

An applicant for a freezing order is required to give an undertaking as to damages. This means that in the event the freezing order is, at a later date, found not to have been justified and also to have caused the defendant loss, the claimant will indemnify the defendant against loss. Such losses can be substantial in the event that a defendant's business is interrupted.

[D] Worldwide Freezing Orders

A 'WFO' will be granted if the applicant can show that the defendant is unlikely to have sufficient assets within England and Wales to satisfy any judgment against it. This requirement is in addition to demonstrating the same requirements as for a domestic freezing order.

Further considerations that the Court will have are the nature of the claim against the defendant, in particular the extent to which there appears to have been fraud or corruption, and the likely ability of the defendant to be able to transfer its assets internationally or 'hide' them in jurisdictions in which it may be difficult to enforce.

It should be noted that a WFO cannot be enforced in other jurisdictions without the permission of the Court. This must be reflected in the terms of the WFO itself.

[E] Freezing Order in Support of Foreign Proceedings

For this relief, the Court will consider the application as if the substantive proceedings were being conducted within this jurisdiction. Assuming the answer to that question is yes, the most important consideration is whether the defendant has assets within this jurisdiction which would render the English Court the most appropriate court to grant the relief. If there are no assets here, then a freezing order will only be granted in exceptional circumstances. Similarly, the English Court is unlikely to be the appropriate Court to grant a WFO in support of foreign proceedings, in circumstances where it has no jurisdiction over the defendant.[9]

[F] Applying for a Freezing Order: Procedure

Applications for freezing orders are made in accordance with CPR 23, which governs applications to the Court generally. As mentioned above, CPR 25.1(1)(f) makes provision for the court to make freezing orders and it sets out the specific requirements. Freezing orders are invariably made without notice to the defendant which means that strict adherence to the procedural requirements is needed. The following steps, amongst others, are required:

9. In *ICICI Bank Uk plc v. Diminco NV [2014]* EWHC 3124 (Comm), Mr Justice Popplewell set out the principles on which a freezing order in aid of foreign proceedings would be considered. He reviewed the established authorities of *Credit Suisse Fides Trust v. Cuoghi* [1998] QB 818, *Motorola Credit Corporation v Uzan and others (No.2) (CA) [2003] EWCA Civ 752, [2004] 1 WLR 113*, amongst others.

- An application notice in the form N244 should be used. In the Commercial Court, the N244 (CC) form is used.
- The application must be supported by evidence in the form of an affidavit. An affidavit must be sworn (before a commissioner for oaths). In practice, it is usually the applicant's solicitor that submits the affidavit. The contents of affidavit are discussed briefly below but the most important feature is that the Court must be satisfied that the applicant (often through its solicitor) has given full and frank disclosure. This means that all arguments in favour of and against granting the freezing order must be put before the Court.
- A draft of the freezing order sought, using the standard form annexed to PD 25A or Appendix 5 of the Admiralty & Commercial Court Guide, must be included with the original application.
- Where possible, an applicant should file copies of application notice, evidence and draft order at court if there is time before the hearing. However, as freezing order applications are usually made without notice and on an urgent basis, this requirement can be dispensed with (see PD 25A.4.3(2)).
- An application for a freezing order will be dealt with at a hearing, rather than on paper. Further, once the order has been served, there will be a return hearing at which the defendant will be entitled to appear to challenge the freezing order. At this point, the Court will decide whether it should be continued, varied or discharged.

[G] Contents of the Affidavit

An applicant for a freezing order must give full and frank disclosure in the supporting affidavit. This should include the following topics:

- The reasons why the application is being made without notice (assuming that it is).[10]
- Full particulars as possible of the claim against the defendant, so that the Court can assess whether the applicant has a good arguable case in respect of the underlying cause of action.
- Identifying as far as possible the sources of information and evidence on which the applicant relies. This is particularly important in the context of full and frank disclosure.
- Evidence of the risk of dissipation of the defendant's assets.

[1] Search Orders

Another form of interim relief which may be used to identify assets is a search order (previously known as an *Anton Piller* order). This allows a claimant's representatives

10. The affidavit in support of the application must state why notice was not given (Practice Direction 25A (Interim Injunctions) paragraph 3.4).

to attend and enter a defendant's premises – without notice – and search for, copy and remove documents or material specified in the search order. It is even more draconian than a freezing order because of its invasive nature. This form of interim relief can be granted against a recalcitrant defendant who has refused to disclose the location and value of its assets pursuant to earlier orders. Therefore search and seizure of the defendant's documents is required to allow the claimant to ascertain the information for itself. It will only be granted in exceptional circumstances.

The High Court's power to grant search orders is now derived from section 7(1) of the Civil Procedure Act 1997. The original power came from the case of *Anton Piller KG v. Manufacturing Processes Ltd* [1976] Ch 55, in which the Court of Appeal set out four requirements for such an order:

- the claimant must show an extremely strong prima facie case against the defendant;
- damage suffered by the claimant must have been very serious;
- whether there was a real possibility that the defendants would destroy relevant documents; and
- whether the effect of the *Anton Piller* order would be out of proportion to the legitimate object of the order.

Obtaining and executing a search order is an expensive process, and the threshold to be met in order to succeed on an application for this relief is high. However, it can bring a major advantage in litigation.

[H] Applying for a Search Order

The procedural requirements for a search order are similar to those for a freezing order, and an application should follow the procedure in CPR 23 and the specific provisions in PD 25A.

Applications for search orders are almost always made without notice, which again necessitates full and frank disclosure and evidence by way of a sworn affidavit. Giving notice would give the defendant an opportunity to destroy or dispose of the materials, defeating the purpose of the order.

A supervising solicitor is required to conduct the search pursuant to the terms of the order and ensure that only relevant documents (or copies) are given to the claimant. This is one of the factors that adds to the cost of a search order.

[I] Appointing a Liquidator

If it is known that a company has transferred funds, then it is possible for an urgent request to be made to the Court to appoint a provisional liquidator if there is a serious risk of dissipation of the company's assets or that its assets will be put beyond the reach of its creditors.

§9.04 ENFORCEMENT OF FOREIGN JUDGMENTS IN ENGLAND AND WALES

The procedures for enforcing foreign judgments vary considerably depending on the country from which the judgment originates, and this has been compounded by the recent (January 2015) change in the regime for enforcing EU judgments. The appropriate regime also depends on the type of judgment that is being enforced (e.g., commercial, insolvency or matrimonial). However many of the procedures are straightforward and efficient. Therefore, once a party is familiar with the requisite enforcement regime, a judgment can often be enforced relatively simply. An overview of the different regimes is set out below. The procedure is dealt with in detail in CPR rule 74.

Although the term 'enforcement' is used, it is technically a two-stage process. For a foreign judgment to be enforced, it must first be recognised by the English Court. The extent to which these two processes are separate depends on the appropriate enforcement regime, but the latter cannot happen without the former. Once a judgment has been recognised, it is treated in the same way as a domestic judgment. Strictly speaking, it is therefore the process of obtaining recognition of the judgment, to the extent that the various regimes require it, which forms the focus of this section.

Broadly speaking, the various enforcement regimes can be split into three categories:

(1) The European enforcement regime, which principally consists of the Recast Judgments Regulation, the 2001 Judgments Regulation,[11] the Lugano Convention and the European Enforcement Order Regulation.
(2) A statutory regime for countries with which the UK has bilateral enforcement conventions in place – typically commonwealth countries and other territories or governorates of the United Kingdom.
(3) The Common Law regime for countries or types of judgment to which neither of the above apply.

[A] European Regime

The European Regime, as described below, applies to civil and commercial judgments from courts and tribunals. It does not apply to arbitration awards, which are addressed in a separate section. Neither does it apply to insolvency, matrimonial or matters relating to wills – which usually come under the Common Law regime but are not addressed substantively in this chapter.

11. These are also known as the Recast Brussels Regulation and 2001 Brussels Regulation respectively.

[1] Recast Judgments Regulation

The Recast Judgments Regulation (Council Regulation (EU) 1215/2012) applies to qualifying judgments from all EU Member States[12] for proceedings commenced on or after 10 January 2015 (note that it is the date proceedings were commenced, not the date of judgment).

The procedure for enforcement under the Recast Judgments Regulation has streamlined that of its predecessor, the 2001 Judgments Regulation (described below). A judgment creditor needs to obtain a certificate from the original court in the form set out in Annex 1 to the Recast Judgments Regulation. This sets out certain basic information, such as details of the judgment, including interest and costs, as well as certifying that the judgment is enforceable.

The judgment creditor must then serve the certificate and judgment on the debtor (with translations if necessary), after which the judgment can be enforced as if it were an English Court judgment (subject to the limited defences that the judgment debtor may have).

[2] Judgments Regulation and 2007 Lugano Convention

The 2001 Judgments Regulation and 2007 Lugano Convention contain similar provisions. They apply to judgments from proceedings commenced before 10 January 2015 between European Union Member States and European Freed Trade Association countries, except Liechtenstein, and continue to apply to those from Switzerland, Norway and Iceland respectively. They require the judgment creditor to apply to the English Court (Queen's Bench Division) to register the judgment. Such an application is usually made without notice and must be accompanied by an authenticated copy of the judgment, a translation of the judgment, a certificate in the form of Annex V of the 2001 Judgments Regulation and information about any interest awarded. Provided the formalities are complied with, the judgment will be recognised and become enforceable.

It is only once the judgment has become enforceable and the order has been served on the judgment debtor that it may challenge its enforceability.

[3] European Enforcement Order ('EEO') Regulation

The EEO Regulation (Council Regulation (EC) 805/2004) applies to money judgments obtained in uncontested claims and is even simpler than the Recast Judgments Regulation. An EEO certificate is required from the originating court, There is no requirement to serve it on the judgment debtor before enforcement can take place.

12. Denmark initially opted-out of the Recast Judgments Regulation but notified the Commission by letter on 20 December 2012 of its decision to implement it. This means that the provisions of the Recast Judgments Regulation will be applied to relations between the EU and Denmark.

Further, as the original claim was not contested, the defences that a judgment debtor may use are even more limited.

[4] Statutory Regime

The primary English statutes governing the enforcement of foreign judgments are the Administration of Justice Act 1920, the Foreign Judgments (Reciprocal Enforcement) Act 1933 and the Civil Jurisdiction and Judgments Act 1982. The first two cover Commonwealth countries, including (but not limited to) Australia, New Zealand, Canada, India, Pakistan and all British Overseas territories, as well as judgments from several European countries that fall outside the European Regime. The 1982 Act covers judgments from Scotland and Northern Ireland. Each of these distinct statutory regimes reflect reciprocal agreements with the countries to which they apply.

In order to be capable of being enforceable under the first two acts, a judgment must be final and conclusive, and also be an award of damages, rather than a penalty or a fine. The scope of the 1982 Act is much wider, but still excludes insolvency judgments (as mentioned above). The first step is to register the judgment, and the procedure for registration is set out in detail in CPR rule 74.4. An application must be made under Part 23, and be supported by written evidence exhibiting the judgment (or a verified copy) and a translation if required.

[5] Common Law

If a country does not fall under any of the above regimes – for example the USA – fresh legal proceedings in England and Wales need to be commenced to enforce a foreign judgment. In effect, the judgment creditor is required to sue on the judgment as a debt. It may be necessary to serve the claim outside the jurisdiction, in which case specific rules apply.

Unless, for example, a fraud is alleged, there should be no need to re-examine the merits of the case at court, so it will often be possible to obtain summary judgment.

§9.05 ENFORCEMENT OF ARBITRAL AWARDS

The party against whom an award is made should voluntarily comply with the award by satisfying the terms of it, for example by making payment of the award sum to the successful party. Most of the leading arbitration rules contain provisions that the parties give an undertaking to carry out the award without delay.

In the absence of voluntary compliance, foreign awards, as well as awards made in England and Wales, can be enforced in this jurisdiction under either section 66 or section 101 of the Arbitration Act 1996. Section 66 will be used predominantly where enforcement of domestic or international awards that do not qualify as New York Convention awards is sought, while section 101 was specifically enacted with respect to the enforcement of New York Convention awards and is therefore most commonly relied upon with respect to the enforcement of international awards.

The defences to enforcement under sections 66 and 101 of the Arbitration Act 1996, although deriving from different sources, are broadly speaking one and the same. They are therefore dealt with in relation to enforcement of New York Convention awards below, but are equally applicable to enforcement of awards via the section 66 route.

[A] New York Convention Awards

The regime for enforcement of awards made in signatory states to the New York Convention are governed by sections 100–104 of the Arbitration Act 1996:

(a) Recognition and enforcement of NY Convention award
If an award falls within the definition of a New York Convention award, it will be recognised as binding on persons who are party to the award.[13]

(b) Summary enforcement of the award
The successful party can apply to the court for permission to enforce the award summarily, and then, if permission is given, he can then enforce the award as if it were a court judgment even though he has not entered a judgment. He can also proceed to enter judgment in the terms of the award if he so wishes.

(c) Requirements for summary enforcement
Section 102 of the Arbitration Act 1996 states what a party must do to have his award recognised or enforced. That party must produce to the court the duly authenticated original award or a duly certified copy of it and the original arbitration agreement or a duly certified copy of it.
If a party produces these documents, the award will be recognised and enforced subject only to the grounds set out in section 103 of the Arbitration Act.

(d) Grounds for objecting to enforcement of an award (section 103)
The Courts adopt a pro-enforcement approach with respect to the enforcement of NY Convention awards and section 103(2) of the Arbitration Act 1996 lists the exhaustive grounds upon which enforcement of such an award may be refused. Indeed, even if one of the grounds is made out, the Courts retain a discretion to enforce an award, though this will be used sparingly.
The grounds for refusing to recognise or enforce an award under section 103(2) of the Arbitration Act 1996 mirror those set forth in Article V of the New York Convention and are as follows:
- incapacity of a party to the arbitration agreement;
- invalidity of arbitration agreement;
- improper notice of appointment of arbitrator or otherwise unable to present case;

13. Section 101(1) Arbitration Act 1996.

- award beyond the scope of submission;
- irregularity in the composition of the arbitral tribunal or failure to conduct arbitration in accordance with applicable arbitral procedure;
- award not yet binding, or has been set aside, or suspended by a competent authority of the country in which or under the law of which the award was made;
- award in respect of a matter not capable of settlement by arbitration; or
- contrary to public policy (the reach of public policy in theory is extremely broad and not capable of being exhaustively defined; however, it is said that it should only be invoked as a defence to enforcement where the enforcement would 'clearly be injurious to public good or wholly offensive to ordinary reasonable and fully informed members of the public'[14]).

A party resisting enforcement can seek a stay of execution of an order granting permission to enforce the award. This usually happens when challenge proceedings are pending in a competent foreign court. If a stay is granted, it will often be granted conditional upon the provision of security in the amount of all or part of the award sum.

In this regard, the courts have highlighted two relevant factors: first, '*if the award is manifestly invalid, there should be an adjournment and no order for security; if it is manifestly valid, there should either be an order for immediate enforcement, or else an order for substantial security*'; secondly '*the court must consider the ease or difficulty of enforcement, and whether it will be rendered more difficult, for example, by movement of assets or by improvident trading, if enforcement is delayed*'.[15]

[B] Challenges to Awards Made in England and Wales

A party against whom an award was made in England and Wales may seek to challenge the award under sections 67–69 of the Arbitration Act 1996, which can be summarised as follows:

- section 67 provides for a challenge to an award on the basis that the tribunal lacked substantive jurisdiction;
- section 68 provides for a challenge to an award on the grounds of serious irregularity affecting the tribunal, the proceedings or the award;[16] and
- under section 69, a party to arbitral proceedings may (upon notice to the other parties and to the tribunal) appeal to the court on a question of law arising out of an award made in the proceedings.[17] Importantly, this provision is non-mandatory: it may be excluded in the parties' arbitration agreement and is effectively excluded by most arbitration rules. In addition, the right to appeal arises only with respect to questions of *English* law. Therefore, an award

14. *Deutsche Schachtbau v. Shell International Petroleum Co. Ltd* [1990] 1 A.C. 295.
15. *Soleh Boneh International Ltd v. Government of the Republic of Uganda* [1993] 2 Lloyd's Rep 208.
16. Section 68 Arbitration Act 1996.
17. Section 69 Arbitration Act 1996.

arising out of an arbitration seated in London in which a tribunal applied a substantive law other than English law would not be capable of appeal under this provision.

[C] Limitation Period

In England, the statutory limitation for enforcing a judgment is six years as per section 7 of the Limitation Act 1980, which also applies to the enforcement of arbitral awards. Although if the arbitration agreement was signed under seal (i.e., in the form of a deed), the limitation period will be twelve years.[18] The limitation period starts on the day of the breach of the express or implied obligation to carry out the award, and not on the date of the arbitration agreement or the award.

§9.06 ENFORCEMENT AGAINST DIRECTORS/OFFICERS

There are numerous causes of action against directors of companies that seek to avoid enforcement. This is particularly the case where a post-judgment freezing order has been made against a Defendant, ensuring that it does not dissipate assets.

The penal notice on a freezing order notifies the Respondent (and anyone else party to it) that a breach of the order may result in contempt proceedings. In many cases, directors are served personally with the freezing order and named in it to ensure the English Court has jurisdiction over them. In such a case, if the assets of a Defendant company are dissipated and the director failed to prevent it, he or she may be personally liable for contempt of Court. It is not required that the director was responsible for the dissipation – failing to ensure that the company complied with an order is sufficient.[19]

Holding a director liable for contempt, however, does not give any damages or compensation – it is simply a punishment for the director. It is usually the company which can take effective measures against directors and officers who attempt to hide or dissipate assets. It is not uncommon, in situations where directors have put the assets out if reach of enforcement, for the company to be put into liquidation and for the insolvency trustee to pursue an action against the directors in the name of the company. Such claims are often brought under sections 213 (Fraudulent Trading) and 214 (Wrongful Trading) of the Insolvency Act 1986 and may require a contribution from the director.

If a situation arises where a company believes a director will destroy documents in order to hide evidence about the misappropriation of assets, the company may apply to the court for a search order (see above). No notice will be given to the director in question. Moreover, the court also has the power to issue a freezing order to prevent

18. Section 8 Limitation Act 1980.
19. *Attorney-General for Tuvalu v. Philatelic Distribution Corp* [1990] 1 WLR 926.

the dissipation of assets (see above). This may be undertaken to freeze bank accounts for instance.

If assets have been diverted to other parties, the court can also make an order to said parties to preserve the assets.

Directors' duties under English law are set out in the Companies Act 2006. The Companies Act 2006 does not provide an exhaustive list and, therefore, common law obligations will provide supplemental obligations. The Companies Act 2006 also provides that certain misconduct committed by directors carries criminal penalties. For instance, if the director conceals information about the affairs of a company by destroying the relevant documents, then he may be guilty of an offence punishable by a maximum of seven years imprisonment and an unlimited fine.

CHAPTER 10

Germany

Jan Heiner Nedden & Friedrich Rosenfeld

§10.01 INTRODUCTION

Germany is a civil law jurisdiction. The legal system distinguishes between public law, criminal law and private law.

The most important source of substantive law in civil matters is the German Civil Code ('*Bürgerliches Gesetzbuch – BGB*'). It comprises five 'books' (sections) covering: (1) the General Part, (2) the Law of Obligations, (3) the Law of Property, (4) the Family Law and (5) the Law of Succession. An official English translation of the German Civil Code is available at: http://www.gesetze-im-internet.de/englisch_bgb/.

The most important source of procedural law in civil matters is the German Code of Civil Procedure ('*Zivilprozessordnung – ZPO*'). It comprises eleven 'books' (sections) covering: (1) General Regulations, (2) Procedural Rules for Proceedings before the Courts of First Instance, (3) Appellate Remedies, (4) the Reopening of Proceedings, (5) Proceedings on Claims arising from a Deed, in which solely Documentary Evidence is submitted, and Proceedings on Claims arising from a Bill of Exchange, (7) Summary Proceedings for a Payment Order,[1] (8) Compulsory Enforcement, (10) Arbitration Proceedings[2] and (11) Judicial Collaboration within the European Union. An official English translation of the German Code of Civil Procedure is available at: http://www.gesetze-im-internet.de/englisch_zpo/index.html.

The part of the German judiciary system which deals with civil matters comprises the following courts: The Federal Court of Justice ('*Bundesgerichtshof*'), higher regional courts ('*Oberlandesgerichte*'), regional courts ('*Landgerichte*') and local courts ('*Amtsgerichte*'). The main German arbitral institution is the German Institution for Arbitration ('*Deutsche Institution für Schiedsgerichtsbarkeit*', or simply 'DIS').

1. The sixth book has been repealed.
2. The ninth book has been repealed.

German law offers a range of fairly efficient mechanisms for identifying a debtor's assets. There is a large number of publicly available registers where relevant information may be retrieved prior to the initiation of a lawsuit or arbitration proceedings. Furthermore, once an enforceable title has been obtained, debtors may be forced to disclose information about their assets in enforcement proceedings. We have dealt with these issues in more detail below under section §10.02.

The German legal system also allows for the freezing of a debtor's assets. Freezing orders may be obtained from State courts or from arbitral tribunals. As described in further detail below in section §10.03, the requirements for obtaining freezing orders are not always easy to meet under German law. For example, the mere fact that a creditor finds itself 'competing' with other creditors provides no sufficient grounds for obtaining a freezing order.

Judgments from courts of Member States of the European Union as well as from Iceland, Norway and Switzerland are enforceable in Germany. Judgments from other States may be enforceable pursuant to bilateral treaties on recognition and enforcement or under the conditions set forth in section 328 of the ZPO.

The enforcement of foreign arbitral awards is governed by sections 1061 et seq. of the ZPO. Germany has ratified the Convention on the Recognition and Enforcement of Foreign Arbitral Awards of 10 June 1958 (the '*New York Convention*'). Also, Germany has adopted the European Convention on International Commercial Arbitration of 21 April 1961, as well as the Convention on the Settlement of Investment Disputes between States and Nationals of Other States of 18 March 1965. German courts are generally regarded as arbitration-friendly. The issue of enforcement of arbitral awards has been addressed in more detail below under section §10.04.

Finally, we have described which remedies German law offers in matters where the enforcement of a judgment or an arbitral award has been unlawfully evaded by the directors or officers of a German company. As will be seen below under section §10.05, attempts to dissipate assets in order to prevent enforcement may trigger both civil and criminal liability under German law.

§10.02 IDENTIFYING ASSETS IN GERMANY

There are various ways to retrieve information about a debtor's assets in Germany.

First of all, there are a large number of public registers and databases, which provide valuable information on the financial situation of debtors. Access to this information does not require the initiation of any legal proceedings. Hence, this way of identifying assets may freely be used prior to and during lawsuits or arbitration proceedings (see in further detail below under section §10.02[A]).

Second, a debtor may be forced to disclose information about his assets in the context of enforcement proceedings. This, however, can only be done if the creditor has obtained an enforceable decision by a court or arbitral tribunal against the debtor (see in further details below under section §10.02[B]).

[A] Identifying Assets outside Enforcement Proceedings

The identification of assets should ideally begin before the initiation of lawsuits or arbitration proceedings. Since creditors do not have an enforceable instrument at this stage, they have to rely on public databases and registers in their efforts to identify assets belonging to a debtor. In relation to legal disputes against German corporations, it is of fundamental importance to first consult: The German insolvency register (see section §10.02[A][1]); the commercial register (section §10.02[A][2]); as well as the company register (see section §10.02[A][3]). These three registers provide essential information about the structure and financial situation of corporations having their seat in Germany. Beyond this, there are registers that provide relevant information about real estate (see section §10.02[A][4]), motor vehicles (see section §10.02[A][5]), vessels (see section §10.02[A][6]), aircrafts (see section §10.02[A][7]) as well as intellectual property rights of debtors (see section §10.02[A][8]).

[1] Insolvency Register

The insolvency register is a public register that contains notifications made by all German insolvency courts. Any initiation of insolvency proceedings is notified through this register. Where reliable data on the economic situation of a given company is missing, it is advisable to check whether any such information has been notified.

The insolvency register may be accessed electronically and is free of charge. Its website can be found here: https://www.insolvenzbekanntmachungen.de/.

[2] Commercial Register

The commercial register ('*Handelsregister*') is a public register that contains various information about companies including their seat, their type of business, their legal form, their authorized representatives as well as their liable principals (if any).

As regards stock companies, the commercial register contains relevant information on the registered capital. In addition, one may find valuable information on the corporate structure of companies in the commercial register. This may also include information about the existence of profit and loss transfer agreements.

The commercial register has its own website and may be accessed electronically against payment of a small fee. The website of the commercial register can be found here: https://www.handelsregister.de.

[3] Company Register

The company register ('*Unternehmensregister*') is the central database for information about German companies. It provides access to the latest financial reports of companies incorporated in Germany. Such financial reports must be filed by: German stock companies ('*Kapitalgesellschaften*'); certain registered partnerships ('*Personenhandelsgesellschaften*'); as well as other companies that fulfil the requirements of section 1 of the German Publicity Act ('*Publizitätsgesetz*'). The company register also contains some of the company information which can be found in the commercial register and in the insolvency register.

The company register has its own website and may be accessed electronically. Some information is free of charge. The website of the company register is as follows: https://www.unternehmensregister.de.

[4] Real Estate

Information about real estate located in Germany is available in the Land Registers ('*Grundbücher*'). The Land Registers are public registers, which contain information about ownership to plots of lands, mortgages, liens and other third-party rights. Under German law, there is a presumption that the contents of the Land Registers are accurate.

The Land Registers are usually administered by the competent local court of the district where the property is located. In the absence of a nationwide Land Register, it is in practice impossible to conduct a general search on all property of a certain debtor. Land Registers are therefore mainly used in order to *verify* the ownership as well as the existence of encumbrances with regard to a specific property at a given location.

Some local courts have created electronic Land Registers, which are available online. Access to information contained in Land Registers will only be given to parties with a justified interest against payment of a small fee.

[5] Motor Vehicles

The Motor Vehicles Register ('*Fahrzeugregister*') contains information about the registered 'keepers' of motor vehicles. A registered keeper is often also the owner of the respective motor vehicle, but this need not necessarily be the case.

The Motor Vehicles Register may only be consulted through public entities. Private persons have no direct access to the information contained therein. In the context of enforcement proceedings, a court-appointed enforcement officer may, however, request such information according to section 802 c l of the ZPO.

[6] Vessels

Information about vessels is available in the German Vessel Registers ('*Schiffsregister*'). The Vessel Registers contain information about the ownership to vessels sailing under German flag and about any rights of third parties to German vessels (including for instance mortgages, attachments, usufructs, etc.). Similar to the Land Registers, there is a presumption that the contents of the Vessel Registers are accurate.

The Vessel Registers are usually administered by the competent local court of the district where the vessel has its home port. In the absence of a nationwide Vessel Register, it is in practice not possible to conduct a general search for all vessels belonging to a certain debtor. Vessel Registers are therefore mainly used in order to verify the ownership as well as the existence of liens or other third-party rights with regard to concrete vessels.

[7] Aircrafts

Information about the ownership of aircrafts is available in the German Aircraft Register (*'Luftfahrzeugrolle'*). The information contained in the German Aircraft Register is generally not accessible to the public. In exceptional circumstances, however, the register may be accessed where this is necessary in order to assert, secure or enforce claims in connection with air traffic.

Information on liens in aircrafts is available in the Register for Liens in Aircrafts (*'Register für Pfandrechte an Luftfahrzeugen'*). This register is administered by the local court of Braunschweig. It can be accessed by the public via the following website: http://www.amtsgericht-braunschweig.niedersachsen.de.

[8] IP Rights

The German Patent and Trademark Office (*'Deutsches Patent- und Markenamt'*) administers the German patent-, utility model-, design- and trademark-registers. Information may be retrieved electronically by the public through this website: https://register.dpma.de/DPMAregister/uebersicht.

Information regarding the ownership of German Internet domain names can be found here: http://www.denic.de/.

[B] Identifying Assets in Enforcement Proceedings

Once a creditor has obtained an enforceable instrument against a certain debtor, he may – insofar as the debtor does not willingly pay the amount owed – initiate enforcement proceedings in order to retrieve information related to the debtor's assets.

In this respect, section 802 c of the ZPO, places an obligation on the debtor to disclose – at the request of the court-appointed enforcement officer – relevant information about his financial situation and about the assets, which he owns, to thereby facilitate the enforcing of the claim. As a general rule, this obligation to provide information extends to *all* assets of the debtor. An exception applies to certain objects that are exempted from enforcement.[3] The debtor is required to confirm by statutory declaration (*in lieu* of an oath) that the information is, to the best of his knowledge, correct and complete.[4]

According to section 802 e of the ZPO, the court-appointed enforcement officer of the local court in the district in which the debtor has his place of residence is competent to take the information related to the debtor's financial circumstances and assets. This

3. Section 802 c paragraph 2 ZPO.
4. Section 802 c paragraph 3 ZPO.

court-appointed enforcement officer is also competent to administer the statutory declaration *in lieu* of an oath.

The procedure of administrating the declaration (*in lieu* of an oath) is governed by section 802 f of the ZPO. According to this provision, the competent court-appointed enforcement officer sets a deadline of two weeks to settle the claims. Concurrently, the court-appointed enforcement officer sets a date for the statutory declaration to be made shortly after expiry of the deadline.

It is worth noting that a false declaration given by the debtor may trigger criminal liability under section 156 of the German Criminal Code ('*Strafgesetzbuch*', '*StGB*').[5]

Should the debtor fail to appear at the hearing, or should he refuse to make the statutory declaration without citing any legitimate reasons for such refusal, the competent court may issue an arrest warrant if the creditor so requests.[6]

§10.03 INTERIM MEASURES

Under German law, it is possible to obtain interim relief providing for the freezing of assets belonging to the debtor. A freezing order may be obtained from the German State courts (see section §10.03[A]) or – where the debtor and the creditor have entered into an arbitration agreement – from a competent arbitral tribunal (see section §10.03[B]). The EU Regulation on Account Preservation Orders,[7] which has been mentioned in several other chapters of this book, will enter into force in Germany as of 18 January 2017.[8]

[A] Freezing Orders Rendered by State Courts

Freezing orders may be obtained pursuant to sections 916 et seq. of the ZPO.

A freezing order is a remedy that secures compulsory enforcement against movable or immovable property. It can be obtained under two main conditions:

(1) the creditor must demonstrate to the satisfaction of the court that he has a monetary claim or a claim that may evolve to become a monetary claim. The admissibility of a freezing order is generally not ruled out by the fact that a claim is subject to conditions or has a fixed maturity date.[9] Exceptions to this main rule are made where the possibility of the condition being met is so remote that the claim is worthless.

(2) the creditor must demonstrate to the satisfaction of the court that there are grounds for a freezing order to be issued. In this respect, section 917 of the

5. Baumbach / Lauterbach / Albers / Hartmann, Zivilprozessordnung, 74th edition 2016, section 802 c ZPO margin no. 2.
6. Section 802 g ZPO.
7. Regulation (EU) No. 655/2014 of the European Parliament and of the Council of 15 May 2014 establishing a European Account Preservation Order procedure to facilitate cross-border debt recovery in civil and commercial matters.
8. With the exception of Article 50, which enters into force as of 18 July 2016.
9. Section 916 paragraph 2 ZPO.

> ZPO specifies that a freezing order is only available wherever there are real concerns that the enforcement of the judgment would become frustrated or significantly more difficult if the freezing order were not rendered. German courts apply a very high standard of proof in this regard. The mere competition with other creditors over the assets of the debtor is, for example, not sufficient for obtaining a freezing order.[10] The situation is different if a future judgment would have to be enforced abroad and if no reciprocity has been granted with respect to the foreign State where the assets are located. In such a situation, a sufficient basis for obtaining a freezing order is deemed to exist.[11]

Section 919 of the ZPO designates the competent court for issuing a freezing order. According to this provision, the competence lies with the court before which the main action is being pursued or, alternatively, the local court in the district of which the asset to be frozen is situated. Pursuant to section 920 of the ZPO, the application for a freezing order has to designate the claim, to specify the amount of money or the monetary value and to demonstrate the existence of grounds for obtaining a freezing order.

The court renders its decision by judgment or court order. Judgments may only be rendered after the debtor has been heard. Decisions without a hearing are rendered by means of a court order against which the debtor may lodge an opposition. In cases where such opposition is lodged, a final judgment on the lawfulness of the freezing order has to be rendered.

A freezing order may be set aside upon corresponding application in situations where the creditor does not start the main proceedings within a period to be determined by the court. Alternatively, the order may be set aside in case of a change in circumstances, including an offer of the debtor to provide security for the creditor's claim.

The enforcement of a freezing order is governed by the rules on compulsory enforcement. According to these rules, bank accounts may be attached and a security right thereto may be created. Should the freezing order prove to have been unfounded from the State or should it turn out that it ought to have been repealed, the party that has obtained the order is under an obligation to compensate the opponent pursuant to section 945 of the ZPO. This liability risk should always be taken into careful consideration by a creditor seeking a freezing order because if it subsequently turns out that the freezing order was unwarranted (e.g., because creditor's claim did not exist) this may give rise to significant claims for damages.

10. Baumbach / Lauterbach / Albers / Hartmann, German Code of Civil Procedure, 74th edition 2016, section 917 ZPO margin no. 7.
11. Section 917 paragraph 2 ZPO.

[B] Freezing Orders Rendered by Arbitral Tribunals

Freezing orders may also be issued by arbitral tribunals. For arbitration proceedings with the seat of the tribunal in Germany, the relevant rules are found in section 1041 of the ZPO. This provision is largely similar to Article 17 of the UNCITRAL Model Law, in its original version. The recently added provisions of the modified UNCITRAL Model Law on interim relief have not (yet) been adopted by the German legislator.[12]

Section 1041 paragraph 1 of the ZPO provides that an arbitral tribunal may direct provisional measures or measures serving to provide security as it deems fit with a view to the subject matter of the arbitration. In connection with such measures, the arbitral tribunal is entitled to order the parties to provide reasonable security.

Upon a corresponding petition, the competent State court may permit the enforcement of such measure. This, however, does not apply in situations where a corresponding measure of *temporary* relief has already been petitioned with a different State court.

Should an order for an interim measure pursuant to section 1041 paragraph 1 of the ZPO prove to have been unfounded from the start, the party that has obtained the measure is under an obligation to compensate the opposing party for any loss suffered as a result of the interim measure.[13] In this respect, the liability risk is similar to the one existing in case of freezing orders being rendered within the framework of civil proceedings.[14]

As an alternative to requesting freezing orders from an arbitral tribunal, the parties may also file an application with the competent court for a preliminary measure. According to section 1033 of the ZPO, an arbitration agreement does not prevent a State court from ordering provisional measures or the provision of security with regard to the subject matter of a dispute that falls within the scope of the arbitration agreement. The application of section 1033 of the ZPO does not presuppose that the place of arbitration is located in Germany.[15]

§10.04 ENFORCEMENT ISSUES

When a creditor seeks enforcement of a foreign judgment or arbitral award in Germany, he or she needs to examine first whether such decision qualifies as an enforceable instrument in Germany (see sub-section §10.04[A] below). Only if this requirement is fulfilled, can the creditor proceed by taking enforcement measures (see sub-section §10.04[B] below).

12. Münch, in: Münchener Kommentar, 4th edition 2013, section 1041 ZPO margin no. 1.
13. Section 1041 paragraph 4 ZPO.
14. See section §10.03[A].
15. This follows from section 1025 paragraph 2 ZPO which reads: *The stipulations of sections 1032, 1033 and 1050 are to be applied also in those cases in which the venue of the arbitration proceedings is located abroad or has not yet been determined.*

[A] Existence of an Enforceable Instrument

[1] Judgments

Judgments rendered by the courts of other European Union Member States qualify as an enforceable instrument according to section 794 paragraph 1 No. 9 of the ZPO in conjunction with Regulation No. 1215/2012 of 12 December 2012 of the European Parliament and of the Council on jurisdiction and the recognition and enforcement of judgments in civil and commercial matters (also known as the '*recast Brussels Regulation*'). Such judgments do not need to be declared enforceable in separate exequatur proceedings.

The same applies to: (i) enforceable European orders for payment according to Regulation (EC) No. 1896/2006;[16] (ii) titles that have been confirmed under the European Enforcement Order for uncontested claims according to Regulation (EC) No. 805/2004;[17] as well as (iii) instruments that have been rendered according to Regulation (EC) No. 861/2007 under the European Small Claims Procedure.[18]

The enforcement of judgments rendered by the courts in Iceland, Norway and Switzerland is governed by the Convention on Jurisdiction and the Recognition and Enforcement of Judgments in Civil and Commercial Matters done in Lugano on 30 October 2007 ('*Lugano Convention 2007*'). The Lugano Convention came into force in Germany on 1 January 2010 and is directly applicable under German law.[19] The German Recognition and Enforcement Implementation Act only contains supplementary provisions[20] and regulates the competence of the German courts in relation to the issuing of certificates that are necessary under Articles 54, 57 and 58 of the Lugano Convention 2007.[21]

In the absence of special rules under European law or international treaties,[22] the enforcement of foreign judgments is governed by the default rules contained in sections 722 and 723 of the ZPO. Pursuant to these provisions, the enforcement of foreign judgments may only be pursued if this has been ruled admissible by a judgment for

16. Section 794 paragraph 1 No. 6 in conjunction with Regulation (EC) No. 1896/2006 of the European Parliament and of the Council of 12 December 2006 creating a European order for payment procedure.
17. Section 794 paragraph 1 No. 7 ZPO in conjunction with Regulation (EC) No. 805/2004 of the European Parliament and of the Council of 21 April 2004 creating a European Enforcement Order for uncontested claims.
18. Section 794 paragraph 1 No. 8 ZPO in conjunction with Regulation (EC) No. 861/2007 of the European Parliament and of the Council of 11 July 2007.
19. Cf. section 1 paragraph 1 No. 2, paragraph 2 of the German Recognition and Enforcement Implementation Act ('*Gesetz zur Ausführung zwischenstaatlicher Verträge und zur Durchführung von Verordnungen und Abkommen der Europäischen Gemeinschaft auf dem Gebiet der Anerkennung und Vollstreckung in Zivil- und Handelssachen – AVAG*').
20. Sections 55, 56 of the German Recognition and Enforcement Implementation Act.
21. Section 57 of the German Recognition and Enforcement Implementation Act.
22. See, e.g., Treaty concerning the reciprocal recognition and enforcement of judicial decisions in civil and commercial matters (with exchange of letters) signed in Jerusalem on 20 July 1977, U.N.T.S. No. 20324.

enforcement. A judgment for enforcement will normally be granted, provided that recognition is not ruled out pursuant to section 328 of the ZPO.

Section 328 ZPO sets forth the general rule that foreign judgments are recognized, *unless*:

- The courts of the State to which the foreign court belongs do not have jurisdiction according to German law.
- The defendant, where the foreign judgment has been rendered by default and the defendant has objected to this, has not been duly served with the writ, or has not been served in such time to allow him to defend himself.
- The judgment is incompatible with a judgment rendered in Germany, or with an earlier judgment handed down abroad that is to be recognized under German law, or if the proceedings on which such judgment is based are incompatible with proceedings that have become pending earlier in Germany.
- The recognition of the judgment would lead to a result that is obviously incompatible with essential principles of German law, and in particular if the recognition is not compatible with fundamental rights.
- Reciprocity has not been granted.

Foreign judgments under section 328 of the ZPO cover all final decisions on the merits that are rendered in civil matters.[23] They must be valid in the jurisdiction in which they have been rendered.[24] The requirement of reciprocity under section 328 no. 5 of the ZPO has the effect that a foreign judgment will only be recognized if a comparable German judgment would be recognized in the jurisdiction where the foreign judgment was rendered.[25]

[2] Foreign Arbitral Awards

Foreign arbitral awards do not as such qualify as an enforceable instrument in Germany. Instead, they have to be declared enforceable.

According to section 1061 paragraph 1 of the ZPO, the recognition and enforcement of foreign arbitral awards is governed by the New York Convention.[26] According to section 1025 of the ZPO, an arbitral award qualifies as a foreign award if it was rendered by a tribunal sitting in a jurisdiction outside Germany.

23. Bach, in: Vorwerk / Wolf, Beck'scher Online Commentary ZPO, date: 1 September 2015, section 328 ZPO margin no. 1.
24. Bach, in: Vorwerk / Wolf, Beck'scher Online Commentary ZPO, date: 1 September 2015, section 328 ZPO margin no. 12.
25. Bach, in: Vorwerk / Wolf, Beck'scher Online Commentary ZPO, date: 1 September 2015, section 328 ZPO margin no. 46.
26. This provision does not cover ICSID awards, which are enforced in accordance with the 'Gesetz zu dem Übereinkommen vom 18. März 1965 zur Beilegung von Investitionsstreitigkeiten zwischen Staaten und Angehörigen anderer Staaten' (Act on the Implementation of the ICSID Convention).

Pursuant to section 1062 paragraph 1 No. 4, paragraph 2 of the ZPO, the Higher Regional Court in the district in which the respondent has his registered seat or his habitual place of residence is competent to declare foreign arbitral awards enforceable.

The petition for a declaration of enforceability has to be accompanied by the award or a certified copy thereof.[27] The certification may be performed by the attorney retained and authorized for the court proceedings.[28]

While a certified translation of the award is not a requirement under section 1064 of the ZPO, it is often recommendable furnishing the German court with at least a certified translation of the conclusions of the award, because German is the official court language in Germany.[29] Further, according to section 142 paragraph 3 of the ZPO, German courts may request that documents prepared in a foreign language be accompanied by a certified translation. It may therefore save time to submit a translation of the award already at the beginning of the proceedings.

The Higher Regional Court renders its decisions in the form of court orders.[30] The court order by which an arbitral award is declared enforceable is to be declared provisionally enforceable.[31]

Prior to the issuing of the court order, the respondent will be heard.[32] The Higher Regional Court may hear the respondent in two ways: (i) it may either order an oral hearing to take place; or (ii) grant the parties a right to file written submissions.[33] The Higher Regional Court enjoys discretion in this regard.[34] According to section 1063 paragraph 2 of the ZPO, an oral hearing is only mandatory if the setting-aside of the arbitral award has been petitioned, or if grounds for setting-aside pursuant to section 1059 paragraph 2 of the ZPO are conceivable.

The court order may be challenged by a complaint based on legal issues. However, this is only possible on limited grounds.[35] It presupposes that the legal matter is of fundamental significance or that the further development of the law is at stake.

It is hardly possible to predict with certainty how long it takes to obtain a decision declaring an arbitral award enforceable. Various factors may have an impact on the length of the proceedings. Among others, it will be relevant whether the respondent defends himself and whether an oral hearing takes place. As a rough estimate, one can expect the proceedings to last between three and twelve months.

Given the time that may be needed to declare an arbitral award enforceable, there may be a need for interim relief according to section 1063 paragraph 3 of the ZPO. This provision entitles the presiding judge to direct that the petitioner may pursue preliminary enforcement under the arbitral award until a decision has been delivered

27. Section 1064 paragraphs 1, 3 ZPO.
28. This deviation from Article IV of the New York Convention is permissible under Article VII.
29. Section 184 Court Organization Act ('*Gerichtsverfassungsgesetz* – GVG').
30. Section 1063 paragraph 1 ZPO.
31. Section 1064 paragraph 2 ZPO.
32. Section 1063 paragraph 1 ZPO.
33. Voit, in: Musielak, 12th edition 2015, section 1063 ZPO margin no. 6.
34. Voit, in: Musielak, 12th edition 2015, section 1063 ZPO margin no. 3.
35. Section 1065 paragraph 1 ZPO in conjunction with section 574 paragraph 1 No. 1 ZPO.

regarding the petition to declare the arbitral award enforceable. Preliminary enforcement may not extend beyond measures serving to provide security. The respondent can avoid preliminary enforcement by providing security for the claim.

[B] Enforcement Measures

Once a creditor has obtained an enforceable instrument, he may proceed with the enforcement against the debtor.

Enforcement generally requires - apart from the existence of an enforceable instrument - a court having issued a 'certificate of enforceability' as well as the instrument having been served on the debtor. The 'certificate of enforceability' is attached to the instrument to evidence its enforceability.[36] It is usually issued by the records clerk of the Higher Regional Court's registry.[37] Further, the instrument has to be served on the debtor.[38] Service may be affected by the court[39] or by a court-appointed enforcement officer.[40] Exceptions from this general rule may apply for certain titles governed by European regulations or international treaties.[41]

Apart from the above-mentioned general conditions of enforcement, there are special requirements that have to be observed for the respective enforcement measure. For the enforcement of monetary claims, three different enforcement measures may be chosen: (1) enforcement against movable property, (2) enforcement against claims and rights, and (3) enforcement against immovable property.

The attachment of tangible assets in the debtor's possession is affected in the form of an attachment order issued by a court-appointed enforcement officer.[42] Tangibles other than money, valuables that can easily be sold and securities will normally be left in the custody of the debtor unless doing so jeopardizes the creditor's chances of enforcing the claim.[43] By means of the attachment order, the creditor acquires a pledge on the tangible assets in question.[44] Any attached cash amount will be surrendered to the creditor.[45] Other objects are to be sold at a public auction.[46]

Enforcement against claims against third parties and other property rights of the debtor is also carried out by means of an order for the attachment and transfer.[47] The competent court is generally the local court where the debtor has his habitual residence

36. Rützl / Krapfl, in: Böckstiegel / Kröll / Nacimiento (eds.), Arbitration in Germany, 2nd edition 2015, p. 1068.
37. Section 724 paragraph 2 ZPO in conjunction with sections 795, 794 ZPO.
38. Section 750 ZPO in conjunction with sections 795, 794 ZPO.
39. Section 317 ZPO.
40. Sections 192 et seq. ZPO.
41. Section 1093 ZPO, for example, provides that the enforcement of a European payment order issued and declared enforceable pursuant to Council Regulation (EC) No. 1896/2006 does not require a court certificate of enforceability.
42. Section 803 ZPO.
43. Section 808 ZPO.
44. Section 804 ZPO.
45. Section 815 ZPO.
46. Section 814 ZPO.
47. Sections 829, 835 ZPO.

in Germany.[48] An application for this form of enforcement must include the names and addresses of the creditor, the debtor and the third party owing the debt (*'Drittschuldner'*). In addition, the alleged claim to be attached and its legal foundation must be specified as precisely as possible.[49]

In order to close the time gap between the application for an attachment and transfer and the actual attachment of the claims or property rights, a creditor may give a notice of imminent attachment pursuant to section 845 of the ZPO. Such notification to third-party debtors has the effect of a seizure, provided that the claim is attached within one month from the date when the notice is served on the debtor.

Enforcement against immovable property is affected by either an entry of a debt-securing mortgage for the claim on the land registry, or enforced action, or by receivership.[50] Enforcement against immovable property presupposes an application with the local court where the property is located.

§10.05 D&O LIABILITY IN RELATION TO ASSET PROTECTION SCHEMES

As a general rule, it is difficult to pierce the corporate veil and hold the officers or directors of a German corporate entity personally liable for any illicit asset protection schemes, which the company has involved itself in. Notwithstanding, certain actions of officers and/or directors of German companies may trigger a civil liability (see sub-section §10.05[A] below) and/or even a criminal liability (see sub-section §10.05[B] below).

[A] Civil Liability

Asset protection schemes may trigger civil liability according to section 826 of the BGB. This provision provides:

> A person who, in a manner contrary to public policy, intentionally inflicts damage on another person is liable to the other person to make compensation for the damage.

Acts that are committed with the aim of foiling the enforcement of valid claims owed by a German company, such as the hiding or dissipation of assets, may be contrary to public policy. Accordingly, officers of companies risk attracting liability under the above provision if their actions result in a foreseeable loss or damages to the creditors of the company and provided that they act intentionally.

In addition, officers and directors of companies may attract a civil liability according to section 823 paragraph 2 of the BGB to the extent that they violate a statute that is designed to protect another person (a so-called *Schutzgesetz*). For example, the

48. Section 828 ZPO.
49. Rützl / Krapfl, in: Böckstiegel / Kröll / Nacimiento (eds.), Arbitration in Germany, 2nd edition 2015, p. 1072; Becker, in: Musielak, 11th edition 2014, section 829 ZPO margin nos 2 et seq.
50. Section 866 ZPO. For details, see Rützl/Krapfl, in: Böckstiegel / Kröll / Nacimiento (eds.), Arbitration in Germany, 2nd edition 2015, p. 1074 et seq.

violation of mandatory accounting obligations, the failure to file for bankruptcy or the commission of the below-mentioned criminal offences may trigger liability according to this provision.

[B] Criminal Liability

The German Criminal Code[51] (*'Strafgesetzbuch - StGB'*) as well as the Insolvency Statute[52] (*'Insolvenzordnung'*) prohibit various actions that are sometimes seen in the context of an insolvency.

The crime of bankruptcy pursuant to section 283 of the StGB, for example, sanctions the disposition or hiding of certain assets in situations of impending inability to pay debts. Other omissions such as the failure to draw up an accurate balance sheet may also trigger criminal liability under this section.

The German Criminal Code also penalizes the evasion of enforcement of judgments.[53] Although this Section presupposes that the debtor *sells* or otherwise disposes of parts of *his* assets with the intent of obstructing enforcement of claims by the creditors, the evasion of enforcement for the benefit of a corporation is also punishable.[54] Other notable provisions in this regard are sections 9, 30, 130 of the Act on Regulatory Offences (*'Gesetz über Ordnungswidrigkeiten – OWiG'*), which may also be applied to sanction certain asset protection schemes.

Asset protection schemes may thus constitute a number of different penal offences including, but not limited to fraud,[55] embezzlement and abuse of trust[56] or unlawful appropriation.[57]

---

51. The official English translation of the German Criminal Code is available at: http://www.gesetze-im-internet.de/englisch_stgb/englisch_stgb.html#p2291.
The official English translation of the German Criminal Code is available at: http://www.gesetze-im-internet.de/englisch_stgb/englisch_stgb.html#p2291.
52. The official English translation of the German Insolvency Statute is available at: http://www.gesetze-im-internet.de/englisch_inso/index.html.
53. Section 288 StGB.
54. Section 14 paragraph 1 StGB.
55. Section 263 StGB.
56. Section 266 StGB.
57. Section 246 StGB.

CHAPTER 11

Hong Kong

Colin Cohen

§11.01 INTRODUCTION

Ever since the handover of sovereignty in 1997, Hong Kong has been governed under the principle of 'One Country, Two Systems'.[1] The Basic Law, the mini-constitution of Hong Kong, has preserved the common law system, which was largely inherited from the legal system of England and Wales during the colonial period.[2] While the judgments of higher courts in Hong Kong are binding to the lower courts, those of all other common law jurisdictions are persuasive precedents, which can be taken into consideration by the courts when making decisions.

In Hong Kong, there are a number of sources open to the public to identify assets. These sources, as described in further detail in section §11.02 below, are easily accessible online.

While there may be risks of dissipating or destroying assets during the course of litigation or arbitration proceedings, interim relief can be sought to preserve and identify assets belonging to the defendant. In section §11.03, we will discuss the interim reliefs available in Hong Kong. To a large extent, the interim reliefs in Hong Kong resemble those of England and Wales. A party can thus apply for a Mareva Injunction to restrain the opposing party, or his agents, from removing or disposing certain assets. He can also seek an Anton Piller order to enter and search the premises of another for the purpose of inspecting or preserving assets.

Regarding the judiciary system in Hong Kong, it comprises of the Court of Final Appeal, the Court of Appeal, the Court of First Instance, the District Court and six Magistracy Courts. Applications for Mareva Injunctions and Anton Piller Orders have

1. Basic Law, Preamble.
2. Basic Law, Article 8.

to be made to the Court of First Instance or to the District Court, depending on the size of the assets involved.

As to the arbitration system, Hong Kong has its own arbitration centre – the Hong Kong Arbitration Centre (HKIAC), which is responsible for appointing arbitrators and determining the number of arbitrators when the parties cannot reach an agreement.[3] Further, the International Court of Arbitration of the Internal Chamber of Commerce, as well as the China International Economic and Trade Arbitration Commission have both set up branches in Hong Kong.[4]

In section §11.04, we will go through the rules concerning the enforcement of foreign judgments and arbitral awards in Hong Kong.

It is not uncommon that directors and owners of a company attempt to remove its assets in order to help the company escape legal liabilities. In the last section of this chapter, we will describe what type of liabilities directors and owners of a company may attract in relation to (illicit) asset protection schemes under the laws of Hong Kong.

§11.02 IDENTIFYING ASSETS IN HONG KONG

In Hong Kong, there are two main ways of identifying the assets of another party without initiating bankruptcy proceedings against such party, namely by (1) obtaining a court order; and (2) by conducting asset searches in publicly available registers.

[A] Court Order: Norwich Pharmacal Order[5]

The Hong Kong Courts may intervene to make orders to request third parties to provide assistance in identifying assets. The so-called Norwich Pharmacal Order is an exception to the rule that the plaintiff is not allowed to require an innocent third party to disclose documents related to the defendant in litigation. In order to apply for such an order, the plaintiff must satisfy the court that there was cogent evidence to demonstrate that serious tortious activities had taken place; and a Norwich Pharmacal Order would, or would very likely, reap substantial and worthwhile benefits for the plaintiff.[6]

Norwich Pharmacal Order is a very useful tool to preserve or identify assets if the plaintiff seeks to trace the assets, which are misappropriated in the third party's activities. It is particularly helpful to discover bank statements (and other documents from banks) to ascertain the assets flow of the defendant.

3. Department of Justice of the HKSAR, *Arbitration*, at http://www.doj.gov.hk/eng/public/arbitration.html.
4. *Ibid.*
5. *Norwich Pharmacal Co v. Customs and Exercise Commissioners* [1974] A.C. 133.
6. *A Co v. B Co* [2002] 3 HKLRD 111, p. 117.

[B] Public Searches

In Hong Kong, it is straightforward to conduct public searches on assets since registers and databases are readily available to the public online.

[1] Land

With its limited land resources, real estate is probably one of the most valuable types of assets in Hong Kong. It is thus very useful to find out the particulars of owners of land. The Hong Kong Land Registry provides the Integrated Registration Information System Online Services for the public to conduct searches on land properties. A land search contains information related to among other things: The previous and current owners of a property; the date of assignments; encumbrances registered on the property; etc. With regards to the encumbrances registered on the property, information as to whether the property is subject to any mortgage or tenancy agreements is also included in the Integrated Registration Information System. Most importantly, the public can apply for copies of the title deeds against payment of the prescribed fees.

The Integrated Registration Information System Online Services of the Hong Kong Land Registry is available here: https://www2.iris.gov.hk/eservices/searchland register/search.jsp.

[2] Motor Vehicles

With regard to information about motor vehicles in Hong Kong, the public can go online to apply for a Certificate of Particulars of Motor Vehicle. The Certificate reveals the history of any motor vehicle registered in Hong Kong.

For more information about the Online Application for a Certificate of Particulars of Motor Vehicle, please refer to the website: http://www.gov.hk/en/residents/transport/vehicle/certofparticulars.htm

[3] Vessels

An application for obtaining particulars of vessels registered in Hong Kong is somewhat more complicated. The application can be made to any district marine office. However, the Marine Department will only accept the application if it is made:

(1) Pursuant to a court order.
(2) By the vessel owner himself.
(3) By a person with written consent of the vessel owner.
(4) To verify the vessel owner and particulars for filing a civil action.

The person making the application has to send a letter signed by himself stating the reasons for the request, enclosing a copy of his identity card. If the application is made with the written consent of the owner, the consent letter must also be produced.

For more information about applications for obtaining particulars of vessels registered in Hong Kong, please refer to this website: http://www.mardep.gov.hk/en/information/home.html.

[4] *Aircrafts*

Even though an application for the *registration* of aircrafts can be made to Civil Aviation Department, online searches *cannot* be done into the particulars of aircrafts registered in Hong Kong.

[C] Intellectual Property Rights

The IPD Online Search System is operated by the Hong Kong Intellectual Property Department. Searches on trademarks, patents and designs registered in Hong Kong can be made via this system.

The IPD Online Search System is available here: http://ipsearch.ipd.gov.hk/index.html.

[D] Bankruptcy and Winding-Up Searches

Even though there are a number of methods available for identifying assets in Hong Kong, there is no mechanism of registering or identifying 'bad debtors' in the jurisdiction.

However, bankruptcy proceedings involving individuals or companies in Hong Kong as well as winding-up proceedings for companies are registered and can be searched online via this website: https://e-services2.oro.gov.hk/search/general/declaration.html?_flowExecutionKey=_cA7BE093E-7C39-5A7F-45AB-387114189EC9_k70C9A197-87A8-016A-54B3-EEB6003D0286.

[E] Financial Reports

Generally speaking, the public can have access to the information of a private company incorporated in Hong Kong by conducting a company search. Information available in a company search includes among other things: Directors' particulars, and a register of charges as well as information about the company's annual return. The Cyber Search Centre of the Integrated Companies Registry Information System is available here: http://www.icris.cr.gov.hk/csci/.

A person, who is neither a shareholder nor a director of a company, is *not* entitled to receive copies of the financial reports of a company incorporated in Hong Kong. Only shareholders and directors can obtain copies of the financial statements of a company.[7] However, information about companies listed on the Hong Kong Stock Exchange,

7. Companies Ordinance (Cap. 622), s. 435(1).

including their interim and annual financial reports, is publicly available on http://www.hkexnews.hk/.

§11.03 INTERIM RELIEFS

The law of Hong Kong related to the granting of Mareva Injunctions and Anton Piller Orders is similar to English law. Both Mareva Injunctions and Anton Piller Orders are generally regarded as draconian reliefs – dramatically described by some as 'nuclear bombs in a litigant's arsenal' – and a party seeking such relief must therefore show clear and solid evidence in support of his application.[8]

As mentioned, whether an application is made to the District Court or to the Court of First Instance depends on the value of the assets involved. The District Court has jurisdiction to grant and enforce injunctions affecting movable property with a value not exceeding HKD 1,000,000 and immovable property with value not exceeding HKD 240,000.[9] The Court of First Instance has jurisdiction over cases concerning assets of a higher value.

Interim reliefs granted by the Court of First Instance are governed by the High Court Ordinance (Cap. 4), the Rules of the High Court (Cap. 4A) and the Practice Direction 11.2.

The Hong Kong Court will exercise discretion in granting interlocutory injunctions. In all circumstances, it will only grant injunctions when it is just or convenient to do so.[10]

In relation to interim reliefs granted in aid of arbitration proceedings, the relevant rules are to be found in the Arbitration Ordinance, the United Nations Commission on Internal Trade Law and the UNCITRAL Model Law on International Commercial Arbitration.

[A] Mareva Injunctions in Hong Kong[11]

The Mareva Injunction is a remedy originated in the United Kingdom. It was designed to restrain a defendant, or its agent, from disposing or even dealing with the assets embraced by the injunction.[12] The Mareva Injunction is an effective measure to prevent the defendant from defeating the plaintiff's interest by dissipating assets.

8. *China Merchants Bank & Orders v. I-China Holdings Ltd & Another* [2003] 1 HKLRD 271, paragraph 9.
9. District Court Ordinance (Cap. 336), s. 52(1).
10. High Court Ordinance (Cap. 4), s. 21L(1).
11. *Mareva Compania Naviera SA v. International Bulk Carriers* SA [1980] 1 All E.R. 213.
12. Judith Sihombing, *Asia Business Guide – Hong Kong Commentary* (Hong Kong: Sweet & Maxwell, 2013), paragraph 70.023.

[1] Procedure

In order to enhance the effectiveness of a Mareva Injunction to prevent any dissipation of assets beforehand, applications in the Hong Kong Court can be made ex parte where the defendant will not be informed until the injunction is ordered.[13] In return, the plaintiff has to make full and frank disclosure of all material facts of the matter.[14] In *Intercontinental Housing Development Ltd v. Quek Teck-huat and Others,*[15] the court stressed the importance of full and frank disclosure. The court would be slow in granting a Mareva Injunction even though non-disclosure is not deliberate since the plaintiff has gained an advantage, which he was not entitled to.[16]

The plaintiff has to make a draft order in the form specified in Practice Direction 11.2, under which undertakings have to be made. If the plaintiff opts to deviate from the standard form in a material respect, the judge should be informed of such changes.[17] In *Jen Kit Josephine v. Chan Sau Wai Shirley,*[18] the defendant contested the Mareva Injuction order, which had been obtained by the plaintiff on the grounds of irregularities. The Judge held that compliance with the order was difficult since it did not provide an exception to the injunction permitting the defendant to spend a specified sum towards his ordinary living expenses and required the defendant to disclose a complete list of her assets, contrary to the standard form in Practice Direction 11.2.[19]

If the court decides to grant a Mareva Injunction, an *inter parte* hearing will usually follow to allow the defendant to present his case for discharge.[20]

[2] Scope

Having said that the Mareva Injunction is a 'draconian' weapon, which requires the Court's careful consideration and restriction, the scope of grating such injunction can be very wide indeed. Under section 21L(3) of the High Court Ordinance,[21] the Court has the power to grant freezing orders over the assets within the jurisdiction of a party 'in cases where he is not, domiciled or resident or present within the jurisdiction'. In order to make the Mareva Injunction order effective, it also binds third parties.[22]

13. The Rules of Hong Kong (Cap. 4A), O.29, r. 1.
14. The Hon. Justice Fok, *Hong Kong Civil Procedure* (Hong Kong: Sweet & Maxwell, 2015), paragraph 29/1/71.
15. [1986] HKLR 1153.
16. *Ibid.*, P. 1162.
17. Practice Direction 11.2, paragraph 3.
18. [2014] HKEC 1851.
19. *Ibid*, paragraphs 20–22.
20. *Supra* n. 14, paragraph 29/1/72.
21. *Supra* n. 10.
22. *Supra* n. 17.

[3] Grounds

Not only does the plaintiff have to make full and frank disclosure and prove that it is just and convenient in granting a Mareva Injunction, but the plaintiff also has to satisfy the following grounds:[23]

(1) He has a good arguable case.
(2) The defendant has assets within the jurisdiction.
(3) There is a real risk of dissipation of assets.
(4) There is balance of convenience in favour of the grant.

(1) Good Arguable Case

It is not necessary for the plaintiff to *win* the case or show a better than 50% chance of success, but the plaintiff needs to show that the case is 'more than barely capable of serious argument'.[24] The Court will look at the evidence through the affirmation presented by the parties.

(2) Assets within Jurisdiction

The amount of 'assets' within the jurisdiction (i.e., Hong Kong) refers to a level which cannot exceed the plaintiff's claim. However, even if the defendant does not have any assets in Hong Kong, the plaintiff could still seek a Worldwide Mareva Injunction, as explained in section §11.03[B] of this chapter.

(3) Real Risk of Dissipation

Whether there is a real risk of dissipation by the defendant has always been a main issue in Mareva Injunction applications or discharge applications. As discussed, the Mareva Injunction is widely regarded as 'nuclear weapon' in litigation, which invades the defendant's right to use his property. As such, the Hong Kong Court requires the plaintiff to show solid evidence of a real risk of dissipation.[25]

Dissipation includes the removal of assets within or outside the jurisdiction. To determine whether there is real risk of dissipation, the Hong Kong Court will look at the circumstances of the case as a whole and draw inferences from the facts.

The Court would take into consideration several factors when assessing whether there is a real risk of dissipation. For instance the court will consider: the nature and financial standing of the defendant and his related business, the domicile or residence of the defendant, the nature of the defendant's assets (inside and outside of the

23. *Supra* n. 14, paragraph 29/1/65.
24. *Akai Holdings Ltd v. Ho* [2009] HKCU 172, paragraph 39 applied *Ninemia Maritime Corporation v. Trave Schiffahrtsgesellschaft mbH & Co KG* [1984] 1 All ER 398, p. 413.
25. *Siu Yuk Hung v. Sin Tung San* [2013] HKEC 2020, paragraph 99.

jurisdiction) and his dealings in relation to them, and the defendant's general behaviour in response to the claim.[26] In *WCL Corp Ltd v. Zhou Jia Jin,*[27] the factors raised by the plaintiff in support of its Mareva Injunction application included the defendant's residence and citizenship in China, the fact that the defendant had no known assets in Hong Kong except the account set out in the application for the injunction, and that he had no reason to keep any of his assets in Hong Kong since the plaintiff was his only Hong Kong client, etc.[28]

The defendant's past and present conduct to transfer or dissipate the assets is another factor, which the court will consider.[29] In *Pacific King Shipping Holdings Pte Ltd v. Huang Ziqiang,*[30] the Hong Kong Court dismissed the defendant's application for discharge of a Mareva Injunction order and found that there was a real risk of dissipation when the defendant sold its Hong Kong properties just prior to the proceedings. The defendant could not explain why the disposal of the properties was done suddenly and in a short period of time.

An unacceptably low standard of commercial morality has been accepted as an important factor in Mareva Injunction cases. The Court should scrutinise the evidence with care when inferring a real risk of dissipation from low commercial morality.[31]

It is trite law that the plaintiff must show that there is a real risk of dissipation in a Mareva Injunction application. However, the law remains ambiguous as to whether the plaintiff has to show the intention of the defendant to frustrate the enforcement of any judgment.

In *Siu Yuk Hung v. Sin Tung San,*[32] the Hong Kong Court looked at the principles for establishing a real risk of dissipation. The authorities cited in this case seem irreconcilable. In *Eastman Chemical Ltd v. Heyro Chemical Co Ltd (No. 2)*[33] where the DHCJ Winnie Tam SC stated that: 'the plaintiff is required to show that at least objectively, the effect of the defendant's conduct would be to frustrate the enforcement of any judgment'.[34] However, the DHCJ John Yan SC's in *Grandview Industries Company Limited v. Leung Yiu Kei trading as AGFA Manufacturing Company*[35] held that the plaintiff does *not* have to show the intention of the defendant. Instead, the test should be an objective one to assess the risk that the judgment may not eventually be fulfilled.

Accordingly, whether it is necessary for a plaintiff in pursuit of a Mareva Injunction to demonstrate that the defendant has an *intention* to frustrate enforcement of a judgment remains unclear. What is clear, however, is that the plaintiff must at least

26. *Pacific King Shipping Holdings Pte Ltd v. Huang Ziqiang* [2014] HKEC 582, paragraph 41.
27. [2014] HKEC 1537.
28. *Ibid*, paragraph 36.
29. Dave Lau, *Civil Procedure in Hong Kong* (Hong Kong: Sweet & Maxwell, 2011), p. 221.
30. [2014] HKEC 582.
31. *Honour Resources (International) Co Ltd v. Savvy Resources Ltd* [2010] 4 HKC 50, at 57.
32. [2013] HKEC 2020.
33. [2012] 3 HKLRD 307.
34. *Ibid*, paragraph 26.
35. HCA 1617/2011.

show that the defendant intends to use his assets for other than normal and proper commercial purposes.[36]

(4) Balance of Convenience

After being satisfied with the first three grounds above, the Court has to decide whether the balance of convenience is in favour of granting a Mareva Injunction. The balancing exercise should be weighed between the needs of both parties. The court will thus assess whether on the one hand the plaintiff could be adequately compensated *without* the injunction and whether on the other hand the defendant's loss of the use of his property embraced by the injunction could be compensated by the plaintiff's undertakings.[37]

[B] Worldwide Mareva Injunctions

The scope of a Mareva Injunction is not limited to assets within Hong Kong. If the defendant does not have any assets in Hong Kong, or if the plaintiff seeks to freeze the defendant's assets outside the jurisdiction, the plaintiff could apply for a Worldwide Mareva Injunction. The main difference between the domestic and Worldwide Mareva Injunction is that the plaintiff has to show that the defendant does not have sufficient assets in Hong Kong to satisfy the judgment, but has assets outside the jurisdiction.[38] Another difference is that the plaintiff has to apply for leave to serve out the injunction order under O.11 of the Rules of the High Court.[39] Apart from the above differences, the principles for a domestic Mareva Injunction are equally applicable to a Worldwide Mareva Injunction.[40]

[C] Anton Piller Order[41] in Hong Kong by Court

While a Mareva Injunction aims to prohibit the respondent from removing or dealing with his assets, an Anton Piller Order is a mandatory injunction allowing the applicant or its agent to enter into and search the respondent's premises in order to obtain and preserve specified property.[42] The purpose of an Anton Piller Order is to 'preserve evidence that a defendant, apprised of impending litigation would be likely to conceal or destroy so that it would not be available as evidence supporting the plaintiff's case'.[43]

36. *Supra* n. 14, paragraph 29/1/70.
37. *Amercian Cynamid, SHL Components Marketing ltd v. Ngan Yuk Shu* [2013] HKEC 1339.
38. *Chau Cham Wong Patrick v. Chau Kar Hon Quinton* [2014] HKEC 1046, paragraph 29.
39. *Supra* n. 13.
40. *Supra* n. 14, paragraph 29/1/83.
41. *Anton Piller KG v. Manufacturing Processes Ltd* [1976] Ch 55.
42. *Supra* n. 19, p. 255.
43. *Columbia Picture Industries Inc v. Robinson* [1987] Ch 38, applied in *Ng Chun Fai Stephen v. Tamco Electronics (HK) Ltd* [1993] 1 HKC 160, P. 174.

[1] Procedures for Anton Piller Orders

One has to bear in mind that an Anton Piller Order is 'contrary to normal principles of justice and can only be done when there is a paramount need to prevent a denial of justice to the plaintiff'.[44] As such, similar to the Mareva Injunction, an Anton Piller order can only be obtained on the basis of an ex parte application with the applicant's full and frank disclosure in the affirmations. Such order may be discharged when there is material non-disclosure, but not automatically. In order to avoid a miscarriage of justice, the Hong Kong Court can exercise its discretion in granting a fresh injunction or continuing the original injunction notwithstanding there has been non-disclosure when the original order was made.[45]

[2] Grounds for Granting an Anton Piller Order

In order to obtain an Anton Piller Order, the applicant must satisfy the following pre-conditions:[46]

(1) There must be an extremely strong prima facie case.
(2) The damage must be very serious for the applicant.
(3) The risk of destruction or removal of evidence must be more than merely possible.
(4) The harm done to the respondent must not be excessive or disproportionate to the legitimate object of the order.

(1) Strong Prima Facie Case

The Hong Kong Court has to look at the merits of the case before granting an Anton Piller Order. Different wordings have been used to describe the first pre-condition, either 'strong prima facie case',[47] 'very strong prima facie case'[48] or 'extremely strong prima facie case'. However, one can expect that the threshold is higher than a 'serious question to be tried', (which is regarded as sufficient for interlocutory injunctions applications).[49]

(2) Very Real Damage for the Applicant

The applicant must prove that the damage, potential or actual, must be real for the applicant. In *Nobs & Another v. Kantec Elctronics Co Ltd*,[50] the plaintiffs sued and

44. *Anton Piller KG v. Manufacturing Processes Ltd* [1976] Ch 55.
45. *C v. L* [2009] HKEC 416, paragraph 29.
46. *Supra* n. 14, paragraph 29/8/22.
47. *Chow Wai Lan v. Cheung Siu Fong and others* [1989] HKEC 84.
48. *Centaline Property Agency Ltd v. Hong Kong Property Services (IC&I) Ltd & Others* [2005] HKEC 170.
49. *Supra* n. 14, paragraph 29/8/22.
50. [1998] 1 HKLRD 935.

sought an Anton Piller Order against the defendant for a copyright infringement as the defendant had plagiarised and marketed the plaintiffs' watches. The Court of First Instance allowed the defendant's application for discharge. One of the reasons was that the plaintiffs had failed to satisfy that there was very serious damage for them as the plaintiffs admitted that they could only sell some hundred watches in Hong Kong each year.

(3) Risk of Destruction of Evidence

This condition requires the plaintiff to show clear evidence that the defendant has, in his or her possession, incriminating documents or things, and that there is a real possibility that he or she may destroy such material before an *inter parte* application can be made.

(4) Proportionality

As aforesaid, an Anton Piller Order is another 'draconian' measure in that it allows searches of the respondent's premises with the aim of obtaining property belonging to the defendant. The applicant's right and the remedy granted must therefore be proportionate. The Hong Kong court has adopted a careful attitude in assessing whether this condition is met. In *Step By Step Ltd,*[51] the plaintiffs sued the defendants who had allegedly misappropriated funds when they were shareholders and directors of the first plaintiff. The plaintiffs obtained an Anton Piller Order to search the defendant's premises for listed items referring to communications with or involving any 'Group Company'. The Hong Kong Court of First Instance discharged the Order and held that the scope of the 'Group Company' including twenty-two companies was too wide while only three of them were the plaintiffs.

[D] Interim Relief in Aid of Arbitration Proceedings

Interim relief has been a useful tool in aid of arbitration proceedings in Hong Kong. The legal basis for granting interim relief in the context of arbitration proceedings can be found in the Arbitration Ordinance,[52] which was reformed on the basis of the UNCITRAL Model Law in 2011.[53]

Under section 35 of the Arbitration Ordinance,[54] with the adoption of Article 17 of UNCITRAL Model Law, the arbitral tribunal has the power at the request of a party[55] to grant interim measures, including an injunction.[56] In other words, the arbitral tribunal can grant a Mareva Injunction in arbitration proceedings.[57]

51. [2009] HKEC 279.
52. (Cap. 609).
53. *Supra* n. 4.
54. *Supra* n. 52.
55. *Ibid*, s. 35(1); UNICITRAL Model Law, Article 17(1).
56. *Supra*, n. 52, s. 35(2).
57. *Katran Shipping Co Ltd v. Kenven Transportation Ltd* [1992] 1 HKC 538.

In addition, an arbitral tribunal has powers similar to that of a court in relation to granting an Anton Piller Order under Hong Kong law. Pursuant to section 56(1)(d) of the Arbitration Ordinance,[58] an arbitral tribunal may make an order directing the inspection, photographing, preservation, custody, detention or sale of relevant property. An Anton Piller Order is thus an available option under this provision.[59]

Furthermore, the Hong Kong courts can also grant Mareva Injunction and Anton Piller Orders in relation to arbitration proceedings.[60] The grounds for applying Mareva Injunctions in aid of arbitration proceedings are the same as the ones in litigation proceedings.[61] Similarly, the pre-conditions of an Anton Piller Order in litigation proceedings are equally applicable to arbitration proceedings.[62]

§11.04 ENFORCEMENT ISSUES

Enforcement issues may arise when a plaintiff starts an action against a defendant outside Hong Kong, but the defendant holds assets here. In this case, there are two ways to assist a plaintiff in freezing or preserving the assets in Hong Kong: (i) by applying for interim relief in aid of foreign proceedings; and (ii) by enforcing the foreign judgment/arbitration award in Hong Kong.

[A] Interim Relief in Aid of Foreign Litigation Proceedings

Even if a plaintiff starts an action in another country, he can still seek interim relief in Hong Kong under certain conditions. Under section 21M of the High Court Ordinance, the Hong Kong Court may grant interim relief in relation to proceedings, which have been or are to be commenced outside Hong Kong, and are capable of giving rise to a judgment, which may be enforced in Hong Kong under any Ordinance or at common law.[63] What amounts to a judgment enforceable in Hong Kong, we will explain further in section §11.04[C] of this chapter.

Section 21M is a 'standalone' provision.[64] Its scope of application is very wide as it covers foreign proceedings, which may not give rise to a cause of action over which the Hong Kong Court would have jurisdiction.[65] Moreover, the interim relief sought does not necessarily have to be ancillary or incidental to any proceedings in Hong Kong.[66]

58. *Supra*, n. 52.
59. The Hon CJ Geoffrey Ma GBM, *Arbitration in Hong Kong – A Practical Guide* (Hong Kong: Thomson Reuters, 2014), paragraph 16.169.
60. *Supra*, n. 51, ss 45 and 60.
61. *Hsin Chong Construction (Asia) Ltd v. Henble Ltd* [2005] HKCU 642: even though this case was adjudicated before the reform of the Arbitration Ordinance, the principles of Mareva Injunction still apply.
62. Christopher To & Damon So, *Hong Kong Arbitration Law Handbook* (Hong Kong: Lexis Nexis Butterworths), paragraph 56.09.
63. *Supra* n. 10, s. 21M(1).
64. *JSC BTA Bank v. Mukhtar Kabulovick Ablyazov* [2014] HKEC 296, paragraph 26.
65. *Supra* n. 10, s. 21M(3)(a).
66. *Supra* n. 10, s. 21M(3)(b).

However, the Hong Kong Court may refuse an application if the Court has no jurisdiction (apart from that provided by section 21M) in relation to the subject matter of the proceedings and it would be unjust or inconvenient to grant such application.[67] Furthermore, the plaintiff should first seek interim relief abroad before applying for such relief in Hong Kong.[68]

The principles applicable to interim relief under section 21M are analogous to those of interim relief granted pursuant to section O.29 except that the good arguable case test or strong prima facie case test must be in relation to the *foreign* proceedings. For instance, in *Minmetals Inc v. Dragon Boom Ltd,*[69] in an action where the plaintiff sought to continue and the defendant sought to discharge the Mareva Injunction in aid of the proceedings started in New Jersey, the Hong Kong Court stated clearly that 'the question is whether there is a good arguable case in the New Jersey proceedings'.[70]

[B] Interim Relief in Aid of Foreign Arbitration Proceedings

The Hong Kong Court has the power to grant a Mareva Injunction and an Anton Piller Order in aid of arbitration proceedings. Such arbitration proceedings include both proceedings commenced in Hong Kong and proceedings before an arbitral tribunal with its seat outside Hong Kong.[71]

Both sub-sections providing for interim relief in aid of foreign arbitration proceedings under section 45 and section 60 are drafted in a way which is consistent with section 21M of the High Court Ordinance. The pre-conditions for granting a Mareva Injunction or an Anton Piller Order include a condition that the arbitral proceedings are capable of giving rise to an arbitral award that may be enforced in Hong Kong under any Ordinance in Hong Kong.[72] The subject matter need not give rise to a cause of action over which the Court would have jurisdiction, and the order sought must not necessarily be ancillary or incidental to any arbitral proceedings in Hong Kong.[73]

[C] Enforcement of Foreign Judgments

For the purposes of private international law, Hong Kong is also regarded as a separate jurisdiction.[74]

The enforcement and recognition of foreign judgments in Hong Kong is generally subject to the conditions laid down in either (i) common law, or (ii) in statutes of Hong Kong.

67. *Supra* n. 10, s. 21M(4).
68. *Deiulemar Shipping SpA v. Transfield* [2011]1 HKLRD 75.
69. [2014] HKEC 778.
70. *Ibid*, paragraphs 22 and 29.
71. *Supra* n. 52, ss 45(2) and 60(1).
72. *Supra* n. 52, s. 45(5) and s. 60(6).
73. *Supra* n. 52, s. 45(6) and s. 60(7).
74. *First Laser v. Fujian Enterprises (Holdings) Ltd* [2012] HKEC 964, paragraph 43.

Under the common law rules, the onus of proof is on the party seeking enforcement of a foreign judgment in Hong Kong to satisfy the Hong Kong Court that the following three conditions are met:[75] First, the foreign court must have had jurisdiction. This means that the judgment debtor submitted to the jurisdiction of the foreign court or that there was a sufficient territorial connection between the judgment debtor and the foreign jurisdiction. Second, the foreign judgment must be final and conclusive, i.e., the foreign judgment has finally ended the litigation proceedings. Last but not least, the foreign judgment must be for a fixed sum of money, but not for a tax or penalty.

If the plaintiff can successfully show that these three conditions are satisfied, the defendant may still attempt to resist enforcement.[76] For instance, enforcement may be successfully denied by the Hong Kong Court if it can be shown that the foreign judgment was obtained by fraud; or if enforcement would amount to a substantial injustice or violate public policy of Hong Kong.

From a procedural point of view, the party seeking enforcement should issue a writ endorsed by or accompanied by a statement of claim pleading the details of the foreign judgment, stating the judgment sum and setting out the above-mentioned three conditions.[77]

[1] Foreign Judgments (Reciprocal Enforcement) Ordinance

The statutory regime related to the enforcement of foreign judgments is dominated by the Foreign Judgments (Reciprocal Enforcement) Ordinance.[78] This Ordinance applies to a list of fifteen foreign jurisdictions specified in the Foreign Judgments (Reciprocal Enforcement) Order.[79] The list includes certain Commonwealth countries, some parts of Australia, New Zealand and Singapore, as well as countries like France, Germany and Italy.

The common law conditions for enforcing foreign judgments are largely incorporated in the Foreign Judgments (Reciprocal Enforcement) Ordinance.[80] The main difference is that the judgment creditor can apply for a *registration* of the foreign judgment within six years after the date of the judgment by proving the conditions[81] under an ex parte application supported by an affidavit.[82] The Hong Kong Court will then register the judgment. The registered judgment will be enforced as if the judgment had been originally rendered by the Hong Kong Court.[83]

---

75. Graeme Johnson, *The Conflict of Laws in Hong Kong* (Hong Kong: Thomson Reuters, 2012), paragraph 9.015.
76. *Ibid*, paragraph 9.015.
77. *Ibid.*
78. (Cap. 319).
79. (Cap. 319A), Schedule 1 and Schedule 2.
80. *Supra* n. 78.
81. *Supra* n. 78, s. 4(1).
82. *Supra* n. 13, O.71, r. 2 and r. 3.
83. *Supra*, n. 78, s. 4(2).

[2] Mainland Foreign Judgments (Reciprocal Enforcement) Ordinance

Given the close connection between Hong Kong and the Peoples Republic of China, it is not uncommon that plaintiffs would like to enforce a Mainland judgment in Hong Kong. Nonetheless, it is intriguing that Mainland judgments are regarded as *inconclusive* since the Mainland courts can review their judgments in the future. This feature renders Mainland judgments unenforceable in Hong Kong.

The Mainland Foreign Judgments (Reciprocal Enforcement) Ordinance[84] was specifically drafted to remedy this legal situation.[85] A plaintiff can apply to register a Mainland judgment in Hong Kong within two years of the judgment date.[86] The judgment will then be recognised by the Hong Kong Court as final and conclusive.[87] However, there are some restrictions in relation to applying to register a Mainland judgment. For example, the judgment must order the defendant to pay a sum of money, but not of tax or penalty. Further, the parties must have agreed on an exclusive jurisdiction clause that excludes the jurisdiction of other countries except for the Mainland.[88] Accordingly, Mainland judgments are not automatically enforceable in Hong Kong.

[D] Enforcement of Foreign Arbitral Awards

Hong Kong is a party to the New York Convention on the Recognition and Enforcement of Foreign Arbitral Awards 1958 (the 'New York Convention'). As a result, Hong Kong has been consistently adopting a pro-enforcement approach in recognising and enforcing foreign arbitral awards before the handover in 1997.[89] Following the implementation of arrangements between Hong Kong and the PRC and the Macao Government, the approach in mutually recognising and enforcing arbitral awards remains in Hong Kong.[90]

Instead of incorporating the *Model Law* in its entirety, the Arbitration Ordinance excludes the Model Law enforcement regime and details its own version in part 10. The enforcement regime in the *Arbitration Ordinance* can be divided into four separate divisions, namely:

(1) Arbitral awards made in Hong Kong or arbitral awards made in a foreign country, which is not a party to the New York Convention, and under UNCITRAL Model Law.
(2) Arbitral awards made in a foreign country, which is a party to the New York Convention.

84. (Cap. 597).
85. *Supra* n. 84, s. 5 and s. 6.
86. *Supra* n. 84, s. 7 and s. 14.
87. *Supra* n. 84, s. 6 and s. 16.
88. *Supra* n. 84, s. 3 and s. 5(b).
89. *Supra* n. 59, p. 626.
90. *Ibid.*

(3) Arbitral awards made by a PRC authority in the PRC Mainland in accordance with the PRC Arbitration Law.
(4) Arbitral awards made in the Macao Special Administrative Region ('Macao').

[1] Hong Kong Awards

The pursuit of summary enforcement under section 84(1) of the Arbitration Ordinance is a quicker and less expensive way of seeking enforcement of an arbitral award. Summary enforcement does not necessarily lead to fresh proceedings in Court before actual enforcement takes place. The only procedural requirement is to seek leave of the Court. Under this section, an arbitral award is enforceable in the same manner and carries the same effect as a judgment of the Court of First Instance of Hong Kong.

The rules governing the grant of leave are stipulated in O.73, r.10 of the Rules of the High Court. An initial application of leave will most often be made on an ex parte basis to avoid costs. The judge in charge of the Construction and Arbitration List will peruse the application, which based on O.73, r. 10(3), must be supported by affidavit, the arbitration agreement and the original award. Apart from the requirement of full and frank disclosure, supporting documents must be in the official languages of Hong Kong, in other words, in Chinese and English. A translation of the award is essential if the required documents are in languages other than the two official ones. Applications for leave to enforce would be refused only if the *validity* of the award is in question or where the form of the award is not one that can be entered as a judgment.

[2] New York Convention Awards

Section 87 of the Arbitration Ordinance[91] stipulates that a New York Convention award is enforceable in Hong Kong either by the action on the award or by summary enforcement. The procedural requirements in seeking leave to enforce a New York Convention award are set out in O.73, r. 10(3) of the Rules of the High Court.[92]

The only difference between enforcing a New York Convention award and a foreign award from a non-New York Convention state is that there are limited exclusive defences against the enforcement of a New York Convention award. These limited grounds for objecting the enforcement are stated in section 89 of the Ordinance.[93] It should also be noted that the public policy defence is rarely permitted unless there are exceptional circumstances.

91. *Supra* n. 52.
92. *Supra* n. 13.
93. *Supra* n. 52.

[3] Mainland Awards

Hong Kong was a party to New York Convention under the United Kingdom's accession before the handover. As already mentioned, it remains a party to the Convention after the handover. Meanwhile, the PRC is also a party to the Convention. This situation has given rise to some complications since the Convention is only applicable to two different countries, but not in two *regions*. The PRC and Hong Kong's governments finally resolve this situation with the enactment and acknowledgment of the 'Arrangement between the Mainland and the Hong Kong Special Administrative Region on the Mutual Enforcement of Arbitration Awards'.

With this legal regime, parties can take action to enforce awards either in Mainland China or in Hong Kong by applying the rules in the relevant courts of the two regions. The relevant court in Mainland China is the Intermediate People's Court of the Mainland City where applications must be filed, whereas the relevant court in Hong Kong is the Court of First Instance. In practice, parties should refer to the procedural and evidential requirements as set out in the Arbitration Ordinance Part IIIA and in the 'Arrangement' as mentioned above. Parties are not entitled to make applications to more than one court in the PRC,[94] nor to make simultaneous applications in courts in both Hong Kong and the PRC.[95]

[4] Macao Awards

The situation between Hong Kong and Macao is similar to that between Hong Kong and the PRC. To resolve this situation, Hong Kong's and Macao's governments have entered into the Arrangement Concerning Reciprocal Recognition and Enforcement of Arbitral Awards (the 'Macao Arrangement') dated 7 January 2013.

Under this special arrangement, parties are entitled to apply to have arbitral awards enforced in Hong Kong or in Macao. The power to entertain applications for the recognition of arbitral awards under the Macao Arrangement is vested in the Court of First Instance of Macao, whereas the jurisdiction to grant enforcement is vested in the Court of Second Instance of Macao. Both application for recognition and enforcement of awards are dealt with by the Court of First Instance of Hong Kong's High Court. The requirements and restrictions under this regime are similar to that between Hong Kong and the PRC.

§11.05 DIRECTORS' AND OWNERS' LIABILITY IN RELATION TO ASSET PROTECTION SCHEMES

If the directors or owners of a company involved in a lawsuit or arbitration transfer the assets of the company to themselves or to a third party in order to thereby protect the

94. Arrangement between the Mainland and the Hong Kong Special Administrative Region on the Mutual Enforcement of Arbitration Awards, Article 2.
95. *Supra* n. 52, s. 93.

company from enforcement, Hong Kong law provides a range of possibilities for suing the directors or the owners. Moreover, the directors or the owners may become criminally liable.

[A] Civil Remedy and Liability

[1] Owners

It is well established under Hong Kong law that a company is a *separate* legal entity.[96] Generally speaking, the company owners are not liable for the company's debts, and if a company owner owns more than one company, a company is not liable for the debts of another company in the same company group.

Accordingly, under normal circumstances, the owner may transfer the assets of a company to himself or to another company owned by him without being held liable. Nonetheless, there is an exception to this rule, which allows the court to pierce the corporate veil when the corporate structure is a mere façade.[97] In *Toptrans Ltd v. Delta Resources Co Inc & Another,*[98] the Hong Kong Court affirmed the principles in *Adams & Others v. Cap Industries Plc & Another*[99] and listed two crucial ingredients to be proven by the plaintiff in order to rely on this exception. First, the plaintiff must show that there is common control of the company and the façade company. Second, the plaintiff has to show that the control is in 'relevant sense'. This means that the owner has the motive to use the façade company to take away attention from the company, leaving the façade company with assets and none of the liabilities. In such circumstances, the Hong Kong Court may hold a company liable for the debts of the other by lifting the corporate veil.

[2] Directors

Directors owe fiduciary duties to the company. One of the fiduciary duties is not to misappropriate the company's assets.[100] However, such duty is owed to the company *only* and not to any third parties. Accordingly, directors are generally not personally liable for the company's actions. There must be some special elements in order to make the directors liable to the plaintiff. If the directors involve themselves in any tortious acts committed by the company or if the elements of tort can be established against them, the directors might be liable as joint tortfeasors.[101]

96. *Salomon v. Saloman* [1897] AC 22.
97. *Adams & Others v. Cape Industries Plc & Another* [1990] Ch 433.
98. [2005] 1 HKLRD 635.
99. *Supra* n. 97.
100. *Re Geeorge Newman & Co* [1895] 1 Ch 674.
101. Lo, Stefan HC and Qu, Charles Z, *Law of Companies in Hong Kong* (Hong Kong: Sweet & Maxwell, 2013), paragraph 12.104.

[B] Criminal Liability

As mentioned, a company is a *separate* legal entity. The assets of the company do not belong to its owners or directors. If, however, the owners or directors transfer assets of the company to themselves without its proper consent, they may become criminally liable for theft under Hong Kong law.

A person commits theft when he dishonestly appropriates property belonging to another with the intention of permanently depriving the other of it.[102] The maximum sentence for theft is ten years of imprisonment.[103] In *HKSAR v. Cheung Ying Kit,*[104] the appellant was a general manager and one of the owners of a company. He falsely represented to the other owner that the company needed to rebate the customers and asked him to sign cheques to transfer money from the company's account. In fact, the money was paid to the appellant. The appellant was held liable for theft at trial by the District Court. The Hong Kong Court of Appeal upheld the District Court's decision.

Finally, the directors cannot hide behind the shield of the company if the company is guilty of any offence with the consent or connivance of the directors.[105] In such cases, the directors may be held liable for the offence committed by the company.

102. Theft Ordinance (Cap. 201), s. 2(1).
103. *Ibid*, s. 9.
104. [2004] HKEC 1471.
105. Criminal Procedure Ordinance (Cap. 221), s. 101E.

CHAPTER 12
Israel

Yonathan Arbel & Elad Peled

§12.01 INTRODUCTION

Israeli law combines features from both common law and civil law.

The territory that nowadays constitutes the State of Israel was administered in the thirty years preceding its establishment by Great Britain, by virtue of a League of Nations Mandate. During that period, the British Mandatory authorities enacted primary legislation in the form of "ordinances," which were based on English legislation or constituted codification of the English common law. When the State was founded in 1948, it incorporated all Mandatory legislation into its law. The dominant British rule and the extensive British legislation left an enduring mark on the domestic legal culture.[1] In recent decades, American law, which also belongs to the common law family, has replaced English law as the major source of impact on the Israeli law. This is attributable to the tremendous influence that the U.S. has on the Israeli society in general, which in turn stems from various political, economic and cultural factors.[2]

One of the salient common law characteristics of Israeli law is the maintenance of an adversarial judicial process. The process is party-centric and depends on the parties for the production of arguments, evidence and claims, whereas the judge is relatively passive and concentrates on deciding between the opposing stances. Another resemblance to the common law concerns the judgments, especially those of the higher instances, which quite often tend to be long and comprehensive and to contain obiter dicta.

---

1. *See* Elad Peled, *The Israeli Law of Defamation: A Comparative Perspective and a Sociological Analysis*, 20 Transnational Law & Contemporary Problems 735, 767 (2012), and the references cited therein.
2. *See Ibid.*, at pp. 774–775, and the references cited therein.

At the same time, Israeli private law has been undergoing a comprehensive reform, utilizing the continental codification technique and its basic concepts. This reform owes primarily to the work of Israeli lawyers with continental education, who reached the country in masses since the 1930s and became a dominant force in shaping and managing the various segments of Israel's legal system. Not only did the form of the legislation follow continental perceptions, but also much of its substantive content.[3] The laws governing the freezing of assets, reviewed below, are mostly codified, although there is still considerable weight to judge-made law.

The Israeli judiciary is composed predominantly of thirty-one Magistrate Courts, six Districts Courts, and the Supreme Court. The vast majority of civil cases are dealt with by those courts. Alongside them there are several types of specialized courts, most notably the Family Courts, which constitute a division of the Magistrate Courts; and the Labor Courts, whose two instances form an administratively separate system.

An important and relatively modern development in Israeli law is the establishment of a government-run enforcement agency, called the Enforcement and Collection Agency (ECA). This agency, overseen by the Ministry of Justice, is headed by registrars with limited judicial powers. They preside over a judicial process whereby they discuss the creditor's motions for enforcement measures, consider the debtor's objections and issue operative decisions to be executed by dedicated agents.

Arbitration proceedings may be initiated privately if the parties agree on their terms and on the identity of the arbitrator, but they can also be organized and facilitated by the Israeli Institute of Commercial Arbitration[4] or by the Arbitration Institute of the Israeli Bar.[5]

This chapter will proceed as follows: The methods for tracing assets in Israel will be described in section §12.02. The process for freezing assets, prescribed by the Israeli rules of civil procedure, will be discussed in section §12.03. The enforcement of foreign judgments and arbitral awards, governed by domestic legislation as well as by international conventions (bilateral conventions in the case of court judgments, as Israel is a party neither to the Brussels Convention nor to the Lugano Convention; and the New York Convention in the case of arbitral awards), will be dealt with in section §12.04. Finally, section §12.05 will touch upon the private liability of directors, corporate officers and shareholders for concealing corporate assets.

§12.02 IDENTIFYING ASSETS

[A] Own Efforts

In many cases, reasonable effort should suffice to identify the defendant's main assets, primarily her motor vehicles and real estate (at least the residential apartment in the case of a natural person, and the business premises in case of a corporation). It should be noted, however, that most public registries are of little assistance in this context, as

3. *See Ibid.*, at p. 769, and the references cited therein.
4. http://www.borerut.com.
5. http://www.israelbar.org.il/english_index.asp.

they do not permit the search of assets by name or identification number but only by asset. The following registries are an exception.

[1] IP Rights

The defendant's patents and trademarks may be searched by their owner's name in the website of the Israel Patent Office, at the following links:

> http://www.ilpatsearch.justice.gov.il/UI/AdvancedSearch.aspx (patents).
> http://www.trademarks.justice.gov.il/TradeMarksWebSiteUI/Trademarks Search/TrademarksSearch.aspx (trademarks).

[2] Company Information

General information about companies may be found in the website of the Israeli Corporations Authority for a small fee of ILS 64. The information contains all of the company's mandatory filings, including but not limited to its Annual Financial Reports, as well as registration of floating charges imposed on all of its assets in favor of creditors. The database is available at the following link: http://havarot.justice.gov.il/OrderForm.aspx

[3] Pledges

Information about pledges may be searched by identification number of the pledger in the website of the Israeli Ministry of Justice. The database refers to various kinds of specific pledged assets (as opposed to floating charges), including real estate, motor vehicles, aircrafts and engineering equipment. It is available at the following link: http://pledges.justice.gov.il/

[4] Land Rights

If the plaintiff already knows or suspects which real estate assets are owned by the defendant, he may verify this and examine whether the property is subject to a mortgage, a previous attachment, a cautionary note etc., through the Land Registry, available (only in Hebrew) at the following link: http://ecom.gov.il/Counter/alternative/tabuNesach/Homepage.aspx?counter = 10&catalog = 1&category = tabuNesach &language = he.

[5] Aircrafts

Information about aircraft ownership is registered with the Civil Aviation Authority. The information is not available online, and it may be obtained from the Authority for a fee of ILS 200, using the following contact options:

Message delivery system:
http://caa.gov.il/index.php?option=com_contact&view=contact&id=14%3A2011-01-16-09-07-37&catid=12%3Acontacts&Itemid=74
Phone: +972-3-9774570
Fax: +972-3-9774621

[6] Vessels

Information about vessel ownership is registered with the Administration of Shipping and Ports. The information is not available online, and it may be obtained from the Administration for a fee of ILS 477, using the following contact options:

Email: sapanut@mot.gov.il
Phone: +972-4-8632136
Fax: +972-4-8632133 / +972-4-8632220
Address: 15A Pal-Yam Blvd., P.O. Box 806, Haifa 31999.

[7] Bad Debtors

The Enforcement and Collection Agency maintains two databases of persons and companies which have been formally recognized as bad debtors. The information may be retrieved from both of those databases by entering the ID number, passport number or company number of the person or company concerned. The first database is the registry of debtors with adequate financial ability who evade paying their debts, available (only in Hebrew) at the following link: http://www.eca.gov.il/index2.php?id=450&lang=HEB.

The second database is the registry of debtors with limited financial ability, available (only in Hebrew) at the following link: http://eca.gov.il/index2.php?id=160&lang=HEB.

[B] Within Interim Measures Process

The normative framework for issuing interim measures, discussed below, provides several routes for identifying the defendant's assets.

[1] Anton Piller Order and Provisional Receivership

Anton Piller order and provisional receivership both allow the plaintiff to trace the defendant's assets or to obtain information on them through the actions of the court-appointed official.

[2] Attachment on All of the Defendant's Assets Held by Third Parties

The issuance of an interim attachment is subject, according to the Civil Procedure Regulations, 5744-1984 (hereinafter: "The Regulations") issued by the Ministry of Justice, to the provisions of the Execution Law, 5727-1967.[6] The Execution Law provides, *inter alia,* for a procedure whereby an attachment is placed on all of the defendant's assets held by specific third parties.

Any third party to whom the attachment order is served must provide information on the defendant's assets in her possession within ten days.[7] This procedure is most efficient in tracing bank accounts, especially due to the small number of banks operating in Israel. In practice, attachment orders pertaining to all of the defendant's financial assets are addressed and served to all Israeli banks and financial institutions, thereby generating high probability of tracing said assets.

[3] Counter Investigation

In certain circumstances in which the defendant objects to the freezing of assets that are already known to the plaintiff, her counter investigation under oath may be employed to extract information about additional assets she owns.

§12.03 INTERIM MEASURES

[A] General

[1] Interim Measures within Court Proceedings

The freezing of assets as an interim measure is governed by the Civil Procedure Regulations. The Regulations contain a detailed chapter on interim measures, which sets forth both the general conditions for issuing interim measures and particular rules for issuing various specific kinds of interim measures. The competence to issue interim measures lies with judges and in certain cases also with court registrars.

For the court to issue an order of interim measures, the following conditions must all be met:[8]

(1) There is reasonable concern, supported by reliable evidence, that the execution of the future judgment will be hampered absent an immediate interim measure.[9]
(2) The plaintiff has a prima facie cause of action supported by reliable evidence.

6. Regulations § 382.
7. Execution Law §§ 43–45B.
8. Regulations §§ 362, 364.
9. This condition is set, in slight variations, by the rules pertaining to the specific interim measures, to be detailed below.

(3) The "balance of convenience" weighs in favor of the plaintiff; namely, the harm he is expected to suffer if the interim measure is not granted is greater than the harm the defendant is expected to suffer if the interim measure is granted. This condition is traded off against the former one using the so-called parallelogram of forces doctrine: meaning, the more solid the cause of action, the less demanding the balance of convenience will have to be, and vice versa.[10]
(4) The plaintiff acts in good faith, most significantly, by disclosing to the court all relevant facts.[11]
(5) The chosen interim measure is proportional; namely, it does not harm the defendant beyond what is necessary.
(6) And, the plaintiff provides a court specified security, usually in the form of a bank guarantee, in order to compensate the defendant for unjustified losses she might suffer due to the interim measure.

As a general rule, an interim measure may only be issued after a claim has been filed against the party subject to the interim measure[12] (although it is possible to have the interim measure issued on the same day shortly after the claim is filed). In exceptional circumstances, however, the court may issue an interim measure before a claim is filed. Such interim measure automatically expires if no claim is filed within seven days, or within a different period of time determined by the court.[13] Additional grounds for the expiration of the interim measure are the dismissal of the claim; the execution of the final judgment; the infringement of the court's orders concerning service to the defendant; and the court's decision to annul the interim measure, which may be rendered at its discretion at any time (mostly when the circumstances change).[14] Upon the expiration, the court may forfeit the security provided by the plaintiff in order to compensate the defendant for her losses. Otherwise, and in case the defendant does not move for forfeiture, the security is returned to the plaintiff after several weeks or months (depending on its kind).[15]

The motion for interim measure must be filed in writing and be accompanied by an affidavit detailing the relevant facts. Both parties' factual and legal arguments are usually heard before the court makes its decision on the interim measure, including within short-counter investigations where appropriate.[16] This is so unless the court is convinced that any prior warning to the defendant would be severely detrimental to the plaintiff's interest, and decides to hold the process ex parte. When the interim measure sought for is an attachment, a Mareva injunction or an *Anton Piller* order, to be discussed below, the process is held ex parte as a default. In such a case, a hearing in

10. For example, PLA 3533/09 *The Condominium Delegation v. Yaron Ayun* (September 1, 2009).
11. For example, PLA 5826/11 *Ariel Tal v. Israel Electric Corporation Ltd.* (August 17, 2011).
12. Regulations § 362.
13. Regulations § 363.
14. Regulations § 370.
15. Regulations § 371.
16. For example, PLA 2508/98 Matan Y. *Communications Systems v. Miltel Communications Ltd.*, 53(3) P.D. 26.

the presence of both parties must be held generally after no more than fourteen days, or seven days when the interim measure at hand is an attachment.[17]

The oral hearing on the interim measure should normally not take more than one day, according to the Regulations, and if further hearing days are required, they should be consecutive to the extent possible.[18] The court's decision must be rendered within fifteen days of the hearing.[19]

The court's decision in the matter of the interim measure may be appealed upon the grant of leave by an upper instance.

With regard to local jurisdiction, the claim as well as its accompanying motion for interim relief should be filed to the court in whose jurisdiction the real estate, which is the subject of the claim, is located. Where the direct subject matter of the claim is not real estate, the local jurisdiction is determined according to the place of the defendant's residence or business, the place in which the obligation at hand was generated or was due to be fulfilled, or the place of the act or omission sued for.[20]

[2] Interim Measures within Arbitration Proceedings

It is unsettled whether an arbitrator may issue enforceable interim measures. The Arbitration Law, 5728-1968, empowers an arbitrator to grant any relief that a court is authorized to grant unless the parties stipulate otherwise in the arbitration agreement,[21] but since it does not refer specifically to interim measures, it is unclear whether the arbitrator's powers extend to them or only to final measures (which would then need to be ratified by a court). Magistrate and District Courts have differed on this matter and the Supreme Court has yet to resolve it.

It should be noted that the Arbitration Law also empowers the arbitrator to give the parties instructions relating to the conduct of the arbitration process, and to render a final ruling against a party who violates such instructions, unless the parties stipulate otherwise in the arbitration agreement.[22] However, if the defendant disposes of assets contrary to the arbitrator's order, this framework does not facilitate its seizure.

In any case, the court may issue certain provisional measures during the course of the arbitration at the request of a party or of the arbitrator, such as an attachment, appointment of a receiver, prohibitory injunction and mandatory injunction.[23]

[B] Attachment

An attachment curbs the negotiability of an asset, prevents it from being altered in a manner that might jeopardize the due payment of the defendant's future debt, and

17. Regulations §§ 366–367.
18. Regulations § 367.
19. Regulations § 373.
20. Regulations §§ 3–4.
21. Arbitration Law, Appendix § 17.
22. Arbitration Law, Appendix § 9.
23. Arbitration Law §§ 16–17.

limits its use.[24] The court is authorized to impose an attachment on any of the defendant's assets,[25] including real estate, movable property of any sort and intangible rights such as contractual rights vis-à-vis third parties.[26] The value of the attached asset must reasonably correspond with the value of the claim.[27]

The attachment may also be imposed on the defendants' assets held by third parties, in which case the party in possession must notify the court whether she indeed holds any of the defendant's assets, and may file an objection to the attachment.[28] If the third party does not respond or does not admit her possession of the assets, the plaintiff must move for the re-approval of the attachment.[29]

When real estate is attached, the court must order the entry of an appropriate note in the land registry, and the plaintiff is responsible for serving that order to the registry.[30] Note that Israeli Land Law does not transfer title in land unless the transaction is registered, and the registrar would refuse to record transactions that violate the terms of the attachment order.[31] Hence, the concealment of real estate and its diversion may prove challenging.

Some types of assets may not be attached; these are assets deemed necessary for basic living expenses, and include, for example, a small part of one's wages and social security payments.[32]

[C] Mareva Injunction

The court is authorized to order the defendant to refrain from taking any of her assets out of her possession or out of the possession of the person holding the assets, and from selling the assets, mortgaging it, altering its status, or altering her rights in the assets. This interim measure is subject to the general conditions applicable to attachment.[33]

[D] Anton Piller Order

The court is authorized to appoint an official to capture the defendant's assets, in a procedure commonly termed *Anton Piller* after the name of the English case in which it was first employed.[34] The official is then empowered to search inside private premises for assets which constitute evidence or are required for holding the judicial process, including computers and media, and to photograph, photocopy or seize them. The person in possession of the premises where the assets are located may be ordered

24. Goren, at p. 963.
25. Regulations § 374.
26. *See* the definition of the term "Assets" in Regulations § 1; Uri Goren, Issues in Civil Procedure 975 (11th ed. 2013) (hereinafter: Goren).
27. Goren, at p. 982.
28. Regulations §§ 374, 376–380.
29. Regulations § 378.
30. Regulations § 375.
31. § 7 to Land Law 5729–1969.
32. Goren, at pp. 976–977.
33. Regulations § 383.
34. *Anton Piller KG v. Manufacturing Processes Ltd.* [1975] EWCA Civ. 12 (December 8, 1975).

to let the official enter the premises.[35] Persons who possess any of the assets or claim to have rights in them may file objection to the order within twenty days.[36] The court may order what will be done with the seized assets at any time and upon the request of any party.[37]

[E] Provisional Receivership

The court is authorized to appoint a provisional receiver for any of the defendant's assets. It may then empower the receiver to enter into private premises; search for the assets; photograph, photocopy or seize the assets; possess the assets; safeguard or insure the assets; manage the assets; and exercise all powers of ownership over the assets.[38] Persons who possess any of the assets or claim to have rights in them may file objection to the order within twenty days.[39] The court may order what will be done with the seized assets at any time and upon the request of any party.[40]

§12.04 ENFORCEMENT ISSUES

[A] Enforcement of Foreign Court Judgments

[1] General

The process for enforcement of foreign judgment is regulated by the Foreign Judgments Enforcement Law, 5718-1958 (FJE). The law provides that a foreign judgment will not be valid in Israel unless it is declared as such by an Israeli court.

A central issue in Israeli law is the distinction between two alternative procedures designed to obtain such a decree, namely: (i) 'enforcement' and (ii) 'recognition'. We will focus on the first type of procedure here, since recognition is rarely relevant in cases concerning the pursuit of monetary claims in Israel based on a foreign judgment or arbitral award.

A declaration of enforceability is necessary when the foreign judgment involves an *in-personam* obligation (e.g., to pay a debt, provide a service, pay damages, etc.). By obtaining an enforceability decree, the foreign judgment may be executed in Israel.

By contrast, a deceleration of recognition is necessary when the foreign judgment involves an issue of personal status or *in-rem* obligations (e.g., a judgment of divorce, validating a will or resolving title in property). In these cases, such a decree will usually not be suitable for execution as it is valid in rem and not against a specific person, although this distinction is not always clear.

35. Regulations §§ 387A, 387E.
36. Regulations § 387I.
37. Regulations § 387H.
38. Regulations § 387B.
39. Regulations § 387I.
40. Regulations § 387H.

An 'enforcement decree' may be obtained by petition to the court directly. A 'recognition decree' may be granted either by direct application or incidentally, while resolving another dispute that partly depends on the validity of the foreign judgment.

The existence of a foreign judgment does not replace the cause of action that gave rise to the foreign judgment, and a new lawsuit may be filed *de-novo* in Israel based on these circumstances.[41] Alternatively, the party may move for recognition or enforcement of the foreign judgment, although in this case, the parties may not be able to contest the logic, factual findings or holdings of the foreign court.[42]

[2] Conditions for Enforcement

The conditions that must be met in order for a foreign judgment to pass the enforcement procedure are set out in § 3 to the FJE:

(1) the courts in the foreign country were competent to render the judgment under that country's law; and
(2) the judgment is no longer appealable; and
(3) the obligation imposed by the judgment is enforceable under the laws of judgment execution in Israel, and the content of the judgment does not contradict public policy in Israel; and
(4) the judgment is executory in the country in which it was rendered.[43]

The competency requirement is interpreted broadly, according to some scholars, and a domestic court would generally not inquire whether the foreign court is the appropriate venue to handle the specific claim, but rather whether courts in general are competent to handle such issues according to the laws of the foreign jurisdiction.[44]

The finality requirement is interpreted narrowly, that is, even if the foreign proceeding may still be vacated or amended, it would still be considered final, if it is no longer subject to appeal.[45] Given that, orders of alimony or child support may be enforced, despite the fact that they are subject to interim revision. Importantly, according to a leading scholar in the field, Professor Fassberg, the finality requirement will not preclude an interim order.[46]

The domestic enforceability requirement is mostly premised on core moral, social, and economic considerations. Courts adopt in this context a relatively narrow view, and will only exclude foreign judgments that run contrary to issues that they

41. Amos Shapira, Recognition and Enforcement of Foreign Judgments, Iyunei Mishpat 4 (1974) 509, 516 (hereinafter: Shapira).
42. Haggai Carmon, Foreign Judgments in Israel: Recognition and Enforcement, (The Israeli Bar Association Publishing), 15 (2011).
43. Foreign Judgments Enforcement Law § 3.
44. Shapira, at p. 523; Carmon, at p. 43; CA 1268/07 *Greenberg v. Bamira* (2009).
45. CA 2214/00 *Carlo Nobili S.p.A Rubinetterie (Italian company) v. Moshe Kattan Ltd.*, 54(4) P.D. 403 (2000).
46. Celia Wasserstein Fassberg, Foreign Judgments in Israeli Law: Deconstruction and Reconstruction, 9 (Jerusalem, 1996).

view as fundamental and essential, and will not decline to enforce a judgment just because it would have been ruled otherwise in Israel on grounds of public policy.[47]

Finally, the executory requirement is understood as limiting the domestic execution of judgments that cannot be executed in the foreign country. Reasons for non-enforceability may include laches and an elapsed statute of limitations, but will generally not include practical constraints in the foreign country.

In summary, then, the elements that the plaintiff must prove to obtain an enforcement decree are interpreted relatively broadly, so as to allow liberal enforcement of foreign judgments. Of the four provisions, three bear a more technical character, whereas one is decidedly substantive (the public policy requirement), although courts do not generally use this provision as a means of deciding on the merits of the case, but only as a safety valve against what would be considered domestically as morally egregious.

[3] Exceptions for Enforcement

When the aforementioned conditions are met, § 3 provides that the court shall enforce the foreign claim.[48] However, there are eight exceptions that the defendant may prove that would render the foreign judgment unenforceable. The first of these is a reciprocity condition (§ 4) whereby a foreign judgment will not be enforced if it originates from a country that does not enforce Israeli judgments. This specific condition, however, may be overcome by an appeal by the Attorney General. As noted, the burden of proof that the originating country does not reciprocate lies with the party contesting the enforceability of the foreign judgment.[49]

When there is uncertainty regarding the enforceability of Israeli judgments – such as in the case of Russia – the Supreme Court held that it suffices to show that a "probable potential of reciprocity" exists in the originating country in order to satisfy the reciprocity requirement.[50] Hence, proving lack of reciprocity may be difficult.

The second exception is set out in § 5. This section states that the court will not hear an application of enforcement if "such application is filed more than five years after the day on which the judgment was given." After the five-year period, the court will not consider the application unless there is a special agreement between Israel and the foreign jurisdiction or the court is convinced that special circumstances mandate it.

Under the third exception, an Israeli court will not enforce a foreign judgment that was obtained by fraud.

Fourth, a foreign judgment will not be enforced if the defendant was not given reasonable opportunity to contest the claim. Consistent with the general approach to exceptions, this exception is interpreted narrowly. A court would not recognize as valid

47. *CA 1137/93 Yael Eshkar v. Tymon Heims*, 48(3) P.D. 641 (1994); CA 4949/03 *Bolos Gad Ltd. v. Globe Master Management Ltd.*, 59(5) P.D. 616 (2005); Carmon, at pp. 53–57.
48. The language of the law is "may enforce," but this is interpreted as "shall enforce". *see* Carmon, p. xix (preface by Deputy Chief Justice of the Supreme Court of Israel, Eliezer Rivlin).
49. CA 1268/07 *Greenberg v. Bamira* (2009).
50. CA 3081/12 *Double K Fuel Products (1996) Ltd. v. Gazprom Transgas Ukhta Ltd.* (2014).

personal difficulties that prevented the defendant from defending her case, but rather would only be willing to consider "objective" difficulties that would prevent anyone from adequately contesting the case.[51]

Fifth, judgments rendered by courts that are internationally incompetent to give them would not be enforced. Importantly, this competency requirement is judged based on the domestic (Israeli) rules of private international law. This requirement is understood as pertaining to the question of whether the foreign court has jurisdiction over the defendant. This is decided, in turn, by examining whether the defendant or the subject matter has had sufficient "connection" with the foreign jurisdiction.[52]

Sixth, if there is a conflict between the foreign judgment and another valid judgment "on the same matter" and between the "same parties", the foreign judgment cannot be enforced. This requirement is meant to prevent the enforcement of conflicting judgments.[53]

Seventh, if the same case is presently being litigated in Israel between the same parties, then a foreign judgment will not be enforced.

Eighth, according to § 7, a court will not give effect to a foreign judgment if its enforcement is "likely to prejudice the sovereignty or security of Israel." Such cases would be rare, and past cases involving this defense involved the relationship between Israel and the Palestinian authority.

In summary, we see that the enforcement procedure is complex. It involves a set of conditions that the party seeking enforcement must demonstrate, and a long list of defenses and exceptions that the defendant may demonstrate to avoid enforcement. Over the years, Israeli courts have developed judge-made law interpreting these provisions, yet much uncertainty still exists over the scope and mode of interpretation of many of these issues.

[4] Interim Measures Pertaining to Foreign Judgments

When a party is prone to shielding assets, fleeing the country or acting otherwise to hinder the future enforcement of a judgment, it may be necessary to enforce interim orders. The problem is that such orders are, by definition, not final, and so they do not meet the condition set out in § 3, requiring the finality of judgments.

In such cases, § 8 provides that the Israeli court has authority to enforce a provisional judgment if the court believes that "the circumstances of the case justify it [the court] doing so." Here, the burden of the proof lies with the petitioner.

In interpreting § 8, the court adopts a somewhat liberal approach. According to the case law, the court would consider, *inter alia,* the difficulties in enforcing the interim order in the foreign country. If it is difficult to do so absent Israeli cooperation, the court would be more willing to grant such an order.[54] The general doctrine that applies in such cases is "balance of convenience," whereby the court seeks to see

51. CA 802/89 *Indurksis v. Indurksis*, 46(2) P.D. 366 (1990).
52. Shapira.
53. Eshkar, at p. 659.
54. DCC (T.A.) 1805/82 *Goldberg v. Goldberg*, 43(2) P.M. 95, 100–101 (1983).

which party will suffer the least harm from a decision in the other party's favor.[55] In addition, the petitioner must show that he has, prime facie, a valid case in court.[56]

[B] Enforcement of Foreign Arbitral Awards

The matter of enforcement of foreign awards is regulated by the Arbitration Law, 5728-1968. According to § 29a, any request by a party to either confirm or reject a foreign award will be decided according to the terms of the treaty with the country issuing this award, should one exist.

Israel is a signatory to the Convention on the Recognition and Enforcement of Foreign Arbitral Awards (the New York Convention) and has ratified it, through an instrument called "Regulations for the Execution of the New York Convention," 5738-1978 (1978).

The regulations set out a simple procedure, whereby a party seeking to enforce a foreign arbitration award needs to submit an authenticated copy of the foreign arbitration award as well as a copy of the underlying arbitration agreement. Translation is required for all awards not written in English, French, Arabic or Hebrew. The translation must be made by a recognized translator.

Moreover, § 4 provides that an Israeli court may postpone the hearing of the enforcement petition, at its discretion, if the foreign award is being disputed at a foreign jurisdiction. The Israeli court may also require guarantees from a party against whom the arbitration award is directed.

Contesting a domestically issued arbitration award has a strict time limit of forty-five days. With foreign awards, Israeli courts allow objections to be issued ten days after the moment the request to recognize the foreign award has been made.[57]

§12.05 D&O LIABILITY FOR SHIELDING ASSETS

The shielding of assets is a significant issue affecting business and the credit market as a whole. Israeli law adopts a strong stance against such behavior and sets several measures aimed at deterring it. These measures stem from various sources – company, insolvency, contract, tort and even employment law. In what follows we will describe the two primary sources for imposition of liability on D&O for the shielding of company assets.

[A] Company Law

D&Os are sometimes shareholders of the company. As such, they may be held liable for the company's debts through the doctrine of "veil piercing." The law provides that, in

55. CA 5603/14 *Marie-Therese Jobe v. Mordechai Molly* (2014).
56. *Ibid.*
57. PLA 4320/11 E.I.M. *Communication Holdings Ltd. v. Michael Wilson & Partners Ltd.* (2012).

exceptional cases, if the court believes that it will be just and right to do so, it may lift the corporate veil if it finds that the company's separate legal personality was used:[58]

(a) To defraud a person or deprive one of the company's creditors from any of his rights.
(b) In a manner that violates the company's objectives while assuming an unreasonable risk with respect to the company's ability to meet its debts.

In other words, the court may lift the veil if the company's separate personality is used as means of fraud, which is a common allegation in cases of asset shielding. Moreover, if the company's assets are mismanaged in a way that runs counter to the company's objectives and an unreasonable risk is assumed, the court may lift the veil. This is, again, a common allegation in cases of asset shielding. Importantly, a shareholder may only be found liable if he was aware or at least suspected that these conditions apply.

The courts repeatedly state that, despite the exceptional nature of veil piercing, they will not allow a party to hide behind the company's veil if it is used to defraud creditors.[59] Additionally, running the company under-capitalized (with respect to its obligations) may be a valid cause for asset lifting, regardless of shareholder's motives.[60]

The liability of directors and officers, known as company's organs, is set out in § 54 to the Companies Law, which provides that:

> (a) Attribution of an act or intention of an organ to a company shall not derogate from the personal liability that individuals in such organ would have borne but for such attribution.

That is, any organ of the company, be it a director or an officer, may still be held liable for wrongdoing even if such an action was made while working for the company. Organ's responsibility is understood as differing from the general question of veil piercing, and an organ would be held responsible for actions it took if the law assigns such a responsibility.[61] To establish such a liability, one would need to show that a cause of action in contract or tort arises, an issue we return to below.

[B] Contractual and Tort Sources of Liability

As noted, D&Os may also be liable in contract or in tort, as the fact that the organ was acting on behalf of the company does not preclude personal liability per § 54 to the Company Law. The § 253 provides that an officer would employ the level of care of a reasonable officer and § 254 establishes a duty of a director to the company. Violating

58. § 6 to Companies Law, 5759-1999 (hereinafter: Companies Law.
59. CA 2223/99 *Vitali Krispi v. H. Electronics (1988) Ltd.*, 57(5) P.D. 116.
60. CA 4263/04 *Kibbutz Mishmar HaEmek v. Adv. Tommy Manor, liquidator of The North's Chicks Ltd.*, 63(1) P.D. 548.
61. CA 407/89 *Tzuk Orr Ltd. v. Car Security Ltd.*, 48(5) P.D. 661.

these duties by, for example, diverting assets for personal use, may give rise to a suit against the director by the shareholders or the company itself.

The cause of action in these cases may either be tort or contract, and the normal conditions of contractual and tort liability must be proven. In tort, this would involve proving that a duty of care exists between the director and the company's creditor and that the director has acted negligently, violating the standard expected from a reasonable director. In contract, one would need to show that contractual relations existed between the director and creditor. This will be of greatest relevance in cases where the director offers his personal surety to the company's debts. Importantly, § 263 prohibits the company from insuring its D&Os against liability arising from actions made in violation of the duty of care to the company, or from actions made to the benefit of the director.

[C] Criminal Liability

There are a few potential sources of criminal liability for the shielding of company assets. The main source is § 424 to the Penal Law, 5737-1977 ("Penal Law"). According to this section, a director or officer of a corporation who has knowingly taken an action, that interferes with the corporation's ability to meet its liabilities or with its proper management, may face up to five years in prison and a fine.

Similarly, § 423 states that a manager of a corporation who falsely reports the financial status of the corporation with an intention to defraud others may face up to five years in prison. Inasmuch as asset shielding involves the misreporting of company's assets, this section would be of relevance.

The § 425 further provides that if a manager of a corporation that acts fraudulently or violates his duty of loyalty to the firm in a manner that harms the corporation, he may face up to three years in prison.

CHAPTER 13
Italy

Marco Padovan, Renato Costagliola & Michele Bonomini

§13.01 INTRODUCTION

After the results of a popular referendum held on 2 June 1946, Italy became a parliamentary republic. The Constitution of Italy was adopted on 22 December 1947.

The Italian legal system is based on Roman law, thus Italy belongs to the wide family of civil law countries.

The Italian legal system has been extensively influenced by the Napoleonic Civil Code and has subsequently been developed on the basis of various statutes on civil and commercial law matters.

Italian civil procedure is largely governed by the Code of Civil Procedure (hereinafter also referred to as the 'CoCP'), adopted by Royal Decree dated 28 October 1940 No. 1443 and in force as of 21 April 1942. The CoCP was supplemented and integrated by Royal Decree dated 19 December 1941 No. 1368 and has, from time to time since the 1950s, been subject to many reviews aimed at simplifying and speeding up civil proceedings.

The CoCP is structured in four so-called *libri* (i.e., books or subject areas), covering general provisions on the competence and powers of the various parties involved in civil procedure (Book I), the conduct of ordinary proceedings and appeals (Book II), enforcement procedures (Book III), and specific proceedings, such as those aimed at obtaining injunctions of payment, interim and conservative measures, release of immovable assets, proceedings related to the state and to family law matters, as well as arbitration (Book IV).

Although the CoCP contains the main basic rules of law on civil procedure matters, other pieces of legislation must be taken into account when describing the Italian procedural landscape, as they regulate certain specific matters such as the organization of the judiciary system,[1] the cost of access to justice,[2] the servicing of writs and other documents by post,[3] and alternative dispute resolution procedures.[4] Finally, specific sets of rules govern bankruptcy proceedings,[5] the procedures for the enforcement of credits of the State and public bodies[6] and class actions.[7] Such proceedings are not dealt with in this chapter.

The enforcement of foreign judgments and arbitral awards is regulated by the Italian law on Private International Law[8] and by the rules adopted at the European Union level. Moreover, Italy has ratified the 1958 New York Convention on the Recognition and Enforcement of Foreign Arbitral Awards as well as the Brussels and Lugano Conventions of 1968 and 1988, respectively, on jurisdiction and the enforcement of judgments in civil and commercial matters.

The procedures for the recognition and enforcement of foreign decisions (including arbitral awards) are dealt with by the Courts of Appeal, and will be analysed in more detail in section §13.04 below. Section §13.02 of this chapter will provide an overview of the rules governing enforcement procedures, and the most important means and tools that can be applied in order to identify assets belonging to debtors. In section §13.03, we will examine the rules applicable to interim measures. Finally, in section §13.05, we will provide an overview of the remedies offered by Italian law to plaintiffs facing illicit asset shielding manoeuvres.

---

1. Royal Decree 30 January 1941 n. 12.
2. Pursuant to Presidential Decree n. 115/2002, access to justice is subject to the payment of a unified contribution tax (and stamps) whose amount is proportionate to the subject matter and to the amount in dispute. The unified contribution tax for civil matters runs from EUR 43.00 to a maximum of EUR 3,372.00 for the judgments in the Court of Cassation. Certain matters such as family law matters and labour and mandatory social security law matters are exempted from the unified contribution tax.

   The unified contribution tax for the proceedings in front of administrative courts runs from a minimum of EUR 300.00 to a maximum of EUR 6,000.00 for disputes relating to public procurement, increased by half in the judgments of appeal. Proceedings against decisions of denial of access to environmental acts and information are exempted from the unified contribution tax.

   In order to limit the filing of claims and/or appeal against first instance decisions, the law provides for certain pecuniary sanctions in cases of proceedings started or resisted in bad faith or gross negligence (the so-called '*liti temerarie*') and in cases of appeals which are manifestly groundless. In such respect, a special system of pecuniary sanctions is also set out in case of '*liti temerarie*' filed in the administrative proceedings with respect to certain categories of public procurement contracts.
3. Law 20 November 1982 n. 890.
4. Law Legislative Decree 4 March 2010 n. 28.
5. Such rules are mainly contained in the Royal Decree dated 16 March 1942 n. 267, published on the Official Gazette n. 81 of 6 April 1942, as subsequently amended and supplemented.
6. Such rules are mainly contained in the Royal Decree dated 14 April 1910 n. 639, published on the Official Gazette n. 227 of 30 September 1910 and in the Decree of the President of the Republic dated 29 September 1973 n. 602, published on the Official Gazette (ordinary supplement n. 2) of 16 October 1973, as subsequently amended and supplemented.
7. Such rules are contained in the Legislative Decree dated 6 September 2005 n. 206, published on the Official gazette (ordinary Supplement) n. 235 of 8 October 2005, also known as which brought the Consumers' Code, as subsequently amended and supplemented.
8. Law 31 May 1995 n. 218, published on the Official gazette (ordinary Supplement) n. 128 of 3 June 1995.

§13.02 IDENTIFYING ASSETS IN ITALY

As indicated, the CoCP regulates in great detail the issue of enforcing judgments or arbitral awards, while very little statutory guidance or leverage is given to a creditor in relation to identifying assets against which enforcement can happen.

Before initiating enforcement proceedings, it is crucial to identify the assets of the debtor in order to start the most appropriate type enforcement procedure; to file the case with the competent court; and generally to increase the chances of enforcing the claim to the fullest possible extent. There are a number of public registers and databases, which contain useful information about different types of assets in Italy belonging to legal and natural persons. In the following, we will provide a brief overview of these registers.

[A] Real Estate

An official database of registered real estate in Italy is accessible to the public via the website of the Italian Tax Authority: www.agenziaentrate.gov.it. To access this database, it is necessary to make a registration with a login and a password. Access can thereafter be made using a PIN code provided by the Italian Tax Authority.

The services are available free of charge. By indicating the tax code of a property owner, the province and the cadastral area where the search is to be carried out, it is possible to obtain information relating to properties situated throughout Italy (excluding, however, the autonomous provinces of Trento and Bolzano).

At the time of the writing of this chapter, searches conducted by individual persons are limited to:

- The name of the property owner.
- Identifying details of the property in question.
- Data relating to the ownership and to the relevant entitlement share.
- The cadastral rent and the location of the property registered in the cadastre of buildings.
- Information about income flowing from the property.

As of today, the search can be carried out only on those property deeds that have been computerized, and on those properties for which the tax code used in the search corresponds to that of the registered holder in the cadastral archives.

[B] Motor Vehicles

Motor vehicles and trailers fall within the specific category of registered movables ('*beni mobili registrati*') mentioned in Article 815 of Italian Civil Code (CC) and are therefore subject to certain rules of evidence to safeguard third-party's rights.

Information about ownership rights and third-party rights (such as retention of title, mortgages and attachments) are available in the Italian Vehicles Registry (in

Italian: '*Pubblico Registro Automobilistico*', usually referred to as the 'PRA'), which is managed by the '*Autobile Club d'Italia*' (briefly referred to as the '*ACI*').

Extract from the PRA are available online at the following website: https://servizi.aci.it/VisureInternet/welcome.do. This is a payment service, and the fees depend on what kind of information and extracts are being requested.

Pursuant to current legislation, private individuals can make current or historical investigations only with reference to their own vehicles, while lawyers and bankruptcy receivers may conduct investigations on a name-specific basis, which enables them to identify all vehicles owned by a person. It is also possible to make investigations on a vehicle specific basis with reference to the vehicle's model and plate.

There are a number of private investigation service agencies that can also provide the creditor with information on a subject-specific basis, allowing the creditor to find all the motor vehicles owned by a natural or legal person registered in the PRA.

[C] Vessels

Under Italian law, commercial vessels can be qualified as major ships ('*navi maggiori*[9]'), which are allowed to navigate beyond 20 nautical miles from the shore; and minor ships and barges ('*navi minori*' e '*galleggianti*'[10]), which are allowed to navigate only within 20 nautical miles from the shore and in internal waters.

Major ships can be registered on the registers of Major Ships, also called '*Matricole*', which is administrated by the local Maritime District Offices.[11] In addition, large vessels can be registered on the International Registers,[12] if the vessel is used for international trade. Minor ships and barges are registered on the Registers of Minor Ships and Barges ('*Registri delle navi minori e galleggianti*'), administrated by the district office and other authorities provided by the regulation.[13] Minor ships and barges for inland navigation are also registered with the '*Registri delle navi minori e galleggianti*', which is administrated by the local Port Inspectorates.[14]

In addition to information about the owner(s) of a vessel, third-party rights over the vessels (such as usufructs, mortgages, liens, conservative sequestrations, attachments, etc.) are also recorded in the above registers, which may be accessed via the local Port Authorities,[15] the Maritime District Offices or the Directorates.[16]

9. Article 136 Italian Maritime Code ('*Codice della navigazione*'), adopted with Royal Decree 30 March 1942, n. 327.
10. Article 136 Italian Maritime Code.
11. Article 146, paragraph 1, Italian Maritime Code.
12. The Italian International Register has been introduced by Law 27 February 1998, n. 30.
13. Article 146, paragraph 2, Italian Maritime Code.
14. Article 146, paragraph 3, Italian Maritime Code.
15. http://guardiacostiera.it/diporto/.
16. The local competent authority can be fined using the registration number of the boat craft.

[D] Aircrafts

As for vessels, under Italian law civil aircrafts need to be registered in the Italian Aircraft Register (*'Registro aeromobili'*), which contains information about the owners of aircrafts and about the rights of third parties (such as usufructs, mortgages, conservative sequestrations, attachments, etc).

The Italian Aircraft Register is held and managed by ENAC – the Italian Civil Aviation Authority (*'Ente Nazionale per l'Aviazione Civile'*).[17]

[E] IP Rights

Information about trademarks, patents, models, Internet domain names and design rights is available at the Italian Trademark and Patent Office (*'Ufficio Italiano Marchi e Brevetti'*), which is administered by the Ministry of Economic Development, Directorate-General for the Fight against Counterfeiting.

Intellectual property rights registered in Italy can be found via the following Internet link: http://www.uibm.gov.it/uibm/dati/.

[F] Financial Reports

Under Italian law subjects who qualify as 'entrepreneurs' (*'imprenditore'*) under Article 2195 CC must be registered with the local office of the Company Register.

The Company Register is managed under the auspices of the Italian Chamber of Commerce, which forms the part of the public administration that deals with business enterprises in Italy.

Under Italian law, entrepreneurs are obliged to make periodical filings with the Company Register. The filings contain valuable information about their economic and financial situation, including: financial statements; bankruptcy filings; resolutions for voluntary liquidation; judicial liquidation orders; etc.

Against payment of a small fee, it is possible to obtain copies of the latest annual financial reports filed by an Italian debtor company via the following link: http://www.registroimprese.it/en/consultazione-dati.

[G] Rights over Plants, Machines and Other Tangible Assets

Information regarding the ownership and sale of machineries can be found in the 'Register of machineries sold with reservation of ownership'[18] (*'Registro vendita di macchine utensili con riserva di proprietà'*), provided that the machinery in question is

17. ENAC was established on 25 July 1997 by Legislative Decree No. 250/97 as the National Authority committed to oversee the technical regulation, the surveillance and the control in the civil aviation field. More information can be obtained at: http://www.enac.gov.it/La_Regolazione_per_la_Sicurezza/Navigabilit-13-/Registro_Aeromobili/index.html.
18. Articles 1524 and 2762 CC and Law 28 November 1965, n. 1329.

worth more than EUR 516,49. The register is held by the local Court (*'Tribunale'*) where the machinery is situated.

The Register is not accessible online, but enquiries can be made with the Clerk's Office in charge of the keeping of the register during opening hours by using the relevant form and against payment of the applicable stamp tax.[19]

[H] Central Credit Register ('Centrale dei Rischi')

The Central Credit Register is an information system related to the debts of the customers of banks and financial companies supervised by the Bank of Italy.

The Bank of Italy collects information about customers' borrowings from intermediary banks and notifies them of the risk position of each customer vis-à-vis the banking system as a whole. By means of the Central Credit Register, the Bank of Italy thus provides intermediaries with a service intended to improve the quality of the credit system with the aim of ultimately enhancing its stability.

The Central Credit Register is available only to persons in whose name the information has been filed and to their receivers or trustees.

[1] 'Anagrafe tributaria'

Finally, Article 492*bis* of the CoCP provides that an Italian enforcement court, during the course of enforcement proceedings and upon request of the creditor, shall investigate the Italian Tax Register (*'Angrafe Tributaria'*) and other public databases in cases where assets cannot be found or where the assets of the debtor are not sufficient to satisfy the claim.[20]

Pursuant to Decree No. 305 dated 29 September 1973, the *'Anagrafe Tributaria'* collects and organizes, on a national level, all information submitted by Italian tax subjects to the Italian tax authorities (*'Agenzia delle Entrate'* whose website is: www.agenziaentrate.it) as well as information stemming from investigations carried out by the tax authorities. The data collected is made available to the employees of the Ministry of Finance in charge of the enforcement and surveillance of tax measures in order to evaluate the financial position of each registered person (be it a natural person, a corporation or other legal entities) identified by the Italian tax authorities with an Italian tax number.

Unfortunately, this database is not available to private parties involved in pre-trial asset searches.

---

19. Currently set at EUR 35.68 for machineries whose value exceeds EUR 2,582.28 and EUR 3.68 for machineries that worth less than such amount.
20. Such provision is not in force, as the operational provisions have not been adopted yet.

§13.03 INTERIM MEASURES

The 4th Book, Title I of the CoCP contains provisions on interim measures, including freezing orders. While section §13.03[A] refers to general provisions (Articles 669*bis* to 669*quattordecies*), section §13.03[B] specifically deals with freezing orders ('*sequestro conservativo*' in Italian).

Furthermore, Italy has adopted EU *Regulation No. 655/2014 of 15 May 2014 establishing a European Account Preservation Order* (the so-called EAPO) *procedure to facilitate cross-border debt recovery in civil and commercial matters.*

[A] European Account Preservation Orders

The EAPO procedure allows a creditor to freeze a debtor's bank accounts in a Member State (except in the UK and Denmark, which have not adopted the regulation) other than in the Member State where the application is made and where the creditor is domiciled. An EAPO can be sought as an alternative to or in addition to pursuing national freezing order proceedings, either before, during or after the legal proceedings concerning the substance of the matter against the debtor.

The EAPO Regulation will apply only as of 18 January 2017. Until this date only the below mentioned national provisions will be available to creditors wishing to freeze assets located in Italy.

[B] Freezing Orders under Italian National Law

Italian Courts do not have a special division for interim measures. Any single presiding judge may handle a request for granting interim relief. However, courts located in larger cities have specialized divisions for certain matters (family law, IP law, contractual law, etc.), which handle interim measures related to those matters.

An application for an interim measure can be filed either with the judge handling a pending proceeding, or prior to the commencement of the proceedings. In the latter case, the following rules apply:

(a) the application must be filed with a Court of First Instance ('*Tribunale*') having territorial jurisdiction over the substance of the matter. Unless the parties have agreed in writing to the exclusive territorial jurisdiction of another particular city court, such jurisdiction belongs to the court either where the debtor is domiciled, or where the obligation related to the proceedings originated or should be performed;
(b) where no Italian court holds jurisdiction, the application must be filed with the court where the interim measure (if granted) is to be enforced;
(c) should the dispute be subject to arbitration, or should an arbitration be already pending, the application must be filed with the court that would have had jurisdiction on the substance of the matter in the absence of the arbitration agreement. It is worth noting that under Italian arbitration law

arbitrators cannot deliver freezing orders or other interim measures (cf. Article 818 of the CoCP).

With regard to the costs of the proceedings, in the Italian judicial system a fixed court fee is charged, the amount of which varies according to the value of the assets in dispute. With reference to freezing orders, the court fee (which is 50% of the fee due for ordinary proceedings) ranges from EUR 21.50 to EUR 843.00.

An application for a freezing order must satisfy the two requirements prescribed by Article 671 of the CoCP:

(i) The plaintiff must demonstrate (normally on the basis of written evidence, although witnesses may also be heard) that he has a plausible claim ('*fumus boni juris*'). Full evidence of the existence of the claim and that it has fallen due is not required.
(ii) The plaintiff must demonstrate a justified concern that he may lose the possibility to secure his claim ('*periculum in mora*') if the freezing order is not granted.

Although not expressly stipulated in the law, an interim measure will not be granted if the plaintiff is in possession of an enforcement order entitling him to seize the defendant's assets directly.

The proceedings for obtaining interim relief are rather informal. The judge fixes a hearing and collects the evidence that he deems necessary. However, if the plaintiff can demonstrate that the effects of the interim measure could be jeopardized pending the time for the hearing, the judge may grant the freezing order '*ex parte*' and instead fix a subsequent hearing, where the measure will be confirmed, amended or revoked.

Whenever delivering a freezing order, the judge may order the plaintiff to provide security for any possible damages to the defendant that may occur as a result of the freezing of his assets.

If the freezing order is issued prior to a lawsuit having been initiated, the judge must also fix a term (up to sixty days) for the plaintiff to commence the proceedings on the substance of the matter. Should the latter be subject to arbitration, the plaintiff must serve the defendant with a request for arbitration (including the nomination of the arbitrator) within the same sixty-day deadline.

The request for a freezing order may be rejected either because of a lack of jurisdiction (in which case a new application may be filed with another court that has jurisdiction), or because the application lacks merit (in which case, the plaintiff may file a new application provided that the factual circumstances have changed, and/or new arguments of law are introduced).

A freezing order is delivered in the form of a 'permission' by the judge to the plaintiff to freeze any assets owned by the defendant, up to the amount of the claim (including interest).

When assets registered on public records (real estate, motor vehicles, ships or aircrafts) are frozen, the plaintiff must also register the relevant act of perfection to secure his right to the assets against bona fide third parties.

As a result of the measure, the defendant cannot dispose of the frozen assets, as this would constitute a criminal offence, sanctioned under the Italian Penal Code. It is worth noting that when a bank account is frozen, neither the bank nor the defendant may dispose of the assets on the account embraced by the freezing order.

Each party may file a complaint against the decision according to which the freezing order was granted or rejected, within fifteen days counting from the hearing when the decision was delivered. The complaint must be submitted to the city where it will be adjudicated by three judges.

The Court will confirm, amend or revoke the appealed decision with a final judgment. The freezing order can be enforced pending the complaint proceedings, unless the court finds it appropriate to suspend enforceability.

A freezing order becomes ineffective should one of the following events occur:

- enforcement is not commenced within thirty days;
- the proceedings on the substance of the matter is not commenced within the prescribed term, or it is cancelled at any time;
- the plaintiff does not lodge the security as ordered by the judge;
- the existence of the right that the freezing order intends to protect is afterwards denied (either through a domestic or foreign judgment, or through an arbitral award); or
- the request for enforcement of the foreign judgment or of the award is not filed within the prescribed term.

During the course of the proceedings on the substance of the matter, the freezing order may be amended or cancelled if new factual circumstances occur or if evidence, which could not have been previously submitted, is discovered.

§13.04 ENFORCEMENT ISSUES

Italy has adopted Council Regulation (EC) No. 44/2001 of 22 December 2000 on jurisdiction and the recognition and enforcement of judgments in civil and commercial matters (the so-called Brussels I Regulation), which has been replaced by the Regulation (EU) No. 1215/2012 of the European Parliament and of the Council of 12 December 2012 (the 'Brussels Regulation Recast'), which applies 'only to legal proceedings instituted, to authentic instruments formally drawn up or registered and to court settlements approved or concluded on or after 10 January 2015'. However, the rules on enforcement of judgments are basically the same.

Furthermore, in 1969 Italy ratified the 1958 New York Convention (the 'NYC') on the Recognition and Enforcement of Foreign Arbitral Awards.

Against this background, foreign judgments and arbitral awards rendered in Brussels regulation and NYC member countries may be enforced in Italy. In the following paragraphs, a brief overview of the respective proceeding will be provided for.

[A] General Comments Concerning Enforcement Proceedings in Italy

Pursuant to Article 474 of the CoCP, enforcement proceedings are commenced on the basis of an enforceable instrument (*'titoli esecutivi'*), such as: judgments and instruments to which the law expressly accords executory effect (e.g., arbitral awards); promissory notes, as well as other negotiable instruments to which the law expressly accords executory effect (e.g., checks); private law instruments including contracts, deeds and other private law instruments executed before a notary, but only as far as pecuniary claims are concerned (e.g., the price to be paid for purchasing a real estate).

Enforcement of a negotiable instrument is based on the original title, while a judgment and any other instrument that is enforceable as a judgment as well as deeds certified by a notary or other public official, must be endorsed with the execution formula (*'formula esecutiva'*) that orders its enforcement.[21]

Save where the law provides otherwise, enforcement must usually be preceded by service of a notice to comply (*'Atto di precetto'*),[22] which is a formal notice issued by the creditor to the debtor to the effect that, if the latter does not fulfil his/her obligation within a given deadline (which may not be less than ten days), enforcement proceedings will be initiated.[23] If delay would be prejudicial, the court may reduce or eliminate the ten-day enforcement period.[24]

If, after service of the notice to comply, the debtor does not pay within the given deadline, enforcement proceedings will be commenced. A file containing all the papers in the proceedings is opened in the registrar's office, and a judge (*'giudice dell'esecuzione'*) is appointed to supervise and conduct the proceedings, which are aimed at allowing the creditor to attach assets belonging to the debtor.[25]

---

21. *Codice di Procedura Civile*, Article 475, paragraph 1 The *formula esecutiva* is inscribed on the instrument by the court registrar or other custodian of the instrument. It commands the bailiff and all other competent officials to enforce the instrument, the public prosecutor office to aid such officers, and the police to render assistance upon request.
22. The notice to comply must indicate that the creditor has his/her residence or elects domicile within the commune in which the court of enforcement sits (*Codice di Procedura Civile*, Article 480, paragraph 3). It must be signed by the creditor or by his/her attorney. It is served personally upon the debtor pursuant to the same rules that apply to service of summons (*Codice di Procedura Civile*, Article 480, paragraph 4). A notice to comply lapses if enforcement proceedings are not commenced within ninety days after its service, but if the debtor takes steps to contest the validity of the notice to comply, the running of the ninety-day period is suspended to permit determination of the contest (*Codice di Procedura Civile*, Article 481). The debtor may challenge the notice to comply pursuant to Article 615 of the CoCP.
23. *Codice di Procedura Civile*, Article 480, paragraph 1.
24. *Codice di Procedura Civile*, Article 482.
25. *Codice di Procedura Civile*, Article 484. This judge is a member of the Court of First Instance (*'tribunale'*) appointed by the president. Territorial competence in proceedings relating to personal and real estate is vested in the court of the place in which the property is located (*Codice di Procedura Civile*, Article 26, paragraph 1), while territorial competence in proceedings concerning liquidation of the debtor's claims is vested in the court of the place in which the debtor resides (*Codice di Procedura Civile*, Article 26*bis*, paragraph 2). These rules of territorial competence may not be modified neither by agreement of the parties (*Codice di Procedura Civile*, Article 28) nor by the possible influence of other special rules. The judge's rulings may be attacked only by instituting a separate proceeding in the tribunal (*giudizio di opposizione*).

In general, attachments and forced liquidations of assets are carried out in several steps:[26] (1) the debtor's assets are identified and attached; (2) other creditors may intervene; (3) the debtor's assets are liquidated; (4) the creditor is paid, or the proceeds from the liquidation of the debtor's assets are distributed amongst the creditors.

[B] Enforcement of Foreign Judgments

A judgment given in an EU country will be recognized in Italy without any special procedural steps, unless the recognition is contested. Under Article 32 of the Brussels Regulation Recast, a 'judgment' means any judgment given by a court of an EU country, whatever its name (such as decrees, orders, decisions or writs of execution), as well as the determination and awarding of procedural costs and expenses.

Under no circumstances will a foreign judgment be revisited as to its substance (cf. Article 36 of the Brussels Regulation Recast) by an Italian court in the context of the enforcement proceedings. Having said this, a judgment will *not* be recognized if:[27]

- such recognition is manifestly contrary to public policy in the EU country in which recognition is sought;
- the defendant was not served with the document that instituted the proceedings in sufficient time and in such a way as to enable the defendant to arrange for his/her defence;
- recognition would be irreconcilable with a judgment given in a dispute between the same parties before an Italian Court;
- recognition would be irreconcilable with an earlier judgment given in another EU or non-EU country involving the same cause of action and the same parties.

An application for enforceability must be submitted to the Court of Appeal having territorial jurisdiction on the basis of the domicile of the defendant or of the place of enforcement. The plaintiff must attach to the application a certified copy of the judgment.

The court before which enforcement is sought may stay the proceedings, if an ordinary appeal against the judgment has been filed.

Once delivered, the declaration of enforceability (the so-called *exequatur*) must be served on the defendant debtor, which is entitled to challenge it in court.

Finally, a foreign judgment that has been declared enforceable in Italy can be enforced in Italy as if it were a judgment delivered by an Italian court.

[C] Enforcement of Foreign Arbitral Awards

With respect to foreign arbitral awards, Article 839 (concerning recognition and enforcement) and Article 840 (concerning appeals) of the CoCP, which mirror the relevant provisions of NYC (Articles V and VI), apply.

26. *Codice di Procedura Civile*, Articles 491-512.
27. Cf. Article 34 of the Brussels Regulation Recast.

The relevant application for enforcement must be filed with the President of the Court of Appeal in which district the other party resides. If the other party does not reside in Italy, the President of the Court of Appeal of Rome holds jurisdiction.

The plaintiff must provide the original award or a certified copy thereof, as well as the original arbitration agreement or a certified copy thereof with the application. If such documents are not in the Italian language, the plaintiff must also file a certified translation into Italian.

The first decision granting or denying recognition can be appealed to the Court of Appeal where a panel of three judges will decide on the matter.

§13.05 D&O LIABILITY IN RELATION TO ASSET PROTECTION SCHEMES

[A] Civil and Company Law Provisions

The general principle on patrimonial liability under Italian Law is stated in Article 2740 CC, according to which: '*(1) A debtor is liable with all his present and future property for the performance of his obligations. (2) Limitations upon such liability are not allowed except in the cases set forth by the law*'.

In order to avoid this broad liability, it is sometimes seen that debtors, be they corporations or private individuals, during the course of, or even before the commencement of a dispute resolution proceeding, attempt to remove valuable assets from their own sphere of ownership, by transfer or assignment to a third party. Further, the use of 'shield corporations' and/or thin or undercapitalized corporations, or the allocation of assets to 'trusts'[28] is also sometimes facing creditors attempting to enforce a judgment or arbitral award against an Italian debtor.[29]

In the following, we will provide an overview of the relevant rules under Italian law that can be applied by creditors facing different types of illicit asset shielding schemes.

[1] Transfer or Assignment of Assets to Third Parties

A creditor can demand that a transfer of assets by a debtor to a third party be declared ineffective when: (1) the debtor was aware that the transfer would prejudice the creditor or that the transfer was fraudulently designed for such purpose; and (2) in cases where the transaction was 'non-gratuitous' and/or where the third party was aware of this and participated regardless.[30]

28. Trust are not expressly regulated under Italian law. However, they are recognized since Italy has ratified the Hague Convention on the law applicable to trusts dated 1 July 1985, entered into force on 1 January 1992. On the regulation of trusts under Italian law see LUPOI, *Trusts*, Milan, 2001.
29. The abuse of insolvency proceedings will not be examined in this report as it falls outside its scope of investigation.
30. Article 2901 CC regulates the so-called ordinary clawback, which shall not be confused with the special bankruptcy clawback, which may be triggered only by the bankruptcy receiver under Article 67 Italian Bankruptcy Act.

Once the declaration of ineffectiveness is obtained, the creditor may institute enforcement proceedings or proceedings to secure precautionary measures on the property, which has been transferred, against the relevant third party.

Another remedy available to a creditor is the action to obtain a declaration that the contract is a sham.[31] The sham can either be relative, when the parties have *formally* executed a contract but have *substantially* intended to execute a *different* contract; or the sham can be absolute, when the parties have formally executed a contract but have substantially intended *not* to execute any contract at all.

According to Article 1416, paragraph 2 CC, the creditors of a debtor who has made a transfer of property according to a sham contract can invoke the sham when it is prejudicial to their rights, and claw back the transferred assets.

[2] The Use of 'Shield Corporations'

With reference to the patrimonial liability of limited liability corporations,[32] the general principle is that the corporation is liable for its obligations only with its assets. This general principle has substantially been reaffirmed during the 2003 corporate law reform in Italy.

The most important exception to this general principle relates to a debtor company, which only has one shareholder in cases where the shareholder has failed to file a registration with the Company Register that there is only one shareholder. In such a situation, the *sole shareholder* is *jointly liable* with the corporation with his own assets.[33]

Other legal principles have sometimes been invoked by creditors in an attempt to extend a company's liability to other subjects. Two such principles should be mentioned here.

[3] The Director's Liability vis-à-vis the Company's Creditors

Article 2394 CC[34] on joint stock companies ('*S.p.A.*') provides, as a general rule, that directors are liable to company creditors for negligently failing to preserve the company's assets, e.g., by having sold or transferred the assets to a third party at a price, which is evidently too low.

Accordingly, where the debtor company's assets prove to be insufficient to satisfy the debts owed by the company, the creditors can bring a direct action for damages

31. Sham contracts are regulated by Articles 1414–1417 CC.
32. Limited liability corporations under Italian Law are joint stock corporations and limited liability corporations. Both corporations can have a sole shareholder or a plurality of shareholders. In limited partnership by shares, regulated by Articles 2452–2461 CC, general partners have joint and unlimited liability for the partnership's obligations, whereas special partners are liable only within the limit of the portion of the capital subscribed.
33. See Articles 2325 and 2362 CC for joint stock companies and Articles 2462 and 2470 CC for limited liability companies.
34. A similar provision is dictated by Article 2476 CC on directors of limited liability companies ('*S.r.l.*').

against the directors of the company if it can be shown that the directors have negligently failed to protect the assets of the company.

The same principle applies to the auditors of the company, who are jointly liable with the directors for damages inflicted on the creditors as a result of a breach of their duties.[35]

The liability of the directors and the auditors is personal and unlimited in these situations.

[4] The 'Shadow Entrepreneur'

The 'shadow entrepreneur' doctrine aims at extending the liability of a company to its persons who, despite the lack of a formal role, are de facto managing the company as if they were shareholders or directors of the same.

This doctrine derives from Article 147 of the Italian Bankruptcy Act, which applies only to partnerships. The rule provides that, in case of a declaration of bankruptcy of a partnership, also its unlimited liability shareholders may be declared bankrupt. This also extends to the shareholders who are not formally registered as such in the Company Register.

Certain scholars[36] have tried to extend this doctrine to corporations, arguing that also dominant 'de facto' shareholders could be held liable vis-à-vis the corporation's creditors. However, so far Italian judges have not adhered to this theory.

[B] Trusts and Allocated Assets

The transfer of assets to a trust may be challenged on the basis of the law governing the trust and/or the above-mentioned rules regarding sham contracts.

With reference to allocated assets, Article 2447*bis* CC provides that a company may allocate assets up to a maximum amount of 10% of its net assets to a specific business activity.

The resolution to settle and allocate asset to a trust must contain the information mentioned in Article 2447*ter* CC, and such resolution should be registered with the Company Register within sixty days. Unless an opposition is filed by the company creditors who were creditors before the registration of the resolution within sixty days from publication, upon registration in the Company Register the company creditors will not be permitted to assert any claim on the allocated assets nor against the proceeds and income arising from the specific business activity to which the assets have been allocated.

The above provisions on allocated assets thus reinforce the principle of the liability of a corporation being limited to its own assets, save for the exceptions mentioned above.

---

35. See Article 2407 CC.
36. See W. Bigiavi, *L'imprenditore occulto*, Padua, 1954; F. GALGANO, *Diritto civile e commerciale*, 4, Padua, 2004.

[C] Criminal Law Provisions

Finally, certain provisions of criminal law are also of importance in relation to the liability of company directors and officers engaged in asset shielding schemes. Some of the relevant provisions are contained in the Italian Civil Code and some in the Penal Code.

Article 2629 CC provides:

> *(1) The directors who, in breach of the provisions of law for the protection of creditors, arrange for the reduction of the capital or for mergers with other companies or for de-mergers, causing a damage to the creditors are punished, subject to the filing of a criminal action by the offended person, with the imprisonment from six months to ten years. (2) The restoration of damages to the creditors prior to the judgment extinguishes the offence.*

Pursuant to Article 2639 CC, the above liability is extended also to subjects other than those formally entrusted with the appointment or the function provided by the law, but who are required to perform the same function, differently qualified, or de facto regularly exercise the powers typically inherent to the appointment or function. The same liability applies also to persons appointed by the judicial authority or the supervisory authority to manage the company or the assets owned by the company or managed by it on behalf of third parties.

Chapter 14
The Netherlands

Sidney J.H.M. Berendsen & Bart-Jaap van Emmerik

§14.01 INTRODUCTION

After the formation of the Republic of the Seven United Netherlands (*Republiek der Zeven Verenigde Nederlanden*) in 1588, the process of codification of the customary law in the Republic slowly started to take place. In the Dutch Golden Age (the seventeenth century), in which the Republic flourished as one of the most powerful countries in the world, Roman law also started to gain significance in the Netherlands.

After France brought down the Republic in 1795, in 1809 Napoleon introduced the French *Code Civil* as well as the *Code Pénal* as the first extensive codification of applicable law in the Netherlands.

Mainly inspired by the French *Code Civil*, in 1838 the first codification of Dutch civil law came into existence. In 1838, the Dutch Supreme Court (*Hoge Raad*) was also founded. The *Code Pénal* was only replaced by the Dutch Wetboek van Strafrecht in 1886.

The rather recent introduction of a new Civil Code in 1992 is unique in Europe. The new code attributes a greater role to considerations of equity and is much more open to other sources of law than just legislation.[1]

As a country which is heavily dependent on (international) trade, the Netherlands has a very creditor friendly juridical system, which provides for far-reaching possibilities in respect of pre-judgment attachments.

However, Dutch law does not provide for specific legal proceedings in respect of asset disclosure, nor does Dutch law provide for a specific obligation pursuant to which one must disclose (and subsequently retain) its assets, unless insolvency proceedings are first initiated against the defendant. As described in further detail below under

1. Lesaffer R.C.H. (2004). A short legal history of the Netherlands. In H. S. Taekema (Ed.), Understanding Dutch law. (pp. 31–58). Den Haag: Boom Juridische Uitgevers.

section §14.02, there are several (online) databases in the Netherlands with detailed information about different types of assets, which are available to the public.

In relation to the possibility of freezing assets, Dutch law provides creditors with far-reaching possibilities, especially compared to other (European) jurisdictions. We will set out the Dutch rules on freezing orders below under section §14.03.

With regard to the judiciary system, the Dutch courts are composed of: the Supreme Court (*Hoge Raad*), four Courts of Appeal (*Gerechtshoven*), and eleven district courts (*Rechtbanken*).[2] The main Dutch arbitral institution is the NAI (*Nederlands Arbitrage Instituut*).

Courts in the Netherlands consist solely of appointed, rather than elected, judges. Judges are civil servants, but act in their judicial capacity with complete independence from the government. Judges are appointed for life.

The enforcement and recognition of judgments and arbitral awards is handled by the district courts, whose decisions can ultimately be appealed to the Supreme Court. The EEX Regulation applies in the Netherlands. Furthermore, the Netherlands has ratified the 1958 New York Convention on the Recognition and Enforcement of Foreign Arbitral Awards as well as the Lugano Convention. Below under section §14.04, we have provided an overview of how foreign judgments and awards can be enforced in the Netherlands.

Finally, under section §14.05, we have addressed the remedies, which Dutch law offers plaintiffs in regard to countering asset shielding manoeuvres.

§14.02 IDENTIFYING ASSETS IN THE NETHERLANDS

Dutch law does – as stated above – not provide for specific legal proceedings in respect of asset disclosure, nor does Dutch law provide for a specific obligation pursuant to which one must disclose its assets. Furthermore, the Netherlands does not have a general register reflecting bad creditors, nor a register in which (security over) tangible assets are registered or a register reflecting the shareholdings in corporations. There are, however, a number of public registers and databases in the Netherlands containing information about different types of assets belonging to corporations and private individuals. The below registers and databases are the most relevant asset research sources.

[A] Real Estate

The land registry in the Netherlands (*Kadaster*) maintains a public database containing information about real estate located in the Netherlands. There are several websites, under which the land registry's official website www.kadaster.nl, that give access to the information about real estate located in the Netherlands. The website makes it possible to search for a specific property using a street address or a zip code.

2. See also http://www.government.nl/issues/administration-of-justice-and-dispute-settlement/the-dutch-court-system.

An extract of the title deed of a property can be retrieved to determine the owner and the purchase price of the property. In order to determine whether the value of a property exceeds the amount of financing in respect of a property, an extract of the mortgage(s) in relation to a property can be retrieved, showing *inter alia* the maximum amount of such mortgage. The database also shows whether or not other creditors have levied attachments on the property.

The website www.funda.nl, which contains a non-exhaustive overview of properties that are for sale, can be used to determine whether the property is for sale.

[B] Motor Vehicles

Although motor vehicles must be registered in the Netherlands, there is no publicly accessible database which contains information about the ownership of a vehicle.

The only information that can be derived from the website of the register (https://ovi.rdw.nl/default.aspx?kenteken), on the basis of the license number of the vehicle, is some limited information such as the year the vehicle has been built, its motor specifications, whether the vehicle is stolen and if it is cleared to be driven on public roads. Pledges and attachments over the vehicle are not registered and are not available to the public.

[C] Vessels

The Dutch land registry (*Kadaster*) maintains a separate vessel register which contains information about *inter alia* ownership, mortgages and attachments in relation to vessels registered in the Netherlands (http://www.kadaster.nl/web/Particulier/Schepen.htm). The name of the vessel, its brand, name of the owner, year of built, properties of the engine and IMO number can be used to identify a vessel.

[D] Aircrafts

There is also a Dutch aircraft register, which contains limited information in respect of registered aircrafts, such as the type of aircraft, the serial number, the engine and the person/corporation that has the aircraft in its possession. Information about ownership and mortgages is not publicly available.

The Dutch Aircraft Register is available via this website: http://www.newfoundland.nl/luchtvaartregister/user/nl/zoeken.htm.

[E] IP Rights

Patents are registered in the Dutch Patent Register, which is available at: http://register.octrooicentrum.nl/register/zoekformulier. Designs and trademarks are registered at the Benelux Office of Intellectual Property (https://register.boip.int/bmbonline/intro

/select.do?language=nl). The owners of the protected intellectual property can be found here, as well as the content that is protected under intellectual property law.

[F] Financial Reports

Dutch corporate entities are registered in the trade register (www.kvk.nl). The trade register contains information about *inter alia* the directors of a corporate entity. If the corporate entity has a sole shareholder, such shareholder is also mentioned. The financial reports of corporate entities can also be obtained from the trade register.

§14.03 INTERIM MEASURES

The Dutch legal system is one of the most creditor friendly legal systems in the world and provides for far-reaching possibilities in respect of freezing assets, both before and after a court judgment regarding the (alleged) claim of the creditor has been obtained.[3]

A prejudgment attachment serves the purpose of preventing a prospective debtor from frustrating recovery by his prospective creditor, for example, by alienating, removing or hiding assets.[4] A direct result of the attachment, and quite often an end in itself, is the pressure it exerts on the debtor. In general, the debtor is not allowed to dispose of any attached property and may not move or transfer it. Although the debtor may be hindered in his business or personal life, and may suffer damages, this does not, in general, constitute a compelling reason for denying or lifting the attachment.

Among the different types of prejudgment attachments are the attachment of assets of the debtor in the possession of the debtor, the garnishment of assets that are owned by the debtor but that are held by a third party, such as bank accounts (usually referred to as 'third-party attachment'), the attachment of shares in a company, the arrest of vessels, the arrest of airplanes, the attachment of real estate and the attachment of property alleged to belong to the creditor. The specific rules governing these types of attachment are to be found primarily in the Dutch Code of Civil Procedures ('DCCP', Articles 700–770c). Statutory law relevant to the arrest of vessels is also found in the Commercial Code (*Wetboek van Koophandel*).

In a number of cases, the (prospective) creditor must state and explain why there is a justified fear that the debtor will embezzle the assets, which the (prospective) creditor seeks to attach, for instance if the (prospective) creditor seeks the attachment of movable or immovable property, intellectual property rights or shares in a corporation.

Any party with an apparently justified claim may request the relief judge of the competent district court to give permission for the attachment, garnishment or arrest of the assets described in the request (Article 700 DCCP). The jurisdiction of the district

3. H.J. Snijders, C.J.M. Klaassen and G.J. Meijer, 'Nederlands burgerlijk procesrecht' (2011), p. 483.
4. W. Hugenholtz and W.H. Heemskerk, 'Hoofdlijnen van Nederlands Burgerlijk Procesrecht' (2009), p. 237.

court may be based on either the location of the assets, the debtor's domicile or, in the case of a garnishment, the domicile of the third party.

A request for permission to make an attachment is made through a petition. The petition must contain a summary description of the facts of the case and the legal basis of the claim (tort, contract or other basis); the possible defence that may be brought forward (including a refutation thereof) and (albeit not a requirement) copies of documents or other evidence. Furthermore, the petition must address whether the requested attachment is the least burdening measure for the debtor, which nevertheless provides sufficient security for the creditor and whether it is in proportion to the interest of the creditor (Article 700 section 2 DCCP).

The relief judge decides after marginal review of the petition, usually without hearing the debtor (ex parte).[5] In the event the relief judge decides to grant permission to make the requested attachment, the relief judge determines a certain period of time (at least eight days but usually fourteen days as of the date the attachment is made), in which the claimant/petitioner must initiate main proceedings against the defendant/debtor, unless such proceedings have already been initiated at the time of the attachment (Article 700 section 3 DCCP).

However, in some cases – for example if the matter is to be decided by a foreign court or by arbitration in another country – Dutch courts tend to allow for a longer period than fourteen days between the attachment and the initiation of the main proceedings. If necessary, this period may be extended by the relief judge upon a motivated request by the claimant. It is noted that a failure to initiate the main proceedings within the set time period automatically renders the attachment void.[6] Sometimes, a relief judge will furthermore decide that the claimant can only make the requested attachment under the condition that he provides the debtor with security up to a certain amount (usually in the form of a bank guarantee) with a view to a possible (counter)claim by the debtor for damages in the event it is later determined that the attachment was unlawful or wrongful (Article 702 section 1 DCCP).

An attachment on assets located in the Netherlands generally establishes jurisdiction over the cause of action for which the attachment is made, even if neither of the parties involved are domiciled in the Netherlands, provided however, that there is no other way through which a judgment can be obtained that can be enforced against the attached assets (Article 767 DCCP). In such cases, the proper court to hear the claim is the district court in whose district the attachment was made (Article 700 DCCP).

An attachment must be lifted if the debtor provides alternative security for the creditor's alleged claim (Article 705 section 2 DCCP). The most common way for a debtor to provide alternative security to the (prospective) creditor is through a bank guarantee.[7] A dispute concerning the sufficiency of the collateral offered may be presented to the authorized relief judge.

5. W. Hugenholtz and W.H. Heemskerk, 'Hoofdlijnen van Nederlands Burgerlijk Procesrecht' (2009), p. 281.
6. Supreme Court judgment of 9 February 2007, ECLI:NL:HR:2007:AZ2587.
7. A.S. Rueb, 'Compendium Burgerlijk Procesrecht' (2013), p. 439.

If the debtor is not willing or able to offer alternative security, he may nevertheless initiate proceedings aimed at lifting the attachment. In either case a hearing can take place at a very short notice; in some cases, if there is a compelling reason for such urgency (such reason could be an attachment on bank accounts that disproportionately frustrates the business of the debtor), even immediately (or within a few days) after attachment of the assets.[8] If the relief judge holds that the claim underlying the attachment is prima facie without merit or that the attachment is unnecessary (e.g., if in all reasonableness the creditor does not need to fear that there will be no or insufficient assets remaining by the time he has obtained an enforceable judgment or award against the debtor), he may order the attachment to be lifted.[9] The decision of the relief judge in these preliminary relief proceedings does not prejudice the decision in the main proceedings.

Finally, it is noted that the arresting party is strictly liable for all damages resulting from a wrongful attachment.[10] An attachment is wrongful, mainly in case the claim of the creditor has been dismissed in main proceedings.[11] Only if the party making a wrongful arrest can demonstrate to the satisfaction of the relevant court that the attachment was made under 'special circumstances' will he have a chance of avoiding such liability. Whether or not such 'special circumstances' apply, always depends on the particular facts and circumstances of a case and is left to the discretion of the courts.

It is noted, however, that a claim for damages resulting from a wrongful attachment will be awarded, even if the arresting party acted with due care and diligence when making the attachment and, for example, the negative outcome (for the arresting party, that is) of the court proceedings regarding the claim following the attachment was by no means predictable or foreseeable.[12]

On the one hand, an attachment provides for a swift and rather far-reaching possibility to preserve the assets of a debtor. On the other hand, such debtor may initiate summary proceedings or issue a bank guarantee to have the attachment lifted at a (very) short notice.

In summary, attachment proceedings can be described as follows:

- the request to place a prejudgment attachment is submitted to the district court where (i) the defendant has his residence or official seat, or (ii) where the assets are located;

8. Provisions Judge of the District Court of Rotterdam judgment of 7 June 2002, ECLI:NL:RBROT:2002:AG8130 and Provisions Judge of the District Court of Roermond judgment of 14 February 2002, ECLI:NL:RBROE:2002:AV7625.
9. Supreme Court judgments of 14 June 1996, ECLI:NL:HR1996:ZC2105 of 13 June 2003, ECLI:NL:HR:2003:AF5529 of 25 November 2005, ECLI:NL:HR:2005:AT9060 and of 30 June 2006, ECLI:NL:HR:2006:AV1559.
10. Supreme Court judgment of 15 April 1965, ECLI:NL:HR:1965:AC4076.
11. A.S. Rueb, 'Compendium Burgerlijk Procesrecht' (2013), p. 441; Supreme Court judgment of 13 January 1995, ECLI:NL:HR:1995:ZC1608.
12. W. Hugenholtz and W.H. Heemskerk, 'Hoofdlijnen van Nederlands Burgerlijk Procesrecht' (2009), p. 283.

- the relief judge decides after marginal review of the petition, usually without hearing the debtor (ex parte);
- after the attachment is placed the creditor must initiate main proceedings on the merits against the debtor to enforce the alleged claim within the term ordered by the court (if the creditor fails to do so, the attachment automatically becomes null and void);
- the debtor may initiate (summary) proceedings at a (very) short notice in which the debtor requests the attachment be lifted;
- the attachment must be lifted if the debtor has issued a bank guarantee; and
- as a general principle, the creditor shall be strictly liable for all damages resulting from wrongful attachment.

§14.04 ENFORCEMENT ISSUES

If the defendant holds assets that are located in the Netherlands, but the dispute resolution proceedings take place in another country, the question arises whether it is possible to enforce the foreign judgment or arbitral award against the Dutch assets.

The Brussels I Regulation applies in the Netherlands. The Netherlands is also a member to the Lugano Convention on Jurisdiction and the Enforcement of Judgments in Civil and Commercial matters (the 'Lugano Convention').

With respect to foreign arbitral awards, the Netherlands is, as are the most European countries, a party to the 1958 New York Convention on the Recognition and Enforcement of Foreign Arbitral Awards (the '1958 New York Convention').[13]

Accordingly, arbitral awards and judgments from most European countries can be enforced in the Netherlands. However, judgments rendered by courts of countries that have not ratified the Brussels or Lugano Conventions will in principle not be enforced by the Dutch courts and will only under certain circumstances be recognized by the Dutch courts.[14]

In the following, we will provide a brief overview as to how foreign judgments rendered by a court in a Lugano Convention or Brussels I Regulation Member State can be enforced in the Netherlands, under section §14.04[A] below. Under section §14.04[B], we will elaborate on the Brussels I Regulation Recast. Under section §14.04[C], we will address enforcement of foreign judgments on the basis of a European Enforcement Order. Under section §14.04[D], we will address how enforcement of foreign judgments takes place if no treaty is applicable and under section §14.04[E], we will set out how international arbitral awards can be enforced in the Netherlands.

13. http://www.uncitral.org/pdf/english/texts/arbitration/NY-conv/XXII_1_e.pdf.
14. H.J. Snijders, C.J.M. Klaassen and G.J. Meijer, 'Nederlands burgerlijk procesrecht' (2011), p. 467. See also Supreme Court judgment of 17 December 1993, ECLI:NL:HR:1993:ZC1183.

[A] Enforcement of Foreign Judgments

Pursuant to Article 33 of the Brussels I Regulation, judgments given in an EU Member State shall be recognized in the other EU Member States without any special procedure being required.[15] The Lugano Convention extends the sphere of mutual recognition and enforcement of civil judgments beyond the borders of the European Union, encompassing also Iceland, Norway and Switzerland.

As is the case with the Brussels I Regulation, the Lugano Convention solely regulates the recognition and enforcement of civil judgments, and the Lugano Convention is, in substance, largely similar to the Brussels I Regulation.[16] Therefore, only the rules of the Brussels I Regulation will be discussed in the following, and the additional rules following from the Brussels I Regulation Recast will be addressed separately.

Under the Brussels I Regulation, a judgment rendered in an EU Member State, which is enforceable there, can be enforced in another Member State after being declared enforceable there, (the so-called *exequatur*), on application by anyone who has an interest in the matter.[17]

The application must be made to the court that has territorial jurisdiction on the basis of the domicile of the defendant or on the basis of the place of enforcement.

The declaration of enforceability, the '*exequatur*', is issued after certain formalities have been completed and must be served on the other party, who may challenge it only in the courts. The plaintiff must present a certified copy of the judgment as well as proof that the judgment is enforceable in the state of origin.

There are no provisions on enforcement as such. Therefore, once a judgment from another Member State has been declared enforceable in the Netherlands, the judgment can be enforced in the same way as judgments rendered by a Dutch court.

The Dutch courts can only refuse to recognize a judgment rendered in another Member State for the following reasons specified in Articles 34 and 35 of the Brussels I Convention:

- such recognition is manifestly contrary to public policy in the EU country in which recognition is sought;
- the defendant was not served with the document that instituted the proceedings in sufficient time and in such a way as to enable the defendant to arrange for his/her defence;
- it is irreconcilable with a judgment given in a dispute between the same parties in the EU country in which recognition is sought;

15. For the purposes of the Brussels I Regulation, 'judgment' means any judgment given by a court or tribunal of a Member State, whatever the judgment may be called, including a decree, order, decision or writ of execution, as well as the determination of costs or expenses by an officer of the court, cf. Article 32.
16. The Lugano Convention was formed as a modified version of the 1968 Brussels Convention and its main purpose was to join the EFTA and the European Union Member States together under one jurisdictional and enforcement system.
17. H.J. Snijders, C.J.M. Klaassen and G.J. Meijer, 'Nederlands burgerlijk procesrecht' (2011), p. 466.

- it is irreconcilable with an earlier judgment given in another EU or non-EU country involving the same cause of action and the same parties.

[B] As of 15 January 2015: Brussels I Regulation Recast

The Brussels I Regulation Recast applies to (judgments given in) legal proceedings instituted, to authentic instruments formally drawn up or registered and to court settlements approved or concluded on or after 10 January 2015 (Article 66(1) of the Brussels I Regulation Recast).

The enforcement procedure under the Brussels I Regulation Recast shows great differences in comparison to the Brussels I Regulation and the Lugano Convention. In short, under the Brussels I Regulation Recast a judgment given in an EU Member State which is enforceable in that EU Member State shall be enforceable in the other EU Member States without any declaration of enforceability being required (Article 39 of the Brussels I Regulation Recast).

The procedure for the enforcement of a judgment given in another EU Member State shall be governed by the law of the EU Member State addressed. The foreign judgment is to be enforced under the same conditions as a judgment given in the EU Member State addressed (Article 41(1) of the Brussels I Regulation).

The grounds for refusal or of suspension of enforcement under the law of the EU Member State addressed shall apply insofar as they are not incompatible with the grounds referred to in Article 45 of the Brussels I Regulation Recast.

On the application of the party against which enforcement is sought, the enforcement of a judgment could be refused on certain grounds, e.g., if a recognition is manifestly contrary to public policy in the EU Member State addressed (Articles 46 and 45 of the Brussels I Regulation Recast).

[C] Enforcement of Foreign Judgments on the Basis of a European Enforcement Order

Further, mention should be made of Regulation (EC) 805/2004 of 21 April 2004 creating a European Enforcement Order for uncontested claims ('European Enforcement Order Regulation'). This regulation is applicable as of 21 October 2005 in all EU Member States, except Denmark. The European Enforcement Order Regulation applies to *inter alia* judgments on uncontested claims. Under this regulation, a claim is regarded as uncontested if, for example, the debtor has expressly agreed to it by admission or the debtor has never objected to it in the course of the legal proceedings (section 3 European Enforcement Order Regulation).[18]

A judgment which has been certified as a European Enforcement Order in the EU Member State of origin of the judgment is to be recognized and enforced in the other EU

18. See also M. Zilinsky, De Europese Executoriale titel, diss. Amsterdam (VU, 2005) and M. Freudenthal, 'Grensoverschrijdende erkenning en tenuitvoerlegging' (2009), ch. 4.

Member States without the need for a declaration of enforceability and without any possibility of opposing its recognition.[19] Enforcement shall, upon application by the debtor, be refused by the competent court in the EU Member State of enforcement if the judgment certified as a European Enforcement Order is irreconcilable with an earlier judgment given in any EU Member State or in a third country, provided that a number of requirements are met. For example, the earlier judgment should involve the same cause of action and be between the same parties.

[D] Enforcement of Foreign Judgments If No Treaty Is Applicable

In the event it does not follow from a treaty or a provision of Dutch law that a judgment which was rendered outside the Netherlands is enforceable in the Netherlands, such judgment cannot be enforced and a retrial of the case in the Netherlands is necessary (section 431 DCCP). In such new legal proceedings in the Netherlands, however, a court could recognize the foreign judgment if the following conditions are met:

(a) the foreign court must have assumed jurisdiction on internationally acceptable grounds;
(b) the foreign judgment must be the result of proceedings that meet the generally accepted fair trial standards;
(c) the foreign judgment must not be in violation of Dutch public policy.

If the foreign judgment is recognized in the Netherlands, a hearing of the case on the merits can be omitted, followed by an order similar to the order which is laid down in the foreign judgment. Subsequently, the judgment of the Dutch court could be enforced in the Netherlands.

[E] Enforcement of International Arbitral Awards

A request for recognition and enforcements of awards made outside of the Netherlands can either be based on a convention (Article 1075 DCCP) or can be made based on Dutch law (Article 1076 DCCP).

With regard to the former option, the 1958 New York Convention is by far the most important treaty.[20]

Article 1075 DCCP confirms once more that an arbitral award made in a foreign State to which a treaty concerning recognition and enforcement is applicable, can be recognized and enforced in the Netherlands. For the avoidance of any doubt: even though according to the text of Article 1075 DCCP an arbitral award can be recognized and enforced in the Netherlands, the Dutch courts are not allowed to refuse recognition and enforcement if this is mandatory pursuant to an international convention. In that

19. H.J. Snijders, C.J.M. Klaassen and G.J. Meijer, 'Nederlands burgerlijk procesrecht' (2011), p. 467.
20. Convention of the Recognition and Enforcement of Foreign Arbitral Awards, New York, 10 June 1958, *Trb.* 1958, 145.

case, the provisions of Articles 985 DCCP up to and including 991 DCCP, which deal with the enforcement of foreign judgments in the Netherlands, also apply to the enforcement of foreign arbitral awards in the Netherlands to the extent that the relevant treaty does not contain provisions deviating therefrom, and provided that the relief judge of the district court shall substitute for the district court and the time limit for appeal from his decision and for recourse to the Supreme Court shall be two months.[21]

If (i) no treaty concerning recognition and enforcement is applicable, or (ii) if an applicable treaty allows a party to rely upon the law of the country in which recognition or enforcement is sought, an arbitral award made in a foreign State may be recognized in the Netherlands and its enforcement may be sought in the Netherlands, upon submission of the original or a certified copy of the arbitration agreement and arbitral award, unless (see Article 1076 section 1 DCCP):

I. The party against whom recognition or enforcement is sought, asserts and proves that:
   (a) there is no valid arbitration agreement between the parties in accordance with the applicable law;
   (b) the arbitral tribunal is constituted in violation of the rules applicable thereto;
   (c) the arbitral tribunal has not complied with its mandate;
   (d) the arbitral award is still open to an appeal to a second arbitral tribunal, or to a court in the country in which the award is made; or
   (e) the arbitral award has been set aside by a competent authority of the country in which that award is made, or

II. The court finds that the recognition or enforcement of the arbitral award would be contrary to public policy.

With regard to the question whether the applicable treaty allows parties to rely on the law of the country in which recognition or enforcement is sought (option (II) above), it is noted that the 1958 New York Convention contains a 'more-favourable-right-provision' (Article 7 section 1). Therefore, it is possible to base the request on both Articles 1075 and 1076 DCCP.[22]

If the award is in excess of, or different from, what was claimed, partial recognition or enforcement is possible to the extent that the part of the award which is in excess of or different from the claim can be separated from the remaining part of the award (Article 1076 section 5 DCCP).

§14.05 D&O LIABILITY IN RELATION TO ASSET PROTECTION SCHEMES

In the course of a dispute, directors of a company may want to shield valuable assets, which could result in the situation that the company's estate provides insufficient opportunity for recovery. Shielding of assets could take place in different forms.

21. See also: H.J. Snijders, 'Groene Serie Burgerlijke Rechtsvordering', Article 1075 DCCP, updated 15 July 2011.
22. H.J. Snijders, C.J.M. Klaassen and G.J. Meijer, 'Nederlands burgerlijk procesrecht' (2011), p. 448.

Directors of a company could transfer assets (undervalued) to an affiliated party, or retrieve the asset from the estate without any judicial grounds. Shielding of assets of course interferes with the recourse of a creditor against the debtor.

The Dutch Civil Code and the Dutch Penal Code provide for several rules concerning D&O liability. In the following, we will provide a brief overview of the relevant rules.

[A] Civil Liability

Dutch civil law provides for several rules on the basis of which the company itself (or a bankruptcy trustee) can hold directors liable for improper performance of their duties (so-called internal liability).

However, third parties that have been harmed by actions of directors can only file proceedings against a director on the basis of the general tort provision of section 6:162 of the Dutch Civil Code (so-called external liability).[23]

In principle, only the company is liable if it commits an unlawful act. Special circumstances may lead to personal liability of a director. From case law, it follows that such special circumstances can be found in the non-payment of outstanding amounts which is caused or allowed by the director or the transfer of assets in order to evade creditors' recourse (*verhaalsfrustratie*).[24]

In the event the managing director breached his duty of care towards the third party such that his actions can be deemed seriously negligent, the managing director can be held liable against such a third party for the loss that third party suffered as a consequence.[25]

[B] Criminal Liability

Section 198 of the Dutch Penal Code declares that a person who intentionally removes any goods that are subject to an attachment or in judicial custody shall be criminally liable. If assets have been frozen by a third party, the act of excluding these assets from the seizure by directors is unlawful and thus punishable.[26]

---

23. See also: A.S. Hartkamp, C.H. Sieburgh, 'Asser/Hartkamp & Sieburgh 6-IV' (2015), nr. 333, updated 1 May 2015.
24. Court of Appeal The Hague judgment of 20 August 1998, ECLI:NL:GHSGR:1998:AG3435.
25. Supreme Court judgment of 8 December 2006, ECLI:NL:HR:2006:AZ0758, (*Ontvanger/ Roelofsen*).
26. For example: Court of Appeal Arnhem judgment of 13 September 2011, ECLI:NL:GHARN: 2011:BT2008.

CHAPTER 15

New Zealand

James Cairney & Kathleen Morrison

§15.01 INTRODUCTION

New Zealand is a parliamentary democracy with a constitutional monarchy that operates as a unitary state, not as a federal system like Australia, Canada or the United States. The Crown or monarch is Queen Elizabeth II, but, for most purposes, she is represented in New Zealand by a Governor-General, whose role is largely ceremonial.

The whole body of existing English law, both legislation and common law, as well as the English constitutional conventions, were received into New Zealand on 14 January 1840. In 1931, the United Kingdom Parliament passed the Statute of Westminster, to facilitate a move towards independence for the Dominions (former colonies) by removing the limitation on their legislative powers. In 1947, New Zealand passed the Statute of Westminster Adoption Act and accepted full responsibility for its own destiny. New Zealand, as a colony, inherited the common law system from Britain, and the English Law Acts of 1854 and 1908 confirmed New Zealand as a common law country.

Statutory law is the supreme law of New Zealand and may specifically overrule an established common law rule. Statutory law will also provide for delegated powers to pass orders and regulations, such as Orders in Council made by the Governor-General on the advice of the executive government, but such power is delegated and must be exercised in accordance with the terms of the empowering statute. New Zealand Courts have no power to strike down statutes or part of statutes as unconstitutional, but the New Zealand Bill of Rights Act 1990 requires that where a statute can be given an interpretation consistent with the Bill of Rights, that interpretation is to be preferred. Until very recently, New Zealand continued to look to the United Kingdom for sources of its own legislation and to the superior English courts for precedents in its own courts. House of Lords and Court of Appeal decisions are still highly persuasive and often cited in New Zealand courts. However, especially in the last twenty years,

New Zealand has looked further afield for legislative models, particularly in commercial law. For example, the New Zealand Commerce Act and Fair Trading Act are modelled directly on the Australian Trade Practices Act, which in turn looks to US models in the American antitrust laws.

The latest Companies Act is based on a Canadian model, as is the Consumer Guarantees Act. On the whole, New Zealand now looks more often to North America than to the United Kingdom for sources of legislation, if not for common law precedent, from which New Zealand courts will consider case authorities, especially in Australia, the Unites Kingdom, Canada and the United States, generally in that order of importance.

The New Zealand High Court has general jurisdiction and responsibility for the administration of justice throughout New Zealand. This includes maintaining the consistent application of the rule of law, supervision of other courts and tribunals and the judicial review of administrative power. It has jurisdiction over both criminal and civil matters, and deals with cases at first instance or on appeal from other courts and certain tribunals.

The High Court comprises the head of the New Zealand Judiciary, the Chief Justice and up to fifty-five other judges (which includes the judges of the Supreme Court and Court of Appeal, which are above the High Court) and are based in most of New Zealand's main cities and regional centres. In addition, Associate Judges of the High Court (formerly known as Masters) supervise the High Court's preliminary processes in most civil proceedings, and have jurisdiction to deal with summary judgment applications, company liquidations, bankruptcy proceedings and some other types of civil proceedings. The High Court has virtually unlimited jurisdiction in civil cases, but generally deals only with those civil claims that exceed the jurisdiction of the District Court or other courts and tribunals, or where particularly complex issues are involved.[1] A plaintiff or applicant seeking a freezing order would have to apply to the High Court for that order, likewise a plaintiff seeking to enforce an award would have to seek enforcement through the High Court's processes (subject in some cases to the amount exceeding lower court jurisdiction).

Above the High Court, the Court of Appeal is New Zealand's intermediate appellate court, dealing with civil and criminal appeals from proceedings heard in the High Court (and some criminal proceedings from District Courts). The highest Court in New Zealand is the Supreme Court, which is the final Court of Appeal and has the role of maintaining overall coherence in New Zealand's legal system.

Below the High Court, there are fifty-seven District Courts around New Zealand that deal with civil matters (where the dispute relates to NZD 200,000 or less) and criminal matters.[2] There are also a number of specialist courts and tribunals set up to deal with specific matters (such as the Family Court).

1. See www.justice.govt.nz/courts.
2. District Courts Act 1947, section 29.

§15.02 IDENTIFYING ASSETS IN NEW ZEALAND

In New Zealand, there are various public registers available to identify assets of a potential defendant. Apart from these public registers, there is currently no legal basis to compel a potential defendant to disclose its assets prior to commencing legal proceedings.[3]

The following public registers are available in New Zealand.

[A] Land

Information regarding property ownership and land is kept electronically by Land Information New Zealand (*LINZ*) (www.linz.govt.nz). If a specific property is known, LINZ will provide a copy of the certificate of title. The certificate of title records encumbrances currently registered against a property (e.g., mortgages, charging orders and caveats) and can list previous dealings with that title. Without a lawyer or other relevant service provider, the public cannot generally request information from LINZ about properties owned by a potential defendant.

The public can personally search for a potential defendant's property through various private databases. The most popular database is Terranet (www.terranet.co.nz). In addition to searching for properties in the name of a defendant, you can search properties previously owned by a defendant and the property history (to identify dispositions to a related party). Information regarding government valuations of the property and its sales history can also be obtained. If a specific property is known, information regarding its government valuation may be provided by some local councils. This however requires knowledge of the governing council.

[B] Vehicles

The New Zealand Transport Agency (*NZTA*) maintains the Motor Vehicle Register which records the current and previous owners of a vehicle. The Register can be searched only using the registration number of a vehicle. The Register will not allow a general search of vehicles registered in a potential defendant's name.

The Register can be searched by applying for a Motochek account with NZTA (www.nzta.govt.nz/motochek). Alternatively, members of the public can use various other private online service providers to search the Register. Since 1 May 2011, information regarding individuals who own vehicles will not be released without a separate application to NZTA being made. The Register will by default only disclose ownership information of companies or other organisations.

3. The Court has jurisdiction to grant a search order (formerly known as Anton Piller Orders) prior to the commencement of legal proceedings, but only for the purpose of entering premises to secure or preserve evidence: High Court Rules, Part 33.

[C] Personal Property Securities Register

An alternative register that may reveal information regarding a defendant's assets (excluding land) is the Personal Property Securities Register (*PPSR*) (www.ppsr.govt.nz). Any member of the public can search the PPSR.

The PPSR holds information regarding security interests that have been granted over personal property. For example, a general security that has been granted over a business and its assets (other than land) may be registered on the PPSR. Similarly, security that has been granted over a vehicle may be registered on the PPSR. The timing of the registration of the security interest on the PPSR has legal implications for the priority of securities over the same property.[4] Consequently, more often than not, secured creditors will register their security interest.

The PPSR is a helpful register to identify various kinds of personal property that a defendant may own and any security interests it is subject to. For a prescribed fee, the PPSR will reveal information on the secured creditor, the debtor and the secured property in question. The key limitation of the PPSR is that no information is held about personal property not subject to a registered security interest.

[D] Shares

All companies are incorporated under the Companies Act 1993 and are registered on the Companies Register (www.companies.govt.nz). The Companies Register predominantly holds information regarding the directors and shareholders of each company. The Companies Register does not generally hold financial information of a company. Accordingly, the annual financial reports of a company incorporated in New Zealand are not publicly available unless the company is listed on the New Zealand Stock Exchange, in which case the annual accounts can typically be found on the website of the company.

The Companies Register can be searched by any member of the public for no charge. Information regarding a defendant's shareholding in or directorship of any company can be easily obtained.[5] If a potential defendant has an interest in a company, it may in turn be beneficial to search for land or personal property owned by that company through the various other public registers.

[E] Intellectual Property Rights, Vessels and Aircrafts

The Intellectual Property Office of New Zealand (IPONZ, www.iponz.govt.nz) maintains registers for various types of intellectual property. Such intellectual property includes trademarks, patents, designs and copyrights. Any member of the public can

4. The PPSR and priority rules are governed by the Personal Property Securities Act 1999.
5. Although, privately owned shares in public listed companies are not disclosed on the Companies Register.

search these registers. The register discloses the currency of the intellectual property right and contact details for its owner (or the owner's agent).

Information can be obtained regarding a ship's registration from the New Zealand Register of Ships (www.maritimenz.govt.nz/Commercial/Ship-registration/Searching-the-register-of-ships). A request must however be made with reference to either the ship's name or the ship's official registration number.

Information regarding aircraft may be obtained from the Civil Aviation Authority's Aircraft Register database (www.caa.govt.nz/Script/Air_Reg_Query). A request must again be made with reference to specific identifying information of the aircraft. Some personal information, such as a registered owner's name, may have been removed at the request of the owners. A special request will need to be made to obtain this information.

[F] Bad Debtors

There are various private databases that hold credit information on both individuals and companies. The most popular database is Veda (www.veda.co.nz).

The Insolvency & Trustee Service (www.insolvency.govt.nz) maintains a register of individuals undergoing, or who have just been released from, an insolvency process (such as bankruptcy). Any member of the public can search the Insolvency Register. Information of a person's bankruptcy must be held on the Insolvency Register for four years after their discharge from bankruptcy.

The Companies Register discloses the current and historic status of the company. In particular, the company in question may no longer be registered or may be in the process of, or just been released from, an insolvency process (such as liquidation or receivership).

[G] After Proceedings Are Commenced

Once judgment is obtained, prior to commencing insolvency proceedings, the judgment creditor is able to compel the judgment debtor to complete a financial statement and be examined before the Court.[6] Both the financial statement and examination are intended to provide the judgment creditor with information on the judgment debtor's: (1) receipts and payments for the preceding fifty-two weeks; (2) assets and liabilities; (3) income and expenditure; and (4) means of satisfying the judgment.

The judgment creditor simply needs to serve a notice on the judgment creditor to complete the financial statement.[7] Alternatively, the judgment creditor may, either prior to or after serving a notice to complete the financial statement, apply to the Court

6. High Court Rules, rule 17.10–17.20.
7. High Court Rules, rule 17.10.

for an order for examination.[8] When granting the application, the Court may order the judgment debtor to produce documents at the examination.

After legal proceedings are commenced, and prior to judgment being entered, the plaintiff may also apply to Court for an order for examination.[9] The threshold is high. The plaintiff must effectively satisfy the Court it is entitled to a pre-judgment charging order (discussed below), or at least persuade the Court that a pre-judgment charging order 'is likely to be granted'.[10]

§15.03 INTERIM MEASURES

In New Zealand, the three main ways to freeze assets of a defendant prior to commencing legal proceedings are: (1) Freezing orders; (2) Pre-judgment charging orders; and (3) Caveats.[11]

[A] Freezing Orders

Freezing orders (formerly known as Mareva injunctions) restrain assets and prevent the defendant from disposing of, dealing with, or diminishing the value of those assets.[12]

Freezing orders can be made in both the High Court[13] and District Court[14] of New Zealand. However, the civil jurisdiction of the District Court is limited to a maximum of NZD 200,000.[15] If the substantive claim is for a greater sum, the application for a freezing order ought to be made to the High Court. Additionally, while the High Court has jurisdiction to grant a freezing order over assets located in or outside New Zealand, the District Court has jurisdiction only over assets in New Zealand.[16]

While a freezing order has the benefit of ensuring that assets are secured, a disadvantage is that freezing orders allow for the payment of the defendant's ordinary living costs and legal expenses relating to the freezing order, and also allow the defendant to dispose of assets or make payments in the ordinary course of business.[17] Secured assets can therefore be depleted in this manner.[18]

8. High Court Rules, rule 17.12.
9. High Court Rules, rule 17.12.
10. *AMP Finance Ltd v. Linecorp Investments Ltd* (HC Auckland, CP351/90, 14 June 1991, Barker J).
11. New Zealand has not implemented the European Union's rules relating to European Account Preservation Orders. New Zealand's Arbitration Act 1996 has adopted the 2006 Model Law rules on interim measures.
12. High Court Rules, rule 32.2.
13. High Court Rules, Part 32.
14. District Court Rules, rule 7.45.
15. This is the present jurisdictional threshold, however, at writing, the New Zealand Government is considering raising the threshold.
16. District Courts Act 1947, section 42.
17. High Court Rules, rule 32.6.
18. Refer *De Alwis v. Chean* (HC Auckland, CIV-2007-404-5357, 5/6/09, Winkelmann J) where household expenses of NZD 1,205 per week were allowed. Refer *De Alwis v. Chean* (HC Auckland, CIV-2007-404-5357, 19/10/09, Courtney J) where legal costs were set with reference to Legal Services Agency guidelines and scale costs claimable under the High Court Rules.

The requisite elements for a freezing order are:[19]

(a) *A good arguable case against the defendant*
The test is more stringent than that normally required for an interlocutory injunction, but the case does not have to be so strong as to entitle summary judgment.[20]

(b) *Assets inside the jurisdiction*
If known, particular assets ought to be identified. However, the Court may in certain circumstances infer there are assets to which an order can apply;[21] for example, a person who claims to have no assets but yet holds no employment and leads an affluent lifestyle. In exceptional circumstances, the Court may extend the order to restrict assets outside New Zealand.[22]

(c) *A risk of dissipation*
The evidence must establish a real risk the assets will be dissipated or moved out of the jurisdiction. However, affirmative proof of the likelihood of dissipation or of nefarious intent is unnecessary.[23] Factors to consider in establishing this element are the defendant's overseas ties, any prior dissipation, the liquidity of the asset, the bona fides of the defendant in prior dealings, or whether there is any apparent or suspected fraud.
The threshold for this element is not overly high. In *Ruakana Moana Fisheries Ltd v. The Ship 'Irina Zharkikh'*,[24] freezing orders were granted on the basis the defendants were foreign companies who had only partially disclosed their financial circumstances and given narrow responses to enquiries about specific matters. The Court was satisfied this indicated a risk of dissipation. However, it is technically an abuse of the Courts process to seek a freezing order where there is no real risk.[25]

(d) *Balance of convenience and interests of justice require the freezing order to be granted*[26]
This element involves a consideration of the respective hardships of the parties. The Court of Appeal has stressed the importance of preserving the flexibility of the remedy, and the need to consider the overall justice of the case, balancing the need to protect the applicant so as to ensure any judgment is not rendered barren against any prejudice or hardship to the defendant or a third party.[27]

19. *Gatx-Fuller Australasia Pty Ltd v. Wilsons (NZ) Portland Cement Ltd* [1985] 2 NZLR 11.
20. *Ibid*, at 21–22.
21. *BNZ v. Hawkins* (1989) 1 PRNZ 451, at 453.
22. As mentioned above, this only applies to the High Court.
23. *BNZ v. Hawkins* (1989) 1 PRNZ 451.
24. *Ruakana Moana Fisheries Ltd v. The Ship 'Irina Zharkikh'* [2001] 2 NZLR 801.
25. *Tranquil Holdings Ltd v. Hudson* (1987) 2 PRNZ 551, at 552.
26. It is noted the High Court Rules do not prescribe this as an element. Its origins are based on earlier case law (*Shaw v. Narain* [1992] 2 NZLR 544) regarding the test for Mareva injunctions, which may have limited continuing application.
27. *Shaw v. Narain* [1992] 2 NZLR 544, at 548.

In addressing this element, factors to consider are the extent of the defendant's assets, whether restraint of some or all is required, effect on the applicant if the assets are dissipated, and the freezing order provides for living and legal costs which mitigates any hardship.

An applicant for a freezing order must file a signed undertaking that the applicant will comply with any order for the payment of damages to compensate the defendant for any damage sustained in consequence of the freezing order.[28] Further, an applicant for a freezing order without notice to the defendant must fully and frankly disclose to the Court all material facts, including any possible defences known to the applicant and information casting doubt on the applicant's ability to discharge the obligation created by the undertaking as to damages.[29]

The former High Court Rule 1985 prescribed that a plaintiff may not make an application for an interlocutory injunction before the commencement of proceedings except in the case of urgency.[30] No equivalent rule is contained in the current High Court Rules 2002, and there is authority for the granting of a freezing order prior to commencement of a proceeding.[31]

The Court may make an ancillary order, in relation to a freezing order or prospective freezing order, if the Court considers it just. An ancillary order may be made to elicit information relating to assets relevant to the freezing order or prospective freezing order, determine whether the freezing order should be made, and appoint a receiver of the assets that are the subject of the freezing order.[32] Freezing orders must reserve leave to the defendant to apply to discharge or vary its terms.

[B] Pre-judgment Charging Order

Prior to judgment being entered, a plaintiff can apply to Court for leave to issue a pre-judgment charging order.[33] A pre-judgment charging order can be over land or personal property, but is only available in the High Court.

The requisite elements for a pre-judgment charging order are that the defendant, with intent to defeat creditors, is either:

(a) Removing, concealing or disposing of property.

28. High Court Rules, rule 32.2. Rule 32.6 does however allow the dispensation of this requirement in 'special circumstances'. This dispensation has been applied to Crown entities: *Registrar of Companies v. Nearzero Inc* (HC Nelson, CIV-2007-442-240); *Official Assignee v. Fry* (HC Auckland, 4/2/09, CIV-2009-404-439, Wylie J); *Official Assignee v. Honk Apartments Ltd* (HC Auckland, 24/9/09, CIV-2009-404-6222, Heath J).
29. High Court Rules, rule 32.2.
30. High Court Rule 1985, rule 238(2).
31. *Official Assignee v. Scott* [2012] NZHC 2579. Although, the issue was not squarely addressed in this case. The freezing order was granted after the Official Assignee issued a voidable notice and received an objection, but prior to the commencement of a legal proceeding to set aside the voidable transaction.
32. High Court Rules, rule 32.3.
33. High Court Rules, rule 17.41.

(b) Is absent from or about to leave NZ.

In proving the required intent, Courts have held that 'not every such disposal qualifies. The one who has the property must be proved to have a particular intent. Not just an intent to dispose of the property but an "intent to defeat" the claim and to do so by "making away" with the property. In short an intent to act illegitimately'.[34]

Prior to the granting of a pre-judgment charging order, the Court must also be satisfied as to the merits of the claim. While the plaintiff 'need not show a serious question to be tried or that he or she is favoured by the balance of convenience and justice overall, [the applicant] must satisfy a test that is equally stringent'.[35] For example, in *Conning v. Martoni Ltd*,[36] the Court found the facts to be 'threatening a serious issue to be tried', later concluding that there was a 'seriously arguable case'.

The significant benefit of a pre-judgment charging order over that of a freezing order is that the charged property will not be dissipated with living costs or legal fees. However, given the need to prove intent to defeat creditors, the threshold is higher than that for freezing orders.

[C] Caveats

Caveats may be registered over land to prevent any dealings with it. A pre-requisite to lodging any caveat over land is that the caveator has a beneficial interest in the land.[37] The lodgement of a caveat generally prevents the Registrar of Land from making any entry on the LINZ Register which will have the effect of charging, transferring or otherwise affecting the estate or interest protected by the caveat.

An interest in land will likely exist, and give rise to a caveatable interest, if the plaintiff has a proprietary claim to the land. For example, land held beneficially on trust for a plaintiff could be secured by registering a caveat disclosing the alleged beneficial interest.[38] Such trusts include not only express trust, but institutional constructive trusts as well.[39] Fraud and breach of confidence often give rise to an interest pursuant to an institutional constructive trust.[40] Additionally, a fiduciary (such as a director of a company) who acts in breach of fiduciary obligations by misapplying property for his or her personal benefit, may hold such misapplied property as constructive trustee for the company.[41]

34. *McKay v. 314 Maunganui Road Limited* (HC, Auckland, 30/04/08, CIV 2007-404-7434, Keane J).
35. *Ibid*, at [34].
36. *Conning v. Martoni Ltd* (HC, Auckland, CIV-2010-404-5351, 1 July 2011, Whata J).
37. Land Transfer Act 1952, section 137.
38. See, for example, *Holt v. Anchorage Management Ltd* [1987] 1 NZLR 108 (CA).
39. Refer *Fortex Group Ltd (in rec and liq) v. MacIntosh* [1998] 3 NZLR 171 (CA) for the distinction between the different types of trusts that may arise.
40. See, for example, *Fletcher Steel Ltd v. Nahal Contractors Ltd* (HC Auckland, CIV-2006-404-498, 24 May 2007, Abbot AJ); *Paugra Holdings Ltd (in liq) v. Harvestfield Holdings Ltd* (2014) 26 NZTC 21-070 (CA); *Attorney-General for Hong Kong v. Reid* [1994] 1 NZLR 1 (PC); and *Trustees Executors Ltd v. Eden Holdings 2010 Ltd* [2010] NZCA 626.
41. See, for example, *Selangor United Rubber Estates Ltd v. Cradock (No 3)* [1968] 2 All ER 1073; and *Karak Runner Co Ltd v. Burden (No 2)* [1972] 1 All ER 1210.

Alternatively, if a guarantor has a claim against the primary debtor to recover amounts paid to the creditor in relation to the guaranteed debt, the guarantor may be able to subrogate to the security interests granted by the primary debtor to the creditor.[42] If any security interests were granted over land, a caveat could be lodged over it.

Disputes involving land may also give rise to interests in land sufficient to support a caveat. Some examples are the interests of a purchaser under a sale and purchase agreement, a lessee under an agreement to lease or a mortgagee under an agreement to mortgage. It is important to note however that in New Zealand, the vendor's equitable lien for non-payment of the purchase price has been abolished.[43] No caveat can therefore be lodged over land by a vendor simply for non-payment of the purchase price.

Finally, if the defendant is a trust, there may be the ability to convert an in personam claim into a proprietary claim and caveat trust property. A trustee has a right of indemnity against trust property for liability incurred as a trustee. The trustee therefore has a proprietary lien/charge over trust property to the extent of this indemnity. The proprietary lien/charge is sufficient to sustain a caveat.[44] Two possible scenarios therefore arise when caveats may be lodged. First, if the trustee is seeking to enforce its indemnity against the trust, a caveat can be lodged to secure the trust assets. Second, a creditor of the trust may subrogate to the trustee's indemnity where the trustee is itself insolvent.[45] In this way, a creditor seeking to recover a debt from the trustee may be able to lodge a caveat over trust assets.

Careful consideration should be given before a caveat is registered. Any person lodging a caveat without reasonable cause must compensate any person who has sustained damage.[46] Additionally, a caveat also only secures the equity in the property. It does not trump an earlier registered mortgage.[47]

§15.04 ENFORCEMENT ISSUES

[A] Enforcing a Foreign Decision against a Defendant's Assets in New Zealand

If a defendant holds assets in New Zealand, but dispute resolution proceedings are taking place in another jurisdiction, the question arises as to whether the foreign judgment or arbitral award can be enforced against the New Zealand assets.

42. Judicature Act 1908, sections 84 and 85. Also *Official Assignee v. Tizard* (HC Dunedin, CP44/92, 19/8/93, Grieg J).
43. Property Law Act 2007, section 67.
44. See, for example, *Apa v. Levin* (CIV-2009-404-4652, HC Auckland, 15/12/09, Robinson AJ); and *Official Assignee v. Menzies* (CIV-2010-404-457, HC Auckland, 14/12/11, Bell AJ).
45. See, for example, *Apa v. Levin* (CIV-2009-404-4652, HC Auckland, 15/12/09, Robinson AJ).
46. Land Transfer Act 1952, section 146.
47. Land Transfer Act 1952, section 105.

In New Zealand, enforcement generally is governed by Part 17 of the New Zealand High Court Rules (the *Rules*). However, the manner of and steps to enforcement in New Zealand will depend on whether the decision is a judgment or an arbitral award, and from which court and jurisdiction the decision came. Each is considered below.

[B] Enforcing a Foreign Judgment

As a starting point, a New Zealand court will not impose sanctions for failing to comply with a foreign judgment. However, a person with a foreign judgment may be able to enforce that foreign judgment by:

(a) first registering the judgment under statute (under the Trans-Tasman Proceedings Act 2010 for certain decisions from Australian courts (the *TTPA*), and under Reciprocal Enforcement of Judgments Act 1936 (the *REJA*) for decisions from other specified jurisdictions); or
(b) bringing an action at common law; or
(c) registering a memorial of the judgment under section 56 of the Judicature Act 1908.

Non-money foreign judgments, such as those in relation to property held overseas or foreign judicial declarations, may be recognised by New Zealand courts without further proceedings in New Zealand. We focus below on the enforcement of money judgments.

[1] Enforcement by Registration under Statute: Australian Decisions – The TTPA

Australian decisions can have specific status in New Zealand law under the TTPA. The TTPA provides for the streamlining of trans-Tasman proceedings to improve efficiencies, reduce costs and minimise existing impediments to enforcing certain Australian judgments.[48] It provides for various New Zealand legal processes to occur in Australia (such as service and remote appearances) and for the recognition in New Zealand of the validity of processes in Australia. The TTPA is also relevant for the recognition and enforcement in New Zealand of specified judgments of Australian courts and tribunals,[49] and in trans-Tasman market proceedings.[50]

In order for an Australian judgment to be enforceable in New Zealand, it must first be registered in a New Zealand Court under section 57 of the TTPA.[51] To be

48. Section 3, TTPA.
49. Part 2, sub-part 5, TTPA.
50. But not including those imposing civil pecuniary penalties. See Trans-Tasman Proceedings Act 2010. Part 28 of the High Court Rules deals specifically with Trans-Tasman competition proceedings; this topic is not covered by this chapter.
51. Section 53, TTPA.

registered, the judgment must be a 'registrable Australian judgment' (which is defined in section 54) and an application for its registration must be made.

Section 56 of the TTPA outlines the process for registering an Australian judgment, including that an application must be in the form and in accordance with the requirements of any regulations, and must be made (broadly speaking) within six years after the day on which the judgment is given.[52]

In terms of the form of an application, the Trans-Tasman Proceedings Regulations and Rules 2013 (New Zealand) provide a specified standard form for an application (form 6 to the Regulations). Regulation 14 specifies the application's specifics and the evidence requirements to accompany it.

Once it is registered, the judgment will have the same force as if the judgment had been given by the New Zealand court.[53] This is subject to a few limited exceptions set out in the TTPA.[54] It will have the same force and effect, and may give rise to the same proceedings for enforcement, as if it was a judgment given by the New Zealand court in which it was registered.[55]

The standard processes for enforcement in New Zealand, as set out in Part 17 of the Rules, will then be available.

[2] Enforcement by Registration under Statute: Jurisdictions Other Than Australia – The REJA

Part 23 of the Rules sets out procedure in New Zealand for the enforcement of foreign judgments under the REJA.[56]

Part 23 defines 'foreign judgment' as any judgment to which, under section 3, 3A, or 3B of the REJA, Part 1 of the REJA applies (Part 1 is the relevant part of the act). The REJA defines 'judgment' broadly, as:[57]

> a [final or interlocutory] judgment or order given or made by a Court in any civil proceedings, or a judgment or order given or made by a Court in any criminal proceedings for the payment of a sum of money in respect of compensation or damages to an injured party; and includes an award in proceedings on an arbitration (not being an award made outside New Zealand within the meaning of the Arbitration Act 1996) if the award has, in pursuance of the law in force in the place where it was made, become enforceable in the same manner as a judgment given by a Court in that place.

52. Section 56(2) TTPA.
53. Section 52(2) TTPA.
54. Section 52(3) TTPA.
55. See section 63(1) TTPA, and the matters which it is subject to at section 63(3).
56. Rule 23.1(1).
57. Section 2 REJA.

In summary, Part 1 applies to certain money judgments from superior courts of the United Kingdom,[58] and from superior and inferior courts of other countries as specified by such Orders in Council.

Orders in Council have been made under section 3 (which provides for directions as to which countries' superior courts the Act applies to in relation to the following countries or states):

- France.
- Belgium.
- New South Wales, Norfolk Island, Queensland, South Australia, Victoria, Western Australia, Solomon Islands, Fiji, Gilbert and Ellice Islands (Kiribati and Tuvalu respectively), Basutoland (Lesotho), Bechuanaland (Botswana), Swaziland.
- Tasmania.
- Federation of Malaya (Malaysia), Singapore, Sarawak.
- North Borneo (Sabah).
- Australian Capital Territory.
- Papua and New Guinea.
- Nigeria and the Cameroons.
- India.
- Hong Kong.
- Northern Territory of Australia.
- Sri Lanka.
- Pakistan.
- Norfolk Island (name change of superior Court).
- Western Samoa.
- Commonwealth of Australia.
- Tonga.

Orders in Council have been made under section 3A (relating to the Act's extension to inferior courts of foreign countries). Section 3B relates to non-money judgments and is not considered in this chapter. However no Orders in Council have been made under section 3B. The Reciprocal Enforcement of Judgments (Australian Inferior Courts) Order 1992 states that the following Australian Courts are specified inferior Courts:

(a) Australian Capital Territory – Magistrate's Court.
(b) Territory of Christmas Island – Magistrate's Court.
(c) Territory of Cocos (Keeling) Islands – Magistrate's Court.
(d) State of New South Wales – District Court; Local Courts.
(e) Northern Territory – Local Courts.
(f) State of Queensland – District Courts; Magistrate's Courts.
(g) State of South Australia – District Court; Magistrate's Court.
(h) State of Tasmania – Magistrate's Court; Courts of Request.
(i) Territory of Norfolk Island – Court of Petty Sessions.

58. The term 'superior court' has been held to mean a court of 'unlimited jurisdiction'; see for example *Saunders v. Saunders* (1994) 7 PRNZ 413, where the Family Court of Australia was held not to be a superior court.

(j) State of Victoria – County Court; Magistrate's Court.
(k) State of Western Australia – District Court; Local Court.

A judgment creditor under a judgment to which Part 1 REJA applies, may apply to the New Zealand High Court at any time within six years after the date of the foreign judgment, or, where there have been proceedings by way of appeal against the judgment, after the date of the last judgment given in those proceedings, to have the judgment registered in the High Court.[59] Upon any such application, the High Court must, subject to proof of the prescribed matters and to the other provisions of the REJA, order the judgment to be registered.[60]

Part 23 of the Rules provides the procedure for registering such foreign decisions. Rule 23.4 provides that an application for registration must be made by originating application in a standard form (form G30, which is provided in a schedule to the Rules). Part 19, which relates to originating applications, then applies except so far as it is necessarily modified by or inconsistent with Part 23. The application may also be made without notice to the judgment debtor, and if so made the requirements for certification apply.[61] The application must be filed in the registry of the court in which the defendant would have been required to file that defendant's statement of defence, had the proceeding been commenced by way of proceeding on the foreign judgment and not by way of application for registration.

Rules 23.6–23.8 provide the procedural requirements as to the application, supporting application and the foreign judgment. A judgment registered in this manner will, for the purposes of enforcement, be of the same force and effect as if the judgment had been a judgment originally given in the High Court on the date of registration.[62] This is subject to the provisions of the REJA with respect to the setting aside of registration.[63]

[3] Bringing an Action at Common Law

In certain circumstances, a foreign judgment may also be enforceable in New Zealand at common law and may give rise to an estoppel as between the parties to the foreign proceeding.

A judgment of a foreign Court (of competent jurisdiction) against a party personally can be regarded as creating a debt owed by the judgment creditor to the judgment debtor. An action may then be brought in the New Zealand High Court on this debt. However, such an action cannot occur for a foreign judgment to which the REJA applies.[64] Such an action must be commenced in accordance with the normal

59. Section 4 REJA.
60. This is subject to it not having been wholly satisfied or not enforceable in the country of the original Court (section 4(2).
61. Rule 23.4(2), and Rule 7.23.
62. The relevant sum will carry interest and the High Court will have the same control over enforcement as if it was a decision of the New Zealand High Court.
63. See sections 6 and 7 REJA.
64. Section 8 REJA.

procedure in New Zealand for civil proceedings, by filing and serving a statement of claim under Part 5 of the Rules.[65]

If a foreign judgment has been given for either party to a proceeding, and proceedings are brought in New Zealand on the same basis, the foreign judgment may also be relied on as the basis for an estoppel by the party in whose favour the claim or issue was determined. Such an estoppel would operate to stop a party from re-litigating an already determined issue. Estoppel, however, is discretionary and is a matter for the relevant Judge.

Also, if a foreign judgment has been fully satisfied, then such satisfaction will be a good defence to an action in New Zealand based on that judgment and will act as a bar to the New Zealand action.

A foreign judgment will be enforced in New Zealand if the foreign Court's jurisdiction over the judgment debtor is recognised by New Zealand law, if the judgment is for a debt or a definite sum of money (but not a penalty) and if the judgment is final. The foreign court's jurisdiction will be recognised only in certain cases, relating to the debtor's presence and participation in the relevant foreign proceeding.

[4] Registering a Memorial of a Judgment under Section 56 of the Judicature Act 1908

Section 56 of the Judicature Act 1908 provides a process for registration and enforcement in New Zealand of judgments or orders for payments of money made by Courts in Commonwealth countries. However, it is of somewhat limited use as it is not available to decisions which are enforceable under Part 1 of the REJA and must be a judgment for a sum of money.[66]

Section 56 permits a person, who has obtained a judgment[67] in any Court of Her Majesty's Dominions,[68] to file in the High Court a memorial of that judgment authenticated by the seal of the original Court. The memorial will then constitute a record of the determination. The Court may, on the application of the person in whose favour the judgment was obtained, require the person against whom it was obtained to show cause (within such time as the Court directs), why execution should not issue on the original determination. If the person fails to appear or fails to show sufficient cause against execution, the Court may make an order for issuing execution. The High Court will not go into the merits of the foreign judgment.[69] Once registered, the foreign judgment can then be enforced in New Zealand.

65. Rule 5.25. Summary judgment under Part 7 of the Rules is also an available process.
66. Section 13, REJA.
67. Including a decree, rule or order and in all cases relating to the payment of money, section 56(1).
68. In *Austin v. Nicholson* (1984) 2 PRNZ 494, Holland J in the High Court noted that 'Her Majesty's Dominions' includes all territories under the sovereignty of the Crown, including the United Kingdom. The provision also applies to each Commonwealth country of which the Queen is not Head of State, Commonwealth Countries Act 1977, section 3.
69. *Platt v. Siegel* [1918] GLR 70.

[5] Examples of Enforcing Foreign Judgments

If the judgment comes from the Australia, all of the above processes are likely to be available to a judgment creditor. Similarly, if the judgment is from a section 3 REJA country (as listed above, including the United Kingdom), then the REJA registration process is likely to be available, as its enforcement at common law (or under the Judicature Act 1908 for Commonwealth countries).

However if, for example, the judgment is from the United States (not an Commonwealth nor a section 3 REJA country) or from a European Union country (other than France or Belgium, both of whom are section 3 REJA countries), then the judgment will only be enforceable at common law. What this will involve however is bringing a fresh proceeding in New Zealand based on the foreign judgment – rather than prove the cases again, the plaintiff/creditor should seek summary judgment on the basis of the foreign judgment debt, as set out above.

[C] Enforcing a Foreign Arbitral Award

The law in New Zealand on the recognition and enforcement of foreign arbitral awards is modelled on the New York Convention (the 1958 Convention on the Recognition and Enforcement of Foreign Arbitral Awards, which New Zealand signed in 1983). It is governed by Articles 35 and 36 of schedule 1 to the Arbitration Act 1995 (*Arbitration Act*). Article 35 provides that an award is to be recognised as binding, irrespective of the country in which it is made, and that, on application to the New Zealand High Court, is to be enforced by entry as a judgment. Recognition and enforcement of an award are subject to procedural requirements, and the grounds for refusing such recognition and enforcement are set out in Article 36.

The starting point for a person seeking the recognition or enforcement of a foreign arbitral award in New Zealand is Article 35(1) of Schedule 1 to the Arbitration Act. The provisions for recognition and enforcement apply 'irrespective of the country' in which the award was made, so no distinction is drawn between awards made in New Zealand or any other jurisdiction. Importantly, provided that the correct procedure is followed, an award must be recognised or enforced subject only to the grounds set out in Article 36.

An award can be enforced by action or by entry of the award as a judgment.[70] A party seeking enforcement of an award by action must commence a proceeding by filing a statement of claim under Part 5 of the Rules.[71] The ordinary rules for proceedings following the filing of a statement of claim will then apply.

An award can be entered as a judgment by agreement of the parties on application by them to a Registrar of High Court[72] (or District Court). The application need simply be made by letter signed by all parties requesting the entry of an award as

70. Article 35(1) of sch 1, Arbitration Act.
71. Rule 26.21(1)(a) and (2). Or, if the sum involved is less than NZD 200,000, then in the District Court under r 2.9 of the District Courts Rules (rr 11.3.1(a) and 11.3.2).
72. Rule 26.20.

a judgment. The Registrar must enter the award as a judgment 'as soon as practicable' or if he or she is satisfied that the parties have agreed to its entry as a judgment, and have provided documents in accordance with Article 35(2) of schedule 1 to the Arbitration Act.

A party electing to enforce an award by its entry as a judgment must file an originating application in the proper registry.[73] The application must be in the prescribed form.[74] The applicant (for enforcement by entry as a judgment) is referred to in the Rules as the plaintiff, being the person on whose behalf the application is brought.[75] The plaintiff must file an affidavit in support providing the matters referred to in Article 35(2) of schedule 1,[76] and attend to ordinary service. Service is not required where the enforcement is sought on a without notice basis.[77] The affidavit must provide the relevant contract (or, at least, the arbitration clause) and proof of the duly authenticated original award.

As to time limits, there is a defence under section 35(1) of the Limitation Act to a claim to enforce a judgment, including an arbitral award entered as a judgment, if the defendant proves that the date on which the claim is filed is at least six years after the date on which the judgment became enforceable in the country in which it was obtained.

The High Court also retains a residual discretion to recognise or enforce an award, even though a ground for refusing such recognition or enforcement may be made out. An award can also be set aside under Articles 34 and 36 of schedule 1 of the Arbitration Act.[78]

Once recognised, the award is actionable under New Zealand law.

§15.05 DIRECTOR AND OWNER LIABILITY IN RELATION TO ASSET PROTECTION SCHEMES

[A] Introduction

This section sets out the circumstances in which directors and/or owners of a company may be held liable where a defendant company attempts to hide assets pending trial.

In New Zealand, a company is a separate legal entity from its directors and shareholders.[79] New Zealand law generally does not allow the piercing of the corporate veil other than to combat fraud (and in a few other limited circumstances not relevant to creditors' claims).

73. District Court Rules 2009, r 11.4.1; High Court Rules 2008, r 26.22.
74. District Courts Rules 2009, rr 11.4.2(a) (form 35) and 11.4.3 (applying High Court Rule 5.44 to the originating application); high Court Rules 2008, r 26.22(2)(a) (form Arb 3) and (3).
75. District Court Rules 2009, r 1.8; High Court Rules 2008, r 1.3.
76. District Court Rules 2009, r 11.5; High Court Rules 2008, r 26.23, In relation to translations see Evidence Act 2006, section 135(1)-(2).
77. District Court Rules 2009, r 11.6.2; High Court Rules 2008, r 26.24(2).
78. See *Downer-Hill Joint Venture v. The Government of Fiji* [2005] 1 NZLR 554 and *Amaltal Corpn Ltd v. Maruha (NZ) Corpn Ltd* [2004] 2 NZLR 614, CA); confirming that the courts' jurisdiction to set aside an award under Article 34 is a limited one.
79. Section 15 Companies Act 1993.

In New Zealand, being a separate legal entity, a company owns its own property. A company's assets do not belong to its shareholders, and a company's creditors are not creditors of the company's shareholders. Accordingly, a creditor's claim must be against the company.

However, where a company is being sued and its directors or shareholders move the company's assets away to avoid enforcement against them, a question arises as to how a plaintiff or creditor can attack the directors and shareholders personally, or otherwise get to the assets. In this respect, three key points are set out below:

(a) claw back provisions in New Zealand insolvency law;
(b) criminal liability of directors and shareholders; and
(c) civil liability of directors and shareholders.

This section does not address the potential for a director to be personally liable for the civil wrongs of a company,[80] nor does it address circumstances where directors who have misapplied a companies assets may become (or see another entity become) constructive trustees of the assets.[81]

[B] Claw Back Provisions

The most useful process for recouping assets from a company is the liquidation of the company through liquidation proceedings. While the process for liquidating a company is beyond the scope of this chapter,[82] if a company has its valuable assets removed – so as to be in a position where it cannot pay a judgment debt – then liquidation ought to able to be achieved through a process commenced by the relevant judgment creditor.

If a company's assets have been transacted away from a company prior to liquidation, then they might be voidable and able to be reversed, or recovery might be possible as against the counterparty (who received the relevant asset). Sections 292, 297 and 298 of the Companies Act 1993 (*Companies Act*) provide powers for recovery – during liquidation – that could be relevant in the case of asset stripping.

[1] Section 292: Voidable Transactions

Section 292 provides that a transaction is voidable by the liquidator if it was an 'insolvent transaction' and if it was entered into during the 'specified period'. Each of the two concepts is described below.

An insolvent transaction is one that is entered into at a time when the company is unable to pay its due debts and enables another person to receive more towards

80. *Trevor Ivory Limited v. Anderson* [1992] 2 NZLR 517 (CA).
81. For a discussion on when this can occur, see *Belmont Finance Corp Limited v. Williams Furniture Limited (No 2)* 1980] 1 All ER 393 (CA), 405.
82. Part 16 of the Companies Act 1993 sets out the process for liquidating a company in New Zealand.

satisfaction of a debt owed by the company than the person would be likely to receive in the company's liquidation.[83] The specified period is (broadly speaking) the period of two years before the date of commencement or initiation of the liquidation.[84]

Accordingly, a transaction in that period – including the payment of money away from the company or the shifting or assets to another company to defeat a claim – that is at a time when the company was unable to pay its due debts and enables another party to receive more than it ought to, is voidable by the company's liquidator. The key issues will likely be whether it can be established that:

(a) at the time of the relevant transaction, the company was 'unable to pay its due debts'; and
(b) whether the transaction in question was one that enabled another party to receive more than it ought to (it must be a payment between creditor and debtor).

This section will be relevant where a company discharges a debt or debts to the detriment of the judgment creditor.

[2] Section 297: Transactions at Undervalue

Section 297 will be relevant where the movement of the assets does not take the form of a discharge of a debt, but instead occurs at below proper value (and in a similar two-year specified period). Under section 297, the liquidator may recover from a person (*X*) the amount C in the formula A – B = C, where:

(a) **A** is the value that X received from a company under a transaction to which the company was or is a party; and
(b) **B** is the value (if any) that the company received from X under the transaction.

The liquidator may recover the difference in value (i.e., C in the formula) from X if the transaction occurred in that two-year period and the company:

(c) was unable to pay its due debts when it entered into the transaction; or
(d) became unable to pay its due debts as a result of entering into the transaction.

While proof of the inability to pay its debts is required, there is also no requirement on the liquidator to prove recipient X knew that the transaction was under

83. Section 292(2). Transactions that occur with a 'restricted period' are presumed to be entered into at a time when the company was unable to pay its due debt, unless it is proved otherwise, section 292(4A); the restricted period is (in summary) the period six months prior to liquidation, section 292(6).
84. Section 292(5).

value or knew of the financial position of the company. This is a useful claw back provision against recipient X, be X a director, shareholder or corporate entity.

[3] Section 298: Transactions for Inappropriate Consideration with Certain Persons

Section 298 will be relevant for movements of assets in a three-year specified period (broadly speaking, prior to the initiation of liquidation), where a company has acquired a business or property from, or the services of a person related in a specified way to the company, including directors and other persons related or in control.[85] The liquidator may recover from the person any amount by which the value of the consideration given for the acquisition of the business, property or services exceeded the value of the business, property or services at the time of the acquisition. Section 298(2) includes where a company has disposed of a business or property, or provided services, or issued shares, to a similar related person.

This is a useful section as it allows a liquidator to attack the insider/counterparty without the need to prove the company was unable to pay its debts at the relevant time. The specified period is also longer than with sections 292 and 297, allowing a period of three years prior to the initiation of liquidation.

[4] The Property Law Act 2007: Creditor Protection

The Property Law Act 2007 (*PLA*) also provides options for creditors in cases where directors or shareholders have removed assets from a company. Sub-part 6 of Part 6 PLA is intended to allow a court to order that property received through certain prejudicial dispositions made by a debtor (or its value) be restored for the benefit of creditors.[86]

Section 345 PLA defines the relevant terms of Sub-part 6, including:[87]

(a) a disposition of property prejudices a creditor if it hinders, delays, or defeats the creditor in the exercise of any right of recourse of the creditor in respect of the property;
(b) a disposition of property is not made with intent to prejudice a creditor if it is made with the intention only of preferring one creditor over another; and
(c) a disposition of property by way of gift includes a disposition made at an undervalue with the intention of making a gift of the difference between the value of the consideration for the disposition and the value of the property comprised in the disposition; and
(d) a debtor must be treated as insolvent if the debtor is unable to pay all his, her, or its debts, as they fall due, from assets other than the property disposed of.

85. Section 298(1) lists those persons to whom the section applies.
86. Section 344 PLA.
87. Disposition is also defined, as are other uncontroversial terms, see section 345(2).

The Sub-part applies to dispositions with intent to prejudice creditors, or by gift, by debtors who:[88]

(a) were insolvent at the time of or as a result of the relevant disposition of assets; or
(b) were engaged, or were about to engage, in a business or transaction for which the remaining assets of the debtor were, given the nature of the business or transaction, unreasonably small; or
(c) intended to incur, or believed, or reasonably should have believed, that the debtor would incur, debts beyond the debtor's ability to pay.

If the Sub-part applies, then a prejudiced creditor (or liquidator) can apply to the court for an order[89] and, if the Court is satisfied that the creditor has been prejudiced by a disposition to which the Sub-part applies, may make an order vesting the property in certain persons or requiring the payment of compensation.[90] Persons who can receive a payment or property under section 348 include a trustee for the relevant creditor (or the company, if it is in liquidation).[91] The Court's power is subject to the matters in section 349, which relate to the protection of persons who have received property under the relevant disposition.

[C] Criminal Liability

As company is a separate legal person and its assets belong to it and not its directors or owners, if a company's directors or owners misappropriate the company's assets, then they may be criminally liable for theft.

The standard for proving theft is high. Proving theft by a director or officer will often be extremely difficult, particularly when they are likely to be able to consent for and on behalf of the company. However, in respect of owners who are not also directors, that difficulty will lessen somewhat. In any event, the requisite elements to prove theft in New Zealand are set out in section 219 of the Crimes Act 1961. They are:

(a) taking property;
(b) an intention to deprive any owner (being the company) permanently of that property; and
(c) it must be dishonestly and without claim of right;
(d) but does not include obtaining property with the consent of the person from whom it is obtained, whether or not consent is obtained by deception.

The standard upon which the element must be proved is 'beyond reasonable doubt', which means the court must be sure of each one.

88. Section 346 PLA.
89. Section 347 PLA.
90. Section 348 PLA.
91. See section 350 as to whom payments can be made to.

The maximum penalty for theft in New Zealand is seven years' imprisonment (for property of over NZD 1,000 value).[92] In addition, a Court, as part of the sentencing process for theft, can order reparation be paid by the offender to any victims of the theft.[93] The victim would, in the above example, be the company and not the company's creditors.

There are also new criminal liability provisions in the Companies Act. Section 138A provides that is an offence for a director to commit a serious breach of the director's duty to act in good faith and in the best interest of the company. It will apply only if a director exercises powers or performs duties as a director of the company *in bad faith towards the company*, believing that the conduct is not in the best interests of the company and *knowing that the conduct will cause serious loss to the company*. Actual knowledge is required. The maximum penalty is imprisonment for a term not exceeding five years or to a fine not exceeding NZD 200,000.

The section was inserted in July 2014 and, as at writing, the section does not appear to have been applied in a New Zealand Court. That said, it is arguable that a director of a company who deliberately moves assets away from a company facing legal proceedings will know that their conduct will cause serious loss to the company. So it is potentially a useful provision to prevent such conduct and, in any event, reminding the other side to litigation of the presence of this criminal sanction might be a practical step that could assist in discouraging the directors from taking steps to remove assets.

[D] Civil Liability

Directors owe fiduciary duties and statutory duties to a company. Any transaction a director undertakes on behalf of a company must be in good faith and in its best interests. But these and other duties are duties owed to the company and not to third parties such as creditors. However, in a position of near insolvency or insolvency, the Court has held that the duty is owed to creditors, not the company's shareholders.

Sections 135 and 136 of the Companies Act provide:

> **135 Reckless trading**
> A director of a company must not—
> (a) Agree to the business of the company being carried on in a manner likely to create a substantial risk of serious loss to the company's creditors; or
> (b) Cause or allow the business of the company to be carried on in a manner *likely to create a substantial risk of serious loss to the company's creditors*.
>
> **136 Duty in relation to obligations**
> A director of a company must not agree to the company incurring an obligation unless the director believes at that time on reasonable grounds that the company will be able to perform the obligation when it is required to do so. [emphasis added]

While still duties owed to the company, sections 135 and 136 concern the interests of third parties, particularly creditors. However, being duties owed to the

92. Section 223(b) Crimes Act 1961.
93. See sub-part 1 of Part 2 of the Sentencing Act 2002.

company, they are not directly actionable by a creditor while the company is not in liquidation. In liquidation however, if assets have been removed by a director in order to defeat a judgment, section 301 of the Companies Act can be utilised to seek an inquiry into the action of the directors or other relevant persons.

Section 301 of the Companies Act provides a Court power to require persons to repay money or return property if, in the course of liquidation, it appears to the Court that a person who has taken part in the formation or promotion of the company (such as a shareholder), or a past or present director or manager,[94] has misapplied, or retained, or become liable or accountable for, money or property of the company, or been guilty of negligence, default, or breach of duty or trust in relation to the company, the Court may, on the application of the liquidator or a creditor:

(a) inquire into the conduct of the relevant person; and
(b) order that person:
  (i) to repay or restore the money or property or any part of it with interest at a rate the Court thinks just; or
  (ii) to contribute such sum to the assets of the company by way of compensation as the Court thinks just; or
  (iii) where the application is made by a creditor, order that person to pay or transfer the money or property or any part of it with interest at a rate the Court thinks just to the creditor.

This section will have effect even though the conduct may constitute an offence, so it can be used alongside criminal liability. Basic misapplications of a company's assets will be caught, but so will breaches of the duties owed to third parties such as creditors, as set out at sections 135 and 136.

94. Section 301(1) provides those persons to whom the section applies, and includes administrators, liquidators and receivers.

CHAPTER 16
Russia

Alexei Panich & Maria Dolotova

§16.01 INTRODUCTION

[A] Russian Legal and Judiciary Systems

Russia's legal system is the result of a long and complicated development. Russian administrative, civil and criminal law has been formed since the tenth century under the influence of the Byzantine and the western European legal systems. The most significant legal reform took place in the middle of the nineteenth century. As a result of the reform, the first Russian Code of Civil Procedure was developed in 1864.

In the beginning of twentieth century, Russia had well-developed legal and judicial systems. However, many legal achievements were lost after 1917 when Russia became a component part of the USSR.

In the period from 1917 to 1991, Russia had a rather simplified legal system aimed at protecting the state property and the interests of the communist party, using mainly administrative tools and methods.

Socialist law recognized only a limited number of private property rights, and the commercial laws (e.g., banking law and securities law) have not developed for decades.

Following the collapse of the USSR, a free market economy and a new legal system were restored in Russia. Numerous lacunas in Russian law have been replaced by the reception of various legal concepts and institutes from the European continental and common law systems. Today Russian legal system is mainly based on the European continental law.

Russia has a dual judiciary system consisting of two branches of courts: (i) the arbitrazh (state commercial) courts, and (ii) the courts of general jurisdiction. Both branches are headed by the Russian Supreme Court and operate on the basis of their respective procedural codes – the Code of Arbitrazh Procedure and the Code of Civil

Procedure. The newly adopted Code of Administrative Procedure will govern administrative proceedings after 15 September 2015.

The Russian Constitutional Court stands apart from the other courts and exercises constitutional justice.

[B] Recovery of Assets from Debtors in Russia

This following chapter is intended to function as a 'first port of call' for anyone who would like to understand the steps, which creditors would have to take to optimize their chance of a successful recovery of assets from debtors in the Russian Federation. The chapter coves the following topics:

- Asset discovery: As discussed in further detail in section §16.02, there are a number of official databases with information about assets located in Russia, which can be accessed by creditors in an asset discovery phase leading up to a lawsuit.
- Interim measures: The Russian courts have wide powers to order various interim remedies pending judgment in support of Russian or foreign court or arbitral proceedings. We will take a close look at the relevant rules on interim measures in section §16.03 of this chapter.
- Enforcement: The rules and procedures relative to recognition and enforcement of foreign judgments and arbitral awards are discussed in detail in section §16.04 of the chapter.
- Return of assets: Finally, in section §16.05 of this chapter, we will describe the measures available to a creditor in a situation where the debtor's assets have been dissipated.

§16.02 DISCOVERING AND RETRIEVING ASSETS IN RUSSIA

[A] Compelling a Debtor to Disclose Assets

A creditor has a limited right to compel a debtor to disclose information about its assets. In general, the right to demand a disclosure of assets is not exercisable unless bankruptcy proceedings have been initiated.[1]

Meanwhile, there are certain practical methods by which a creditor can obtain information about a legal entity's or private individual's assets via public databases and registers. In the following, we will provide an overview of the available sources of information about assets located in Russia.

1. According to Article 37 of the Federal law as of 26 October 2002 No. 127-FZ on Bankruptcy (the 'Bankruptcy law'), a debtor shall disclose information about its assets in a bankruptcy petition. If the application for bankruptcy is filed by a creditor, the debtor shall disclose information about its accounts in the statement of defence (cf. Article 47 of the Bankruptcy law).

[B] Publicly Available Information

There are a number of public databases and registers in Russia, which contain important details about certain types of assets owned by corporations and private individuals. These databases can offer an initial step to identify property of a debtor.

[1] Real Estate

[a] Legal Identification of an Asset

As a matter of Russian law, 'real estate' includes land plots, land plots with mineral deposits and any other asset, which is closely connected with land, such as buildings and construction in progress ('genuine' real estate).

In this context, it is worth noting that aircrafts and sea going vessels, inland navigation ships and space objects[2] are classified as immovable property ('legal' immovables). However, there are separate registers for 'genuine' real estate and 'legal' immovables. The following section of this chapter is concerned with 'genuine' real estate objects only.

Information on current and former rights to real estate objects, encumbrances, identifying information, peculiarities (for instance, cultural heritage sites) and ownership information are registered with the Unified State Register of Legal Rights (USRLR), which is administrated by the Federal Service for State Registration, Cadastre and Cartography ('Rosreestr'). The register contains information about all land plots, subsoil plots, other objects closely connected with land including buildings, constructions, residential and non-residential premises, and factories as unified objects. There is one exception, which is that title to objects which pre-date 1997[3] cannot be included on the register.

Information contained in the USRLR is publicly available and can usually be received in the form of an extract from the USRLR. It is provided within five business days following payment of a small state fee of RUB 200[4] for a hardcopy extract and RUB 150[5] for an extract in electronic form. Extracts from the USRLR contain descriptions of real estate objects, registered title, encumbrances, information on registered claims and objections, and of course the registered proprietor. Documents contained in the registration file related to the object and overall information about all real estate owned by a particular person or entity are not accessible for a creditor without the consent of the registered proprietor or his/her authorized representative.

To obtain an extract from the register, a creditor will need to provide a request indicating the address or cadastral/base number of the applicable real estate object. The request may be filed in person with the relevant regional branch of Rosreestr, or a

2. Article 130 of the Russian Civil Code.
3. Federal Law On State Registration of Immovable Property and Transactions with it dated 21 July 1997 No. 122-FZ (which entered into force on 28 January 1998).
4. Approximately USD 3.5 at the applicable exchange rate as of 26 March 2015.
5. Approximately USD 2.5 at the applicable exchange rate as of 26 March 2015.

multifunctional centre, or by post with the regional branch of Rosreestr at the location of the real estate. The list and addresses of these regional bodies and multifunctional centres can be found at – https://rosreestr.ru/site/fiz/poluchit-svedeniya-iz-egrp/. A request may also be lodged electronically via this website: https://rosreestr.ru/wps/portal/cc_egrp_form_new.

[b] Technical Identification

Since 2007, creditors pursuing debts in Russia have been able to claim information about the technical characteristics and cadastral value of real estate belonging to debtors. Whilst this system initially only applied to land plots, it has in recent years been extended to all types of real estate.

The cadastral register contains the following information:[6]

- Type of object (land plot, building, etc).
- Cadastral number.
- Identification of the object's borders.
- Description of the place of the object on the land plot.
- Size of the object.
- Historical data regarding the object (for instance, on cadastral or registration numbers).
- Information about title to the object and encumbrances.
- Information about permitted exploitation.
- Technical description (so far as it relates to the buildings and construction).
- Cadastral price of the object, etc.

As noted above, information in the State Cadastre of Real Estate (SCRE) is (subject to certain exceptions) publicly available[7] and can be received in the form of a cadastral extract, a cadastral 'passport', a cadastral plan of the territory and a copy of the document under which entries to the SCRE have been made as well as a note on the cadastral value of the object. However pursuant to Order No. 75 dated 27 February 2010, issued by the Ministry of Economic Development of the Russian Federation, which sets forth the procedure for granting access to the information contained in the SCRE, any interested party may access the register, provided that *personal* data is protected in accordance with the applicable data protection laws.[8] In other words, any personal data contained in the documents or extracts from the SCRE will be deleted in the hardcopies to be received by the creditors.

As with applications relating to the USRLR, requests for information from the SCRE may be filed in person with any regional body of the Rosreestr or with any cadastre chamber of the Rosreestr, or with a multifunctional centre, or by post with the regional body of the Rosreestr or cadastre chamber at the place where the real estate is

6. Article 7 of the Federal Law On State Cadastre of Real Estate dated 24 July 2007 No. 221-FZ.
7. Article 4 of the Federal Law On State Cadastre of Real Estate dated 24 July 2007 No. 221-FZ.
8. Letter of the FSBE 'FCC Rosreestr' dated 5 May 2014 No. 11-1635-KL.

located. The list and addresses of the relevant regional bodies and multifunctional centres of services can be found at https://rosreestr.ru/site/fiz/poluchit-svedeniya-iz-gkn/. A request may also be lodged electronically on the following website: https://rosreestr.ru/wps/portal/cc_gkn_form_new.

Most requests are processed within five business days, although cadastral plans of the territory are provided within fifteen business days of the date of the request. Fees for provision of information depend on the type of document requested and may vary from RUB 200 to RUB 800[9] for individuals and from RUB 600 to RUB 2,400 for entities. There is no fee for obtaining a not on cadastral value.[10] The cadastral value is a specific administrative instrument (which is reviewed every five years[11]) and is used to calculate land taxes and lease payments (in state/municipal contracts). It should be noted, however, that this value does not necessarily coincide with the object's real market value.

[c] Public Cadastral Map

As an alternative to the above-described research option, a creditor seeking information about real estate in Russia may access the 'Public cadastral map'. Access is free of charge from – http://maps.rosreestr.ru/PortalOnline/.

A search can be initiated using either the ID of the land plot or a visual references. The following information is available from the Public cadastral map database:

- borders of the Russian Federation, units of the Russian Federation, territorial divisions, etc.;
- borders of land plots;
- frames of buildings;
- cadastral numbers of real estate;
- information about the type of title;
- cadastral value;
- square and primary technical characteristics of buildings, construction;
- permitted use, etc.

[2] Movable Assets

[a] Motor Vehicles

There is no publicly available register for motor vehicles in Russia.

9. Approximately between USD 3.5 and USD 13.5 and USD 10 and USD 40, respectively (as of 26 March 2015).
10. Article 14 of the Federal Law On State Cadastre of Real Estate dated 24 July 2007 No. 221-FZ.
11. Ruling of the Government of the Russian Federation dated 8 April 2000 No. 316 approving rules for the arrangement of the cadastral land assessment.

However recent changes[12] in the legislation concerning collateralizations has led to the creation of a register containing information about pledges registered on movable property (including motor vehicles and machinery), which is administrated by Federal Notary Chamber. The public section of the Register is available at www.reestr-zalogov.ru. It allows the user to conduct a search using a vehicle's ID number or the name of the owner.

It is worth noting that the system has only recently been implemented, and that registration is not mandatory. Accordingly, the register does not provide up to date and a full scope of information about pledged, tangible assets in Russia.

[b] Vessels

A vessel (depending on its purpose, size and technical characteristics) must be registered with one of the following vessel registers of the Russian Federation:[13]

- National Register of Ships.
- Register of Small Vessels.
- Register of Leased Foreign Vessels (Bareboat Charter Register).
- Russian International Register of Ships.
- Register of Ships under Construction.

The registers include information covering technical characteristics and descriptions, ownership, transactions involving vessels and encumbrances. Information and documents (related to any pledges) contained in the registers can be requested by any interested party on payment of a small fee.[14]

However, there is no unified register of vessels or publicly available electronic database in Russia. Registration of vessels (depending of their type) is administrated by the Captains of Sea Ports,[15] State Inspections for Small Vessels of the EMERCOM of Russia[16] and the Administration for the Inland Waterway Basins.[17] To access a particular register, it is necessary to submit a written application (indicating the name and identification number of the vessel) to the relevant registration authority.

12. Federal Law dated 21 December 2013 No. 379-FZ on Amendments to the Legal Acts of the Russian Federation.
13. Article 16 of the Inland Water Transport Code dated 7 March 2001 No. 24-FZ, Article 33 of the Merchant Shipping Code of the Russian Federation dated 20 April 1999 No. 81-FZ.
14. Article 50 and paragraph 6 Article 377 of the Merchant Shipping Code of the Russian Federation.
15. According to a Ruling of the Government of the Russian Federation dated 25 April 2006 No. 583-p registration in the Russian International Register of Ships is arranged by the Captains of the Sea Ports in the cities of Arkhangelsk, Astrakhan, Vladivostok, Kaliningrad, Korsakov, Murmansk, Nakhodka, Novorossiysk, Saint-Petersburg, Taganrog, Tuapse and Kholmsk.
16. Ministry of the Russian Federation for Affairs for Civil Defence, Emergencies and Elimination of Consequences of Natural disasters.
17. Orders of the Ministry of Transport dated 26 September 2001 No. 144 and 9 December 2010 No. 277.

[c] Aircrafts

On 14 March 2009, Federal law No. 31-FZ on State Registration of Rights to Aircraft and Transactions involving Aircraft was adopted. In accordance with this law, the Unified State Register of Rights to the Aircraft (USRRT) was created, which is administered by the Federal Aircraft Agency.[18] The Register includes a description of the registered aircraft, information on the registered title, information of claims related to the aircraft and relevant objections thereto and encumbrances.

Information contained in the USRRT is publicly available. Thus, third parties may receive an extract from the register containing the most sensitive information (including descriptions, owner and encumbrances). Owners and authorized persons are able to access the full register (including documents contained on the aircraft's file).[19]

The law only entered into force on 16 September 2009. Accordingly, unless voluntarily registered information about titles to aircrafts, which pre-date the law, is unlikely to be available.

A request to access the USRRT must be submitted in writing to Federal Aircraft Agency. If approved, the extract is usually issued within five business days against payment of a fee of RUB 100 for individuals and RUB 300 for entities.[20]

In addition to the USRRT, the Federal Aircraft Agency maintains the State Register of Civil Aircrafts of the Russian Federation.[21] On registration of an aircraft with this registry, the state authorities will issue a certificate of registration and allocate state and registration numbers to the aircraft. The certificate does not deal with issues of title, but acts as a certificate of airworthiness. However, the register itself contains information on the technical characteristics of the aircraft, its owner and encumbrances, if any.

An interested party may receive an extract from the State Register of Civil Aircraft by filing a written request in relation to a particular aircraft with the Federal Aircraft Agency. A response is usually provided within thirty calendar days of the date of registration of the request.[22]

[3] IP Rights

Trademarks, patents and models have only in recent years become valuable assets worth searching in Russia. In 2006, the 4th Part of the Russian Civil Code was adopted. This new legislation provided for the systematic regulation of IP rights and provided rules concerning the transfer of IP rights and the registration of certain types of IP

18. Ruling of the Government of the Russian Federation dated 28 November 2009 No. 958, which sets forth the regulatory provisions for the management of this register.
19. Article 6 of the Federal Law dated 14 March 2009 No. 31 –FZ On State Registration of Rights to Aircraft and Transactions with them.
20. Approximately USD 1.7 for individuals and USD 5 for entities at the applicable exchange rate as of 26 March 2015. The fees may change from time to time.
21. Article 33 of the Air Code of the Russian Federation.
22. Paragraph 6 Article 18 of the Federal Law dated 9 February 2009 No. 8-FZ.

rights.[23] In particular, inventions, trademarks, utility models, programmes, databases and appellations of origin must be registered with the relevant registers under Russian law. The registers of IP rights are administrated by the Federal Institute of Industrial Property of the Federal Service for Intellectual property (Rospatent). Information from the registers is available at this website: http://www1.fips.ru/wps/portal/Registers/. The portal provides access to the registers of trademarks and service marks, inventions, models, international trademarks, appellation of origin, trademarks notorious in Russia, programmes and databases as well access to pending applications for the registration of IP rights.

In addition, applicants can, against payment, gain access to databases, which contain information about patent documents covering the period from 1924 to 1993, including inventory and models document, etc.

[4] Financial and Related Reports

All legal entities incorporated in the Russian Federation that are obliged to file financial reports must file a copy of their annual report to the statistic registrar.[24] The annual report – which, as in other jurisdictions, must include a balance sheet, accounting statements, information about the turnover, expenses, taxes, etc. and an audit report – is publicly available and can be requested from the Federal Service for State Statistics. Electronic copies of reports for 2012–2014 are available at http://www.gks.ru/accounting_report and can be located by using an entity's tax number.

In addition, listed joint stock companies[25] are obliged to disclose their annual financial reports and annual accounting reports on their official websites and on one or more of the following websites: http://www.e-disclosure.ru/, http://www.disclosure.ru/index.shtml, http://disclosure.1prime.ru/, http://disclosure.skrin.ru/.

Moreover, starting form 1 January 2013, the Federal Tax Service has been required to establish and maintain the so-called Unified Federal Register of Information on the Facts of Business of Legal Entities. This register contains company data such as incorporation details, reorganization history, liquidation, changes in the registered capital, alteration of address and net assets, etc. The register is available at www.fedresurs.ru.

Finally, information about companies involved in insolvency proceedings is also publicly available and can be accessed at http://bankrot.fedresurs.ru/DebtorsSearch.aspx.

[C] Register of 'Bad' Debtors

There is only one official register of 'bad debtors' in Russia. It is administrated by the Federal Antimonopoly Service of the Russian Federation and contains a list of entities

23. Articles 1262, 1353, 1452, 1480 of the Russian Civil Code.
24. Paragraph 1 Article 18 of the Federal Law dated 6 December 2011 No. 402-FZ On Accounting.
25. Article 92 of the Federal Law dated 26 December 1995 No. 208-FZ On Joint Stock Companies.

and entrepreneurs who have failed to perform a state or a municipal contract. The register is available at http://rnp.fas.gov.ru/ for free. Information is removed from the register upon expiration of two years from the date of the violation.

In addition, there are a number of unofficial 'black lists' in Russia, which offer a useful way to collect information about a contractual counterparty.[26]

§16.03 INTERIM MEASURES

Russian courts have the power to grant interim measures upon request of a party involved in the proceedings, if a failure to grant interim relief would impede or render the execution of a judicial decision impossible and result in extensive harm to the applicant.[27] It is possible to apply for interim measures at any stage during the proceedings, and even prior to initiating litigation.[28] In practice, the claimant will often file an application for interim measures simultaneously with its statement of claim or writ.

A party involved in arbitration either in Russia or abroad may also file a request for interim measures with a Russian state court.[29] In this case, interim relief can be granted by the state court at the place where the tribunal has its seat, at the debtor's place of residence or at the location of the debtor's asset(s).[30]

Recent case law confirms that a party to proceedings in a foreign state court is also entitled to request interim measures in a Russian state court.[31]

The Russian Procedural Act does not contain an exhaustive list of possible interim measures. The most commonly used interim measures involve:[32]

- The freezing of monetary assets (in particular bank accounts) or other property owned by the respondent and held by him or other persons.
- Forbidding the respondent or other persons to perform certain actions relating to the assets in dispute.
- Placing on the respondent a duty to perform certain actions to prevent damage to, or the deterioration of, the assets in dispute.
- Transfer of the assets in dispute to the claimant or a third-party trustee.
- Suspending a sale of real property.

Several security measures may be granted simultaneously.

26. See for example the following two websites: http://www.mgodeloros.ru/register/search and http://zakupki.rosatom.ru/Web.aspx?node=unscrupulous.
27. Article 90 of the Russian Arbitrazh Procedure Code.
28. Article 99 of the Russian Arbitrazh Procedure Code.
29. Articles 90 and 92 of the Russian Arbitrazh Procedure Code.
30. Article 90.3 of the Russian Arbitrazh Procedure Code.
31. Clause 30 of Information Letter of the Presidium of the Supreme Arbitrazh Court of the Russian Federation No. 158 dated 9 July 2013.
32. Article 91 of the Russian Arbitrazh Procedure Code.

A violation of an injunction may result in an administrative fine being levied by a court.[33] Interestingly, however, the amount of the fine cannot exceed RUB 2,500 for individuals, RUB 5,000 for officials and RUB 100,000 for legal entities.[34]

An interim measure can be granted on an ex-parte basis by a single judge no later than on the day after the filing of the application.[35] The court grants interim measures by issuing an order, which has an immediate legal effect. Rulings in favour of or against interim measures are subject to appeal.[36] However an appeal does not suspend the effect of interim measures.

The court granting interim measures will often order the applicant to provide security[37] to ensure compensation of the respondent's possible losses if the interim relief subsequently turns out to be unwarranted. Security may be provided by depositing funds into the court's bank account or by way of providing a bank guarantee. The amount of the security is determined by the court within the limits of the assets in dispute. Generally, guarantee amount is not less than 50% of the assets in dispute.[38]

The court must rule on the issue of the applicant's obligation to place security within one day following the date of receipt of the application for interim relief. The ruling must state the amount of the security and the deadline for providing it, which may not exceed fifteen days following the date of the court's decision. A ruling concerning security may be appealed.[39]

As indicated, it is possible to obtain interim relief before filing a lawsuit.[40] An application for such a 'preliminary' interim measure must be accompanied by a document showing that security equal to the amount of the claim has been furnished. A ruling on preliminary interim measures will be rendered by a court in the same manner as a ruling on interim measures. Any preliminary interim measures granted will remain in force for the period indicated in the ruling. The term of the measures shall not exceed fifteen days from the day of the announcement of the ruling. The applicant who has claimed preliminary interim measures must file a relevant lawsuit within this fifteen-day period. A failure to file a lawsuit within this period will result in the interim measure being revoked and expose the applicant to liability for any loss suffered by the counterparty as a result of the interim measure.

An order for an interim measure is enforced pursuant to the general rules of the Russian enforcement procedure. When granting interim relief, the court issues a so-called writ of execution. The requirements to such a writ are the same as the requirements related to a writ of execution issued pursuant to a judgment. The claimant may serve the writ either on the respondent's bank (where the interim measure is granted in the form of a freezing order targeting the respondent's bank

33. Article 119.1 of the Russian Arbitrazh Procedure Code.
34. Approximately USD 40, USD 80 and USD 1,650 respectively.
35. Article 93.1.1 of the Russian Arbitrazh Procedure Code.
36. Article 93.7 of the Russian Arbitrazh Procedure Code.
37. Article 94 of the Russian Arbitrazh Procedure Code.
38. Article 94.1 of the Russian Arbitrazh Procedure Code.
39. Article 94.3 of the Russian Arbitrazh Procedure Code.
40. Article 99 of the Russian Arbitrazh Procedure Code.

account(s)) or on the office of bailiffs. In the latter case, the bailiff will seek to enforce the interim measures against relevant third parties and the debtor. No preliminary notification of the defendant in relation to enforcement is required.

§16.04 ENFORCEMENT ISSUES

Foreign judgments are usually only enforceable in Russia if there is a bilateral treaty between Russia and the relevant foreign country whose court has rendered the judgment providing for the mutual recognition and enforcement of judgments. However, certain exceptions to this approach exist in the state commercial courts (the so-called arbitrazh).

As far as foreign arbitral awards are concerned, Russia is a party to the 1958 New York Convention on the Recognition and Enforcement of Foreign Arbitral Awards (the 'New York Convention'). The grounds for refusing enforcement of an arbitral award rendered by a tribunal having its seat in a country other than Russia are accordingly very limited. Having said this, the applicable Russian procedural rules applicable to the enforcement of foreign awards in Russia are not always consistently applied.

The limitation period for submitting a foreign judgment or arbitral award to the Russian court for recognition and enforcement is three years. A party seeking to enforce an international arbitral award or foreign judgment must file a written application with the competent state court. After hearing the application, the Russian court renders a ruling declaring the award enforceable and issues a writ of enforcement. There is a right of appeal to the upper (cassation) court within one month from the date when the ruling is rendered. Once a writ of execution has been issued, a creditor may enforce the judgment or award in the same way as judgments rendered by a Russian court are enforced under Federal law No. 229-FZ dated 2 October 2007 on Enforcement Procedures.

[A] Recognition and Enforcement of Foreign Judgments

Russian law[41] provides that foreign judgments can be recognized and enforced only if there is a relevant international treaty between the Russian Federation and the country where the judgment was delivered. The Russian Arbitrazh Procedural Code, however, also provides for the recognition and enforcement of foreign judgments in cases provided for in federal laws.[42]

41. In particular, the Federal Constitutional Law dated 31 December 1996 No. 1-FCL On judicial system in the Russian Federation, Article 241 of the Russian Arbitrazh Procedure Code and Article 409 of the Russian Civil Procedure Code.
42. These exceptions cover judgments in bankruptcy cases (paragraph 1 Article 6 of the Federal Law on Insolvency (Bankruptcy)) and judgments on dissolution of marriage between Russian and foreign nationals (or stateless persons), provided that several conditions are met (Article 160 of the Family Code of the Russian Federation).

Russia[43] has ratified a number of bilateral treaties with foreign countries. For instance, relevant treaties were concluded with: Greece (1981), Italy (1979), Spain (1990), Cyprus (1984), China (1992), Poland (1996), Hungary (1958), Estonia (1993), Lithuania (1992), Latvia (1993), Vietnam (1998), Argentina (2000), India (2000), and Egypt (1997). In total there are more than thirty bilateral treaties, which provide for mutual recognition of judgments in a wide range of disputes. In addition, the CIS members are parties to the Convention on Legal Assistance and Legal Relations in Civil, Family and Criminal Cases (executed in Minsk in 1993) and the Treaty on the Mechanism for Resolution of Disputes related to Performance of Business Activities (executed in Kiev in 1992). Nevertheless, Russia has no treaties providing for mutual recognition and enforcement of foreign judgments with the majority of the European Union Member States.

In circumstances where no treaty exists, the approach to recognition and enforcement of foreign judgments differs in the courts of general jurisdiction and in the state commercial courts (the 'arbitrazh').

The courts of general jurisdiction consistently adhere to the rule that recognition and enforcement is only possible if a treaty on mutual recognition and enforcement is in place and consequently refuses to enforce foreign judgments rendered by courts of countries which Russia has no treaty relationship with.[44]

The state commercial courts, on the other hand, follow a more flexible approach. In particular, in the Ruling of the Federal Arbitrazh court of the North-Western Circuit dated 11 January 2008 in Case No. F56-22667/2007, the court explained that an applicant filing a request for recognition and enforcement of the foreign judgment in the absence of a relevant international treaty must provide sufficient evidence that judgments of the Russian courts are recognized and enforced in the country where the judgment under consideration has been rendered. A plaintiff may seek to meet this burden of evidence by reference to legislation, other sources of law and case law of the relevant country. If the burden of proof for showing 'de facto enforcement reciprocity' is met, the state commercial court may decide to order the enforcement of the foreign judgment in question. Having said this, the case law seems to indicate that the judges, when deciding on the issue of enforcement of a foreign judgment from a jurisdiction, which is not covered by a bilateral treaty with Russia, sometimes also attach importance to the existence of other types of treaties such as the UN Convention on Human Rights and the ECHR.[45]

43. Some of these treaties have been initially concluded by the USSR and subsequently recognized by Russia as a legal successor of the USSR.
44. Determination of the Supreme Court of Russia dated 28 January 1999 Case No. 78-G98-46, Determination of the Supreme Court of Russia dated 1 December 2009 Case No. 4-G09-27, Determination of the Supreme Court of Russia dated 28 July 2009 No. 38-G09-7 (which refused recognition of judgments issued in Finland, Germany and Moldova), Determination of the Supreme Court of Russia 2013 Case No. 5-KG12-92, Determination of the Constitutional Court of Russia dated 17 June 2013 No. 890-O.
45. For instance, in a relatively recent Ruling the Presidium of the Supreme Arbitrazh Court of the Russian Federation dated 8 October 2013 No. 6004/13 recognized a judgment of the High Court of Justice of the Northern Ireland citing joint participation of Russia and the Northern Ireland in the UN Convention against Corruption (2003), Agreement on Partnership and Cooperation

Foreign parties should take this into account if choosing to litigate in their own local courts against a Russian entity (except for the countries which are the parties to the above-mentioned bilateral treaties).

[1] Rules of Procedure[46]

A creditor may request enforcement of a foreign judgment within three years from the date from which it can be enforced. If expired, the enforcement period may be extended, provided that reasonable grounds exist for doing so.

An application for enforcement must be filed by the judgment creditor at the local arbitrazh court at the debtor's location or place of residence or, if the debtor's location and place of residence are unknown, at the place where the debtor's property is located.

The application must indicate the name of the local arbitrazh (state commercial) court, with which the application is filed; the name and location of the foreign court; the name of the parties to the dispute, their location or place of residence; information regarding the foreign judgment; and a list of exhibits, including:

- A properly certified copy of the foreign judgment.
- A document confirming that the judgment is enforceable (unless indicated in the text of the judgment itself).
- A properly certified document confirming that the debtor was duly notified of the proceedings in the foreign court.
- A court fee in the amount of RUB 3,000.[47]

All foreign documents must be accompanied by a certified translation into Russian.

The application and the documents attached thereto may be filed with the court either in hardcopy or in electronic form at this website: https://my.arbitr.ru/#index.[48]

(1994) and Treaty on Economic Cooperation (1992). Neither of these international agreements refers to mutual recognition and enforcement. Other examples are the Ruling of the Supreme Court dated 12 October 2004 Case No. 5- Г04-91, Ruling of the Federal Arbitrazh Court of the Moscow Circuit dated 9 September 2008 Case No. KG-A40/7229-08; Determination of the Supreme Arbitrazh Court of the Russian Federation dated 7 December 2009 No.BAC-13688/09. The same approach was demonstrated in the Determination of the Supreme Court of Russia dated 7 June 2002 Case No. 5-G02-64, Ruling of the Federal Arbitrazh Court of Moscow Circuit dated 29 November 2012 No. F05-3492/12, Determination of the Arbitration Court of the Saint-Petersburg and Leningrad Region dated 4 June 2013 Case No. A56-68674/2012.

46. The rules of procedure are largely the same in the Arbitrazh (state commercial) courts and the courts of general jurisdiction. As such, for the sake of convenience, we refer only to the rules of the Arbitrazh courts.
47. At the exchange rate effective as of 25 March 2015, the fee is equal to approximately USD 52 (Article 333.21 ((11), paragraph 1) of the Russian Tax Code). However the law does not require payment of the state fee when applying for recognition and enforcement with the courts of general jurisdiction.
48. There is no mechanism for online filing in the courts of general jurisdiction.

[2] *Applications for Recognition and Enforcement: Grounds for Denial*

An application for recognition and enforcement of a foreign judgment is subject to an open hearing by a single judge. The hearing must be held within three months from the date when the arbitrazh (state commercial) court receives the application. When considering this type of case, the court has no right to review the judgment on its merits. The court may refuse to recognize and enforce a foreign judgment fully or in part, if:

(i) the judgment has not become enforceable in the country where it was rendered;[49]
(ii) the judgment debtor was not properly notified of the proceedings or was otherwise prevented from presenting its case;
(iii) according to an international treaty of the Russian Federation or a federal law, the subject matter of the dispute falls within the exclusive competence of a court in the Russian Federation;[50]
(iv) there is a Russian court decision involving the same parties and subject matter of the dispute;
(v) proceedings involving the same persons, subject matter and grounds are currently pending before courts in the Russian Federation, and those proceedings were commenced first in time, or the Russian courts were the first forum in which an application relating to the dispute was heard (litis pendens);
(vi) the term for enforcement has expired, and this term has not been extended;
(vii) enforcement would contradict the public policy of the Russian Federation.

In practice, the 'failure of due notification' and 'public policy' grounds are most often cited as reasons why enforcement should be denied. If a foreign court judgment is rendered on the matter, which falls within 'exclusive jurisdiction' of Russian state courts, enforcement of such judgment will also be denied (a few examples of such 'exclusive jurisdiction' are indicated below under section §16.04[B][2] in relation to the concept of 'arbitrability').

[a] *Faulty Notification*

Judgment creditors should bear in mind that the Russian Federation is a party to the Hague Convention on Service Abroad of Judicial and Extrajudicial documents in Civil and Commercial Matters (1965). This said, Russian parties to foreign proceeding shall be notified in accordance with the order envisaged in the Convention.

49. The courts of general jurisdiction can also reject enforcement if the judgment is not enforceable in the country where it was adopted (Article 412 of the Civil Procedure code of the Russian Federation).
50. For instance, disputes related to corporate relations involving a Russian legal entity, ownership of shares and stakes in Russian entities fall within exclusive competence of Russian courts – please, see Ruling of the Presidium of the Supreme Arbitrazh Court of the Russian Federation dated 23 October 2012 No. 7805/12.

A request for the service of foreign process under the Hague Convention should be sent by the authorized authority of the country of process to the Russian Central Authority[51] (being the Ministry of Justice). Following receipt of a request for service:[52]

(i) The Ministry of Justice forwards the request to the Russian court nearest to the addressee.
(ii) The court issues a domestic summons notifying the defendant that a hearing will be convened for the purposes of serving the defendant with a foreign process. In the arbitrazh (state commercial) court, this takes the form of a court ruling. In the courts of general jurisdiction, a court summons is used rather than a ruling.
(iii) The defendant attends the local court to accept service. If a summons is not validly served (or deemed served), the hearing for the acceptance of the foreign process will be adjourned until such time as the court has been provided with evidence of actual or deemed service.[53]
(iv) The Russian court then confirms due service to the Ministry of Justice which, in turn, responds to the authorized agency of the country where the proceedings take place in accordance with the Hague Convention.

As a matter of practice, following receipt of the request for service of a foreign process, serving the defendant can take up to approximately six months (whether through the arbitrazh courts or the courts of general jurisdiction). A failure to follow the procedure set out in the Hague Service Convention (even if the judgment debtor has been effectively notified of the proceedings) may result in the Russian courts refusing to recognize and enforce the foreign judgment.[54]

[b] Public Policy

An alleged violation of public policy is another cornerstone in most enforcement evasion strategies, because Russian courts often refuse to recognize and enforce

51. Article 10 of the Hague Convention provides that foreign judicial documents may be served on the parties in contracting states by postal channels. However, in 2004 the Russian Federation opted out of Article 10. It also excluded service through the diplomatic channels under Article 8 (except for citizens of the requesting country).
52. Articles 63, 113–117 and 407 of the Russian Civil Procedure Code and Articles 74, 121–123 and 256 of the Russian Arbitrazh Procedure Code.
53. If a defendant has been properly served (or deemed served), but fails to attend court to accept service, then service cannot usually take place (based on the available court decisions, we note that this approach prevailed in twenty out of twenty-nine cases in which this issue was raised in the period from 1 September to 15 November 2014). However the case law in this area is contradictory, and there are a small minority of cases where, notwithstanding the fact that the defendant has failed to attend the court, service of foreign process was deemed to have succeeded (see for example, Cases No. A53-19502/14 (15 September 2014) A41-41568/14 (19 September 2014) and A53-22447/2014 (29 October 2014).
54. Please see clause 6 of the Information letter of the Plenum of the Supreme Arbitrazh Court of the Russian Federation dated 22 December 2005 No. 96, Ruling of the Presidium of the Supreme Arbitrazh Court of the Russian Federation dated 28 January 2014 No. 3366/13, Ruling of the Federal Arbitrazh Court of the Moscow Circuit dated 6 February 2013 Case No. A40-99083/12-50-2011.

foreign judgments on public policy grounds. These are discussed in more detail below, however, it is worth bearing in mind that the Russian courts adopt an expansive interpretation of public policy.

Besides, it should be noted that the Russian courts have the right to refuse recognition and enforcement at their own initiative if there is a violation of public policy requirements.[55] This rule emphasizes the importance of the public policy protection mechanism.

[B] Recognition and Enforcement of Arbitral Awards

Most disputes involving Russian and foreign entities are resolved by way of international arbitration, with the most popular venues being London, Stockholm, Paris and New York. As a result of the current sanctions regime, however, Hong Kong and Singapore are also becoming increasingly popular venues.

As mentioned above, pursuant to the New York Convention, Russia must recognize and enforce awards made in signatory states, unless certain limited exceptions apply. At the outset, it is worth noting that recognition and enforcement are often easier to obtain in Moscow and St Petersburg, as they are more familiar with the New York Convention compared to the courts in Russia's regions. The statistics show that over the past few years there has been an increase from 79 in 2008 to 158 in 2013 in claims for recognition and enforcement of foreign judgments and arbitral awards.

Although the case law varies, the past decade or so has seen a marked improvement in enforcement rates and the grounds for challenging awards have become more sophisticated and in line with international practice.

[1] Rules of Procedure

The procedural aspects of enforcement are set out in the Russian Arbitrazh Procedure Code and in the Civil Procedure Code.[56] A foreign arbitral award is enforceable for three years from the date of the award.

Enforcement of foreign arbitral awards rendered in commercial disputes falls within the exclusive competence of the arbitrazh (state commercial) courts of Russia.[57] Decisions regarding enforcement must be rendered within three months[58] and may be appealed.

The procedure for enforcing a foreign arbitral award in Russia is as follows:

---

55. Paragraph 1 of the Information letter of the Presidium of the Supreme Arbitrazh Court of the Russian Federation dated 26 February 2013 No. 156, Ruling of the Federal Arbirazh Court of the Moscow Circuit dated 23 August 2013 Case No. A40-16783/2013, Ruling of the Federal Arbirazh Court of the North-West Circuit dated 28 December 2009 Case No. A21-802/2009.
56. The rules of procedure are largely the same in the arbitrazh courts and the courts of general jurisdiction. As such for the sake of convenience we will refer only to the rules for the arbitrazh courts.
57. Article 32 of the Russian Arbitrazh Procedure Code.
58. The terms for consideration of the application in the courts of general jurisdiction are not specified in procedural rules.

(i) The applicant prepares and files an application for recognition and enforcement of the award with the judgment debtor's local court or, if the judgment debtor's location is unknown, where the defendant's assets are situated.

(ii) The application must be accompanied by: (i) the arbitral award (or a copy) duly certified (for instance, by the relevant arbitral institution), notarized and apostilled; and (ii) the arbitration agreement or a duly certified copy thereof. These documents must be accompanied by certified Russian translations.

(iii) The court will initiate proceedings, notify the judgment debtor that an application has been filed and schedule a hearing. A number of hearings may be required depending on the circumstances. When considering the application, the court is not allowed to review the case on the merits.

(iv) If the court finds that there are no grounds for refusing the application, it will issue an order for recognition and enforcement of the arbitral award. This order may be appealed to the upper (cassation) court within one month.

(v) The court will also provide the judgment creditor with a writ of execution based on which the bailiffs will commence enforcement proceedings (and will search for the defendant's assets, freeze cash in bank accounts, attach property, etc.).

[a] Stay of Proceedings

The Russian court may stay the proceedings for recognition and enforcement pending the outcome of an application for setting aside or suspending the award,[59] provided the judgment debtor deposits sufficient funds or guarantees to compensate any harm suffered by the judgment creditor as a result of the suspension of the recognition and enforcement proceedings.

[2] Denial of Enforcement

The Russian law on International Commercial Arbitration 1993 (the 'Arbitration Law') and the Russian Code of Civil Procedure[60] largely replicates the relevant provisions of the New York Convention. As such, recognition and enforcement of international arbitral awards can only be refused on the following grounds:[61]

59. Paragraph 2 Article 36 of the Law of the Russian Federation on International Commercial arbitration No. 5338-1 as of 7 July 1993. There is a little case law where a suspension was granted on these grounds (see, Ruling of the Presidium of the Supreme Arbitrazh Court of the Russian Federation dated 13 September 2011 No. 9899/09).

60. Article 417 of Civil Procedure Code.

61. An arbitral award which does not need to be 'performed' (e.g., confirmation of title to movable property) can simply be 'recognized' by a Russian court and does not need to be 'enforced'. As such, non-monetary relief can also be enforced in Russia. All other awards need to be 'recognized and enforced'.

(i) One of the parties did not have legal capacity to enter into the arbitration agreement, or the arbitration agreement was otherwise void.
(ii) The respondent was not duly informed of the appointment of the arbitrator or commencement of the arbitration proceedings, or for other reasons was unable to present its case.
(iii) The award relates to a dispute, which is not covered by the arbitration agreement.
(iv) The arbitration procedure or composition of the tribunal was inconsistent with the law of the agreement.
(v) The award is not yet final or has been revoked, or its enforcement has been suspended by the court at the seat of the arbitration.
(vi) The subject matter of the dispute is not arbitrable under Russian law.
(vii) Recognition and enforcement of the award would be contrary to Russian public policy.

In practice, the 'arbitrability' and 'public policy' grounds are often cited in enforcement proceedings, although the Russian courts are required to consider these grounds ex officio, i.e., even when they have not been raised by the parties to the dispute.[62]

[a] Arbitrability

As a matter of Russian law and recent case law, certain types of disputes cannot be settled through arbitration, including:

(i) Disputes related to rent of forest land plots.[63]
(ii) Disputes under public procurement contracts.[64]
(iii) Disputes related to title to immovable property.

As a result of a ruling of the Constitutional Court No. 10-P dated 26 May 2011, disputes relating to immovable property (including those related to the title to immovable property) may now be referred to domestic arbitration tribunals. However Russian legal scholars have not elaborated a unilateral approach as to whether the Constitutional court's guidance shall also apply to international commercial arbitral tribunals. Relevant case law is not available so far. This said, there is a risk that Russian courts will reject recognition and enforcement of a foreign arbitral award related to the title to immovable property in Russia.

(iv) Corporate disputes

62. Please see Rulings of the Presidium of the Supreme Arbitrazh Court of the Russian Federation dated 13 November 2012 No. 8141/12 and 5 February 2013 No. 11606/12.
63. Please see Ruling of the Presidium of the Supreme Arbitrazh Court of the Russian Federation dated 11 February 2014 No. 11059/13.
64. Please see Ruling of the Presidium of the Supreme Arbitrazh Court of the Russian Federation dated 28 January 2014 No. 11535/12.

In recent years, Russian courts have sought to exert exclusive jurisdiction over 'corporate disputes' involving Russian entities, regardless of agreed dispute resolution procedures. For example, the Constitutional Court of the RF in Determinations No. 1488-O as of 17 July 2012 and No. 1804-O-O dated 21 December 2011 noted that:

> a reference in the Russian Arbitrazh Procedure Code to special jurisdiction over corporate disputes means not only that there exists a split of competence between the courts of the general jurisdiction and the arbitrazh courts but also indicates that these types of disputes cannot be referred to arbitration due to the character and specific features of the relationships from which these disputes arise. These conclusions follow from a systematic construction of Articles 4 and 33 of the Russian Arbitrazh Procedure Code.[65]

The notion of 'corporate disputes' was introduced into Russian law in July 2009 and covers disputes related to (among other things):

(i) incorporation, reorganization or liquidation of companies;
(ii) title to shares, encumbrances over shares or the exercise of rights attached to shares;
(iii) registration of rights to shares;
(iv) challenging a company's corporate resolutions or transactions;
(v) appointment, suspension or termination of officers;
(vi) issuance of securities; and
(vii) convocation of general meetings.

In light of the above, all disputes arising out of shareholders' agreements (or similar agreements) fall within this category. Indeed, it is fair to say that 'corporate disputes' involve practically any dispute in relation to the exercising of shareholders'/participants' rights in Russian entities. Furthermore, there have been cases where Russian courts have claimed exclusive jurisdiction even with respect to share purchase agreements related to Russian companies.[66]

The risks associated with the enforcement of awards in relation to corporate disputes are therefore twofold: (i) any arbitral award issued in connection with a 'corporate dispute' may not be enforceable in Russia; and (ii) a counterparty could commence parallel proceedings in the Russian courts, resulting in conflicting decisions and increased costs.[67]

65. However some courts have adopted a more flexible approach: please see Determination of the Supreme Arbitrazh Court of the Russian Federation dated 6 March 2012 No. SAC-2489/12, Ruling of the Federal Arbitrazh Court of the North-West Circuit dated 19 December 2011 Case No. A42-4871/2011, Ruling of the Federal Arbitrazh Court of the Moscow Circuit dated 15 November 2010 Case No. A40-3775/10-138-31.
66. Please see Ruling of the Federal Arbitrazh Court of the Moscow Circuit dated 10 October 2011 No. A40-35844/11-69-311, Determinations of the Supreme Arbitration Court dated 30 January 2012 No. SAC-15384/11, Ruling of the Arbitration Court of the Moscow Circuit dated 17 December 2014 No. A40-26424/11-83-201.
67. Enforcement of an award conflicting with the Russian court judgment denied (see, Determination of the Supreme Arbitrazh Court of the Russian Federation dated 2 December 2013 No. SAC-16350/13).

[b] Public Policy

'Public policy' is broadly interpreted, and Russian courts frequently reject recognition and enforcement of awards the enforcement of which could entail a necessity to perform actions, which are prohibited by Russian law, may imperil the safety and sovereignty of Russia or large social groups, are inconsistent with the principles of Russian economic, political, legal system and violate the basic principles of Russian civil legislation.[68] Certain uniformity on issues related to the 'public policy' was set out by the Supreme Arbitrazh Court of the Russian Federation in its Information letter dated 26 February 2013 No. 156. The Supreme Arbitrazh Court ruled that the following types of awards can involve public policy violations:

(i) Awards rendered pursuant to an optional arbitration or litigation clause (usually contained in finance contracts).
There is recent, but unfortunately not very helpful, case law[69] regarding unilateral (or one-way) option clauses, which allow one party to choose the forum (for instance, LCIA arbitration, litigation in English courts or any other court with jurisdiction), while the other party is only entitled to initiate proceedings in one forum (for instance, LCIA arbitration). The Supreme Arbitrazh Court of the Russian Federation has recently held such clauses to be void, although the consequences of this ruling are not yet clear. The liberal view is that the Supreme Arbitrazh Court has simply transformed a unilateral option into a bilateral option, in effect giving both parties the option to commence arbitration or court proceedings. There is, however, another view, which is that the dispute resolution clause is void in its entirety, so that the parties have no option but to litigate their dispute in Russia's state courts.

(ii) Awards of a penal character (e.g., which impose a fine or non-compensatory damages).[70]
The court will likely deny recognition and enforcement of an award if the amount of damages awarded is abnormally high and significantly increase the amount, which the parties could reasonably foresee when entering into the contract. Also the amount of awarded damages will be acknowledged as violating public policy if there is obvious evidence of an abuse of the freedom of contracts with respect to the volume of such damages.

68. Please see the Ruling of the Federal Arbitrazh Court of the North-West Circuit dated 10 March 2011 Case No. 05-10560/2010, Determination of the Supreme Arbitrazh Court of the Russian Federation dated 26 May 2011 No. SAC-436/11.
69. Please see the Ruling of the Presidium of the Supreme Arbitrazh Court of the Russian Federation dated 19 June 2012 No. 1831/12 in Case No. A40-49223/11-112-401.
70. Paragraph 6 of the Information letter of the Supreme Arbitrazh Court of the Russian Federation dated 26 February 2013 No. 156, Ruling of the Presidium of the Supreme Arbitrazh Court of the Russian Federation dated 23 April 2013 No. 16497/12.

(iii) Awards issued by an 'impaired' tribunal[71] (for instance, if an arbitrator died before rendering an award) or by an arbitrator whose impartiality may be questioned.[72]

In general, however, it should be noted that the recent case law and directive recommendations of the Supreme Arbirazh Court aim at prohibiting a broad construction of the 'public policy' principle, which formerly prevented successful enforcement of foreign arbitral awards in Russia.

§16.05 CONSEQUENCES OF ASSETS DISSIPATING

When it comes to immediate opposition between a creditor and a debtor and when the risk of attachment and seizure of assets arise, debtors frequently introduce various schemes and manoeuvres to conceal and dissipate their assets. In order to guard creditors against the risk of asset dissipation in the context of threatening or actual proceedings against a debtor, creditors may seek to freeze the debtor's assets, or take other steps aimed at discovering the nature and location of the debtor's assets, as we have described in the foregoing sections of this chapter.

Bankruptcy legislation provides the most effective 'ammunition' for these purposes. However, initiating and conducting bankruptcy proceedings is an extensive and expensive way forward.

Certain measures are proposed by the amended Russian Civil Code and corporate legislation to safeguard the interest of creditors. Below we briefly discuss some of the remedies, which can be available to a creditor seeking to claw back assets removed by the debtor in an attempt to dodge enforcement.

[A] Return of Assets

According to the general rules of Russian civil law, a creditor has no rights to claim a return of assets dissipated by a debtor. However, recent changes in the Russian Civil Code and developments in Russian insolvency case law supports claw back claims.

[1] Asset Tracking Attachment

The year 2013 was marked by significant reforms in Russia's civil legislation. The reform is still pending. One new rule, which came in force on 1 September 2013, and which shall apply to transaction executed from this date, relates to the distribution of property in violation of a court order prohibiting the disposal of such property.

One measure, which is usually used by a creditor to prevent the dissipation of assets is the attachment of the debtor's property. However, an attachment order does

71. Please see the Ruling of the Presidium of the Supreme Arbitrazh Court of the Russian Federation dated 20 July 2012 No. 4325/10.

72. Paragraph 12 of the Information letter of the Supreme Arbitrazh Court of the Russian Federation dated 26 February 2013 No. 156.

not always prevent a sale of the debtor's property, even if a sale would reduce the value of the debtor's assets. Until recently, it was necessary for creditors to file a fresh lawsuit challenging such transactions and seeking restitution of the disposed assets.

Currently, Article 174.1 of the Russian Civil Code stipulates that a transaction executed in violation of a ban to dispose assets applied by the court (or otherwise in the order prescribed by the law) in the favour of a creditor (another authorized person) shall not prevent this creditor (authorized person) to exercise the rights, which were secured by this ban. Exceptions are established for situations where a purchaser of the property did not know and should not have known about the prohibition.

This having been said, the recent revisions to the Civil Code entitle a creditor to exercise its right against the attached property, (save against bona fides purchasers). Needless to say that there is no guiding case law with respect to the application of this new rule. However, recent judgments demonstrate that the rule has been adequately perceived by the courts, and is likely to be properly applied.[73]

[2] Liability of Successors and Controlling Persons during a Corporate Reorganization

Debtors sometimes seek to conceal their property through corporate restructurings, which result in the debtor being left with liabilities, but no assets of real significance.

Amendments to Article 60 of the Russian Civil Code aim to guard creditors against such corporate reorganization:

(i) Paragraph 5 accordingly provides that all entities involved in a restructuring are jointly and severally liable to a creditor if assets and liabilities are unfairly distributed during the reorganization.[74]

(ii) In addition, pursuant to paragraph 3, (i) individuals who direct the reorganized entities, (ii) members of entities' collective bodies, and (iii) their executives are also jointly and severally liable to creditors if creditors' debts are not discharged as a result of a reorganization, and the said individuals assisted infliction of negative consequences to the creditors.

Even if one of the entities was liquidated during or after a reorganization (or insolvency), a creditor may still be able to claw back assets. According to a new draft of Article 64 of the Russian Civil Code,[75] an interested party has the right to file an application with the court seeking the distribution of property, which a debtor has managed to put beyond the reach of its creditors through a restructuring (liquidation). These proceedings can be initiated within five years from the relevant entity's

73. Ruling of the Arbitration Court of the Ural Circuit dated 1 September 2014 Case No. A60-13790/2013, the Arbitration Court of the Central Circuit dated 1 October 2014 Case No. A08-147/2013.
74. Ruling of the Seventeenth Arbitrazh Appellate Court dated 9 December 2014 Case No. A60-28238/2014.
75. Effective from 1 September 2014.

liquidation, and will result in the appointment of an administrator to claw back the relevant assets.

[B] Recovery of Damages from Third Parties

[1] 'Piercing the Corporate Veil'

Russian law adheres to the principle of individual liability. As such, debtors alone are civilly liable to their creditors. Under Article 56 of the Russian Civil Code, a participant in the Russian legal entity is not therefore liable for the obligations of its subsidiaries, unless otherwise set forth by law. There are only limited grounds for when a beneficiary / parent company may be held liable for the debtor's actions.

[a] Liability for a Subsidiary

At present, Russian law provides that a shareholder/participant is responsible under the obligations of its subsidiary only in case of bringing the subsidiary into insolvency.[76] To establish subsidiary liability it is necessary to:

(i) initiate bankruptcy proceedings against the subsidiary;
(ii) demonstrate that the subsidiary's assets are insufficient to satisfy the claims of its creditors;
(iii) show that bankruptcy was caused by the actions/instructions/omissions of the parent company.

The Bankruptcy law does not expressly refer to a 'parent company', but to a 'controlling person'. A 'controlling person' is defined as a company (or individual) who possesses over 50% of the voting shares of a joint-stock company or over 50% of the authorized capital of a limited liability company.

Even then, a controlling person will avoid liability if it acted reasonably and in good faith in accordance with the interests of the debtor (subsidiary). Its liability may also be reduced by a court at its discretion if the creditors' losses are significantly lower than their claims against the debtor.

[b] Joint and Several Liability

A parent company and its subsidiary are jointly and severally liable for deals executed under the instructions or with the consent of the parent company.[77] Although the case law has not yet developed a uniform approach to the term 'consent', academics agree

76. Article 3 of Federal Law No. 14-FZ of 8 February 1998 On Limited Liability Companies, Article 3 of the Federal Law No. 208-FZ of 26 December 1995 On Joint-Stock Companies; Determination of the Supreme Arbitrazh Court of the Russian Federation dated 29 April 2013 No. 11134/12.
77. Article 67.3 of the Russian Civil Code.

that 'consent' excludes ordinary corporate approvals which are usually required under Russian law for major or interested transactions.

[c] Damages

Recent changes to Russian civil legislation extend the grounds on which shareholders may be held liable for damages incurred by entity subsidiary. As follows from the Russian Civil Code a person (both entity and individual) with the ability to determine the actions of a legal entity (including the right, capability to instruct the director of the entity) shall act reasonably, in good faith and is obliged to make good any harm as a result of its failure to act accordingly.[78]

The rules setting forth the right of a shareholder or company to claim damages from a controlling person have only recently been incorporated into Russian law. As such, court practice in this area is still developing.[79]

These rules do not allow the creditor itself to benefit from bringing the beneficiaries of a company to liability.

[2] Liability of Directors and Officials

A creditor does not have a right to commence proceedings against a director of the company – debtor for wrongs committed by the director. Such claims are bought by or on behalf of a company against its directors.

The right to file such a claim rests with shareholders (participants), the company itself and members of its collective executive body. Claims can be filed against directors, controlling persons,[80] members of the board or other collective executive bodies of the company and members of a liquidation commission and are often commenced for harm to the company as a result of a failure to act fairly, prudently and in accordance with business norms and practice.[81] Liability may be joint and several.

In 2013, the Supreme Arbitrazh Court of the Russian Federation in the Ruling No. 62 of 30 July 2013 established that directors are presumed to act fairly and reasonably with a view to maximizing corporate value. However, there is a presumption that they have acted unfairly if they:[82]

78. Article 53.1 of the Russian Civil Code, Article 6 of the Federal Law No. 208-FZ of 26 December 1995 On joint-stock companies.
79. Ruling of the Eighth Arbitrazh Appellate Court dated 16 January 2015 Case No. A46-1517/2014.
80. For more details, please, see §16.05[B][1].
81. Article 53.1 of the Russian Civil law, Article 71 of the Federal Law On Joint Stock Companies, Article 44 of the Federal Law of Limited Liability Companies.
82. Paragraph 2 of the Ruling of the Plenum of the Supreme Arbitrazh Court of the Russian Federation dated 30 July 2013 No. 62. The case law demonstrates that unfair practice may include undue issuance of a power of attorney (Ruling of the Presidium of the Supreme Arbitrazh Court of the Russian Federation dated 21 January 2014 No. 9324/12), signing of an act of acceptance for the works, which have not been performed (Ruling of the Presidium of the Supreme Arbitrazh Court of the Russian Federation dated 24 June 2014 No. 3159/14), actions resulted in administrative liability of the company (Ruling of the Federal Arbitrazh Court of the

(i) acted in a situation where there was a conflict of interest and failed to disclose information about the conflict;
(ii) concealed sensitive information from the shareholders;
(iii) executed a transaction without the necessary corporate approvals;
(iv) upon termination of employment retained documents relating to circumstances resulted or may result in the entity suffering negative consequences.

Directors are presumed to have acted imprudently if they:

(i) took a decision without regard to available information;
(ii) failed to take necessary measures (ordinary for business practice) to obtain information required before making a decision;
(iii) executed a transaction without complying with internal procedures.

The said clarifications of the Supreme Arbitrazh Court of the Russian Federation shall apply to the members of the collective, executive bodies of the company. Damages inflicted on a legal entity by several officials or executives shall be compensated jointly and severally.

Finally, in 2009, the Bankruptcy law established that chief executive officers of a debtor (in particular, the general director) are liable to its creditors for the loss or falsification of the debtor's accounting statements prior to the initiation of bankruptcy proceedings. Also the director shall be liable for losses which resulted from the late submission of a bankruptcy petition.[83]

[C] Criminal Proceedings in Connection with Asset Dissipation

The implementation of various schemes aimed at dissipation of assets may sometimes qualify as a fraud, abuse of power, debt payment evasion, intentional bankruptcy or another crime punishable under Russian criminal law.

Since there is no criminal liability for legal entities in Russia, the persons who may be prosecuted for dissipation of company assets are the officials or shareholders of the respective companies. In practice, Russian authorities are rather reluctant to start criminal proceedings against officials and shareholders of legal entities when no damage was caused to the interests of the state or state-owned companies. If a criminal case is nevertheless opened against such individuals, there is a possibility for the creditors to file a civil lawsuit in the criminal proceedings and to seek compensation for damages from those individuals. Attachment of the assets of the accused person will also be available for the creditors in such cases.

Far-East Circuit dated 14 July 2014 Case No. A51-192397/2011, Determination of the Supreme Arbitrazh Court of the Russian Federation dated 17 July 2014 No. SAC-9063/14.

83. Article 10 of the Bankruptcy law. In practice, the courts are currently reluctant to bring official to accounts under these provisions.

§16.06 CONCLUSION

Generally, an analysis of Russian legislation and court practice shows that a creditor has limited practical tools in Russia to discover and attach assets of its debtor. A significant number of remedies available in western countries are not recognized or do not work in Russia (e.g., proceedings for the disclosure of documents, unified search bases, etc.). Therefore a cautious approach to potential debt collection in Russia is required.

CHAPTER 17
Sweden

Finn Madsen & Daniel Prawitz

§17.01 INTRODUCTION

It is not a rash guess that the Swedish legal system is unknown to most lawyers outside of Sweden, or at least outside of Scandinavia. In fact Scandinavian law is often considered to be a unity composed of the legal systems of Denmark, Finland, Iceland, Norway and Sweden. There are indeed similarities, but it is important to stress that there are considerable differences as well.

It is also occasionally argued that the Swedish legal system holds an intermediate position between continental law and common law.[1] Swedish law does have characteristics found in both these legal traditions. For example, written and enacted statutes are the main source of law in Sweden. On the other hand, case law holds a more prominent position as a source of law in Sweden than in many countries where continental law tradition is predominant.

The latter is certainly true when it comes to civil law, and in particular property law. The Swedish legal system does not contain a general all-embracing civil act, like for example the German *Bürgerliches Gesetzbuch* or the French *Code civil*. Instead, Swedish civil law may be described as a patchwork quilt of enacted statutes and general legal principles, supplemented by the contents of the preparatory works, case law and jurisprudence. Parts of Swedish civil law legislation are old. For example, the Swedish Contracts Act (Sw. *Lag (1915:218) om avtal och andra rättshandlingar på förmögenhetsrättens område*) celebrated its centenary in 2015, and the Swedish Commercial Code (Sw. *Handelsbalk (1736:0123)*), which contains important statutes regarding, *inter alia*, pledges and securities and the authority of representatives and agents, has been in force for nearly three hundred years.

1. See, for example, Stig Strömholm, *General Features of Swedish Law*, 1st edition, 2000, p. 11.

The Swedish sources of law and the hierarchy between these have been debated thoroughly. However, in simplified terms, the sources of Swedish law are commonly considered to be the following, in a descending hierarchical order:[2]

- Laws of the European Union.
- The Swedish constitution.
- Statutes (in the meaning of acts enacted by the Swedish Parliament (Sw. *Riksdagen*)) and other officially binding government regulations, in said order.
- Government bills and other preparatory works.
- Judicial practice and precedent (case law).
- Works by legal scholars.

As regards the Swedish court system, the courts are primarily constituted by the general courts and the administrative courts. In addition hereto, the court system also consists of a few courts specifically designated for certain matters such as, for example, market law, employment law and patent issues.

The general courts handle all criminal and civil cases. The general courts are, in descending hierarchical order: (i) the Swedish Supreme Court; (ii) the Courts of Appeal; and (iii) the district courts. There are forty-eight district courts throughout Sweden with jurisdiction within certain geographical areas, as well as six Courts of Appeal, each exercising jurisdiction over a number of district courts.

The administrative courts handle cases concerning administrative law, which includes many different types of matters such as matters involving taxes, social security, migration and environmental issues. The administrative courts are in descending hierarchical order: (i) the Swedish Supreme Administrative Court; (ii) the administrative courts of appeal; and (iii) the administrative courts. There are twelve administrative courts, with jurisdiction within certain geographical areas, as well as four administrative courts of appeal, each exercising jurisdiction over two or more administrative courts.

The enforcement of judgments and arbitral awards is executed by the Swedish Enforcement Authority (Sw. *Kronofogdemyndigheten*), which also enforces freezing orders and other types of interim measures. The Enforcement Authority is free standing from the courts, and the activities of the Enforcement Authority are regulated in the Swedish Enforcement Code (Sw. *Utsökningsbalken (1981:774)*). Enforcement of a judgment, award or any other court decision must upon its rendering be actively pursued by a creditor by a written application to the Enforcement Authority.

Given this brief introduction to the Swedish legal system, the following presentation will focus on: how a claimant may identify assets of a debtor located in Sweden (section §17.02); safety measures to secure assets in Sweden, in particular freezing orders (section §17.03); enforceability of foreign judgments and arbitral awards (section §17.04); and to what extent the directors and officers of a debtor may be held

2. See for example Aleksander Peczenik, *Juridikens metodproblem: rättskällelära och lagtolkning*, 2nd edition, 1980.

liable in the event that the company attempts to dissipate or hide assets from its creditors (section §17.05).

§17.02 IDENTIFYING ASSETS IN SWEDEN

[A] Introduction

Naturally, prior to initiating what can sometimes prove to be costly legal proceedings, a creditor must always consider whether the debtor is in fact capable of satisfying the creditor's claim as well as any legal costs which the debtor may be ordered to pay to the creditor in connection with a judgment or award.

Swedish procedural law does, in principle, not provide for any instrument or method to be used to force access to information regarding a debtor's assets, either in a pre-trial stage or during pending legal proceedings.[3] However, in connection with the enforcement of a judgment or any other court decision, such as a freezing order, the debtor may be ordered to disclose information abort any assets he may have, and this may be done under oath, making any non-disclosure by the debtor a criminal offence. Further, any third party may be ordered to disclose any economic relationship that such third party has with the debtor. This could include orders to banks to disclose assets held in bank accounts in the debtor's name, as well as the disclosure of any contractual rights (e.g., right to payment) that the debtor may have towards a third party which could be subject to seizure.[4] As mentioned, in order for these measures to be available before or during legal proceedings (i.e., prior to a final judgment or award has been rendered), a creditor would require a freezing order.

However, although a defendant as a general rule may not be forced to disclose its assets, access to information on possible assets is to a large extent publicly available. The Swedish principle of public access to official records (Sw. *Offentlighetsprincipen*) provides, in simplified terms, that all documents and other types of information, which are in the possession of an official authority are public and shall be provided to anyone requesting a copy of the documentation in question or the opportunity to review such information. Refusal to disclose such information is permitted only in cases provided for in the Public Access to Information and Secrecy Act (Sw. *Offentlighets- och sekretesslagen (2009:400)*).

There are a number of public registers in Sweden containing information regarding property rights with respect to different types of assets. As a result of the principle of public access to official records, these public registers are open and available to anyone, and most of them may also be easily browsed on the Internet. In a pre-trial phase, such public records constitute an important source of information regarding a debtor's financial situation.

This chapter outlines the main sources of information available on possibly valuable assets.

3. There are certain such instruments in connection with bankruptcy proceedings, but these will not be elaborated on in this presentation.
4. The rules in this respect are contained in Chapter 4 sections 14–16 of the Enforcement Code.

[B] Real Property

Real property represents large financial values in Sweden, as it does in most countries. The Swedish Mapping, Cadastral and Land Registration Authority (Sw. *Lantmäteriet*) administrates the Swedish Real Property Register (Sw. *Fastighetsregistret*). The register gives access to relevant information such as data on legally qualified owners, mortgage deeds, encumbrances, tax assessed property values, the price the current owner paid in connection with the purchase, etc.

All relevant information may be retrieved directly from the authority by contacts with the authority. The Real Property Register has not been made accessible online by the authority, however, there are a number of private companies that gather, assemble and present information from the Real Property Register, easily accessible online for a small fee.

[C] Motor Vehicles

The Swedish Road Traffic Register (Sw. *Fordonsregistret*) is administrated by the Swedish Transport Agency (Sw. *Transportstyrelsen*). The register contains detailed information regarding all civilian, Swedish registered vehicles, such as registered ownership, acquisition date and the date on which the vehicle was first used on a public road. Although the register does not provide information regarding the condition and status of the vehicle, the information found therein normally allows for a fair valuation of the vehicle. The Road Traffic Register is accessible at http://www.transportstyrelsen.se.

Information on registered ownership of vehicles may be used in order to find assets to attach in connection with a freezing order or in connection with the enforcement of a judgment. However, in this context it should be highlighted that registered ownership may not necessarily reflect the actual legal ownership of a vehicle.

[D] Vessels

The Swedish Transport Agency also administrates the Swedish Register of Ships (Sw. *Skeppsregistret*). According to Chapter 1, section 2 of the Swedish Maritime Code (Sw. *Sjölagen (1994:1009)*), a vessel is defined as a *ship* if it has an overall length of at least 12 metres and a minimum beam of at least 4 metres. Other vessels are called boats. All Swedish[5] ships must be registered in the Register of Ships. Boats used commercially for tugging, towing, transporting goods or passengers and for fishing must also be registered. The register contains detailed information regarding registered ownership to Swedish ships and such boats subject to registration. The register further contains registrations of third-party rights in ships, including mortgages, attachments, etc.

5. According to Chapter 1, section 1 of the Maritime Code, a ship is, in general, considered to be Swedish if a Swedish citizen or legal entity owns 50% or more of the ship.

The Register of Ships is not as easily accessible as, for example, the Real Property Register or the Road Traffic Register. Access to the register requires a written application to the Swedish Transport Agency in which the applicant must state the purpose for which access is requested. Access may be granted, e.g., if the applicant in its public or private activities is in need of information contained in the register to form the basis for, e.g., a legal claim or other commercial decisions. Hence, it should be considered sufficient in order to gain access that a creditor is investigating whether a debtor has any assets in order to be able to decide whether to proceed with an appropriate legal remedy.

As there is no requirement to register boats with an overall length of under 12 metres, many valuable boats for leisure purposes may not be found in the register.

[E] Aircrafts

The Swedish Aircraft Register (Sw. *Luftfartygsregistret*) is also administrated by the Swedish Transport Agency. The register contains information about all civilian aircraft registered in Sweden, including information regarding, e.g., registered ownership and mortgages.

The register is accessible at http://www.transportstyrelsen.se/sv/luftfart/Luftfartyg-och-luftvardighet/Luftfartygsregistret/Sok-luftfartyg/.

[F] Intellectual Property Rights

The Swedish Patent and Registration Office (Sw. *Patent- och Registreringsverket*) administrates the Swedish patent, model, design and trademark registers, which are all available at http://www.prv.se/sv/vara-tjanster/databaser/. So-called Community Trademarks which are administered by OHIM (*Office for Harmonization in the Internal Market*) are also recognized in Sweden and information regarding all Community Trademarks may be retrieved from OHIM at https://oami.europa.eu/ohimportal/en/home.

It should be pointed out that although intellectual property rights may represent substantial value, the matter of to what extent intellectual property rights may be attached or seized has been debated in Sweden and often gives rise to specific problems from a property right perspective. Some intellectual property rights are subject to explicit regulation with respect to the possibilities to attach or seize such property. For example, copyrights may not be seized.

[G] Annual Financial Reports

The majority of all types of legal forms of business activity (Sw. *Associationsformer*) existing in Sweden are obliged to file annual reports with the Swedish Companies Registration Office (Sw. *Bolagsverket*) or other such authority designated for a specific type of legal entity. The predominant form of business activity in Sweden, the limited liability company (Sw. *Aktiebolag*), are always required to file annual reports.

An annual report shall contain true and relevant information regarding the financial status of the company it concerns as per the end of the company's financial year and is an important source of information in a pre-trial stage. However, seeing that the applicable rules provide that the annual report shall be filed annually, i.e., only once a year, and within seven months after the end of the financial year, the information found in the report may not always reflect the current situation of a company, even if it has been filed very recently.

All annual reports are available online at the Swedish Companies Registration Office's website (http://www.bolagsverket.se/) against a small fee, and there are also several private organizations which supply the same service.

[H] Tangible Assets Belonging to a Company

The Companies Registration Office also administers the Swedish Business Mortgage Register (Sw. *Företagsinteckningsregistret*). The register contains information regarding third-party rights in rem to a business's tangible assets such as machinery, stock of merchandise, raw materials, etc.[6] Obviously, the register does not contain any information regarding what tangible assets a company in fact has.

Any third party holding a business mortgage in a business has priority in case of bankruptcy. It should thus be evaluated whether the assets of a debtor will suffice for any creditors other than such creditors holding a business mortgage. The information is public and may be acquired by contacting the Companies Registration Office. The Business Mortgage Register has not been made accessible online by the authority; however, there are a number of private companies that present information from the Business Mortgage Register, easily accessible online for a small fee.

[I] The Enforcement Authority's Register

The Swedish Enforcement Authority registers all debts which have been confirmed through a court order or a simplified payment procedure and in respect of which enforcement has been attempted but has proven unsuccessful. The Enforcement Authority will provide all relevant information by telephone or in written form upon request. Also, there are a number of private companies that offer the same information easily accessible online for a small fee

Obviously, if the investigation shows that the debtor has large unpaid debts registered by the Enforcement Authority, a creditor must consider whether the chances that any additional attempts by the Enforcement Authority to enforce such creditors claim would be successful.

6. For further information on the Swedish regulations on security in chattel mortgages see, for example, Torgny Håstad, *Sakrätt: avseende lös egendon*, 6th edition, 2000.

§17.03 SECURITY MEASURES IN ORDER TO SECURE ASSETS

Chapter 15 of the Swedish Code of Judicial Procedure (Sw. *Rättegångsbalken (1942:740)*) provides effective methods to be used in order to prevent a debtor from dissipating assets. Although the freezing order[7] is the most frequently used security measure, the Code of Judicial Procedure provides the courts with the discretion to decide on the interim restoration of possession of a specific asset[8] as well as to decide on any other appropriate action to be taken in order to prevent the dissipation of assets.[9] The courts may, for example, order a defendant to conduct, or refrain from conducting, certain activities if such activities may affect a creditor's chances of enforcing a claim, which is or may become subject to legal proceedings.

As the freezing order is the most important and most frequently used security measure, the legal qualifications for receiving a freezing order will be outlined below, although the principles are also applicable to the application of any other security measure under Chapter 15 of the Code of Judicial Procedure.

[A] Freezing Orders

The primary consequence of a freezing order is that the assets of the defendant are secured until a final judgment in favour of the claimant has become legally binding. The fact that assets have been subject to a freezing order does not mean that the claimant has obtained any preferential title to them, should a defendant enter into bankruptcy. In addition, a freezing order does not prevent the same assets from being seized as a result of any third-party claim against the same defendant.

To obtain a freezing order in a civil case the claimant must show *probable cause* that the claimant has a valid claim against the defendant. This implies a lower evidentiary requirement compared to that which is required in order to be ultimately successful. The requirement implies that the claimant is not required to present full evidence in order to show that he has a legitimate claim, but only sufficient evidence making it more probable than not that the claimant will ultimately be successful with the claim.

In addition to the above, the claimant must demonstrate that it is reasonable to suspect that the defendant, in the absence of the security measure sought, will attempt to evade its responsibilities towards the claimant by disposing of property or otherwise taking measures to hide or dissipate its assets. The defendant's behaviour in this regard shall be imminent or ongoing. The fact that a defendant has a poor financial status is never in itself enough to bring about a freezing order, although it may be relevant when deciding whether the claimant is in need of a security measure. Finally, the claimant must deposit security with respect to any damage that the defendant may incur as a

7. Chapter 15, sections 1–2 of the Code of Judicial Procedure.
8. Chapter 15, section 3 of the Code of Judicial Procedure.
9. Chapter 15, section 4 of the Code of Judicial Procedure.

result of the freezing order, if the claimant is ultimately unsuccessful in his pursuit of the claim based on which the freezing order was granted.[10]

Should the matter be urgent with respect to the actions of the defendant, the court may upon request decide to grant a freezing order or another security measure without any prior communication with the defendant. The fact that security measures are required at all usually implies at least some degree of urgency. Therefore, if the claimant can demonstrate that the defendant's actions are ongoing or imminently at hand, then this will often be sufficient for the court to accept the need to grant an security measure on an ex parte basis. Within no more than a day or two – giving the claimant an opportunity to secure assets – the claimant's application for a freezing order and the court's interim decision shall be communicated to the defendant. Upon receipt of the defendant's response, the court shall reassess its decision.

The enforcement of a freezing order is executed by the Enforcement Authority. The Enforcement Authority will search all available public registers for assets and will also request all major banks to state whether the defendant has funds in the bank. Further, if the defendant rents or owns for example an office or warehouse or any other premises, the Enforcement Authority will literally break locks and grant itself access if it has to secure any assets belonging to the defendant. When enforcing a freezing order, time is often of the essence, and the claimant should have prepared thoroughly by investigating what assets the defendant may have and inform the Enforcement Authority accordingly as this will help ensure a swift and effective enforcement.

Upon a decision to grant a freezing order, the claimant must initiate legal proceedings within one month from when the decision was rendered, unless of course the decision to grant a freezing order has been rendered during pending proceedings. If proceedings are not initiated within one month, the freezing order shall be cancelled immediately.

[B] Arbitration and Security Measures

The security measures regulated in Chapter 15 of the Swedish Code of Judicial Procedure may, pursuant to section 4 in the Swedish Arbitration Act (Sw. *Lag (1999:116) om skiljeförfarande*), also be utilized to secure a claim, which is or may become subject to arbitral proceedings.

In this context, something should also be said regarding the Arbitration Institute of the Stockholm Chamber of Commerce (Sw. *Stockholms Handelskammares Skiljedomsinstitut*) (the 'SCC'). The SCC has for a long time had a prominent position in international arbitration. In 2010, as one of the first arbitration institutes in the world, the SCC introduced into the Arbitration Rules of the SCC a possibility to request the appointment of an emergency arbitrator. Such emergency arbitrator may, if appointed by the SCC, decide on any security measures, which the emergency arbitrator deems appropriate to secure the claimant's claim. The provisions are not available on an ex

10. If the applicant is not able to deposit any security, the court may discharge him of such obligation, provided that the applicant can show exceptional cause for his claim.

parte basis. A decision for an security measure shall be rendered within five days from when the request was handed over to the emergency arbitrator and is valid and binding until otherwise decided. The emergency decision ceases to be binding if arbitration is not commenced within thirty days from the date of the decision, or – if a referral is not made – within ninety days. An application for the appointment of an emergency arbitrator may be made until the arbitration has been referred to the arbitral tribunal. The fee is EUR 15,000 and is paid by the claimant. The number of applications for appointment of an emergency arbitrator has been steady since the introduction of this possibility, and several other international arbitration institutes have followed this lead and introduced similar rules into their arbitration rules.

[C] European Account Preservation Orders (EAPOs)

On 15 May 2014, *Regulation (EU) 655/2014 of the European Parliament and of the Council of 15 May 2014 establishing a European Account Preservation Order procedure to facilitate cross-border debt recovery in civil and commercial matters* was adopted. Being a member of the European Union, Sweden is bound by this regulation. The regulation will apply from 18 January 2017.

The regulation aims to provide preservation measures to be used in order to locate and seize bank assets throughout the EU. The regulation applies to pecuniary claims only, and its main feature is that it will be possible for a court in one Member State to freeze assets on bank accounts held in any bank in another Member State. An EAPO granted in a Member State shall be recognized and enforced in all other Member States without any exequatur means. In that context, it may be noted that the UK and Denmark has an opt-out in this area and are not bound by the regulation. Hence, courts in the UK and Denmark will not be able to grant EAPOs, nor will a court in another Member State be able to freeze assets held in bank accounts in the UK or Denmark.

The requirements for granting an EAPO are much alike those described in the foregoing regarding freezing orders under the Swedish Code of Judicial Procedure.

If an EAPO has been granted prior to any legal proceedings being initiated, the creditor shall initiate such proceedings within thirty days of the date on which he lodged the application or within fourteen days of the date of the issue of the order, whichever date is the later. If proof that proceedings have been initiated is not presented to the court that has granted the order within this thirty-day deadline, the order shall be revoked.

As the regulation has not yet begun to apply, the practical use of EAPOs and the benefits thereof are yet to be assessed.

§17.04 RECOGNITION AND ENFORCEMENT OF FOREIGN JUDGMENTS AND AWARDS

[A] Introduction

The enforceability of foreign judgments in Sweden is dependent on what the judgment concerns and where it has been rendered.[11]

As a point of departure, foreign judgments and court decisions are neither recognized, nor enforceable in Sweden and may be recognized and enforced only if statutory support provides for it. This follows from Chapter 3, section 2 of the Swedish Enforcement Code.

There are a few cases where such statutory support exists, mainly based on international conventions or EU regulations. Within the area of civil and commercial law, the most important examples are the *Council Regulation (EC) No. 1215/2012 of 12 December 2012 on Jurisdiction and the Recognition and Enforcement of Judgments in Civil and Commercial Matters*, commonly referred to as the Brussels I Regulation, the *Convention of 13 October 2007 on Jurisdiction and the Enforcement of Judgments in Civil and Commercial Matters*, commonly referred to as the Lugano Convention, and the Act on the Recognition and Enforcement of Judgments in Civil Cases Rendered in the Nordic States (Sw. *Lag (1977:595) om erkännande och verkställighet av nordiska domar på privaträttens område*).

Being a member of the European Union, Sweden is bound by the Brussels I Regulation. Sweden has also ratified the Lugano Convention.

[B] Recognition and Enforcement of Judgments Rendered in Another EU Member State

Under the Brussels I Regulation, a judgment rendered in any other Member State, which is enforceable in such state, shall be recognized and enforced in all other Member States. According to the original version of the Brussels I Regulation (Council Regulation (EC 44/2001)), enforcement was subject to an exequatur procedure, meaning that a designated national court would first declare the judgment enforceable in the Member State where enforcement was sought. For Sweden's part, the designated court to handle all exequatur procedures was Svea Court of Appeal (Sw. *Svea hovrätt*). However, on 10 January 2015, a recast version of the Brussels I Regulation – Council Regulation (EC) 1215/2012 – entered into force, replacing Council Regulation (EC) 44/2001. One of the most significant changes in the recast version is that the exequatur procedure has been abolished. According to the recast version of the Brussels I Regulation, judgments from another Member State shall now be recognized and enforced without the need for any additional actions from the party seeking enforcement. A party seeking enforcement according to Council Regulation (EC) 1215/2012

11. See, for example, Michael Bogdan, *Svensk internationell privat- och processrätt*, 8th edition, 2014, p. 280.

must merely submit the judgment to the national authority handling enforcement in the form set out in the Brussels I Regulation. If enforcement is sought in Sweden, the application for enforcement shall be submitted to the Enforcement Authority.

However, Council Regulation (EC) 1215/2012 applies only to judgments and other court decisions if the proceedings preceding said judgment or decision were initiated *after* 10 January 2015. If the proceedings were initiated *prior to* 10 January 2015, Council Regulation (EC) 44/2001 shall apply when enforcement of such judgment or decision is sought. Hence, the rules on exequatur procedure will be of importance for a few years to follow. Therefore, the provisions in connections therewith deserve mentioning.

According to Article 41 of Council Regulation (EC) 44/2001, a foreign judgment is to be declared enforceable by the Svea Court of Appeal immediately upon the fulfilment of the formalities stipulated in Article 53.[12] The court's decision shall be served on the defendant.

Svea Court of Appeal may refuse recognition of a judgment rendered in another Member State only in such cases provided for in Articles 34–35 of the Council Regulation (EC) 44/2001, most importantly:

- if recognition is manifestly contrary to public policy in the Member State in which recognition is sought; or
- where it was given in default of appearance, if the defendant was not served with the document which instituted the proceedings or with an equivalent document in sufficient time and in such a way as to enable him to arrange for his defence, unless the defendant failed to commence proceedings to challenge the judgment when it was possible for him to do so; or
- if it is irreconcilable with a judgment given in a dispute between the same parties in the Member State in which recognition is sought; or
- if it is irreconcilable with an earlier judgment given in another Member State or in a third state involving the same cause of action and between the same parties, provided that the earlier judgment fulfils the conditions necessary for its recognition in the Member State addressed.

[C] Recognition and Enforcement of Judgments Rendered in Non-EU Member States

With respect to foreign judgments and court decisions from non-EU Member States, the Brussels I Regulation is not applicable. As for countries within the European Free Trade Association (EFTA), the Lugano Convention is applicable and contains, in principle, the same provisions as the Brussels I Regulation. The EFTA Member States are Iceland, Liechtenstein, Norway and Switzerland, but Lichtenstein has not ratified the Lugano Convention, and the Convention is thus not applicable to judgments rendered in

12. The formalities consist of certain measures provided to guarantee the authenticity of the original judgment.

Lichtenstein. One important difference to the Brussels I Regulation, however, is that the Lugano Convention has not been amended in order to reflect the new rules under the Brussels I Regulation abolishing the exequatur procedure. Hence, exequatur procedure is still required under the Lugano Convention. This means that judgments rendered in Iceland, Norway and Switzerland would be subject to an exequatur procedure if enforcement is sought in an EU Member State. The exequatur procedure is in principle the same as described above in connection with Council Regulation 44/2001.

However, with respect to the close historical relationship and cooperation between the Nordic countries, i.e., Norway, Denmark, Iceland and Finland, the Nordic countries have for a long time allowed recognition and enforcement of judgments rendered in the other Nordic countries. In Sweden, the provisions in this respect are mainly contained in the Act (1977:595) on the Recognition and Enforcement of Judgments in Civil Cases Rendered in the Nordic States. According to this act, judgments and court decisions rendered in Norway, Denmark, Iceland and Finland shall be recognized and enforced as were they a Swedish judgment or court decision.

As for judgments rendered in non-EU or EFTA Member States, there is no 'all in one body' regulation under Swedish international procedural law to be referred to in relation to issues of recognition and enforcement. There are a number of different statutes containing provisions dealing with enforcement issues of foreign rulings on different areas of the law. These statutes are based on international conventions and thus are only effective in relation to judgments rendered in countries which have ratified such convention.

Non-enforceable judgments may, in line with the Swedish principle of free sifting of evidence, be given evidential value with regards to factual circumstances, but a claimant would always have to initiate new court proceedings in Sweden, or in another EU Member State or Lugano Convention Member State, in order to receive a judgment, which can be enforced in respect of assets located in Sweden.

[D] Enforcement of International Arbitral Awards

The issue of recognition and enforcement of foreign arbitration awards is far less complex than is the case in relation to foreign judgments.

In 1972, Sweden ratified *the 1958 New York Convention on the Recognition and Enforcement of Foreign Arbitral Awards* (the 'NYC'). The NYC applies to the recognition and enforcement of arbitration awards rendered in a state other than the state in which the recognition and enforcement of the judgment are sought. A vast number of states have ratified the NYC. As there is currently no world encompassing convention on the recognition and enforcement of court judgments, arbitration is often preferred for parties domiciled in different jurisdictions.

The NYC has been implemented in the Swedish legal system by means of certain provisions in the Swedish Arbitration Act *in fine*.[13] It should be noted that these

13. See sections 52–60 of the Arbitration Act.

provisions are applicable to all foreign arbitral awards, i.e., also awards rendered in a non-signatory state would thus in principle be enforceable in Sweden.

The Arbitration Act provides that foreign awards may be enforced in Sweden after having passed an exequatur procedure similar to that which is stipulated in the Council Regulation (EC) 44/2001 regarding judgments rendered in another EU Member State. An application for exequatur shall be submitted to the Svea Court of Appeal.

A foreign award shall be declared enforceable in Sweden unless the defendant shows that any of the circumstances in section 54 of the Arbitration Act are at hand, or if the Svea Court of Appeal during the exequatur procedure ex officio finds that any of the circumstances in section 55 of the Arbitration Act are at hand. Section 54 of the Arbitration Act corresponds to Article 5.1 of the NYC and section 55 of the Arbitration Act corresponds to Article 5.2 of the NYC.

§17.05 LIABILITY FOR DIRECTORS AND OFFICERS

Virtually all business activities in Sweden are conducted as either a partnership (Sw. *handelsbolag*), limited partnership (Sw. *kommanditbolag*) or as a limited liability company. All three are legal persons capable of conducting business activities in their own name. As regards partnerships, the partners to such venture are always jointly and severally liable with the partnership for all the partnership's debts. As regards limited partnerships, one or more partners have reserved the right to limit their liability. Not all partners may be limited partners. Hence, there are always one or more partners, which are jointly and severally liable with the limited partnership for all the limited partnership's debts.

As the absolute majority of all businesses in Sweden are run as limited liability companies, the prerequisites for liability for such company's debts shall be elaborated on further.

[A] The Swedish Companies Act

As the name implies, the foremost characteristics of the limited liability company is that that the liability for the shareholders is limited to what has been invested in the company. As a general rule, it is thus not possible to pursue claims against shareholders with respect to the company's inability to pay its debts. Nor is it, as a general rule, possible to pursue such claims against a company's directors or officers. However, like any other general rule, there are exceptions hereto.

First, the members of a board of a company may under certain circumstances become liable for the satisfaction of the company's debts. Chapter 25 of the Swedish Companies Act (Sw. *Aktiebolagslagen (2005:551)*) provides rules on what measures need to be taken by the board if it is suspected that the company's equity is below a certain threshold, and when the board of a company is required to decide to place the company into a winding-up procedure.

When the board has reason to suspect that the company's equity is less than half of the registered share capital (the so-called critical juncture), the board is required to prepare a balance sheet for liquidation purposes (Sw. *kontrollbalansräkning*). If their suspicions prove to be correct, and the balance sheet in question shows that the company's equity is less than half of the company's registered share capital, the board shall as soon as possible summon the shareholders to a first extraordinary general meeting (Sw. *första kontrollstämma*) in order to decide whether the company should enter into a winding-up procedure. If at such extraordinary general meeting, the balance sheet does not show that the company's equity corresponds with at least the registered share capital and if the company has not been entered into a winding-up procedure, the board shall summon a second extraordinary general meeting (Sw. *andra kontrollstämma*) to be held within eight months from such general meeting, in order to reassess the decision whether the company should enter into a winding-up procedure. The board shall, prior to the second extraordinary general meeting, have a renewed balance sheet drafted, and if such balance sheet does not show that the company's equity corresponds with at least the registered share capital, the board is thereupon obliged to apply for the immediate winding-up of the company.

If the board fails to fulfil all of its duties set forth in Chapter 25 of the Companies Act, the members of the board are jointly and severally liable with the company for any debts and other obligations of the company incurred after the critical juncture. To avoid such liability, a board member must show that he or she has not acted negligently. Thus, liability is presumed and the burden of proof in this respect lies with the board member against whom a claim has been lodged.

Second, a member of the board of directors or a managing director may become liable if he or she, in the performance of his or her duties, intentionally or negligently causes damage to the company, to a shareholder or to any third party as a consequence of a violation of the provisions of the Companies Act, the company's articles of association or the applicable legislation regarding annual reports. This liability is sometime referred to as the management's external liability.[14]

Hence, a creditor who has incurred damage as a result of such violation may lodge a claim against a member of the board or the managing director.

[B] The Swedish Criminal Code

Chapter 11 of the Swedish Criminal Code (Sw. *Brottsbalken*) contains provisions relating to crimes against creditors. An asset protection scheme through which a debtor's assets are transferred from the debtor in connection with a company's imminent insolvency would normally constitute a criminal offence under Chapter 11, section 1 of the Criminal Code (Sw. *oredlighet mot borgenärer*), but Chapter 11 of the Criminal Code encompasses a number of different actions which are frequently found to have been taken by the directors of a debtor in connection with a company becoming insolvent.

14. See, for example, Carl Svernlöv, *Styrelse- och VD-ansvar i aktiebolaget – en introduktion*, 2nd edition, 2012, p. 73.

The provisions regarding fraud and embezzlement contained in Chapters 9 and 10 of the Criminal Code should also be mentioned. If a creditor's claim derives from a fraudulent act by an officer of a company, a claim for damages as a result hereof may of course be pursued against such officer by virtue of the provisions under Chapter 9 of the Criminal Code. If it is the company itself that has been targeted by the fraudulent behaviour, the provisions concerning embezzlement and other breaches of trust found in Chapter 10 may be applied.

As regards damages, the Swedish Tort Liability Act (Sw. *skadeståndslagen (1972:207)*) provides that anyone who causes personal injury or damage to property shall compensate any loss as a result thereof, provided the damage was caused by negligence or intent. Hence, in Swedish tort law, pure economic loss is normally not compensated (unlike contractual liability, where pure economic loss shall be compensated unless otherwise agreed). However, if the damage is a result of a criminal action, compensation shall also be paid for all pure economic loss. Hence, if a director or officer of a company has caused pure economic damages to a third party through a criminal action, such director or officer shall compensate all such damage.

In this context, it deserves to be highlighted that the defendant to such a claim need not have been convicted of any crime in order to incur liability for damages towards a third party. A claimant may nevertheless claim that the defendant has committed a crime which, in turn, has caused the damage and may demonstrate to the court that this is the case. Of course, this would not entail any criminal liability for such defendant, but only liability in damages.

It should further be noted that although a prosecutor may have withdrawn any charges against such person as a result of the prosecutor not anticipating that it will be possible to prove *beyond reasonable doubt* that the person is guilty of a crime, this should not necessarily deter a claimant from pursuing a claim for damages in a civil lawsuit under the assertion that the defendant has committed said crime. The reason for this is that a claimant would not need to demonstrate *beyond reasonable doubt* that the defendant has committed a crime. In civil procedure, the evidentiary requirements are lower than those applied in criminal procedure. Hence, in civil procedure it is generally sufficient that the claimant *shows* that he has a legitimate claim, whether it is based on a crime having been committed or not, which entails a lower standard of proof than the prosecutor's requirement to prove *beyond reasonable doubt* that a crime has been committed.

CHAPTER 18

Switzerland

Alexander Jolles & Stefan Leimgruber[*]

§18.01 INTRODUCTION

The Swiss legal system is based on the civil law tradition. Switzerland is a Confederation comprising of twenty-six cantons, which generally enjoy broad political autonomy. However, over time, since the beginning of the twentieth century, legislative powers have been shifted to a federal level in order to harmonize relevant fields of law. This includes, in particular, civil and commercial law, criminal law, and the rules on civil and criminal procedure. It also includes the rules on international assistance in civil and criminal matters.[1]

A Federal Code of Civil Procedure (the "CPC") was introduced at the beginning of 2011. At the same time, other acts relating to civil procedure were revised, particularly the Lugano Convention on Jurisdiction and the Enforcement of Judgments in Civil and Commercial Matters (the "Lugano Convention") and the Federal Debt Enforcement and Bankruptcy Act (the "DEBA"). These changes had a considerable effect on the procedural regime related to the attachment of assets in Switzerland.

While civil proceedings are governed by the CPC, the cantons still control the organization and functioning of their own courts. Accordingly, the structure and certain rules applying to cantonal courts may differ from canton to canton. The language of the proceedings (German, French or Italian) depends on the geographic location of the court.

The court system is structured as follows:

* The authors thank Stefan Jud, Junior Associate with Schellenberg Wittmer Ltd., for his valuable assistance in preparing this chapter.

1. As a non-Member State, the laws or rules of the European Union or the European Economic Area do not directly apply in Switzerland.

- Courts of First Instance (*District Courts*): Every canton has at least one, whereas larger cantons have several District Courts.
- *High Courts*: Every canton has a High Court (Court of Appeals) handling appeals against District Court judgments.
- *The Federal Supreme Court*: Under certain circumstances, decisions of the High Courts can be appealed to the Swiss Federal Supreme Court, which is situated in Lausanne.
- *Special courts*: Various cantons have special courts handling, e.g., commercial, labor or landlord and tenant matters. In addition, there are special administrative tribunals dealing with administrative and public law cases (e.g., tax matters, zoning and construction permit matters, etc.).

Applications for attachment orders or for the enforcement of foreign judgments or awards are dealt with by the cantonal Courts of First Instance, usually by a single judge. The debt collection offices are in charge of executing the attachment orders or other enforcement measures ordered by the courts.

Swiss civil procedure and debt enforcement laws do not provide specific means for a pre-trial search for assets in civil law matters, unless insolvency proceedings are initiated. Accordingly, if no specific information is available to a creditor about assets belonging to a debtor, the creditor is limited to consulting public registries and databases containing information about certain types of assets. Such registries and databases are described below under section §18.02.

Section §18.03 describes the procedure and the requirements for the attachment of assets in civil proceedings in Switzerland. The respective rules are, to a large extent, not part of the CPC, but have traditionally been set forth in the DEBA.

Regarding the enforcement of foreign decisions, Switzerland has ratified the Lugano Convention as well as the 1958 New York Convention on the Recognition and Enforcement of Foreign Arbitral Awards (the "New York Convention"). An overview of the enforcement procedures regarding foreign judgments and awards is provided below under section §18.04.

Lastly, with respect to the risk of illicit asset protection schemes, section §18.05 of this chapter contains a brief analysis as to when a direct action can be taken against directors and officers of a company engaging in such activities.

§18.02 IDENTIFYING ASSETS IN SWITZERLAND

Under Swiss law, courts or other authorities involved in the granting and execution of an attachment order do not search for or provide information about a debtor's assets. Rather, it is for the creditor to specify and prove on a prima facie basis the existence of the debtor's assets in Switzerland (*see* below section §18.03). Hence, Swiss law does not permit "fishing expeditions" that would allow a creditor to obtain relevant information about the debtor's assets by filing an attachment request. Nor will a debtor be compelled to reveal the existence and whereabouts of assets in the course of attachment or enforcement proceedings.[2]

There are public registries and databases containing information about certain types of assets belonging to corporations and private individuals. These registries and databases (*see* immediately below section §18.02[A]–[H]) are the most obvious sources to search for assets of a debtor in the pre-trial phase. Further information may be obtained from private databases such as credit information services providing background details as to the solvency of a debtor, media databases or through a general internet search. Often, however, relevant information about a debtor's assets is not publicly available and is even well protected, e.g., by Swiss banking secrecy law or rules on data protection.

[A] Real Estate

The Swiss land register contains registrations of rights to immovable property located in Switzerland. Although regulated nationally, the cantons are responsible for setting up and keeping the land registers. Accordingly, there is no land register for the whole of Switzerland. Instead each canton has its own register, sometimes even kept on a district or communal level.[3]

Certain information in the land register is publicly available without restriction. In particular, any person is entitled to obtain information about the name and description of an immovable property, the name and identity of the owner, the form of ownership, the date of acquisition and some additional information, e.g., on easements (*Grunddienstbarkeiten*) and real burdens (*Grundlasten*).[4] The cantons may make this information accessible via the internet.[5]

In addition to the above, any person showing a legitimate interest is entitled to request additional information,[6] e.g., about charges and liens and priority notices (*Vormerkungen*).

Information will, however, only be provided for a specific property at a specific location; it is not possible to make a general search for real estate of a specific owner covering a certain territory or even the whole country.[7] Furthermore, a request for an extract from a land register can entail significant fees, depending on the level of detail of the extract and the land registry in charge.

The following website provides direct links to the various cantonal land registries and allows a search for a specific property. If the property can be found, information about the competent land registry is available: www.cadastre.ch.

To estimate the value of a property, the website https://en.comparis.ch/immobilien/verkaufen/default.aspx offers a basic valuation tool free of charge. A

2. Decision of the Swiss Federal Supreme Court BGer 5P.256/2006 of October 4, 2006, consid. 2.4.
3. Article 953 of the Swiss Civil Code (the "CC").
4. Article 970(2) CC in connection with Article 26(1) Grundbuchverordnung.
5. Article 27 Grundbuchverordnung. It remains to be seen to what extent the cantons will make use of this opportunity.
6. Article 970(1) CC.
7. Article 26(2) Grundbuchverordnung.

somewhat more sophisticated valuation is offered at www.iazicifi.ch for a fee of approximately CHF 300.

[B] Motor Vehicles

The Swiss car register lists every vehicle admitted in Switzerland including its license plate number, as well as information regarding the holder of the vehicle such as the name, address, nationality and the liability insurance.[8] The name and address of the holder of a registered vehicle may be disclosed to every person.[9]

As the car register is organized on a cantonal level, there is no register covering the whole of Switzerland. All cantons offer online access to the names and addresses of vehicle holders. In most cantons, however, information is only provided for a specific license plate number, while research by the name of the vehicle owner is not possible. At www.fahrzeugindex.ch, links to all cantonal online car registers are available.

[C] Vessels and Boats

The Swiss ship register contains information about the ownership of registered boats as well as information about the liens and usufructs associated with the boats. The register of inland ships is organized by canton and kept by the competent cantonal land registry (ship registration office).[10] For Swiss deep-sea vessels as well as for Swiss ocean-going yachts and small boats sailing under Swiss flag, the Swiss maritime navigation registry office keeps a separate register ("Schweizerisches Seeschiffsregister" or "SSA") that also informs about the ownership, liens and usufructs of the vessels. The SSA is managed by the land registry office of the canton of Basel-Stadt.[11]

As with the land register, certain information of the ship register is publicly available without the requesting person having to show a legitimate interest. Such information encompasses the name and identity of the owner, the form of ownership, the acquisition date and the usufructs. By showing a legitimate interest, information on liens will also be provided.[12]

No online access to the ship register is available. However, the website www.swiss-ships.ch contains a list of all deep-sea vessels sailing under Swiss flag and provides some information about the vessels, including about the ownership. Given that the website is run by a private foundation, no guarantee as to the completeness and content of the information is given.

8. Article 104a Strassenverkehrsgesetz.
9. Article 126 Verkehrszulassungsverordnung.
10. Article 1 and Article 26(1) Schiffsregistergesetz.
11. Article 10 Seeschifffahrtsgesetz in connection with Article 26(1) Schiffsregistergesetz.
12. Article 28 Schiffsregistergesetz in connection with Article 970 CC.

[D] Aircrafts

The Swiss Aircraft Registry is kept by the Federal Office of Civil Aviation ("Bundesamt für Zivilluftfahrt" or "BAZL") and contains a record of Swiss registered aircrafts, that is, information regarding the owner and the holder, the type of aircraft, the year of construction, the serial number and further details.[13]

At https://www.bazl.admin.ch/bazl/en/home/specialists/aircraft/swiss-aircraft-registry.html, the aircraft registry can be accessed online. It is not only possible to search by aircraft, but also by owner or holder.

Additionally, rights in rem relating to aircrafts (e.g., aircraft liens, notifications) can be recorded in the Aircraft records register. Entries may include lease agreements, notifications regarding restricted availability, etc. Every person is entitled to obtain information without having to show a legitimate interest.[14]

[E] IP Rights

The Swiss Federal Institute of Intellectual Property ("Institut für Geistiges Eigentum" or "IGE") with headquarters in Bern is the federal agency for matters concerning intellectual property in Switzerland. The IGE is the point of contact with regard to industrial protective rights (trademarks, patents and designs). Copyrights cannot be registered in Switzerland.

At https://www.swissreg.ch/srclient/faces/jsp/start.jsp, the IGE offers a free of charge online database containing registered data on trademarks, patents and designs as well as protected topographies.[15] It is possible to search by owner, i.e., for the IP rights of a particular individual or corporation.[16]

Online queries for registered internet domain names can be submitted at www.nic.ch.

[F] Financial Reports

Companies listed on a Swiss stock exchange - either on the SIX Swiss exchange (main Swiss stock exchange) or on the BX Berne eXchange - are required to publish annual reports, comprising the audited annual financial statements in accordance with the applicable financial reporting standards, as well as the corresponding audit report.[17]

---

13. Article 8 Luftfahrtverordnung.
14. Articles 4 et seq. and 13 Luftfahrzeugbuchgesetz.
15. International trademark registrations with effect in Switzerland are not contained in this database. They can be found in the online register of the World Intellectual Property Organization at www.wipo.int/romarin.
16. Swissreg is the official publication of the IGE, but is not the Swiss register of protective titles for trademarks, patents, designs and topographies. Only the particulars about protective rights from the register excerpts are legally binding. Excerpts can be obtained through the IGE at www.ige.ch.
17. Article 49 Listing Rules of the SIX Swiss Exchange and Article 16 Listing Rules of the BX Berne eXchange.

The reports are available via the websites of the stock exchanges at www.six-swiss-exchange.com or www.berne-x.com.

Regardless of the listing rules, companies having outstanding debentures or shares listed on a stock market (home or abroad) must either publish the annual accounts and consolidated accounts together with the audit reports in the Swiss Official Gazette of Commerce (www.shab.ch) or send an official copy to any person who requests the same within one year of their approval. Other companies are not required to publish their annual reports, but must allow creditors showing a legitimate interest to inspect the annual report and the audit reports.[18]

[G] Tangible Assets

The reservation of ownership with respect to a chattel that has been transferred to an acquirer is only effective if it is entered in the register on reservation of ownership kept by the debt collection office at the domicile of the acquirer.[19] Every person is entitled to consult the register.[20]

[H] Debt Collection and Bankruptcy Records and Registers

The debt collection and bankruptcy offices keep records and registers about debt enforcement and bankruptcy proceedings.[21] These records and registers contain information about "critical debtors," i.e., individuals and corporations domiciled in Switzerland that are involved in debt enforcement or bankruptcy proceedings. The records also include names of debtors against whom payment orders have been issued, identity of creditors having applied for the issuance of payment orders, information on amounts claimed by creditors and the date of such orders.

Any person credibly showing an interest in such information may consult the records and registers of the debt collection and bankruptcy offices and request extracts thereof.[22] However, information is accessible only for the five years preceding the request.

§18.03 INTERIM MEASURES

In Switzerland, the rules on interim measures in state court proceedings are set out in Articles 261 et seq. CPC, while Article 374 CPC and Article 183 of the Swiss Private International Law Act (PILA) deal with interim measures in arbitration proceedings.

18. Article 958e CO. In practice, a party has a sufficient interest if the enforceability of a claim is deemed at risk or if there are indications that the debtor is in financial trouble (Decision of the Swiss Federal Supreme Court BGer 4C.129/2004 of July 6, 2004, consid. 4.2.1).
19. Article 715 CC.
20. Article 17 Verordnung des Bundesgerichts betreffend die Eintragung der Eigentumsvorbehalte.
21. Article 8 DEBA.
22. Article 8a(1) DEBA; *see* F.C. Meier-Dieterle, in: D. Hunkeler (ed.), *Kurzkommentar SchKG*, 2nd ed., Basel 2014, Article 8a N 12, as to the prerequisite of a credible interest.

Protective measures in the context of enforcing monetary claims are, however, exhaustively governed by the DEBA. Specifically, the procedures and requirements with regard to civil attachment, i.e., the freezing of assets, are set out in Articles 271–281 DEBA. Since Switzerland is not a Member State of the European Union, the EU rules on European Account Preservation Orders do not apply.

[A] Attachment Orders Issued by Swiss Courts

[1] Requirements

In order to obtain an attachment order, a creditor must credibly show, i.e., establish on a prima facie basis, that the following requirements are met:

(i) the creditor has a mature and unsecured claim against the debtor;
(ii) the creditor can rely on one of the statutory reasons for an attachment set forth in Article 271(1) DEBA, that is:
  (1) the debtor has no permanent place of residence in Switzerland;
  (2) the debtor is concealing his or her assets, absconding or making preparations to abscond so as to evade the fulfillment of his or her obligations;
  (3) the debtor is on a journey through Switzerland or belongs to the persons visiting trade fairs and markets and the creditor's claim is to be fulfilled immediately;
  (4) the debtor does not live in Switzerland, no other reason for an attachment is fulfilled and the claim has a sufficient connection with Switzerland or is based on a signed acknowledgment of debt pursuant to Article 82(1) of the DEBA;
  (5) the creditor holds a provisional or definitive loss certificate against the debtor; or
  (6) the creditor holds an enforceable title to set aside an objection in debt enforcement proceedings ("definitiver Rechtsöffnungstitel") within the meaning of Article 80 DEBA, that is, an enforceable judgment, award or similar.
(iii) there are assets located in Switzerland belonging to the debtor.[23]

The most important and most frequently used grounds for attaching assets are Article 271(1)(4) and (6) DEBA. Article 271(1)(6), which was introduced upon entry into force of the CPC in 2011, provides that an attachment order will be granted if a creditor holds an enforceable title within the meaning of Article 80 DEBA (*"definitiver Rechtsöffnungstitel"*), such as a judgment of a Swiss or a foreign state court,[24] a domestic or foreign arbitral award,[25] or a domestic or foreign public deed.[26]

---

23. Article 272(1) DEBA in conjunction with Article 271(1) DEBA.
24. Articles 80(1), 80(2)(1) and 81(3) DEBA.
25. Article 387 CPC and Article 194 PILA.
26. Article 80(2)(1*bis*) DEBA, Article 57 Lugano Convention and Article 31 PILA.

This statutory ground for an attachment of a debtor's assets applies irrespective of whether the debtor is domiciled in Switzerland or abroad. There has been a lively debate among scholars after the introduction of the new attachment ground with regard to the interpretation of the term "definitiver Rechtsöffnungstitel," In a recent decision, the Swiss Federal Supreme Court held that the term must not be construed narrowly so that not only domestic judgments and awards or judgments rendered in a Member State of the Lugano Convention fall under this provision, but also foreign arbitral awards or foreign judgments rendered by a court of a non-contracting state of the Lugano Convention.[27] In these cases, the attachment may be granted even if there has not been a previous decision on the recognition and enforceability of the foreign judgment or award. It is sufficient for a creditor to demonstrate on a prima facie basis that the title is recognizable and enforceable in Switzerland.[28]

If no enforceable judgment or award is available and an attachment order is sought against a debtor not domiciled in Switzerland, Article 271(1)(4) DEBA allows a creditor to attach the debtor's assets, if – in addition to the absence of a Swiss domicile of the debtor – no other reason for an attachment is fulfilled, and the claim has a sufficient link to Switzerland or is based on a signed acknowledgment of debt as defined in Article 82(1) DEBA.

Whether a claim has a sufficient link to Switzerland is not interpreted restrictively. A sufficient connection has been assumed for example, if the creditor is domiciled in Switzerland, or if the place of jurisdiction or the place of performance is in Switzerland, or if the creditor's claim is governed by Swiss law or if the contract was negotiated or entered into in Switzerland.[29]

On the other hand, the mere fact that a debtor's assets are located in Switzerland is not sufficient to establish a Swiss connection within the meaning of Article 271(1)(4) DEBA, unless the transfer of the assets to Switzerland was part of the debtor's wrongful conduct.[30]

[2] ***Procedure***

[a] *Request for Attachment*

Pursuant to Article 272 of the DEBA, a creditor's application for an attachment order is brought by way of ex parte summary proceedings before the cantonal Court of First Instance at the place where the assets are located or at the debtor's regular place of debt enforcement (i.e., at the debtor's domicile or seat). Thus, the debtor will not be heard in this initial phase and, if the creditor's request is rejected, the debtor will not be

27. Decision of the Swiss Federal Supreme Court (reported, "*BGE*") 139 III 135 consid. 4.
28. BGE 139 III 135 consid. 4.5.2.
29. F.C. Meier-Dieterle, in: D. Hunkeler (ed.), *Kurzkommentar SchKG*, 2nd ed., Basel 2014, Article 271 N 14 et seq.
30. Decision of the High Court of Zurich of January 27, 1999, AJP 1999, 1023.

informed.[31] The court has discretion to order a creditor to furnish security for the damages, which the debtor might incur as a result of an unjustified attachment.[32]

An attachment order is granted on the basis of the creditor's application and supporting documentary evidence, which must include evidence with regard to the existence of assets in Switzerland. While, prior to the revision of the DEBA, the authority of a court was limited to attaching assets in its local jurisdiction, an attachment order may now cover assets located in any Swiss canton.

If the court grants a creditor's request, it will notify the debt collection office(s) at the place(s) where the assets are located, which in turn will notify the debtor and any third parties holding assets belonging to the debtor, e.g., a bank, that they are prohibited from disposing of such assets. The debt collection office then draws up a certificate specifying the assets that have been attached and serves a copy of the attachment certificate to the parties.[33] However, due to Swiss banking secrecy laws, Swiss banks usually refuse to provide information as to the existence of a debtor's assets at this stage.

The debtor, or a third party whose rights are affected, may contest the attachment order by filing an "objection" with the cantonal Court of First Instance within ten days of learning of the attachment.[34] This objection will be dealt with in *inter partes* proceedings. The decision of the cantonal Court of First Instance is subject to appeal to a higher cantonal court and ultimately to the Swiss Federal Supreme Court. The attachment order will remain in place during objection and appeal proceedings.

[b] Validation of the Attachment

If the attachment order is granted, the creditor must commence debt collection proceedings to validate the attachment. Alternatively, if the creditor's claim is not based on an enforceable judgment or award or a signed acknowledgment of debt, the creditor may choose to first start litigation on the merits. If the creditor does not commence debt collection, court or arbitral proceedings within ten days from receipt of the certificate of attachment, the attachment order will no longer be effective.[35]

The request for debt collection is a simple one-page form setting out the details of the creditor, the debtor and the nature, the cause and the amount of the claim. The debt collection office serves a payment order on the debtor, if necessary by way of international legal assistance. The debtor may file an objection within ten days of receipt of the payment order.

If the debtor does not object to the payment order, the debt collection office will proceed to enforce the debt. If the debtor files an objection, the creditor, again within ten days of being informed thereof, must commence summary *inter partes* proceedings

31. F.C. Meier-Dieterle, in: D. Hunkeler (ed.), *Kurzkommentar SchKG*, 2nd ed., Basel 2014, Article 272 paragraphs 19 et seq.; J. Schwaller & G. Naegeli, in: *Global Insolvency & Restructuring Review 2013/14*, pp. 118–120.
32. Article 273(1) DEBA.
33. Article 276 DEBA.
34. Article 278 DEBA.
35. Article 279 DEBA.

before the cantonal Court of First Instance to set aside the objection. At this stage, the court will also decide on the recognition and enforcement of the award or the foreign judgment.

The decision of the cantonal Court of First Instance is subject to appeal to the cantonal High Court and eventually to the Swiss Federal Supreme Court.

Once the judgment setting aside the debtor's objection to the payment order becomes final, the creditor must file an application to continue the debt collection proceedings within ten days, in order for the debt collection office to proceed with the seizure and the liquidation of the debtor's assets.[36]

[B] Attachment Orders by Arbitral Tribunals?

Swiss legislation on arbitration is based on a dual concept. Chapter 12 of the PILA applies to international arbitral proceedings seated in Switzerland. Chapter 12 is not based on the UNCITRAL Model Law, but has been influenced by it to a certain degree.[37] Domestic arbitration, on the other hand, is governed by Part 3 of the CPC, which replaced the Swiss Cantonal Concordat on Arbitration of 1969.

Pursuant to Article 183 PILA and Article 374 CPC, the Swiss state courts and arbitral tribunals have concurrent jurisdiction to order interim measures.[38] Therefore, a requesting party has the possibility to choose the forum it deems appropriate to order an interim measure, if the parties have not excluded the arbitral tribunal's competence in this respect.[39] However, with regard to enforceability and urgency, it will often be preferable to seek an order through the ordinary courts.

Although, in general, an arbitral tribunal is allowed to order any interim measures that can be ordered by ordinary courts at the place of enforcement, it is a matter of debate whether, under Article 183 PILA and Article 374 CCP, arbitral tribunals may order an attachment of assets. The prevailing view denies the arbitral tribunal's competence in this respect, thus suggesting that a creditor should always direct its request for an attachment order to the ordinary courts.[40]

36. Article 88 DEBA.
37. B. Berger & F. Kellerhals, *International and Domestic Arbitration in Switzerland*, Bern 2015, paragraphs 20, 70 et seq.
38. *See* B. Berger & F. Kellerhals, *International and Domestic Arbitration in Switzerland*, Bern 2015, paragraphs 1273 et seq.
39. Article 183 PILA and Article 374 CPC provide that the parties may agree that the arbitral tribunal shall not have the authority to grant interim measures. In contrast, it is a matter of debate among legal scholars whether the competence of the state courts can be excluded by party agreement; *see* F. Dasser, in: P. Oberhammer (ed.), *Kurzkommentar ZPO*, Basel 2010, Article 374 N 3 et seq.; B. Berger & F. Kellerhals, *International and Domestic Arbitration in Switzerland*, Bern 2015, paragraphs 1273 et seq.
40. B. Berger & F. Kellerhals, *International and Domestic Arbitration in Switzerland*, Bern 2015, paragraphs 1248 et seq. with further references.

[C] Other Freezing Measures

An alternative route, based on Swiss law of criminal procedure, for obtaining a freezing order may be available to creditors insofar as they have become the victim of an act of fraud.

In general terms, the Swiss prosecuting authorities have the power to block assets, which are relevant as evidence in a criminal case, or which are the proceeds of a crime or necessary to secure a claim for compensation by the state, regardless of whether those authorities are acting in execution of a foreign request for legal assistance or within the framework of a domestic Swiss criminal investigation. Criminal freezing orders can be very efficient and fast.[41]

Furthermore, if a party has reasons to believe that it has been the victim of a criminal offense, in particular a fraud, an immediate de facto freezing of funds may be obtained, without the involvement of Swiss courts or prosecuting authorities. The party must give a reasoned written notice to the bank where the proceeds of the crime have been deposited, making the bank aware of its potential liability in the event that it allows the funds to be withdrawn or transferred. If such a notice is supported by sufficient documentary evidence, the bank will usually decide to block the funds.[42]

§18.04 ENFORCEMENT ISSUES

The most efficient way to have a foreign monetary judgment or a foreign monetary arbitral award enforced in Switzerland is to initiate debt enforcement proceedings under the DEBA. However, a party may also choose to first seek a court declaration on the recognition and enforceability of a foreign judgment or award in separate exequatur proceedings. In such a case, the application must be directed to the cantonal Court of First Instance.

As described above, upon a request by a creditor, the debt collection office serves a payment order on the debtor. The debtor may file an objection within ten days of service of the payment order. If the debtor does not object to the payment order, the debt collection office will proceed to enforce the debt. If the debtor files an objection, the creditor, within ten days of being informed thereof, must commence summary *inter partes* proceedings before the cantonal Court of First Instance to have the objection set aside.

It is at this stage that the court will decide, as a preliminary issue, on the recognition and enforcement of the foreign judgment. Judgments rendered in civil and commercial matters by courts of Member States of the Lugano Convention are recognized and enforced in accordance with the provisions of that convention. Recognition and enforcement of other foreign judgments is subject to the provisions of

41. For a more detailed discussion *see* M. Bernet & P. Burckhardt, *Freezing Assets in Switzerland – a Creditor's Option*, in: Business Law International, Vol. 8 No. 2, p. 127 et seq.
42. M. Bernet & P. Burckhardt, *Freezing Assets in Switzerland – a Creditor's Option*, in: Business Law International, Vol. 8 No. 2, p. 127 et seq.

the PILA, while the NYC governs the enforcement of foreign arbitral awards (*see* section §18.04[B] below).

[A] Enforcement of Foreign Judgments

[1] Enforcement under the Lugano Convention

Under the Lugano Convention, the competent court declares a foreign judgment enforceable, if the application meets the formal requirements set out in Article 53.[43] The requesting party must present the original judgment or a certified copy thereof (Article 53 of the Lugano Convention) and provide the standard form of Annex V as per Article 54 of the Lugano Convention or other documents proving that the judgment is enforceable in its state of origin.

Recognition under the Lugano Convention does not involve a review by the Swiss courts of the merits of the foreign judgment. Moreover, material objections to the recognition, if any, are not possible at this first stage, as the judgment is declared enforceable without regard to Articles 34 and 35 Lugano Convention. Only in a second stage, during appellate proceedings, can the defendant raise objections based on the limited grounds set out in Articles 34 and 35.[44] These objections include:

- the foreign judgment manifestly violates Swiss public policy;
- the judgment is a default judgment and the defendant was not served with the document which instituted the proceedings or with an equivalent document in sufficient time and in such a way as to enable him to arrange for his defense (unless the defendant failed to commence proceedings to challenge the judgment when it was possible for him to do so);
- the judgment is irreconcilable with a judgment given in a dispute between the same parties in the country in which recognition is sought, i.e., in Switzerland;
- the judgment is irreconcilable with an earlier judgment rendered in another Member State of the Lugano Convention or in a non-contracting state involving the same cause of action and the same parties, provided that the earlier judgment meets the requirements for recognition in Switzerland.

[2] Enforcement under the PILA

In the absence of a multi- or bilateral treaty, the recognition and enforcement of foreign judgments in Switzerland is governed by the PILA. Under Articles 25 et seq. PILA, a foreign judgment will be recognized in Switzerland if the following requirements are cumulatively met:

---

43. Article 41 Lugano Convention.
44. M. Plutschow, in: A. K. Schnyder (ed.), *Lugano-Übereinkommen (LugÜ) zum internationalen Zivilverfahrensrecht: Kommentar*, Zurich 2011, Article 41 N 7 et seq.

(i) the judgment has by Swiss standards been rendered by a competent court (so-called indirect jurisdiction); and
(ii) the judgment is final or no longer subject to an ordinary appeal; and
(iii) no grounds for refusal of recognition pursuant to Article 27 PILA exist: According to this provision, the judgment must not manifestly violate Swiss public policy. The judgment must furthermore emanate from proceedings that guaranteed the defendant due process and a right to be heard. If the judgment was given in default, the defendant must have received proper notice of the proceedings. Finally, the recognition of a foreign judgment is denied if a claim regarding the same dispute was first filed in Switzerland or if an earlier judgment pertaining to the same claim has been rendered in Switzerland. The same applies to earlier third-state judgments if they meet the requirements for recognition in Switzerland.

In addition, if enforcement of a monetary judgment is sought in the framework of debt collection proceedings (as described above), the defendant may resist enforcement if he or she can prove by means of documentary evidence that the debt has been discharged, deferred or become time-barred after the judgment was rendered.[45]

In terms of formalities and evidence, the following requirements have to be met (Article 29(1) PILA):

(i) An application for recognition of a foreign judgment must be accompanied by a full and certified copy of the judgment.
(ii) The application must contain a confirmation from a public authority in the state of origin that the judgment is final or no longer subject to an ordinary appeal.
(iii) In case of a default judgment, the applicant must adduce documentary evidence for the fact that the defendant was given proper notice of the proceedings and had enough time to arrange for his defense.
(iv) All documents filed with the application must, upon the court's request, be translated into the official language of the place where enforcement is sought (i.e., German, French or Italian).

[B] Enforcement of Arbitral Awards

The recognition and enforcement of a foreign arbitral award in Switzerland is governed by the New York Convention (cf. Article 194 of the PILA).

Swiss court proceedings for the enforcement of foreign monetary arbitral awards are, with some exceptions, the same as those for foreign court judgments. The creditor files a request for debt collection at the debt collection office, usually at the debtor's domicile. If the debtor does not have a domicile or branch in Switzerland, the creditor must first obtain a civil attachment order against the debtor's assets in Switzerland

45. Article 81(1) DEBA.

from the court where these assets are situated in order to establish a forum.[46] The creditor may also choose to seek a declaration of enforceability in separate proceedings, which will be the only route in case of a non-monetary award.

If the creditor initiates debt collection proceedings, the debt collection office issues and serves a payment order on the debtor, requiring the debtor to either pay the debt within twenty days or to file an objection within ten days (*see* above section §18.03[A][2][b]). If an objection is filed, the creditor must commence summary court proceedings in order to have the objection set aside.

In these proceedings, the Court of First Instance also decides on the recognition and enforceability of the award under the New York Convention. Pursuant to Article 81(3) DEBA, the debtor may raise any of the defenses to recognition and enforcement provided under the New York Convention. In principle, it is for the defendant to prove that recognition and enforcement should be refused because at least one of the exhaustive[47] grounds listed in Article V(1) of the New York Convention to refuse enforcement is met.[48] However, pursuant to Article V(2) of the New York Convention, recognition and enforcement must be denied by the court on its own motion (ex officio) if the award violates public policy or if the dispute is not arbitrable.

For the enforcement of an arbitral award under the New York Convention, the creditor is (only) required to file:

(i) the original duly authenticated award (in its entirety) or a duly certified copy thereof;
(ii) the original arbitration agreement or a duly certified copy thereof; and
(iii) full translations of the award and the arbitration agreement into French, German or Italian (depending on the place of enforcement within Switzerland) certified by an official or sworn translator or by a Swiss diplomatic or consular agent.[49]

Swiss courts interpret the grounds for denying recognition and enforcement set out in Article V of the New York Convention rather restrictively and rarely refuse recognition of foreign arbitral awards.[50]

The decision of the cantonal Court of First Instance as to the enforceability of the award is subject to appeal to the cantonal High Court. Furthermore, there is a final appeal to the Swiss Federal Supreme Court. The Swiss Federal Supreme Court may fully review the enforcement decision but not the merits of the arbitral award. An

46. Article 52 DEBA.
47. E. Geisinger, *Implementing the New York Convention in Switzerland*, in: Journal of International Arbitration 2008, p. 694.
48. Among the various grounds listed in Article V(1) of the New York Convention, the debtor may raise the following objections: invalidity of the agreement to arbitrate, lack of proper service of process, the award not yet having become binding, having been set aside or having been suspended. Also, the debtor may claim that the debt under the award has been paid, deferred or become time-barred (Article 81(1) DEBA).
49. Article IV New York Convention.
50. E. Geisinger, *Implementing the New York Convention in Switzerland*, in: Journal of International Arbitration 2008, p. 694.

appeal to the Federal Supreme Court does not automatically stay execution, but the Court may order a stay in appropriate cases.

§18.05 MEASURES AGAINST ASSET PROTECTION SCHEMES

[A] Piercing the Corporate Veil

As a matter of principle, the attachment of assets is restricted to the *debtor's* assets, while no attachment is granted with regard to assets belonging to a third party. Therefore, if a debtor has removed assets or taken others steps to protect its assets, e.g., by holding assets indirectly as beneficial but not legal owner, or by transferring assets – possibly through complex (offshore) structures – from one corporate entity to another, a creditor may be prevented from enforcing its claim against such assets.

Under narrowly restricted circumstances, the attachment of assets owned by a third party is possible based on the concept of piercing the corporate veil. Case law generally requires for the concept to be applicable that the use of the third party, or *alter ego*, formally holding the assets amounts to an abuse of rights; mere economic identity between the debtor and the third party is not sufficient.[51] In our experience, it is fairly difficult to rely on this concept in the context of enforcement proceedings.

[B] D&O Liability

The question, therefore, arises whether it is possible to take action directly against directors and officers of an entity engaging in asset shielding. As the below overview will show, the risk of liability is rather limited for directors and officers, unless improper activities occur in the context of or prior to the opening of insolvency proceedings.

[1] Company Law

The key provision on D&O liability under Swiss company law is Article 754 of the Swiss Code of Obligations (CO). Article 754 CO provides that the members of the board of directors and all persons engaged in the business management or liquidation of the company are liable both to the company and to the individual shareholders and creditors for any losses or damage arising from intentional or negligent breach of their duties. It is possible under Swiss law, and also common, to insure the directors and officers against such liability.[52]

---

51. F.C. Meier-Dieterle, in: D. Hunkeler (ed.), *Kurzkommentar SchKG*, 2nd ed., ed. Daniel Hunkeler, Basel 2014, Article 271 paragraph 25; Blätter für Zürcherische Rechtsprechung 104 (2005) No. 8; *see also* BGE 107 III 33 (= Pra 70 (1981) No. 194); BGE 126 III 95 (= Pra 90 (2001) No. 52); BGE 102 III 165 (= Pra 1977 No. 17).
52. D. Gericke & S. Waller, in: *Basler Kommentar Obligationenrecht II*, 4th ed., Heinrich Honsell, Nedim P. Vogt & Rolf Watter (eds.), Basel 2012, Article 754 N 51 et seq.

The duties of directors and officers encompass, among others, the duty of care and loyalty pursuant to Article 717 CO. This provision prohibits actions like the distribution of hidden profits to certain shareholders, competing behavior, all sorts of criminal offenses, as well as unjustified transfers of assets – even within the same corporate group.[53] Thus, if a member of the board of directors (or any other person engaged in the business management) has initiated or accepted improper activities aimed at asset shielding, in particular transferring valuable assets against no or insufficient consideration, such action would likely amount to a breach of the duty of care and loyalty.

Notwithstanding this, the threat of liability of a director or officer is limited because a creditor's capacity to sue a director or officer is limited outside insolvency proceedings under Swiss law. Specifically, the Swiss Federal Supreme Court distinguishes between direct and indirect damage of creditors (and shareholders). The assets of creditors are only damaged *directly* by a director's breach of duty if at the same time the assets of the underlying entity are not affected.[54] On the other hand, the creditor sustains *indirect* damage if the damage only arises because the underlying entity has been damaged.[55]

Outside insolvency proceedings, a creditor can only take action against a director for restitution of *direct* damage. Yet direct damage of a creditor is rare and usually not given in a situation involving asset shielding maneuvers, as such maneuvers primarily affect and diminish the assets of the entity and only *indirectly* affect the creditor's assets.

As a consequence, a creditor affected by asset shielding maneuvers may only start legal action against directors and officers if the entity is already involved in insolvency proceedings. Moreover, even if such claim is successful, compensation is due to the insolvent company and not to the creditor directly. Therefore, the likelihood of deterring directors and officers from removing assets by the mere threat of a potential liability claim is limited.

[2] Criminal Law

In addition to the above rules regarding D&O liability under Swiss company law, the Swiss Criminal Code (SCC) lists specific criminal offenses that are relevant for the conduct of a business and may lead to criminal liability of directors or officers. In particular, the following provisions are of significance in the present context:

---

53. BGE 130 III 213, consid. 2.2.2; D. Gericke & S. Waller, in: *Basler Kommentar Obligationenrecht II*, 4th ed., Heinrich Honsell, Nedim P. Vogt & Rolf Watter (eds.), Basel 2012, Article 754 N 29 et seq.
54. For example if a creditor grants a loan to an overindebted entity, which he or she would not have done if the board had executed its duty to notify such overindebtedness according to Article 725 CO in time (BGE 125 III 86).
55. D. Gericke & S. Waller, in: *Basler Kommentar Obligationenrecht II*, 4th ed., Heinrich Honsell, Nedim P. Vogt & Rolf Watter (eds.), Basel 2012, Article 754 N 15 et seq.

- Fraudulent bankruptcy and fraud against seizure (Article 163 SCC): the criminal offense consists in the fictitious diminishment of assets to the detriment of creditors, namely by disposing of or concealing assets, by simulating debts or by acknowledging fictitious claims.
- Harming of creditors by diminishing assets (Article 164 SCC): culpability requires the intentional (but not necessarily fraudulent) actual diminishment of assets to the detriment of creditors by (i) damaging, destroying, devaluating or disabling assets, (ii) disposing of assets against no consideration or consideration of evidently lower value, or (iii) waiving rights or claims without any justified reason.

These provisions only apply if bankruptcy proceedings have been commenced against the debtor or a certificate of unsatisfied claims has been issued as a result of previous debt enforcement proceedings. However, it is irrelevant whether the removal of assets has taken place before, during or after the bankruptcy proceedings were initiated.[56] Where the debtor is a legal entity, the criminal liability is attributed to a natural person, in particular a governing officer or a member of a governing body of the entity.[57]

Asset shielding maneuvers may also potentially amount to a violation of Article 158 SCC. According to this provision, a person who: (i) has been entrusted with the management of the property of another or the supervision of such management, and (ii) in the course of and in breach of his duties causes or permits that entity to sustain financial loss is liable. To the extent that asset shielding maneuvers cause (also) the company to sustain financial loss, a liability of directors and officers under Article 158 SCC is possible.

56. N. Hagenstein, in: Marcel A. Niggli & Hans Wiprächtiger (eds.), *Basler Kommentar Strafrecht II*, 3rd ed., Basel 2013, Article 163 paragraph 63 and Article 164 paragraph 31.
57. Article 29(a) SCC.

CHAPTER 19

Turkey

Suat Sarı & Utku Coşar

§19.01 INTRODUCTION

Turkish law, similar to the judicial systems found in most continental European states, is structured according to the division between private and public law. In this context, disputes concerning private law fall within the jurisdiction of civil courts, while disputes related to administrative law fall within the jurisdiction of administrative courts. The Turkish civil court system does not utilize a jury; disputes are resolved by a judge or a panel of judges.

Structurally, the civil court system in Turkey functions on three levels:

- Civil courts are comprised of civil courts of peace and Courts of First Instance. The Court of First Instance is the general competent court, unless another court is specified as competent by law. There are two types of Courts of First Instance: the civil Court of First Instance and the commercial Court of First Instance, with the latter mainly established in large cities. Specialized courts have been established for specific areas of disputes, such as maritime law, labour law, consumer rights and intellectual property.
- According to the new Turkish Code of Civil Procedure, No. 6100 (CCP), decisions of the Court of First Instance may be appealed to the Regional Appeal Courts. Yet due to the fact that the Regional Appeal Courts have not yet been established, the Court of Appeals will, for the time being, continue to serve as the appellate body for first instance decisions.
- The highest court is the Court of Appeals, which is currently the appellate body for decisions of the First Instance Courts and, once established, will be the appellate body for decisions of the Regional Appeal Courts.

Turkey is a signatory to the 1958 New York Convention on the Recognition and Enforcement of Foreign Arbitral Awards ('New York Convention'). However, Turkey is not a party to the Lugano Convention or the Brussels Convention, both of which regulate jurisdiction and the enforcement of judgments in civil and commercial matters. Nor has Turkey implemented the European Account Preservation Order, which only directly applies in the EU Member States (except for the UK and Denmark, which have an opt-out).

Within the Turkish court system, it is possible for a party to freeze assets belonging to a counterparty prior to trial. A party may apply for interim injunction in case the dispute is regarding non-monetary claims (as governed by the CCP) or interim attachment in case the dispute is regarding monetary claims (as governed by the Code of Execution and Bankruptcy, No. 2004 or 'CEB'). Interim attachment may concern the assets, rights and other claims falling outside the scope of interim injunction. Yet in practice, these two forms of interim remedies are often confused with one another.[1] This is discussed further under section §19.03 below.

§19.02 IDENTIFYING ASSETS IN TURKEY

In general, it is not possible under Turkish law to obtain a court order compelling a counterparty to reveal its assets before initiating a lawsuit, arbitration or execution proceedings. However, it is possible to request an interim injunction or attachment order from a court prior to filing the actual case[2] and, as part of this request, to ask the court to write a writ to certain registries, including those listed below, for the location of the debtor's assets. The public registries are obliged to provide relevant information to the courts upon such written request.

The following public registries may be used to uncover information on a counterparty's assets before the initiation of any legal proceedings.

[A] Real Estate

According to Article 997 of the Turkish Civil Code ('Civil Code'), the land registry is maintained in order to display existing rights over immovable properties. Land, independent and permanent rights over immovables, and independent parts that constitute the subject matter of condominium ownership are registered in the land registry as immovable properties (Civil Code, Article 998). Immovables intended for

1. Pekcanıtez, Atalay, Özekes, Law of Civil Procedure, 14th Edition (Pekcanıtez), p. 1048.
2. Please note that if the interim injunction order is granted before the case on the merits is filed, the requesting party should file its case within two weeks after it requests the execution of the interim injunction order (see §19.03 [A], last paragraph below). In case an interim attachment order is granted before filing a lawsuit or before commencing an execution proceeding, the creditor is required to file a lawsuit or initiate an execution proceeding within seven days after the execution of the attachment order or after the notification of the attachment minutes if the execution is conducted in the absence of the creditor (see §19.03 [B], thirteenth paragraph below).

public enjoyment and not privately owned are not registered in the land registry unless a right in rem that is required to be registered is established (Civil Code, Article 999).[3]

Land registry records may appear as registrations, annotations or declarations.[4] Information on ownership, liens, and easement or encumbrance of rights over an immovable appear as registrations, whereas certain rights arising from agreements, such as construction agreements in return for land share, or other rights explicitly foreseen by law as capable of being annotated, appear as annotations (Civil Code, Articles 1008, 1009).

An individual may learn about certain restrictions on an immovable from examining the land registry's annotations. Articles 1009 and 1010 of the Civil Code require the following to be marked as annotations in the land registry: (i) restrictions on the right of disposal stemming from court decisions protecting contentious rights, (ii) attachment and bankruptcy orders or the period granted with composition, and (iii) acts such as the establishment of a homestead and the appointment of a reversionary heir.

Anyone can access the land registry, as long as she can demonstrate her interest. The individual may ask the registry officer to show her the relevant page and documents, and provide her with copies thereof (Civil Code, Article 1020, Land Registry Rules, Article 85/2).

By making an individual 'demonstrate her interest', the Civil Code has conditioned access to the land registry, a policy that has been endorsed by the Turkish Court of Appeals. According to the Court of Appeals, the principle of public access does not mean that any random person can examine the land registry. Only persons who demonstrate their interest may benefit from this principle.[5] However, it cannot be understood to mean that only the owner or the representatives of the owner of the property may examine said property's listing in the land registry.[6]

Certain aspects of the principle of public access to the land registry have been dealt with in a circular issued by the General Directorate of Land Registry and Cadastre (dated 8 August 2001 (updated on 20 March 2013) and numbered 1556–2001/11). It states, among other things, that:

- Upon written request, the Land Registry Offices will provide Courts, Offices of the Chief Public Prosecutors, and persons who are assigned and authorized under the relevant laws and rules with information and documents within the scope of examinations and investigations.
- Pursuant to Article 2/3 of the Attorneyship Law, upon written request, attorneys may examine the land registry in the presence of a land registry

3. According to Article 18 of the Law No. 3402, state-owned lands which may be subject to private ownership in the future or may gain economic value may be registered to the Treasury (Court of Appeals, 1st Civil Law Chamber, 16 January 2003, F. 2002/14196, D. 2003/409).
4. Civil Code Articles 1008–11012 (Ömer Uğur Gençcan, Turkish Civil Code with No. 4721, Articles 531–1030 Expanded 2nd Edition, 2007, p. 4636.
5. Court of Appeals, 6th Civil Law Chamber, 10 May 2011, F. 2011/3325, D. 2011/6125.
6. Court of Appeals, 4th Criminal Law Chamber, 16 October 2000, F. 2000/6286, D. 2000/6646.

officer. To obtain a copy of the land registry, attorneys are required to present a power of attorney and demonstrate their interest in obtaining a copy.

Recently an electronic project called TAKBIS (Turkish Land Registry and Cadastre Information System) was created in order to transfer the land registry information to an electronic environment and enable digital research (Land Registry Rules, Articles 12–15).[7]

[B] Tangibles (Cars, Machinery, Inventory, Etc.)

Traffic registries are established in cities (and in certain districts) and maintain information on vehicles, drivers, and technical and legal changes, in addition to gathering and evaluating statistical data (Highway Traffic Law No. 2918, Article 5). Information regarding pledges and attachments on vehicles is also contained in these registries. The registration of vehicles is compulsory in Turkey (Highway Traffic Law No. 2918, Article 19). However, these traffic registries are not open to the public.[8]

General information regarding a vehicle, such as its model, brand, registration place and whether there are any limitations on the ownership, may be found by using the plate/license number at https://www.turkiye.gov.tr/arac-sorgulama. Identifying information, such as the owner's name and address, is not provided. However, in order to access this website an individual must have an e-Government password, an e-signature or a mobile signature.[9]

Information relating to the establishment, operations, capital, and machinery and facilities (such as capacity, type, quality and quantity) of industrial enterprises are recorded in the Industrial Registry, which may only be accessed by individuals with a permit from the Ministry of Science, Industry and Technology (Industrial Registry Law No. 6948, Articles 3 and 7). Limitations on machinery are also recorded in this registry.

Furthermore, if a commercial enterprise is pledged together with its tangibles, this pledge should be registered to the relevant Trade Registry (Commercial Enterprise Pledge Law No. 1447, Article 5). Following the registration of the commercial enterprise pledge with the Trade Registry, this pledge must also be registered with the relevant registry offices with respect to the assets that are listed in the commercial enterprise pledge, such as vehicles, machinery and trademarks (Commercial Enterprise Pledge Law No. 1447, Article 7).

7. According to Article 14 the Land Registry Rules, prosecutors, execution offices, courts and public entities and professional organizations with public institution status may access TAKBIS within the scope of their duties through a protocol to be signed with the General Directorate of Land Registry and Cadaster. Moreover, the owners of the immovable or right owners on the immovable may obtain information within the scope of the contract to be signed.
8. Court of Appeals 13th Civil Law Chambers, 14 April 2004, F. 2003/14592, D. 2004/5348.
9. https://www.turkiye.gov.tr/non-citizens.

[C] Vessels

According to Article 954/1 of the Turkish Commercial Code (TCC), national ship registries (NSR) are kept for Turkish vessels in the locations determined by the Ministry of Transport, Maritime Affairs and Communications. NSR are kept by registry offices within port authorities and under the supervision of designated maritime courts or, in the absence of such court, the civil Court of First Instance designated for adjudicating commercial disputes (TCC, Article 954/2). Pursuant to Article 1 of the Ship Registry Regulation dated 31 December 1956 and numbered 4/8520, NSR have been established in Trabzon, Samsun, Zonguldak, Istanbul, Bandırma, Çanakkale, Izmir, Antalya, Mersin and Iskenderun. Registration is voluntary except for commercial vessels with a gross tonnage of 18 or more, which must be registered (TCC, Article 957).

A ship is registered in the registry office assigned to its home port, namely the port where its journeys are administered (TCC, Article 955/1). If the vessel's owner has no place of residence or commercial enterprise in Turkey, then he is required to name a representative who resides in the region to exercise the rights and perform the duties under the TCC (TCC, Article 955/3).

NSR are public records; anyone who can convincingly demonstrate that they have a valid interest may examine them and obtain certified or non-certified copies, subject to a fee (TCC, Article 973).

In addition to NSR, there is the Turkish International Ship Registry (TISR), which was established pursuant to the Law Numbered 4490 on the Turkish Ship Registry Law and the Amendments to the Statutory Decree Numbered 491 (Law No. 4490). Pursuant to Article 4 of Law No. 4490 and the Turkish International Ship Registry Regulation, which was published in the Official Gazette dated 23 June 2000, the following vessels are registered in the TISR:

(a) All vessels and yachts that were already registered on NSR on the date which the Law No. 4490 entered into force.
(b) Regardless of tonnage limit, vessels, yachts and specially constructed vessels that are built in Turkey.[10]
(c) Any kind of freighter or open sea fishing vessel above 3,000 DWT to be imported and used for commercial purposes, and passenger ships and specially built vessels above 300 gross tonnes.[11]

10. The vessels and yachts which are built within Turkey for export purposes or built in Turkey for Turkish originated real or legal persons and then exported abroad and then imported in Turkey again shall be accepted as built within the country.
11. Article 5 of the Law No. 4490 and Article 7 of the Turkish International Ship Registry Regulation state that the vessels which are owned by Turkish citizens and foreigners who are resident in Turkey and the vessels that are owned by companies established as per the Turkish regulations may be registered in the TISR.
The ships and yachts registered in the TISR are exempted from certain tax liabilities according to Article 12 of Law No. 4490.

Moreover, Article 986 of the TCC provides that ships which are under construction may be registered in a special ship registry for ships under construction in the following situations: (i) upon the request of the owner; (ii) if a ship mortgage is taken out for the construction; (iii) if the construction is attached due to interim or conclusive attachment; or (iv) if the registration of an annotation is required in order to secure the owner of the shipyard's right to claim the establishment of a lien. The above-mentioned Article 954 (regarding the establishment of registries) and Article 957 (regarding availability to public) of the TCC also apply to this special registry pursuant to Article 991 of the TCC.

Both NSR and the TISR contain information on ownership, technical information, any existing ship mortgage, attachment arising from public debt and other encumbrances.

[D] Airplanes

According to Article 50 of the Turkish Civil Aviation Law, the Ministry of Transport, Maritime Affairs and Transportation maintains a Civil Aircraft Registry for Turkish civil aircraft.[12] This registry, which contains information on the owner, the aircraft, and any mortgage or other rights over the aircraft, is open to the public; individuals who can prove their connection to the request may examine the documents underlying an entry, pending registration procedures and registration files, and take copies thereof, subject to a fee (Civil Aviation Law, Aricles 51 and 57).

Turkish civil aircraft are those aircraft owned by the state that fall outside the definition of state aircraft, and aircraft owned by public entities or Turkish citizens (Civil Aviation Law, Article 3). According to Article 49 of the same law: (a) aircraft owned by occupational institutions (in the nature of a public entity), associations, political parties, unions or foundations are deemed Turkish civil aircraft, provided that Turkish citizens make up the majority of its administrative body; and (b) aircraft owned individually by companies and cooperatives registered in the Turkish Trade Registry and those owned jointly by said companies and cooperatives are deemed Turkish civil aircraft, provided that the majority of the persons authorized to represent and manage the company in question are Turkish citizens and vote majority is held by Turkish shareholders.

[E] Financial Reports

Under the regime governed by the TCC and relevant regulations, companies are not required to make their financial reports, audit reports or supporting documents publicly available unless the companies are publicly traded (Capital Markets Law, Article 14/5, Communique regarding Financial Reports in Capital Markets, Article 10).

12. According to the Law No. 5431 on the Organization and Functions of the General Directorate of Civil Aviation, the General Directorate of Civil Aviation is in charge of the registrations.

According to Article 14 of the Communique on the Rules with Respect to Financial Reporting in Capital Markets, enterprises are obliged to publish their annual and interim reports and financial statements prepared in compliance with the Communique, as well as their independent audit reports in such a way that they can easily be accessed by users on their websites after they have been disclosed to public. This information must be kept available to the public on the relevant website for a period of at least five years. In case there are several websites belonging to the enterprise, the website that is most widely known by the public shall be used for disclosure.

[F] IP Rights

Patent applications and patent rights are registered in the Patent Registry in accordance with the relevant regulation (Statutory Decree No. 551 on Protection of Patent Rights, Article 92/1). This registry is open to the public (Statutory Decree No. 551 on Protection of Patent Rights, Article 92/4).

Industrial designs are registered in the Design Registry (Statutory Decree No. 554 on Protection of Industrial Design Rights, Article 34/1). According to Article 16 of the Regulation on the Implementation of the Statutory Decree on Protection of Industrial Design Rights, registrations are published in a periodical basis (pursuant to the amendment published in the Official Gazette dated 24 November 2015) on the Official Industrial Design Bulletin. Also, an online search engine is available at the Turkish Patent Institute: http://online.tpe.gov.tr/EDESIGN/servlet/IDSearchRequestManager.

Trademarks are registered in the Trademark Registry, which is open to the public (Statutory Decree No. 556 on Protection of Trademarks, Article 39). It is possible to obtain copies of the registry upon request and payment of the prescribed fee. Pursuant to Article 14 of the Regulation on Implementation of the Statutory Decree No. 556, a trademark registered in accordance with Article 39 of the Statutory Decree is published in the bi-monthly Official Trademark Gazette, which indicates the information contained in the Registry. An online search engine is available at the Turkish Patent Institute: http://online.tpe.gov.tr/trademark-search/pub/trademark_search.

[G] Information on 'Bad' Debtors

A Risk Centre has been established as part of the Banks Association of Turkey by an amendment to the Banking Law No. 5411, which was published in the Official Gazette dated 25 February 2011. The aim of this Centre, which began operating in June 2013,[13] is to gather risk information about the customers of crediting institutions and other financial institutions that are deemed appropriate by the Banking Regulation and Supervision Board, and to share such information with the said institutions and with natural persons or legal entities themselves or, subject to prior consent thereof, with third parties (Banking Law, Additional Article 1; The Risk Center of the Banks Association Regulation, Article 13).

13. http://www.riskmerkezi.org/en-EN/about/39.aspx.

§19.03 INTERIM REMEDIES

[A] Interim Injunction

Under Turkish law, as a general rule, the court may grant a suitable interim injunction in certain situations. According to Article 389 of the CCP, an interim injunction may be granted in case: (i) securing the right may become significantly difficult or impossible due to a change in the existing situation, or (ii) an inconvenience or a substantial damage is likely to occur due to a delay.

Grounds for interim remedies are not limited by law and, as per the wording of Article 391 of the CCP, the court may decide on any kind of suitable interim injunction to secure the right according to the specifics of the case at hand.[14] Therefore it may order the protection of the right or asset in question, the consignment to a trustee or the performance/avoidance of a specific action in order to prevent the inconvenience or damages.[15]

Prior to trial, requests for interim injunction may be filed before a competent court that has jurisdiction over the merits of the dispute. During trial, however, these requests may only be filed before the court hearing the case. Requests for interim remedies must be in writing, and the requesting party must clearly state: (i) its grounds, (ii) the type of the interim injunction it requests, and (iii) prove its rightfulness on the merits with plausible proof (CCP, Article 390).[16] The court may order the interim injunction without hearing the counterparty in cases where an immediate protection of the rights of the requesting party is required (CCP, Article 390/2). Decisions rejecting the requests of interim injunctions may be appealed to the Court of Appeals.[17]

The interim injunction order must include, among other things, the type and amount of the security that shall be provided by the requesting party (CCP, Article 391/2), which is required to compensate the potential damages of the counterparty and other third parties. The court may decide not to order security if the request is based on an official document or another piece of conclusive evidence, or if it is required by the conditions of the situation, provided that the court's justifications are expressly stated. The security shall be returned after the decision on the merits becomes final or in case a lawsuit for damages was not filed within a month of the interim injunction order being lifted (CCP, Article 392).

The party who was not heard when the interim injunction order was given may object to such an order.[18] The objection itself does not suspend the execution of an

14. Pekcanıtez, p. 1035.
15. Ejder Yılmaz, Commentary on Civil Procedure, 2012, p. 1634; Pekcanıtez, p. 1035.
16. Pekcanıtez, p. 1026.
17. Pekcanıtez, p. 1028. The new appeal provisions in the CCP will be applicable once the Regional Appeal Courts are established.
18. This is as a result of the 'right to be heard'. This possibility is not provided to the parties who were present when the court was giving the interim injunction order since the change to be heard was provided to them at that time (Pekcanıtez, p. 1039); M. Kılıçoğlu, Hand Book Commentary on the Code of Civil Procedure, No. 6100, 2012 (Kılıçoğlu), p. 1426.

interim injunction order, although the court may still decide to temporarily suspend the order's execution (CCP, Article 394/1).[19] Moreover, third parties whose interests are clearly violated due to the execution of the interim injunction order may object to the conditions of the interim injunction or the security within a week of learning about the interim injunction (CCP, Article 394/3). Upon receiving an objection, the court may decide to lift or amend the interim injunction (CCP, Article 394/4). The court's decision regarding the objection may be appealed,[20] but appellate review does not suspend the execution of the interim injunction (CCP, Article 394/5).

Moreover, CCP Article 395 provides that, depending on the circumstances, the court may decide to lift or amend the interim injunction if the person whom the interim injunction order is levied on or executed against provides a security which is accepted by the court. Furthermore, if it is proven that the situation and the conditions have changed, the court may amend or lift the interim injunction without seeking security. These decisions are also subject to objection and appellate review (CCP, Articles 395/3, 396/1, 396/2).

The execution of the interim injunction order must be requested within a week after the granting of the decision; otherwise, the injunction is automatically lifted even if the case is filed within the legal time period (CCP, Article 393/1). The execution may be requested from the execution office within the judicial locality of the court which granted the interim injunction order, or from the execution offices where the assets or rights subject to the injunction are located. The court itself may also assign the clerk for the execution of the injunction (CCP, Article 393/2). Law enforcement officers may use force as necessary upon the written request of the officer executing the injunction (CCP, Article 393/3).

If the interim injunction order is granted before the case on the merits is filed, the requesting party must file its case within two weeks after it requests the execution of the interim injunction order. The party must then provide the documents showing that the case is filed to the execution officers, and obtain a document from them in return. Otherwise, the injunction shall be automatically lifted (CCP, Article 397/1).

[B] Interim Attachment

Interim attachment is regulated under the Code of Execution and Bankruptcy (CEB), and it is a special type of interim remedy that serves the purpose of securing the performance of a particular monetary debt.

According to Article 257 of the CEB, a court may order an interim attachment of the debtor's movable and immovable property held by either the debtor or third parties in order to secure the creditors' monetary debts which are due and are not secured by

19. Pekcanıtez, p. 1041.
20. As stated, new provisions relating to appeals in the CCP are not applicable until the Regional Appeal Courts are established. Thus, the appellate review would be done by the Court of Appeals.

a pledge. Unlike interim injunctions, interim attachment can only be granted where the claim requested to be secured relates to a particular amount of money.[21]

Interim attachment may also be requested for undue monetary debts (CEB, Article 257/2), provided that:

- The debtor does not have a habitual residence.
- The debtor is attempting to hide or transfer assets, is planning to leave Turkey to evade fulfilling his obligation, leaves Turkey or conducts fraudulent transactions for this purpose in violation of the creditor's rights.[22]

The competent court for interim attachment requests is determined by the CCP provisions regarding jurisdiction (CEB, Articles 258/1, 50); the creditor is required to present sufficient evidence regarding its receivable and the grounds for interim attachment. Article 258/3 of the CEB provides that the decisions rejecting interim attachment may be challenged, and at the moment these challenges will be reviewed and decided by the Court of Appeals.[23]

The creditor requesting the interim attachment must provide a security in order to satisfy the damages of the debtor or third parties in case the interim attachment is later regarded as unjust. However, if the interim attachment request is based on a document deemed to be a judgment (such as settlement agreements executed before courts or statutory notary public papers acknowledging monetary debts), the court may decide whether such guarantee is necessary. Furthermore, security is not required if the interim attachment is based on a court decision. (CEB, Article 259).

The court has the discretion whether to hear both parties (CEB, Article 258/2). Thus, if it considers that notifying the debtor would hinder the purpose of the interim attachment and its application, the court may grant the attachment without prior notice to the defendant.[24]

If the interim attachment order has been granted without the debtor being heard, the debtor may object to: (i) the reasoning of the interim attachment order, (ii) the jurisdiction of the court, or (iii) the security. This objection should be filed within seven days of the execution of the attachment if the interim attachment was executed in presence of the debtor, or within seven days following notification of the attachment record if the attachment was executed in the absence of the debtor (CEB, Article 265/1).

Third parties whose interests are affected may object to the grounds of the interim attachment or to the security within seven days of becoming aware of the order (CEB, Article 265/2).

21. Baki Kuru, Ramazan Arslan, Ejder Yılmaz, Law of Execution and Bankruptcy Text Book, 21st Edition (Kuru/Arslan/Yılmaz), p. 435; Pekcanıtez, p. 1048.
22. Hakan Pekcanıtez/ Oğuz Atalay/ Meral Sungurtekin Özkan/ Muhammet Özekes, Execution and Bankruptcy Law, 6th Edition, Ankara 2008 (Pekcanıtez/Atalay/Sungurtekin/Özekes), pp. 429-430.
23. 16th Civil Law Chamber of the Court of Appeals, 16 October 2003, F. 2003/8822, D. 2003/10013 (Pekcanıtez/Atalay/Sungurtekin/Özekes, p. 433). As previously mentioned, once the Regional Appeal Courts are established, they will review and decide on these appeals.
24. Kuru/Arslan/Yılmaz, p. 436.

In case of an objection, the court will review the reasons, decide to reject or accept the objection, and may change its decision or lift the attachment after hearing the parties (CEB, Article 265/3 and 265/4). The decision of the court may be challenged before the Court of Appeals.[25]

An interim attachment order should set out the justifications and the amount of the receivable, and identify the things that are subject to attachment, such as the debtor's immovable and movable properties and/or other rights and receivables held by third parties (CEB, Article 260).

The creditor must request the execution of the interim attachment decision within ten days after the granting of such an order from the execution office within the judicial locality of the court who has made the interim attachment decision. Otherwise, the interim attachment order is automatically lifted (CEB, Article 261).

If the debtor provides security, the attached assets may be left to the debtor or the third parties (provided that the assets were being held by such third party when they were attached). This request is managed by the execution officers (CEB, Article 263) and is not the same as lifting the interim attachment order since only the attached assets are left to the debtor or third parties in return for a security,[26] and the debtor is obliged to return the assets or the money if requested.[27] On the other hand, pursuant to Article 266 of the CEB, the debtor may request from the court the release of the attachment if the debtor provides a security. The execution courts will decide on this matter after the execution proceedings are initiated. If this request is accepted, the interim attachment is lifted over the attached property but it continues over the provided security.[28]

If a creditor obtains an interim attachment order before filing a lawsuit or before commencing an execution proceeding, the creditor is required to file a lawsuit or initiate an execution proceeding within seven days of the execution of the attachment order or after the notification of the attachment minutes (in case the execution is conducted in the absence of the creditor) (CEB, Article 264/1).

If the debtor objects to the execution order in an execution proceeding, this is immediately notified to the creditor and in this case, the creditor is obliged to request the cancellation of the objection from the execution court or file a lawsuit before the court. If the execution court refuses to cancel the objection, the creditor is required to file a case within seven days of the announcement or notification of the decision (CEB, Article 264/2).

If the debtor does not object to the execution order or if the objection is rejected by the execution court, the interim attachment is deemed to be conclusive (CEB, Article 264/5).[29]

25. As previously mentioned, once the Regional Appeal Courts are established, they will review and decide on these appeals.
26. Pekcanıtez/Atalay/Sungurtekin/Özekes, p. 436; 12th Law Chamber of the Court of Appeals (28 September 1981, F. 1981/5628, D. 1981/7109 (Talih Uyar, Code of Execution and Bankruptcy with Case Law and Explanations, Volume 10, January 2009, [Uyar], pp. 17171-17172).
27. Pekcanıtez/Atalay/Sungurtekin/Özekes, p. 439.
28. Pekcanıtez/Atalay/Sungurtekin/Özekes, p. 441.
29. Pekcanıtez/Atalay/Sungurtekin/Özekes, p. 444.

The execution of the attachment order differs based on the type of property or right to be attached. For example, with respect to real estate, the execution office notifies the land registry and the interim attachment is recorded in the registry. The execution office also notifies any tenants and requests the rent to be paid to the execution office (CEB, Article 91).

With respect to shares held by the debtor in a joint stock company, the execution office sends an attachment notification to the company, and this should be registered in the company's books (CEB, Article 94/1). However, if the said company has issued share certificates, then attachment thereof must be done in accordance with the procedure applicable to attachment of movable properties. Due to the fact that share certificates are valuable instruments, they are attached and taken into the custody of the execution office (CEB, Article 88).

[C] Foreign Creditors/Claimants

In addition to the security that must be provided in accordance with Article 259 of the CEB and Article 391 of the CCP, foreign creditors must also provide security in accordance with International Private and Procedural Law (IPPL) Article 48 for the commencement of execution proceedings for the attachment order or for the filing of a lawsuit in order to cover the potential loss and damages. In the event that there is reciprocity between Turkey and the country of which the creditor is a national, the court may exempt the creditor from this obligation.

[D] Interim Remedies under the International Arbitration Law

Under Turkish law, international arbitrations are subject to the International Arbitration Law (IAL),[30] which came into effect on 5 July 2001 and is largely based on the UNCITRAL Model Law on International Commercial Arbitration dated 1985. The IAL has not been updated with the 2006 Model Law rules on interim measures. According to the IAL, parties may request an interim injunction or an attachment decision before or during the arbitration proceedings. Unless agreed otherwise, the arbitral tribunal may order an interim attachment or interim injunction upon the request of the parties and they may hold the ordering of such attachment or injunction subject to an appropriate security. Moreover, in case one of the parties does not abide by the arbitral tribunal's decision regarding the interim attachment or injunction, the other party may seek assistance and request an interim attachment or injunction from the competent court (IAL, Article 6). The interim attachment or injunction ordered by the tribunal shall be automatically lifted when the arbitral award becomes enforceable or if the case is rejected by the tribunal (IAL, Article 6).

30. The IAL applies to disputes that are seated in Turkey and contain a 'foreign element', which is defined in Article 2 of the IAL.

An interim attachment order may be granted based on a foreign arbitral award before applying for an enforcement decision.[31]

§19.04 ENFORCEMENT OF FOREIGN JUDGMENTS AND ARBITRAL AWARDS

[A] Enforcement of Foreign Court Decisions and Arbitral Awards

The recognition and enforcement of foreign court decisions and arbitral awards are regulated under the IPPL and the New York Convention. Arbitral awards rendered in countries that are party to the New York Convention will be recognized and enforced under Article V of the Convention. Foreign court decisions and arbitral awards rendered in countries that are not party to the New York Convention will be recognized and enforced under the IPPL. The party requesting the enforcement of a foreign arbitral award should apply with a petition and the necessary documents.

[B] Enforcement of Foreign Judgments

Only foreign civil judgments which are final in the jurisdiction where they were rendered can be subject to enforcement in Turkey. With respect to criminal judgments, orders that relate to personal rights may also be enforced (IPPL, Article 50). Anyone with a legal interest in the enforcement of the judgment may request it via a petition to the Court of First Instance located in the domicile or place of residence of the party against whom enforcement is being sought. In case the said party does not have a domicile or residence in Turkey, then enforcement may be requested at the Ankara, Istanbul or Izmir civil Courts of First Instance (IPPL, Article 51).

Pursuant to IPPL Article 54, the following conditions must be satisfied before an enforcement decision can be given:

- There must be an agreement based on the principle of reciprocity between Turkey and the foreign country in which the judgment was made, or a similar legal provision or practice in that country allowing the enforcement of foreign judgments.
- The judgment must not relate to a subject that is within the exclusive jurisdiction of Turkish courts or must not have been made by a non-competent court.
- The judgment must not manifestly contradict Turkish public order.
- The principles of due process, including proper notice, must not have been violated.

31. 11th Civil Law Chamber of the Court of Appeals 8 May 2006, F. 2005/5401, D. 2006/5335; Court of Appeals, 6th Civil Law Chamber, 14 April 2014, File No. 2014/3906, Decision No. 2014/4941.

Enforcement applications are subject to the simplified trial procedures foreseen in the CCP.[32] In this simplified trial procedure, parties must specify and include all evidence and information regarding collection of such evidence in their statement of claim/defence petitions, as it is not possible to submit joinder and rejoinder. The court may decide to enforce the judgment in full or in part, or dismiss the enforcement application. The court enters its decision below the foreign judgment, and the judge signs and affixes the court's seal. This decision is subject to appeal and rectification before the Court of Appeals within fifteen days of notification. An appeal stays the enforcement of the decision. Foreign judgments which are found to be enforceable by the courts are enforced in the same way as judgments given by the Turkish courts (IPPL, Articles 55–57).

[C] Enforcement of Foreign Arbitral Awards

According to Article 60 of the IPPL, the enforcement of foreign arbitral awards is requested via a petition to the Court of First Instance at the location agreed upon by the parties. In the absence of such an agreement, the competent court shall be the Court of First Instance where the losing party is domiciled in Turkey. In case there is no domicile, the court where the losing party is habitually resident, and in the absence thereof, the court where the assets which may be subject to enforcement reside, shall be the competent court.

Upon service of the enforcement request, the other party may object to enforcement of the foreign arbitral award on grounds stated in Article 62 of the IPPL, which are very similar to those in the New York Convention. Under Article 62 of the IPPL, the court will reject enforcement of a foreign arbitral award if:

(a) there is no arbitration agreement, or there is no arbitration clause in the contract;
(b) the arbitral award is contrary to morals or public order;
(c) the dispute resolved in the award is not arbitrable under Turkish law;
(d) one of the parties was not represented before the arbitral tribunal in accordance with due process and did not explicitly consent to the latter actions;
(e) the party against which enforcement is requested was not informed of the appointment of an arbitrator (or arbitrators) or was deprived of defence rights;
(f) the arbitration agreement (or clause) is invalid under the law to which it was subject to or, where there is no agreement on this, under the law of the state in which the award was made;
(g) the appointment of the arbitrators, or procedural rules applied by the arbitrators, is contrary to the parties' agreement, or if there is no agreement, is contrary to the law of the country in which the award was made;

32. This simplified procedure is applied to cases that can be concluded in a shorter time or with simpler examination (e.g., those that are subject to the jurisdiction of the civil courts of peace, those related to recognition and enforcement of foreign arbitral awards).

(h) the arbitral award relates to a matter that was not in the arbitration agreement (or clause), or it exceeds the scope of the arbitration agreement (in which case the court only refuses to enforce the part which exceeds the scope of the arbitral agreement);
(i) if the arbitral award has not become final or enforceable or binding under:
- the law which it was subject to;
- the law of the state where it was made;
- pursuant to the procedural rules to which it was subject; or
- if the arbitral award was annulled by the competent body of the place where it was made.[33]

[D] Execution of Foreign Judgments and Arbitral Awards

After the court decides for the enforcement of the foreign judgment or arbitral award, the foreign judgment or arbitral award can then be executed through execution courts and offices. The execution procedures are the same as the ones foreseen for local judgments, and depend on the type of execution required and the conditions under which it is to take place.

The issue of court fees to be collected during the application for an enforcement decision is clarified by the Court of Appeals. According to the Court of Appeals, a decision fee shall be collected from the requesting party and the fee shall be determined pursuant to the nature of the arbitral award. It held that in cases which are subject to a proportional fee, a proportional decision fee shall be collected.[34] Similarly, the Court of Appeals found that if enforcement of a foreign arbitral award regarding the collection of a receivable is sought, the enforcement proceedings must be subject to a proportional decision fee.[35]

[E] Enforcement of International Arbitral Awards Made Pursuant to the IAL

Pursuant to the IAL, which regulates international arbitration in Turkey, a certificate of enforcement is required from the court for the enforcement of international arbitral awards. An application for annulment of the award that is filed within the prescribed time limit stays the enforcement of the award. A decision rejecting the annulment application must become final before the certificate of enforcement can be issued.

In case the time limit for annulment application expires or the parties have waived their right to apply for annulment, the party seeking to enforce the award should apply to the competent court to receive a certificate of enforcement. The competent court accords a limited review for this certificate, which consists of

33. The burden of proof regarding the issues provided under subparagraphs (d), (e), (f), (g), (h) and (i) belongs to the party against which enforcement is sought.
34. Court of Appeals, 19th Civil Law Chamber, 15 September 2009, F. 2009/5703, D. 2009/8256.
35. Court of Appeals, 19th Civil Law Chamber, 14 April 2012, F. 2012/1885, D. 2012/5598.

determining whether the dispute is arbitrable according to Turkish law and whether the award is against the public order (IAL, Article 15).

Pursuant to Article 3 of the IAL, the competent court that issues the certificate of enforcement is the civil Court of First Instance of the respondent's domicile, habitual residence or place of business; where none of these is in Turkey, the competent court is the Istanbul civil Court of First Instance.

§19.05 LIABILITY OF MEMBERS OF THE BOARD OF DIRECTORS AND COMPANY MANAGERS IN ATTEMPTS TO HIDE ASSETS

Under certain circumstances, board members and company managers may be held liable for attempts to hide assets.

[A] Liability under the Turkish Commercial Code

The TCC includes special provisions regarding the civil liability of the Board of Directors or managers of a company. Pursuant to the TCC, members of the Board of Directors and company managers shall be liable against the company, the shareholders and the creditors of the company for the damages they caused if they violate their obligations arising from law and the company's articles of association by fault (TCC, Articles 553(1) and 644(1)(a)). On the other hand, pursuant to Article 553/2 of the TCC, the persons/bodies who delegate the duties and powers that are arising from law and the articles of association to others shall not be liable for the actions and the decisions taken by these individuals, unless it is proven that they did not act in due case when assigning those persons. Thus, no one can be held liable for breaches of the law or articles of association or for irregularities that are out of their control. This non-liability cannot be invalidated based on supervisory and fiduciary duties (TCC, Article 553/3).

The company or its shareholders may request the relevant members to reimburse the company for its damages where the members' actions have caused damage to the company (TCC, Article 555/1). In case such company becomes bankrupt, then company creditors also have the right to request payment of damages to the company. However, the bankruptcy trustee has priority in filing such a request (TCC, Article 556/1).[36]

Therefore, damage must have been caused by board members' faulty actions for them to be held liable. A lawsuit for liability is subject to a statute of limitations. According to Article 560 of the TCC:

> The claim for damages against any liable person becomes time-barred two years after the date on which the injured party learned of the damages and of the person liable for it, but in any event five years after the date of the act which caused the

36. Soner Altaş, Joint Stock Companies Pursuant to the Turkish Commercial Code with Comparisons, Explanations and Examples, 4th Edition, January 2013, p. 639.

> damages. Where the action requires criminal penalty and the criminal law provides a longer time limit, the latter also applies to the claim for damages.

The TCC, under Article 562,[37,38] also provides criminal sanctions for certain situations. This article provides, amongst others, that those who forge documents as specified in Article 549 of the TCC (such as undertakings, declarations and guarantees regarding the establishment of the company, increase or decrease of its capital, merger, division, change of type or issuance of securities) and those who intentionally make false declarations in commercial books shall be punished with imprisonment from one to three years.

[B] Liability under the Code of Execution and Bankruptcy

The CEB also provides certain punishments for debtors who try to hide their assets with the intention to harm the creditor (CEB, Articles 331, 333/a, and 311[39]).

Regarding the liability of directors and officers, Article 333/a of the CEB states that the persons who have administrative powers in commercial companies shall be punished with imprisonment from six months to two years and an administrative punitive fine of up to 5,000 days upon the complaint of the creditor, if they cause damages to their creditors by not paying their debts partially or completely with the intention to harm the creditor, provided that these transactions and actions do not constitute another crime. In case the crime specified in Article 333/a of the CEB is conducted by negligence, the debtor shall be punished with an administrative punitive fine of up to 2,000 days. The Court of Appeals found that for the application of Article 333/a of the CEB, the actions of the suspects must not constitute another crime.[40]

---

37. Moreover, Article 562(8)-(10) provides that:

    > (8) Those who forge the documents specified in Article 549 and those who intentionally make false declarations in commercial books shall be punished by imprisonment from one to three years.
    > (9) Those who act in violation of Article 550 shall be punished with a judicial fine or imprisonment from three months to two years.
    > (10) Those who act in contradiction with Article 551 shall be subject to a judicial fine of not less than 90 days.

38. Mustafa Yavuz, Legal Liability of the Managers in Limited Liability Companies, Journal of Financial Solutions, January-February 2013, p. 185.
39. Article 311 is specifically regarding insolvency proceedings.
40. Court of Appeals, 16th Civil Law Chamber, 2 March 2009, F. 2008/3443, D 2009/ 1148. In this case, the Court held that the debtor should not be punished under Article 333/a of the CEB because the debtor's actions already constituted a crime under Article 331 of the CEB, which states that upon the complaint of the creditor, the debtor shall be punished with imprisonment from if the debtor, with the intention to harm the creditor, artificially decreases its assets by taking its property or certain properties out of its assets, destroying them, depreciating their value or collusively transferring the property to others or acknowledging unreal debts.

CHAPTER 20
United States of America

John Daerr

§20.01 INTRODUCTION

The legal system in the United States consists of a variety of codified and uncodified forms of law. The foundation is of course the United States Constitution which is considered the "supreme law of the land." It is the Constitution that establishes the federal government and creates the hierarchy for the development of the federal laws which consist of acts of Congress, treaties ratified by the Senate, regulations promulgated by the executive branch, and case law originating from the federal judiciary.

The federal courts consist of the United States Supreme Court, thirteen U.S. Courts of Appeals, ninety-four U.S. District Courts, the U.S. Court of Claims, the U.S. Court of International Trade and U.S. Bankruptcy Courts. Decisions from a U.S. District Court, the U.S. Court of Claims, and the U.S. Court of International Trade may be appealed to a U.S. Court of Appeals. The U.S. Supreme Court can review a decision of the U.S. Court of Appeals, but is under no obligation to do so.[1]

A "second," but not less important, legal system is found at the state level with each of the fifty states possessing its own state government, state constitution, and state courts.[2] Thus, each state has a legislative branch to enact state statutes, an executive branch to establish state regulations, and a judicial branch to apply and interpret the numerous statutes, regulations and local ordinances. State courts sitting at the first level consist of the state trial courts (civil and criminal) and courts that handle a variety of specific legal matters such as juvenile issues and family law matters. Parties

1. Each year, the United States Supreme Court receives approximately 10,000 requests to hear a case, but only accepts between 75 and 80.
2. Each state's laws are independent from those of other states. Thus the United States cannot be regarded as having one legal system under control of the federal government. Rather, there are federal laws and then fifty separate state-based systems of tort law, property law, contract law, criminal law, family law etc.

dissatisfied with the decision of a trial court may appeal their case to the intermediate Court of Appeals. In most instances state Supreme Courts are the final interpreters of state constitutions and state law, unless their interpretation presents a federal issue, in which case a decision may be appealed to the U.S. Supreme. It is important to note that state courts maintain their own separate power to make laws covering anything not preempted by the United States Constitution, federal statutes, or international treaties ratified by the federal government. Recognizing that it is important to have some degree of similarity between the laws of each state, "uniform" laws are often drafted by various commissions and then presented to the states for adoption, amendment or rejection.[3]

Although the United States has a well-known reputation for its court-based litigation, arbitration is well recognized and frequently used as a means for resolving disputes of all types. The Federal Arbitration Act[4] (FAA) was initially enacted in 1925 to make valid, and enforceable, written provisions or agreements for arbitration of disputes arising out of contracts, maritime transactions, or commerce among the states, territories or foreign nations. In addition, most states have adopted their own individual arbitration statutes.[5]

The United States has further supported international arbitration by becoming a signatory to and/or adopting a number of significant treaties in support of international arbitration. These include the New York Convention on the Recognition and Enforcement of Foreign Arbitral Awards,[6] the Inter-American Convention on International Commercial Arbitration of 1975 (the Panama Convention),[7] and the Convention on the Settlement of Investment Disputes between States and Nationals of Other States (the ICSID Convention).

For purposes of this chapter, it is perhaps important to know that freezing orders and enforcement proceedings are most frequently seen at the trial court levels – they typically have the authority to issue the necessary orders to seize or freeze assets and enforce judgments. As will be discussed in more detail throughout this chapter, there exits a variety of rules and legislation, at both the state and federal levels, that can be utilized to locate, freeze, and attach assets that are located within the US. These include, in part, the state and federal rules of trial procedure relating to discovery and the issuance of temporary restraining orders (TRO), preliminary injunctions and prejudgment writs of attachment as well as state and federal legislation such as Uniform Foreign Money-Judgments Recognition Act (UFMJRA), Uniform Voidable

3. The Uniform Law Commission was established in 1892 to provide states with non-partisan, well-conceived and well-drafted legislation that brings clarity and stability ("uniformity") to critical areas of state statutory law.
4. 9 U.S.C. 1 et seq. (United States Code).
5. When arbitration takes place within the United States, the FAA should be considered along with the individual state's own arbitration statutes. In most instances, the FAA preempts the state's law, but there are numerous cases that have called this into question for a variety of reasons.
6. The New Your Convention became effective in the United States on December 29, 1970.
7. In situations where both the New York Convention and the Panama Convention apply, the Panama Convention takes precedence if a majority of the parties to the arbitration agreement are from Member States of the Organization of American States and from states that have ratified or acceded to the Panama Convention. *See* 9 USC § 307.

Transactions Act (UVTA), the Federal Bankruptcy Code, the New York Convention, the Federal Arbitration Act and a particular state's version of the Uniform Arbitration Act (Uniform Act).

§20.02 IDENTIFYING ASSETS IN THE UNITED STATES

There are essentially two time periods during which a creditor might be able to identify the assets belonging to a debtor; prior to the initiation of litigation and after litigation is pending. Of course this is obvious, but the reason this can be significant to a creditor is because once viable legal proceedings are in place a creditor/plaintiff might be able to take advantage of the processes and leverage provided by the United States judicial system; namely, the discovery procedures,[8] proceedings supplemental[9] and a variety of related court orders.[10]

[A] Legal Proceedings and Court Orders

Once litigation has been initiated, a creditor/plaintiff has, to some degree, pretrial discovery procedures available to assist with "asset identification", but only to a reasonable extent. These procedures will, in most instances, permit the creditor/plaintiff to ask the debtor/defendant a variety of questions about their personal identification[11] which in turn will aid in asset searches. In some instances, albeit rare, a creditor/plaintiff might be able to learn about the debtor/defendant's finances and assets in an effort to determine whether any judgment that might be obtained at the conclusion of the litigation can be satisfied.[12]

[B] Public Searches

Unfortunately, identifying potential debtor's assets before litigation has been initiated is more challenging, in the sense that there is less assistance or leverage to be offered

8. The discovery procedures in the United States are unique and well known for permitting a party to litigation to have great latitude with regard to the collection of information that might lead to the discovery of admissible evidence. As a result, the discovery procedures can be a useful tool in identifying a debtor/defendant's assets.
9. These are proceedings in which a judgment debtor is summoned into court for questioning by a judgment creditor who has not received payment. This provides the creditor with a chance to discover whether the debtor has any assets that can be used to satisfy the judgment.
10. Such orders can consist of orders to produce information held by the debtor/defendant and third parties as well as orders permitting the attachment and seizure of assets.
11. Information including birth dates, addresses, employers, social security numbers, family members, and ownership of real property.
12. Such information is often sought under the guise of preparing the damages portion of a plaintiffs/creditor's claim, but most courts will not require a defendant to reveal a great deal of his detailed financial information. Such financial information is often an issue when a claim for punitive damages is made (although the courts differ on whether this is permitted) or when it is likely that a defendant would have insurance policies that cover the complained of activity. If revealed, such private information may be subject to a Court's Protective Order thereby limiting its use and preventing it from being made public.

by the court system. That is, there is a great deal of "private information" that cannot be released without a court order. Fortunately, there exist public records, online databases, and registers that can provide detailed information about different types of assets an individual or company may possess. The following sections will set forth several of the publicly available resources.[13]

[C] "Secretary of State"

Each individual state compiles a registry of corporations that can provide helpful information relating to the assets and financial stability of businesses and their owners. This service is most frequently performed by a division of the local "secretary of state" office.[14] Here, one can search for records relating to business entities that include corporations, limited liability companies, limited partnerships, general partnerships, limited liability partnerships, and a variety of other business filings.

In addition, the local Secretary of state's office is often the central filing office for certain Uniform Commercial Code financing statements[15] and other documents such as liens relating to judgments, attachments, federal and state taxes, and security interests in collateral. The Uniform Commercial Code filings can be a vital source when investigating business dealings since the law requires that a financial statement be filed whenever transactions take place that involve the use of personal property as collateral.[16]

Finally, it is important to consider that some secretary of state offices maintain information relating to the state trademarks, service marks, container brands, and the names of farms, ranches, or other estates.

[D] Dun & Bradstreet

Dun & Bradstreet has a massive database of businesses and records and can provide information such as public filings, payment history, financial statements, and credit scores and ratings.[17]

---

13. It can be beneficial to retain the services of professional asset locators and online database information providers. They typically have experience with researching public records and can efficiently conduct all of a needed asset search.
14. Here the "Secretary of State" refers to a particular state's local government office and not the federal government's office responsible for foreign relations.
15. A Uniform Commercial Code financing statement is a legal form that a creditor files to give notice that it has or may have an interest in the personal property of a debtor. This form is filed in order to "perfect" a creditor's security interest by giving notice that there is a right to take possession of certain assets for repayment of a specific debt.
16. Records are indexed by the name of the debtor and can list the names of secured parties with regard to the particular debt. An accurate description of collateral used as security is also provided.
17. *See*, creditreports.dnb.com.

[E] Real Property

Records relating to the buying, selling, transferring and taxation of real property are public information in the United States and can generally be found in a variety of government offices in the local (county) municipality. The first agency to check with regard to real property is the office of the county *tax assessor*. The tax assessor has detailed records of where and to whom property tax bills are sent. In many cases, the recipient of the tax bill is often the owner.

In addition, the county's *recorder's* and *registrar's* offices can also be beneficial. These offices will most likely have copies of deeds and information that relate to the sale or transfer of the property. Cross-checking tax records and deeds is the most reliable way of finding the owner of a property.[18]

[F] Motor Vehicles

Each state has its own Department of Motor Vehicles where vehicles are registered either under the individual's name or, in some states, under the name of a company. Motor vehicle records will also indicate whether there is a lien on the vehicle.

[G] Boats

In each state, the department of natural resources will most likely possess information regarding boats or other water-operated craft that are owned by individuals or companies. Small watercraft or boats are typically registered in a state, while the larger boats must be registered with the U.S. Coast Guard.

[H] Aircraft

The registration of aircraft is performed through the Federal Aviation Administration. This information is similar in nature to that collected for motor vehicles and boats.

[I] Intellectual Property

The United States Patent and Trademark Office possess registers relating to patents and trademarks and can therefore be a useful database in identifying assets. Here you can find information relating to ownership and related parties. It is also important to note that some states take the position that intellectual property may not be subject to attachment or to execution after judgment. A court may, however, appoint a receiver to sell intellectual property in order to satisfy a judgment, and rights to payment arising

18. Unfortunately, the largest obstacle in searching property ownership records is that the method for filing those records can vary greatly among the different jurisdictions, with some being extremely inefficient and time consuming. In some municipalities, the tax and deed records may be available online while in others it may be necessary to search records at the offices.

out of intellectual property generally are subject to attachment, to execution after judgment, and to other post-judgment enforcement proceedings.[19]

[J] Bank Accounts

There is no central database that maintains bank account information for specific debtors. It used to be that locating bank account information for a debtor was relatively easy; a variety of techniques such as use of credit reports, information subpoenas and pretext calling were used to uncover bank account information. Now, bank customers have greater protection from searches and such tactics as pretext calls are no longer permitted.[20]

Many people with means have more than one bank account, insurance policy, brokerage account or safety deposit box. An individual tax return is a good source of information regarding any type of account that pays interest. A court subpoena is required to retrieve tax returns.

[K] Securities Exchange Commission

Publicly traded companies are required to make certain disclosures with the Securities Exchange Commission. These disclosures may include stock options to executives, significant stock holdings by third parties, compensation agreements or even independent contractor agreements with outside parties.

Most forms filed by publicly traded companies with the U.S. Securities and Exchange Commission are accessible online through the SEC's EDGAR system (www.sec.gov/edgar/searchedgar/webusers.htm).

[L] Court Records

In most instances, but not all, court records in the US are public and available for review by anyone for any reason or "no reason." Searches to determine whether a person or business entity has court-based litigation pending against it can be conducted with similar ease, but it will require some time and effort. In these instances, where one is attempting to determine whether pending litigation even exists, it is important to have as much identifying information as possible so that a proper and thorough search can be conducted (e.g., full names, addresses, social security, and other tax identification numbers). Fortunately, central databases often exist at the federal level so such

19. The USPTO online research system can be found at http://www.uspto.gov/main/profiles/acadres.htm.
20. Pretext calling is a deceptive practice for obtaining private information. For example, a fake or deceptive caller might contact bank employees, posing as their customers, to access personal account information and status on a particular debtor. Such Information can then be used by debt collectors, attorneys, and private investigators to ascertain assets for use in court or arbitration proceedings. For obvious reasons it is not a recommended practice.

searches can be relatively easy, but sadly this is not always the case at the state court level and thus much more time and effort will be required.[21]

[1] Civil Litigation

A review of court filings relating to civil litigation involving a corporation or individual may not be the most obvious place to identify potential assets. However, in certain situations an individual or company may have been awarded a large financial settlement as part of the litigation. In other situations, parties may have had to supply financial statements or asset information as part of the litigation and that information will be preserved in the public record. Finally, litigation typically requires witnesses, and the witness lists that have been filed with the court can provide the names and contact information for a wide variety of professionals, such as attorneys or accountants, who might have information about the debtor's assets.

Federal Court cases can be searched online via PACER Case Locator.[22] State court cases may be more difficult to search depending upon what state is involved.

[2] Divorce Filings

The identification and evaluation of assets in a divorce proceeding is standard procedure, and in many jurisdictions, these records are publicly available documents which contain a great deal wealth of information relating to bank accounts, employment information, investment income, and other sources of income.

[3] Probate Filings

An inheritance from a wealthy distant relative or a well-to-do grandparent can be identified in local probate filings. Identifying key family members and distant relatives who recently passed away can lead you to a significant inheritance and a list of other possible assets.

§20.03 INTERIM MEASURES

As might be expected, in all but the rarest of circumstances, the property belonging to another party cannot be attached without being a defendant. The same is true for attempts to control one's conduct. That is, the allegedly detrimental behavior of another which may lead to the dissipation of assets cannot be restrained without being

21. In most instances, it will be necessary for you to communicate with the particular court's clerk to determine how best to conduct your search. Phone calls and in-person visits are recommended as a court's staff is typically understaffed and simply not able to send a great deal of time assisting. Politeness, respect and smiles will go along way toward getting the information you need. While access to the federal courts' data system is relatively easy and inexpensive, search of state courts' records are likely to be more time consuming.
22. www.pacer.gov/findcase.html.

a defendant. Some form of litigation, whether it be court-based or arbitral proceedings, is likely to be required to have been initiated at the time of, or before, seeking either a prejudgment writ of attachment, temporary restraining order or some other form of injunctive relief.[23] Once the litigation is initiated, the most frequently used tools for "freezing" assets before a judgment or award is rendered are prejudgment writs of attachment, temporary restraining orders and preliminary injunctions.

[A] Prejudgment Writs of Attachment

The statutes authorizing prejudgment attachment vary widely among the states with each having their own rules to govern: (1) what property can be attached, (2) what rights a defendant has to notice of the proceedings, and (3) the procedure for obtaining the prejudgment attachment. In rare instances, a plaintiff might be able to obtain an "ex parte" order for a prejudgment writ of attachment, but this only occurs when a court is convinced that the failure to issue an immediate prejudgment writ of attachment may mean that the debtor's asset are likely to be unavailable at a future time. The requirements for obtaining a prejudgment attachment may be different in each state, but in general they will necessitate the: (1) existence of a suit for damages, (2) identification of property of the defendant, (3) to which the plaintiff claims a legal right, and (4) demonstration of some need (most often that irreparable harm will occur) to secure the property prior to the conclusion of the lawsuit.[24] Frequently, a plaintiff seeking a prejudgment writ of attachment must post some form of bond in an amount equal to or, in some instances even greater,[25] than the amount of the damages claimed by the plaintiff and any damages that might be caused to the defendant should the defendant prevail.

[B] Temporary Restraining Orders and Preliminary Injunctions

Temporary restraining orders (TRO) and preliminary injunctions are short-term pre-trial and temporary injunctions that are often used to prevent behavior that causes the dissipation of valuable assets. Such orders are considered to be extreme measures and are not taken lightly by the courts who are asked to grant them.

---

23. In some instances, it may be sufficient to have a binding arbitration agreement. *See.* e.g., *California Code of Civil Procedure section 1281.8* which provides that a party to an arbitration agreement may file in the court in the county in which an arbitration proceeding is pending, or if an arbitration proceeding has not commenced, in any proper court, an application for a provisional remedy in connection with an arbitral controversy, but only upon the ground that the award to which the applicant may be entitled may be rendered ineffectual without provisional relief. The application shall be accompanied by a complaint or by copies of the demand for arbitration and any response thereto. If accompanied by a complaint, the application shall also be accompanied by a statement stating whether the party is or is not reserving the party's right to arbitration.
24. *See* e.g., Indiana Code 34-25-2-1: Attachment of Property at or After Filing Complaint.
25. Each state will have its own requirements or formulas for determining the amount of such a bond.

To obtain a TRO, and eventually a preliminary injunction a party must convince a judge that he or she will suffer immediate and irreparable harm unless the order is issued and the complaint of conduct is stopped.[26] If the judge is convinced that such injunctive relief is warranted, then he or she may issue the order immediately, without informing the other parties and without holding a hearing. These orders for a TRO are intended to be an immediate stop-gap measures and will only last for as long as it takes for the court to hold a hearing on whether to grant a preliminary injunction.[27]

[C] Requirements with Respect to Arbitral Proceedings

In essence, this same process for obtaining a prejudgment writ of attachment or some form of injunctive relief may be available to a claimant after beginning arbitration proceedings, but this is much more controversial issues among the various courts. While the Federal Arbitration Act does not expressly permit courts to grant injunctive or other provisional relief, many federal courts have taken the position that the FAA does not prevent a court from granting such measures so long as the requisite elements are met.[28] In addition, many states have taken steps to permit such actions via their own rules of procedures and state court decisions.[29]

§20.04 ENFORCEMENT OF FOREIGN JUDGMENTS AND AWARDS

There exist a number of ways that a foreign judgment or arbitral award can be enforced against a defendant's assets held in the United States.

[A] Foreign Judgments

The United States is not a party to any treaties which provide for the recognition of judgments rendered by non-U.S. courts. In addition, there is no federal legislation with respect to enforcing non-U.S. judgments. As a result, the recognition and subsequent enforcement of judgments issued by non-U.S. courts in the U.S. is left to the laws of the

26. In many instances, irreparable harm can be shown if there is a danger that the property to be attached may be concealed, substantially impaired in value, or made unavailable to attachment.
27. In the federal courts, injunctions and restraining orders are governed by Rule 65(b) of the Federal Rules of Civil Procedure. State rules of procedures will likely have a similar rule.
28. The majority of the Federal Circuits (First, Second, Third, Fourth, Sixth, Seventh, Ninth, and Tenth) have all held that under the right circumstances, and with the right proof, a court has jurisdiction to grant injunctive relief in an arbitral dispute. The remaining circuits have seemed to be more hesitant.
29. *See* e.g., New York Civil Practice Laws and Rules 7502; California Code of Civil Procedure section 1281.8.; *California Retail Portfolio Fund GMBH & Co. v. Hopkins Real Estate Group* (Cal. App. Second Dist., Div. 8; March 22, 2011) 193 Cal.App.4th 849, [122 Cal.Rptr.3d 614] (during arbitration proceedings, plaintiff applied to the court for a writ of attachment supported by a showing of potential insolvency of defendant which might render an award in arbitration ineffectual. The court issued the writ and the Court of Appeal affirmed).

individual states.[30] Thus, a party seeking to enforce such a judgment in the U.S. must file an action before a competent court and seek enforcement under state law.

[1] Uniform Foreign Money-Judgments Recognition Act

In 1962, the Uniform Law Commissioners put forth the Uniform Foreign Money-Judgments Recognition Act (UFMJRA) which provided for the enforcement of foreign country judgments in a state court in the United States.[31] However, in order to meet the increased needs for enforcement of foreign country money-judgments, revision to the 1962 Uniform Act were made in 2005.[32] Currently, approximately half of the states have enacted one version or the other of the UFMJRA.[33]

[2] Basic Requirements for Recognition and Enforcement

Whether established by their enactment of UFMJRA or through relevant case law, most states provide that a non-U.S. court judgment will be recognized, provided that it is final, conclusive, and enforceable where rendered. The U.S. court's may refuse to recognize the foreign judgment if it is determined that the tribunal did not have personal jurisdiction over the defendant or that the tribunal was not impartial or failed to provide proper due process of law.

If all the prerequisites for enforcement are satisfied, then the non-U.S. court judgment will be converted to a state court judgment. This is generally perfected by commencing a new action in the state court requesting the conversion or "domestication" of the foreign judgment. Once the non-U.S. court judgment is domesticated and converted to a state court judgment it is enforceable as a judgment.

[B] Foreign Arbitral Awards

As mentioned above, the United States is a signatory to the New York Convention on the Recognition and Enforcement of Foreign Arbitral Awards and ratified it in 1970. This Convention has been incorporated into Chapter 2 of the Federal Arbitration Act[34] which was designed to validate and enforce written agreements for arbitration of disputes arising out of contracts, maritime transactions, and commerce among the states or territories or with foreign nations. Thus, when the proper United States

30. *See Restatement (Third) Foreign Relations Law* § 481a (1987).
31. This 1962 Act has been enacted by approximately thirty states.
32. Approximately twenty states have enacted the 2005 version.
33. The differences between the two versions of UFMJRA are not many, but there are nuances that make the newer version a bit more user friendly. For example, the newer version discusses which party maintains the burden of proof for certain issues and establishes a statute of limitations. The newer version also discusses the procedures that must be followed in more clear detail.
34. 9 U.S.C. 201. The United States Arbitration Act was enacted in 1925 and became effective in January of 1926. It is now known as the Federal Arbitration Act (FAA) and can be found within the United States Code at 9 U.S.C. 1 et seq).

District Court is petitioned to confirm a foreign award under the New York Convention, it *shall* confirm the award unless it finds one of the grounds for refusal or deferral of recognition or enforcement as specified in the New York Convention.[35]

It should be noted that the general process for enforcing a foreign arbitral award is quite easy and essentially requires that the arbitral award, since it is not initially equivalent to a court issued judgment be "converted" into a judicial judgment before it can be properly enforced. All that is required is that the enforcing party provides an authenticated original award or a certified copy of the award and the original or certified copy of the arbitration agreement to a United States District Court. The application to confirm the award, as well as any challenge to it, is then litigated as motions before the court (not before a jury).

[C] Domestic Arbitral Awards

Arbitrations conducted in the United States are primarily governed by the Federal Arbitration Act (FAA).[36] The FAA applies to contracts involving "commerce among the several states or with foreign nations" that provide for arbitration of controversies arising out of the contracts.[37]

Enforcement procedures for arbitration awards are governed by the FAA and a state's version of the Uniform Arbitration Act (Uniform Act).[38] If an arbitration case involves interstate commerce or maritime issues, the FAA applies. State arbitration statutes, including those which derive from the Uniform Act, apply to the extent the FAA does not apply or has not preempted them. As a general matter, both Acts provide simplified enforcement procedures which require only that the winning party file a motion in an appropriate court to confirm the arbitration award. The court must confirm the award and enter judgment on it unless, upon timely motion of the unsuccessful party, it is challenged for one of the very few reasons allowed by the FAA or the Uniform Act. There is a presumption in favor of the validity of the award, and under either Act a party's ability to successfully challenge an entry of judgment is limited. Once a court enters judgment, relatively simple procedures exist to execute the judgment and pursue collection from the losing party's assets.[39]

35. United States Federal Arbitration Act, 9 U.S.C. § 207. This is similar to Article V(1) of the New York Convention.
36. 9 U.S.C. 1-16.
37. 9 U.S.C. 2.
38. The Uniform Arbitration Act originated in 1955 through the efforts of the National Conference of Commissioners on Uniform State Laws. Its purpose is to provide the fifty states one universal way to function when it comes to arbitration. The law was adopted by Congress in the year 2000 and requires each state to adopt their own version. Many states have enacted a similar version of the 1955 Act.
39. Many of these procedures are discussed *supra*.

§20.05 D&O LIABILITY IN RELATION TO ASSET PROTECTION SCHEMES

In general, the decisions made by corporate directors, officers and shareholders, even bad decisions, do not subject them to personal liability. However, when those decisions are fraught with unlawful, fraudulent or tortious misconduct arguments can be made that the protections provided by the corporate identity should crumble and personal liability become an issue. A director or officer likely will be found personally liable if they were actively participating in a wrongful act. Thus, the degree of involvement in the wrongful activity will likely determine whether a court will pierce the corporate veil and impose personal liability. In most instances, lawsuits brought against the directors or officers claim there was a breach of a duty owed to the corporation, that there was a violation of a federal or state law, or that the individual(s) engaged in some other wrongful conduct.

Although corporate law in the United States is largely a creation state law, the laws governing corporations, and especially the behavior of their directors and officers, received a national spotlight in 2001 and 2002 and changed a great deal as a result of federal legislation. This is especially true with regard to directors or officers who make decisions that cause financial harm to a corporation, who act in their own interests to the detriment of the corporation, or who commit a wrongful act or crime.

In 2001 the Enron Corporation, a large energy company based in Houston, Texas, collapsed and filed the largest bankruptcy ever seen in the U.S. After months of intense investigation, it was determined that the corporate officers, as well as others, committed various acts of fraud that resulted in the corporation's ultimate demise. As a result, the officers and directors faced civil liability,[40] and the U.S. Securities and Exchange Commission (SEC) pursued criminal charges. Sadly, during this same general time period similar misconduct was found to exist on the part of officers and directors of other large corporations, such as WorldCom, Tyco International, and Global Crossing. The federal government took notice of the behaviors and quickly passed legislation that would become known best as the Sarbanes-Oxley Act of 2002 (Public Company Accounting Reform and Investor Protection Act of 2002). This Act is generally recognized as the most important new law since the Securities and Exchange Act of 1934.[41]

40. Many of whom paid millions of dollars out of their own pockets as a result of settlements.
41. Sarbones-Oxley addresses among other things: (1) the reform of auditing and accounting procedures, including internal controls, (2) the oversight responsibilities of corporate directors and officers and regulation of conflicts of interest, insider dealings, and the disclosure of special compensation and bonuses, (3) conflicts of interest by stock analysts, (4) earlier and more complete disclosure of information on anything that directly and indirectly influences or might influence financial results, (5) criminalization of fraudulent handling of documents, interference with investigations, and violation of disclosure rules, and (6) requiring chief executives to certify financial results personally and to sign federal income tax documents.

[A] Fraudulent Transfer / Conveyance Acts

Fraudulent transfers are essentially governed by two sets of laws that are generally consistent with each other. The first is the Uniform Voidable Transactions Act (UVTA)[42] and the second is found in the federal Bankruptcy Code.[43] Both of these laws provide that a transfer made by a debtor with the intent to hinder, delay or defraud any creditor of the debtor is fraudulent.[44] Under the UVTA a transfer is fraudulent (whether the creditor's claim arose before or after the transfer was made) if the debtor made the transfer with actual intent to hinder, delay, or defraud any creditor.[45] Likewise, the Bankruptcy Code authorizes a bankruptcy trustee to recover property that was transferred fraudulently if the transfer took place within the codes specified time frame.[46] If a debtor decides to make such an improper transfer he may face federal criminal penalties. In addition, the person who received the property may also face criminal penalties if that person had the intent to keep the property out of the bankruptcy process. Such penalties are serious and can include monetary fines as well as incarceration.

It should be noted that many states have enacted laws as part of their criminal codes which make it a crime for anyone who is a party to any fraudulent conveyance with intent to deceive and defraud others, or to defeat, hinder, or delay creditors or others of their just debts, damages, or demands.[47]

42. The Uniform Voidable Transactions Act (formerly known as the Uniform Fraudulent Transfer Act), recently amended renamed in 2014, was originally completed by the Uniform Law Commissioners in 1984, and revised the Uniform Fraudulent Conveyance Act of 1918. As a result of a series of amendments in 2014, the act has been renamed the Uniform Voidable Transactions Act. It is designed to prevent debtors from divesting themselves of assets while claims are pending or potential claims might arise. Moat states have adopted some version of the Uniform Fraudulent Transfer Act – Alaska, Kentucky, Louisiana, Maryland, New York, South Carolina, and Virginia.
43. 11 U.S. Code § 548 Fraudulent transfers and obligations.
44. It is perhaps at least historically interesting to know that the doctrine against fraudulent conveyance can be traced back to the English *Twynes* Case (1601) 76 ER 809. Here a man named Pierce was indebted to Twyne and another. The other creditor brought an action against Pierce. Pending the writ, Pierce, in secret, made a general deed of gift of all his goods and chattels real and personal (primarily sheep) to Twyne, in satisfaction of the debt to Twyne. However, Pierce continued in possession of the sheep and even marked them with his own brand. The court held that Pierce attempted to defraud his creditor under the Fraudulent Conveyances Act 1571 (13 Eliz c 5).
45. Section 4(a)(1):
46. The transfer may also be recovered by a bankruptcy trustee under the UVTA if the state in which the transfer took place has adopted it and the transfer took place within the specified time periods. Creditors may also pursue remedies under the UVTA without the necessity of a bankruptcy.
47. *See* e.g., California Penal Code 154 PC and 531 PC.

[B] Civil and Criminal Fraud

In many instances, a wronged creditor will contend that a debtor's wrongful attempt to hide assets to the detriment of the creditor constitutes fraud.[48] After all, fraud typically includes some form of false statement, misrepresentation, or *deceitful conduct* and hiding assets certainly seems deceitful. However, it is important to note that fraud in this context can be difficult to prove since the elements include proving the intent of the perpetrator and the state of mind of the victim. Difficulties also arise since each element must be proven with "particularity"; that is, each and every element must be separately proven for a fraud charge to stand.

The exact elements which need to be proved to support a claim for fraud will vary from state to state, can be different between state laws and federal laws, and can vary depending upon whether one is trying to prove a civil fraud or a criminal fraud.[49] In general, the requisite elements of fraud as a tort (civil fraud) consist of: the intentional misrepresentation or concealment of an important fact upon which the victim is meant to rely, and in fact does rely, to the harm of the victim. When it comes to fraud as a crime the elements generally consist of: the intentional deception of a victim by false representation or pretense with the intent of persuading the victim to part with property and with the victim parting with property in reliance on the representation or pretense and with the perpetrator intending to keep the property from the victim.

Penalties for fraud offenses may include criminal penalties, civil penalties, or both. Civil penalties may include restitution (paying the person what he is owed) and/or substantial fines (intended to punish the behavior). Criminal fraud offenses are often considered felony crimes (the most severe) and can be punishable by fines, jail, and/or probation.

48. The main purpose of fraud is to gain something of value (usually money or property) by misleading or deceiving someone into thinking something which the fraud perpetrator knows to be false. While not every instance of dishonesty is fraud, knowing the warning signs may help stop someone from gaining any unfair advantage over your personal, financial, or business affairs.
49. Civil fraud applies more broadly to circumstances where bad faith is usually involved, and where the penalties are meant to punish the actor and put the victim back in the same position before the fraud took place. Criminal fraud requires criminal intent on the part of the actor, and is punishable by fines as well as imprisonment.